Advance Praise for *21 Leaders for the 21st Century*

This book takes one very deeply into the nature of effective
leadership, hence understanding of it, more than most books. It
provides a better basis than has been available for selecting effective
leaders from among candidates for the job.

> —Russell L. Ackoff
> Anheuser-Busch Professor Emeritus
> of Management Science
> The Wharton School
> University of Pennsylvania

Trompenaars and Hampden-Turner bring a unique perspective to the
field of leadership in this fascinating analysis of the behaviour of a
broad spectrum of effective leaders. The capacity to resolve dilemmas
may be the essential competence for leaders in the 21st century.

> —David K. Hurst, speaker, consultant, and
> author of *Crisis & Renewal: Meeting the
> Challenge of Organizational Change*

With the bookshelves full of "one size fits all" approaches—a book
that examines leadership applied across cultures, values, and situations
is a refreshing change.

> —John Luff
> Vice President Brand
> BT Worldwide

A fascinating, spellbinding text blending the intercultural dilemmas of
management with the reconciling forces of leadership to create innovative leaders. Examples from 21 business leaders prove again and
again that Trompenaars and Hampden-Turner have hit enough nails
on the head to build a solid model for the future.

> —David C. Wigglesworth
> Interculturalist Management Consultant and President
> D.C.W. Research Associates International

21 Leaders for the 21st Century

How Innovative Leaders Manage in the Digital Age

FONS TROMPENAARS
CHARLES HAMPDEN-TURNER

McGraw-Hill

New York   Chicago   San Francisco
Lisbon   London   Madrid   Mexico City
Milan   New Delhi   San Juan   Seoul
Singapore   Sydney   Toronto

Library of Congress Cataloging-in-Publication Data

Trompenaars, Alfons.
    21 leaders for the 21st century / by Fons Trompenaars and
    Charles Hampden-Turner.
      p. cm.
    ISBN 0-07-136294-0
    1. Leadership—Case studies. 2. Industrial management—Case
studies. 3. Corporations—Growth—Case studies. 4. Technological
innovations—Economic aspects—Case studies. 5. Success in business—
Case studies. I. Title: Twenty-one leaders for the twenty-first century.
II. Hampden-Turner, Charles. III. Title.

HD38.2.T76 2001
658.4'092—dc21   00-052722

To Neil Young

McGraw-Hill

A Division of The **McGraw·Hill** Companies

1 2 3 4 5 6 7 8 9 0   DOC/DOC   0 9 8 7 6 5 4 3 2 1

ISBN 0-07-136294-0

This book was set in Janson MT by North Market Street Graphics.

Printed and bound by R. R. Donnelley & Sons Company.

This publication is designed to provide accurate and authoritative information in
regard to the subject matter covered. It is sold with the understanding that the pub-
lisher is not engaged in rendering legal, accounting, or other professional service.
If legal advice or other expert assistance is required, the services of a competent
professional person should be sought.
        —From a declaration of principles jointly adopted by a committee of the
        American Bar Association and a committee of publishers.

This book is printed on recycled, acid-free paper containing a minimum of 50% recycled de-inked fiber.

McGraw-Hill books are available at special quantity discounts to use as premiums
and sales promotions, or for use in corporate training programs. For more information, please write to the Director of Special Sales, Professional Publishing,
McGraw-Hill, Two Penn Plaza, New York, NY 10121-2298. Or contact your local
bookstore.

Contents

Foreword

A generation ago two world wars had so influenced our concept of leadership as to cast it in a military mode. To "lead" was to know sooner than others and convince them that harsh realities had to be faced and sacrifices had to be made. Winston Churchill, Charles de Gaulle, and Dwight D. Eisenhower led; the rest of us followed. There was an inevitable feeling of uncertainty about those times. We were right, and the enemy was wrong. We all knew what had to be done even if the doing was hard and dangerous. Our leaders had been the first to proclaim this necessity.

How different are the circumstances now! Today it is much easier to get things done. Gone are the blood, toil, tears, and sweat. Kosovo is bombed from a safe height. However, we are now much less sure about what *ought* to be done. We see people trying to lead but question whether we should follow. Why go in this direction and not that one?

Studies of leadership have attempted to duck the issue of what should be done by grounding themselves in what the leader was trying to do, not in the critiquing of values. The test became performance: Does this or that leader accomplish what he or she set out to do?

In 1983 Warren Bennis, a well-known writer on leadership, traveled across the United States, proclaiming four universal traits of leadership:

- Management of attention (the leader draws you to him or her and makes you want to join the cause).
- Management of trust (leaders can be trusted because they are consistent—even if you disagree with their views).
- Management of self (leaders know their own skills and deploy them effectively).
- Management of meaning (leaders are great communicators).

This kind of prescription is largely value free and regards leadership as a skill or technique.

Hersey and Blanchard (1983) propose a "situational leadership" model. Styles of leadership are appropriate to different paradigms. The trick is to identify the paradigm and adjust your style to the attitudinal and knowledge stance of the followers. This kind of prescription is largely reactive and unidirectional.

In *The Future of Leadership*, White and associates (1996) assert five key skills of a leader, gleaned from their observations:

- Continually learning things that are hard to learn
- Maximizing energy as a master of uncertainty
- Capturing an issue's essence to achieve by resonant simplicity
- Balancing the long term and the short term in a multiple focus
- Applying an inner sense or gut feeling in the absence of decision support data

Many other authors and researchers have faced this struggle, and many prescriptions and explanations have been published. However, those explanations lack a coherent underlying rationale or fundamental principle that predicts effective leadership behaviors. These models tend to seek the same end but differ in approach as they try to encapsulate the existing body of knowledge about what makes an effective leader. Because of their methodology, these are only prescriptive lists. There is no underlying rationale or unifying theme that defines the holistic experience.

Such approaches create considerable confusion for today's world transcultural manager. Because most management theory comes from the United States and other English-speaking countries, there is a real danger of ethnocentrism. We do not know, for example, how the lists cited here fare outside the United States or how diverse might be the conceptions of leadership elsewhere. Do different cultures necessitate different styles? Can we reasonably expect other cultures to follow a lead from outside those cultures?

The approach to leadership in this book is completely different. It developed from the convergence of two separate strands of thinking, one from each of the principal authors. The earlier research by Fons Trompenaars, developed since the early 1990s, was based on getting people to consider where they were coming from in terms of norms, values, and attitudes. This approach helped identify and model the source not only of national cultural differences but also of corporate culture and how to deal with diversity in a local workforce. It helped managers structure their experiences and provided new insights for them and their organizations into the real source of problems in managing across cultures or dealing with diversity. The second strand was the work of Charles Hampden-Turner, who developed a methodology for reconciling seemingly opposed values. In his research, constructs such as universalism (adherence to rules) and particularism (each case is an exception) are not separate notions but different, reconcilable points on a sliding scale. Universal rules are tested against a variety of exceptions and re-formed to take account of them.

The result of combining the two strands of research is that differences are progressively reconciled. Managers work to accomplish this or that objective; effective *leaders* deal with the dilemmas of seemingly opposed objectives that they continually seek to *reconcile*. As is discussed throughout the body of this book, the contributing authors have collected primary evidence to support this proposition through questionnaires, workshops, simulations, and interviews. Furthermore, it is confirmed that these behaviors correlate with bottom-line business results.

The 21 leaders described in this book were approached deductively. The authors started with a proposition centered on the reconciliation of dilemmas and set out to demonstrate these concepts with evidence gathered from high-performing leaders. Thus, unlike other approaches that result from postrationalizing observations into an ad hoc theory, they had the advantage of a conceptual framework when they approached and interviewed the target list of leaders. The overall aim of this book is to render leadership practice tangible by showing how 21 world-class leaders reconcile the dilemmas that face their companies.

Peter Woolliams, PhD
Professor of International Business
Anglia Business School, United Kingdom

Acknowledgments

This book is the result of much teamwork. Many people have contributed. First, we want to thank all our colleagues at Trompenaars Hampden-Turner Intercultural Management Consulting. All have acted as professional authors. They have interviewed many leaders with great care and have captured the essence of the fruits their subjects brought into existence. We want to thank Professor Peter Woolliams for his ever-fresh enthusiasm and great insights into many aspects of this complex field. We owe Dirk Devos for giving us the fruits of his interviews. Finally, we want to thank all the leaders who have contributed to the book. The majority also took the time to complete our Intercultural Competence Questionnaire—quite an effort in view of their hectic schedules!

Fons Trompenaars

Charles Hampden-Turner

Introduction to the Metatheory of Leadership

Fons Trompenaars and Charles Hampden-Turner

*T*HE MAIN DIFFERENCE between managers and leaders is that some managers cannot sleep because they have not met their objectives, while some leaders cannot sleep because their various objectives appear to be in conflict and they cannot reconcile them. It goes without saying that when objectives clash and impede one another, they will be difficult to attain, and *no one* will sleep! It is tough when you cannot "make it," but even tougher when you do not know what you should be making. When objectives are achieved, the problem disappears, but the dilemma of needing to combine objectives *never* disappears. You can reconcile a dilemma so that its horns are transformed into something new, but other dilemmas will appear and will have to be reconciled. This challenge to leadership never ends.

A leader is here conceived as one suspended between contrasting values. So numerous are the value conflicts within large organizations that their leaders must deal with the human condition itself. This idea was well conveyed by Alexander Pope in his "Essay on Man," whom he saw as

Placed on the isthmus of a middle state,
A being darkly wise and rudely great:

I

With too much knowledge for the sceptic side,
With too much weakness for the stoic's pride,
He hangs between; in doubt to act or rest;
In doubt to deem himself a god, or beast;
In doubt his mind or body to prefer;
Born but to die, and reas'ning but to err;
. . . .
Created half to rise, and half to fall;
Great lord of all things, yet a prey to all;
Sole judge of truth, in endless error hurled;
The glory, jest, and riddle of the world!

The reason leaders must mediate values is that corporations have reached such levels of complexity that "giving orders" rarely works anymore. What increasingly happens is that leaders "manage culture" by fine-tuning values and dilemmas, and then *that culture runs the organization.* The leader defines excellence and develops an appropriate culture, and then *that culture does the excelling.*

Consider a few of the "dilemmas of leadership." You are supposed to inspire and motivate yet listen, decide yet delegate, and centralize business units that must have locally decentralized responsibilities. You are supposed to be professionally detached yet passionate about the mission of the organization, be a brilliant analyst when not synthesizing others' contributions, and be a model and rewarder of achievement when not eliciting the potential of those who have yet to achieve. You are supposed to develop priorities and strict sequences, although parallel processing is currently all the rage and saves time. You must enunciate a clear strategy but never miss an opportunity even when the strategy has not anticipated it. Finally, you must encourage participation while not forgetting to model decisive leadership. No wonder the characteristics of good leadership are so elusive!

One reason leaders must know themselves is that they have to pick people to work with them who will supplement and complement their own powers. We all have weaknesses, but unless the leader recognizes his or hers, the team surrounding the leader will fail to compensate for that weakness.

To rise to a position of leadership is to experience ever more numerous and more various claims on your allegiance. You are no longer *in* manufacturing, marketing, finance, or human relations but *between* them. You must satisfy shareholders, but how can you do that without first sparking enthusiasm in your own people, who then delight customers, who in turn provide the revenues you all seek? You are between such constituencies, and you must learn how to reconcile their claims.

In several earlier books the main authors researched and described how different nations and their management cultures approach dilemmas, choosing one horn of the dilemma in preference to another and making choices that are mirror images of each other. Cultures also are more or less capable of reconciling opposing values. This book will demonstrate that outstanding leaders are particularly adept at resolving dilemmas, a process that has become our definition of good leadership.

Great psychologists have not agreed on the vital entities the mind includes. However, they do agree that the life of the mind is a series of dilemmas. Freud saw the superego contending with the id, a struggle mediated by the ego. C. J. Jung saw the collective unconscious contending with the libido in a conflict mediated by the psyche. Otto Rank saw the death fear contending with the life fear. Brain researchers have identified opposing characteristics of the left and right brain hemispheres generating conflicts mediated by the corpus callosum and the neocortex struggling against the limbic system. It can be said of leaders that they have voluntarily shouldered far more dilemmas than the life of their own minds presents to them. Along with psychic conflicts, they must struggle with all the oppositions identified by organizational thinkers: formal versus informal systems, mass production versus customization, competition versus cooperation, adaptation to external reality versus maintenance of internal integrity, and so on.

Among these many dilemmas is a vital tension around which this book is organized. Can you make the *distinctions* necessary to leadership yet *integrate* them into a viable whole? It is to meet this challenge that *21 Leaders for the 21st Century* is offered. Our view is that value is not "added" by corporations, because only in the simplest cases do values "add up." Values are *combined:* a high-performing vehicle *and* a safe one, a luxury food *and* a convenient one. No one pretends that combining such values is easy, but it is *possible.* A computer of amazing complexity can, with difficulty, be made user-friendly. It is these ever more extensive systems of satisfaction that successful leaders help create.

The Main Concepts in This Book

Cultures consist of values in some kind of reciprocal balance, and so it is important to ask what values *are.* Much of the life of people consists of managing *things,* and things are identified through a logic as old as Aristotle, a logic of noncontradiction. Two different things cannot occupy the same physical space at the same moment.

For example, we choose to buy this car or that one, choose to live in one house instead of another, choose between airlines, and put out a contract and choose among the bids. But values are not things. You cannot acquire courage, hope, or innocence. You will not meet evil at the street corner, or honesty, or compassion. Values are *differences,* and any difference posits a continuum with two contrasting ends. For example, we can be honest or tactful, courageous or cautious, patient or insistent, trusting or supervising, and truthful or loyal. In many cases it does not make sense to say that one end of such a continuum is "good" and the other is "bad." Should you be honest and hurt someone's feelings or be tactful and hide what you really believe? Should you trust a subordinate or check up on that person from time to time? When should you show courage, and when should you cautiously husband your strength? Is it better to be patient or insistent? In all such cases good conflicts with good, and we face a dilemma.

Moreover, it would be ridiculous to live one's life continuously at one end of a continuum, forever proving one's courage and insisting on hard truths. Those who trust everyone on principle will surely get cheated—you might as well present your throat to a vampire. In fact, we move to and fro along the values continuum, now tactful and now honest, now trusting and now supervising.

Does this mean that all values are relative? Are they like a shell game: Now you see it, now you don't? Fortunately not. There is a test of the skill with which one "dances" to and fro on a continuum. At the end of this dance the values at both ends of the continuum *should be stronger than they were before.* Here are some examples: As a result of your tact, you were able to communicate a more honest account; because you cautiously conserved your strength and summoned help, your courage saved the day; in patiently listening to many points of view, you could insist on the best of them; your trusting of a subordinate for a longer period caused your supervision to increase in significance; such was your loyalty to a colleague that she was able to confide the truth to you.

In all these cases the values continuum has been cleverly traversed to vindicate the values at *both* ends of the continuum, allowing seemingly opposed values to be reconciled and achieving a higher level of integration.

The Example of Centralization-Decentralization

Values in tension, which appear at first glance to be negations of one another, can in fact work in synergy (from the Greek *syn* and *ergos,* "working together"). We illustrate this proposition in detail with the example of centralization-decentralization. This is a particularly important dilemma for leaders. On the one hand, they are responsible to shareholders for the combined profitability of the whole company, over which they exercise centralized control. On the other hand, the many business units must have the decentralized autonomy to engage their very different environments effectively.

At their simplest, centralization and decentralization are the opposite ends of a "rope" or "string." Each end represents contrasting characteristics. We illustrate this in Figure I–1.

When we draw the dilemma like this, our chief interest lies in the *difference* between centralized and decentralized activities. Typically, some people in a company believe that the firm is overcentralized—a view common among outlying business units. Others complain that the firm is too decentralized—a view common among those supplying shared resources. Does the corporation risk disintegrating, or does it suffer from overcontrol? The "rope" is frequently stretched between rival factions as in a tug-of-war, with each believing that to "save" the company it needs to pull harder toward its own end—more centralization or more decentralization.

But conceiving of values as being in opposition is not wholly satisfactory. After all, without decentralized activities, what is the purpose of centralized controls? Putting the two values so far apart misses the important connection between them. Is there anything we could do with our "rope" that would reveal this connection? We could join both ends of the rope to make a circle, as in Figure I–2.

Note that there is a subtle change of wording: "centralization" has become *centralizing* (*knowledge*) and "decentralization" has become *decentralizing* (*activity*). Control comes from the center, activity comes from the field. Instead of the two values negating each other, they complement each other. Now, even though our single dimension has

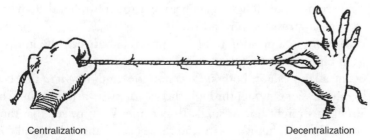

Centralization   Decentralization

Figure I–I

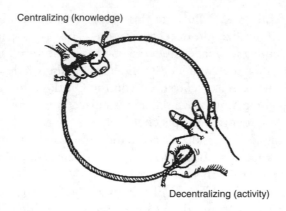

Centralizing (knowledge)

Decentralizing (activity)

Figure I–2

become a circle, there are still two sides as we move between the two former polarities. Can we do this? Of course! Who says thoughts are static? The more we play with such constructs, the more we can see and grasp while recognizing that what we have are merely variations on our original dimension.

The advantage of the metaphorical circle is that we can now see that central *controls* follow upon peripheral *activities,* and vice versa. You cannot have one without the other; they constitute a system.

So now we have two figures, each with a distinct advantage. Figure I–1 differentiates decentralized activity from centralized control; Figure I–2 integrates them. Both are useful viewpoints. Is there a way to combine them in a single illustration? There is. First we take our original dimension and break it at a right angle, as shown in Figure I–3.

This conceptualization gives us two axes or, if you like, two horns of a dilemma that create a culture space; notice how much more freedom to move our thoughts have in two dimensions rather than along a line. Different organizations with different cultures deal with the dilemma of decentralizing and having to control decentralized activities in different ways: Some are afraid of peripheral activity, while others are accepting; some take delight in learning from peripheral activities, while others suppress the very possibility.

Now we are in a position to place our circle between the horns or axes, as in Figure I–4.

Decentralizing is now both *differentiated from* and *integrated with* centralizing in the same model through the use of two variations on what was initially a straight line or single dimension. We now see that those performing the peripheral activity and those exercising the central control are different parties. (The control is *about* the activity and inquires

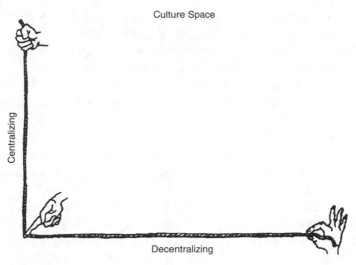

Figure I–3

into it.) Nor do the two processes occur at the same time. Rather, activity *precedes* control, which checks at intervals to make sure that everything is all right. But our model still has problems: It seems to lack direction and purpose and goes around and around in one place. This is why we have suggested the effect of a treadmill, with activity recompensing the energy of central control. Is there some way to learn through this experience and make progress? Yes! We can add a third

Figure I–4

dimension—progression through time—to generate the synthesis between a circle and a straight line, a helix, as in Figure I–5.

The helix shows how a circle looks from the side as it winds between our two polarities. Here we decentralize in order to have more to centralize, and we communicate our conclusions about the myriad activities of the corporation to each business unit so that it can compose itself to, and learn from, the activities of other units. Which have performed well, which badly, and why?

Helix-shaped molecular structures are the basis of life, and so we should take this metaphor seriously. We can superimpose the helix on our culture space in the manner illustrated in Figure I–6.

Here the helix winds progressively between peripheral activity and central control of that activity. If a company is well led, its activities will become *both* more and more decentralized *and* better monitored and centralized, with the center acting as does the central nervous system of the human body, which coordinates inputs from semiautonomous peripheries, such as the hands of an artist. What is being centralized is information *about* decentralized activities, which, by using this feedback, become more effective at achieving their goals.

Would we be better off if we were totally decentralized, that is, if we occupied the lower right position in Figure I–6? Hardly. What is the point of being parts of one company and one system if we cannot learn from each other? The problem with total freedom not to communicate is that the poorer units no longer learn from the better ones, and the

Helix as Synthesis between Line and Circle

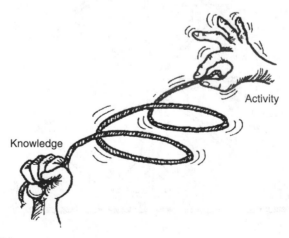

Activity

Knowledge

Figure I–5

A Helical Progression toward Better Knowledge of Better Activities

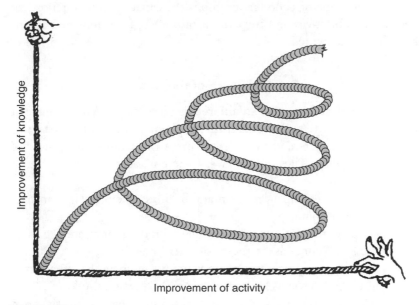

Figure I–6

point of being one corporation generating a body of shared knowledge from multiple sources is then lost. There are many pathways to success. The experience of a hundred business units is far more valuable than the experience of any single unit.

Would we be better off if we were tightly centralized—if we occupied the upper left position in Figure I–6? Hardly. Every business unit has a local market with key variations. The environment is constantly changing, and such changes show up in some environments but not in others. Unless business units can adapt swiftly to changing customer demands, the whole corporation will lose touch. The reason the center cannot give detailed orders to the business units is that the complexity is too great. No single leader can process so much information; moreover, the center is farther from customers than the local business unit is.

The answer has to be at the upper right of the figure: an inquiring system- and knowledge-generating corporation that gathers information from scores of business units and transforms it into a body of knowledge that is sharable with each unit so that each peripheral part has the wisdom of the whole centralized system. As the saying goes, you must "act locally" but "think globally." Local actions provide the information from which global conclusions are drawn.

Our definition of good leadership is the capacity to reconcile such contrasting objectives and turn them into a single system that learns from its own activities.

The Structure of the Book

This text will attempt to explain reconciliation theory and make it more accessible. We seek to illustrate its principles through the practice of successful leaders and thus demonstrate the vitality and power of synergizing values. The book intends to help leaders

- Elicit and become aware of major business dilemmas in transcultural environments
- See dilemma resolution as a crucial ingredient of strategy
- Utilize dilemmas as strategic contexts for action
- Learn the art of achieving one value through another in a virtuous circle (a process known as "through–through thinking")
- Learn how transnational entrepreneurs take their stands (*preneur*) between (*entre*) contrasting values

In *Chapters 1 and 2* we introduce seven dimensions that we habitually use in distinguishing between different national cultures. We seek to show that these dimensions also illuminate the way leaders think and act. Chapter 1 deals with the first three dimensions:

Universalism	Particularism
Individualism	Communitarianism
Specificity	Diffusion

We continue our exposition in Chapter 2 with four additional dimensions characterizing the dilemmas faced by major leaders:

Neutral	Affective
Achieved status	Ascribed status
Inner-directed	Outer-directed
Sequential time	Synchronous time

Chapters 3 through 19 deal with major dilemmas faced by prominent business leaders as the twenty-first century begins. *Chapter 3* looks at the well-publicized personality and career of Sir Richard Branson, the "Virgin tongue in cheek." On these pages are reconciled a wide diversity of opposite endowments, so that Branson is both a critic of traditional capitalism and an agent of its profitable transformation. We start with Branson because he is living proof that enlightened leadership can change the whole spirit of capitalism.

Chapter 4 features the conscious design of a "hyperculture," a purpose-built corporate environment of superlatively high performance created from the values of its participants (East Germans, West Germans, and Americans). In this particular case the cross-cultural convenor, Martin Gillo, was familiar with dilemma theory and used it to design a culture *of* cultures that broke all records. His interpretations add to the theory expounded in Chapters 1 and 2.

Chapters 5 through 7 deal with the dilemmas and dynamics of corporate turnaround. How do those who save a company in crisis think and act? Each of three companies was suffering from a surfeit of its traditional strengths; it had overplayed a winning streak and found itself facing catastrophe. Philippe Bourguignon of Club Med had to save the company from the runaway costs of its own stylish hospitality. Christian Majgaard of LEGO survived a sea of red ink to restore "the children's toy of the twentieth century" to its former glory. Anders Knutsen of Bang and Olufsen saved the Danish company from its own technological perfectionism, which had scorned marketing and pricing.

Chapter 8 looks at how private enterprise provides long-term public service; the chapter examines the deeds of Gérard Mestrallet at Suez Lyonnaise des Eaux. *Chapter 9* shows how Val Gooding inspires a corporate form that makes the private insurance of health work again.

In *Chapters 10 through 12* we look at three global giants of the electronics and computer revolution whose dynamism has outdistanced their rivals. Jim Morgan of Applied Materials made a detailed study of, and even wrote a book on, Japanese electronics strategy that is now widely copied throughout East Asia. Morgan's global strategy is based squarely on an East-West dialogue in which the machinery made for microchip manufacturing takes on various meanings in different cultures. Michael Dell of Dell Computers, a latecomer to the maturing personal computer industry, has nonetheless thrust his company into the position of second in the world through direct sales over the Internet, on which all customers have their "Premier Pages." Finally, Stan Shih of Acer has shown what a company with a traditional Taiwanese management style can achieve in a global marketplace by adhering to, while reconceiving, its homegrown Taiwanese values.

Chapter 13 revisits the ferocious force fields and destructive cross-pressures described by the dilemma model. These forces are particularly severe in cultures that are in transition from communism to capitalism. We pick up the spectacular banking career of Russia's former prime minister, Sergei Kiriyenko, whose resistance to disintegrative forces within the system borders on the heroic.

Chapter 14 examines a rare yet impressive instance of changing a company by changing its values. Edgar Bronfman of Seagram's transformed the company's performance through a dialogue on values that all parties agreed to, committed themselves to, and operationalized, with notable success. Crucial to Bronfman's success was walking the talk and monitoring the results.

Chapters 15 and 16 examine two examples of "success" that the respective leaders realize cannot continue for much longer without important changes. Without waiting for a crisis to strike, Karel Vuursteen of Heineken and Hugo Levecke of ABN AMRO instituted changes that will stop the coming squeeze of future dilemmas.

Chapters 17 and 18 pick up on two companies in the fast-changing financial services industry. Merrill Lynch, symbolised by a bull's horns, confronts genuine dilemmas provoked by the cut-rate Internet brokerage services offered by Charles Schwab and other competitors. Should it beat them or join them? AEGON, the Dutch insurer, confronts a consolidating global industry. It must acquire or be acquired, but will it learn how to digest foreign acquisitions?

Chapter 19 tells the story of Rahmi Koç of Turkey. Koç built a family business into a powerhouse that by itself accounts for 6 percent of Turkey's gross national product and pays 11 percent of that nation's taxes. The Koç Group, as the business is known, is admiringly referred to as Turkey's "third sector," behind the public and private sectors.

Chapter 20 shows that global activities generate dilemmas through conflicts with local cultures.

Chapter 21 looks at the dilemmas of three start-ups in family ownership. How do acorns become oaks? What are the dilemmas that kill off most small companies? Is it possible to "incubate" small companies to prevent their early demise? Three leaders tell their stories.

Chapter 22 seeks to generalize the particular models, frameworks, and discussion from the body of the text about the 21 leaders to a generic framework for reconciling each dimension of cultural values.

Following Chapter 22 are short biographies of the main and contributing authors, and references that support and supplement the chapter material.

A full and comprehensive version of our diagnostic tools and questionnaires, the associated statistical analyses, and data mining can be downloaded free from the support website www.twentyoneleaders.com.

Chapter 1

Transcultural Competence: Learning to Lead by Through-Through Thinking and Acting, Part I

Fons Trompenaars and Charles Hampden-Turner

*T*HERE WAS A time when globalism was merely a question of extending American influence ever farther around the globe, propelled by the digital revolution. The world's only remaining superpower had a universal methodology for economic development and leadership. Free markets were one with economic science. The American way extended to social sciences in general and management theories in particular. Then some disturbing signs began to appear. Why was China, although still communist, growing faster over a decade than any capitalist economy had ever grown? Why was newly capitalist Russia moving backward toward total economic collapse? Why had the Japanese and East Asian economies grown "miraculously" for 30 years and then relapsed? The same business values that appear to have given U.S. businesses a new creative surge have had quite opposite effects elsewhere. The hope for a world system of economic development has dimmed perceptibly.

This chapter will argue that business cultures are so different as to be in some respects diametrically opposed and that because business is run differently around the globe, we need different managerial and leadership competencies. Yet from those differences, from that seeming Babel of discordant values, there is emerging a new capacity for bridging business differences. We call this *transcultural competence*. It has a logic that unifies differences. It is the logic that differentiates the manager from the leader and the successful leader from the failing one. The leader of the twenty-first century needs a new way of thinking, to which we refer here as *through-through* thinking. It goes beyond *either-or* and even *and-and* thinking. It synthesizes seemingly opposed values into coherence.

For more than a decade we have researched the cultures and values of managers in more than 50 nations. Recently there has emerged a new phenomenon among managers for whom crossing borders and engaging foreigners is a way of life. We will show that this competence can be described, measured, and identified for the purposes of recruitment, selection, assessment, and training. We believe that it reveals the competitive advantage of the managing of diversities of many kinds and origins. Most especially, it allows us to revisit the neglected field of values and ethics.

Before we can describe this competence convincingly, we must first dislodge the huge boulders of misapprehension that block the path to understanding how values affect cultures. For at least two centuries scholars have tried to give ethics a status borrowed from physics by pretending that values are like things or objects. Even industry has spoken of *goods* (good things). At a recent human rights conference three speakers, inspired by each other's examples, pulled from their pockets a piece of the Berlin Wall, a stone from a Muslim temple destroyed by Serbs, and a small rock symbolizing the steadfast nature of an insurance company. We seem to want our values to be hard, durable, solid, and exact. Yet in truth, the attempt to reify our values and give them rocklike certainty has proved a disaster. Historians almost certainly will recall the twentieth century as an era of genocide in which rigid convictions clashed mercilessly. Many of those engaged in scientific inquiry have abandoned moral questions entirely. These questions are said to have no testable meaning, no connection with observable behaviors.

We view values quite differently: as information, as differences that make a difference to people communicating with each other. Values have no physical existence. They are not bags of coins or jewels, but, like the binary digits in computers, they contrast 0 with 1. "Be flexible" means move down the conviction-flexibility continuum in the direction of flexibility, and "be steadfast" means move toward the conviction end—but if we have been very flexible in reaching a position, we should become more convinced that that position is right.

Leaders Recognize, Respect, and Reconcile Differences

The main thesis of this book is that leaders who reconcile value dilemmas are more successful than leaders who don't. Leaders face similar dilemmas. In our series of interviews with successful leaders we have seen that seven basic dilemmas show up time and time again in different shapes.

Take the question of giving gifts. Suppose my American or West European headquarters has a code of conduct banning gifts, which are considered a form of bribery. Suppose an important supplier gives me a piece of jade not because he wants to corrupt me but because I mentioned over lunch that my daughter collects jade figurines. The gift is small in value, a token of friendship and respect. It is even inscribed with birthday greetings. Should I "follow the code of conduct" prescribed from 8000 miles away? Or should I "be flexible" and follow the norms of East Asian friendship networks?

At the moment we lack the logic to decide such issues. British analytical philosophy tells us that values are mere "exclamations of preference," akin to liking or disliking strawberry ice cream. Economists tell us that all values are subjective and relative until an objective price is fixed by markets, at which point their value becomes verifiable. The logic of dilemma resolution is circular or cybernetic. "Follow the code" forbids all reception of gifts, but it needs to learn from Southeast Asian flexibility that *some* gifts are not bribes but tokens of friendship—in short, that there are reasonable exceptions to this rule. Therefore, the rule is modified; now the prohibition is against accepting *bribes,* which are defined as gifts exceeding $75 in value. Note that the rule as qualified allows executives abroad *both* to "follow the code" *and* to "be flexible" about friendship tokens. No longer do we have to insult gift givers by returning their presents and thus lose business. Another variation is to accept gifts "equal to the value of an evening meal for two at a good restaurant" but no more. This makes sense because Westerners tend to treat entertainment expense as a nonbribe; others do not make this distinction and are puzzled by our acceptance of meals and our refusal of gifts.

The ideal of reconciliation upholds the important principle that the best product should win the business and that bribes distort this outcome—yet service is also important, and so small gifts may be used to show that friendship, consideration, and good relations are also on offer. Clearly, some gifts *are* bribes, but many are not. By thinking carefully about these exceptions, you can learn to develop rules that will work in foreign countries, moving tactically along the continuum of *new rules–new exceptions*. This is the way to make your rules better while appreciating the truly exceptional.

Consider two international businesses and how they confront two common dilemmas of overseas operations:

Competing strongly   versus   Making friends

Following rules   versus   Finding exceptions

Suppose one of our businesses is extremely successful and the other is on the edge of bankruptcy. Can we explain their good and ill fortunes by the dilemmas they face? No, because the dilemmas are the same. Can we explain it by the relative fervor with which they compete or follow rules? Not really; a failing company may be competing with desperate intensity and clinging to the rules as one would to a life raft. Feeling very strongly about any of these four values cannot distinguish triumph from disaster. So where does the difference lie? Not *in* each value itself or in the strength of one or both. The answer lies *between* them, in the patterns of competing strongly and making friends and the patterns of following rules and finding exceptions. In successful wealth creation these two pairs of values are integrated and synergistic; hence the judgment that such leaders have "integrity." In wealth or value destruction the two pairs of values frustrate, impede, and ultimately confound each other. We call the first pattern a *virtuous circle*, the second a *vicious circle*. The logic of the former is shown in the following diagram:

The Virtuous Circle

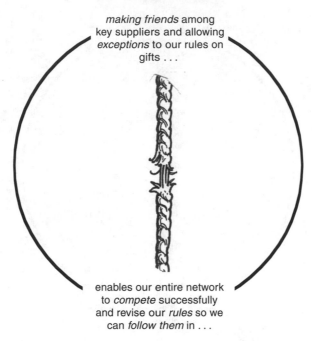

making friends among key suppliers and allowing *exceptions* to our rules on gifts . . .

enables our entire network to *compete* successfully and revise our *rules* so we can *follow them* in . . .

In the preceding example making friends and competing fiercely on the merits of the product or service have been synergized, and the exception of gift giving has been encouraged by revised rules that allow genuine expressions of respect but not bribes. All four values work together, but it could have turned out quite differently—as in this vicious circle:

The Vicious Circle

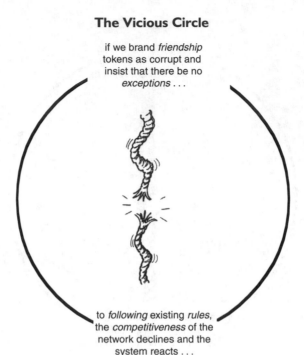

if we brand *friendship* tokens as corrupt and insist that there be no *exceptions* . . .

to *following* existing *rules*, the *competitiveness* of the network declines and the system reacts . . .

In the vicious circle one value—sticking to the rules—is deemed "right"; the opposite—making an exception for small gifts—is deemed "wrong." As a result, network competitiveness falls, business is in real jeopardy, and in desperation, someone probably *will* pay a bribe where friendship has failed! The result is a *downward* spiral: Rules that exclude more and more of what is necessary to survive and the failure of friendship drive competitiveness ever lower, making friendship ever more costly and unwise. In virtuous circles the values are mutually reinforcing and intensifying. In vicious circles the values are split apart and provoke each other to greater excess. A failing competitiveness under outmoded rules is extremely likely to swing over into flagrant illegality among crony capitalists. As the crisis looms, people grow desperate. As the values they once clung to fail, they veer to their opposites, which fail too. The vicious circle goes into "run-away," oscillating wildly from Draconian rules to glaring exceptions, from competitive failure to conspiratorial cliques, as people attempt to save themselves from the consequences of failure. When we communicate with each other about values, we are not uttering meaningless subjective words. On the contrary, we can help each other develop or damn each other to destruction.

This insight into how values connect or disconnect also helps us solve the age-old puzzle of whether values are absolute or relative. Cross-cultural researchers often are accused of cultural relativism—say, equating the Taliban militia with Western democracy. Values are of course absolute in one sense and relative in another sense, and we will be healthier, wealthier, and wiser if we can combine these two senses. Adapting and following rules in some measure is absolutely necessary to wealth creation. In the absence of these values, no wealth will be created anywhere, ever. Yet the proportions in which these values are combined to meet this challenge are relative. They are acts of judgment, art forms. Yes, we must have values to draw on—the requirement that they be present is absolute—but no, their expression is relative. They must be artfully combined in ever-changing syntheses appropriate to particular circumstances.

Take the question of loving and correcting one's children. Both the value of love and the value of correction are absolute in the sense that if either is not present, the child has no hope of growing up properly. Unloved and uncorrected children do not become effective citizens.

Yet how loving and correcting are best *combined* remains an art form—relative to the challenge encountered. The way your criticism and support are expressed must vary with the child, the relationship, and the seriousness of the situation. Whether your child experiences your anger as loving depends very much on communication skills. Even with love and correction in abundant supply, you could get the expression all wrong and fail to convey your meaning. Hence, it is *absolutely* necessary both to love and to correct, yet the proportions of these factors in any communication are *relative* to the person being addressed.

In approaching transcultural competence, we have chosen seven major dimensions of difference, the first of which we have already touched on. Each has contrasting value poles. These dimensions were selected because we have found that they best account for the major differences between national cultures.

The seven dimensions are as follows:

1. Rule making   Exception finding
   (universalism)   (particularism)

2. Self-interest and personal fulfillment (individualism)

Group interest and social concern (communitarianism)

3. Preference for precise, singular "hard" standards (specificity)

Preference for pervasive, patterned "soft" processes (diffusion)

4. Emotions inhibited (neutral)

Emotions expressed (affective)

5. Status earned through success and track record (achievement)

Status ascribed to person's potential, e.g., age, family, education (ascription)

6. Control and effective direction from within (inner-directed)

Control and effective direction from outside (outer-directed)

7. Time conceived of as a "race" with passing increments (sequential)

Time conceived of as a "dance" with circular iterations (synchronous)

The first three dimensions will be considered in this chapter. The last four will be considered in Chapter 2. Each of these seven dimensions can be polarized with the others, in which case we get spectacular, amusing, and sometimes tragic contrasts; alternatively, all seven can be integrated and synergized, in which case we achieve transcultural competence.

We will now go through the seven dimensions in turn and consider the following in each case:

a. The sophisticated stereotypes
b.
Some typical misunderstandings
c. What effective leaders know and have learned
d. How we measured transcultural competence

Before we proceed, let us explain what is meant by "sophisticated stereotypes." We mean by this term the stereotypes (or sociotypes) of a culture that have been researched carefully and found to be true. They therefore are not the product of prejudice or denigration, but they remain nonetheless surface manifestations. We cannot avoid stereotypes for several reasons—mainly because cultures stereotype themselves: to sell popular culture, to sell tourism, to idealize themselves, and to contrast themselves favorably with perceived enemies.

For 20 years or more Geert Hofstede with his IBM samples and Charles Hampden-Turner and Fons Trompenaars with their dilemma methodology have classified respondents as belonging at one or the other end of various continua. Americans, for example, are individualist, not collectivist. The problem with sophisticated stereotypes is what they miss. How do Americans use groups, teams, and communities? How do the Japanese create? Hiding beneath the stereotype is much crucial information.

We therefore must note the sophisticated stereotype, observe the trouble it causes, and move beyond it. This we will try to do by delineating transcultural competence.

Dimension I. Rule Making   *versus*   Exception Finding
(Universalism)   (Particularism)

The Sophisticated Stereotype

Here the contrast is between the desire to make, discover, and enforce rules of wide applicability, whether they are scientific, legal, moral, or industrial standards, and the desire to find a way to be exceptional, unique, unprecedented, particular, and one of a kind.

As Box 1-1 shows, the United States, Finland, Canada, Denmark, and the United Kingdom are all high in the desire for universal rule making. In contrast, South Korea, China, Japan, Singapore, and France are all relatively particularistic. One theme in universalism is Protestantism, which sees the word of God as encoded in the Bible; a second is the common law tradition; a third is the concept of America as the New World, with rules designed to attract immigrants. That America has 22 times as many lawyers per capita as Japan is one consequence of the universalistic preference. Among the well-known manifestations of high universalism are scientific management, Fordism, fast food, benchmarking, "100 percent American," how to win friends and influence people, and similar moral commandments. In contrast, China is a culture much higher in particularism. Box 1-2 contains an excerpt from an eighteenth-century Chinese encyclope-

Box 1-1

Fourteen Nations Compared

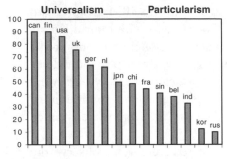

Universalism_____Particularism

© THT Consulting 2001

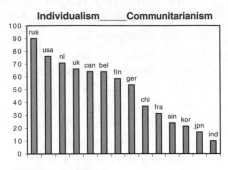

Individualism_____Communitarianism

© THT Consulting 2001

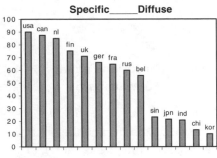

Specific_____Diffuse

© THT Consulting 2001

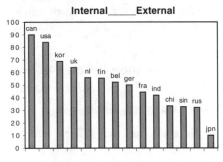

Internal_____External

© THT Consulting 2001

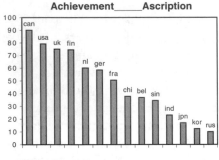

Achievement_____Ascription

© THT Consulting 2001

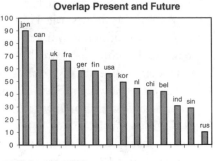

Overlap Present and Future

© THT Consulting 2001

Box 1-2

Chinese Particularism

Jorge Luis Borges offers the following excerpt from an early Chinese encyclopedia:

Animals are divided into (a) Belonging to the Emperor, (b) Embalmed, (c) Tamed, (d) Suckling pigs, (e) Sirens, (f) Fabulous, (g) Stray dogs, (h) Included in the present classification, (I) Frenzied, (j) Innumerable, (k) Drawn with a very fine camel hairbrush, (l) Having just broken the water pitcher, (m) "that from a long way off look like flies."

We need have no fear of the variety and uniqueness of such a civilization, but some might doubt its rule-making and classificatory powers.

dia that attempts to describe and classify "animals." The particularity of detail astounds, yet the rules of classification are, by Western standards, very strange indeed!

Some Typical Misunderstandings

In its dealings with the world, the United States tends to see itself as the rule maker and global policeman. In its trade disputes with Japan, the United States tries to personify the rules of capitalism: "Rice is a commodity. It must be freely traded." The Japanese say, "But we are different. Rice is the sacred symbol of our culture, something very particular."

A famous dispute about sugar prices broke out between Australia and Japan in the middle of the 1970s. Japan signed a long-term contract to buy Australian sugar at a price below the then world market price. Weeks later the bottom fell out of the market. Japan wanted to renegotiate a new contract on the basis that its particular relationship with sugar exporters preceded the contract's terms. Australia wanted the original contract honored as part of a universal obligation to keep one's word. Does particular partnership override the law? Or is legal conduct to be expected from true partners, however inconvenient?

Is the United States an "obvious" culture because it makes highly standardized "universal" goods—MS Windows, Levi's, Big Macs, Coca-Cola? Is France a "snobbish" culture because it prefers products of high particularity—haute couture, haute cuisine, fine wines? Such arguments can entertain us, but they are not fruitful.

Source: Michel Foucault, *The Order of Things,* Editions Gallimard, 1966.

What Effective Leaders Know and Have Learned

As we noted before, the secret of creating wealth lies not *in* the values of rule making and exception finding but *between* them, for these values are complementary. How do you improve your rules except by noting each exception and revising the rules accordingly? However, this assumes that legislating better is your prime purpose. Suppose you were a particularist, seeking to be exceptional and unique. Would the same complementarity apply? It would, but in reverse order: How do you develop exceptional abilities except by noting the highest standards and exceeding them?

Either way, a transculturally competent leader can make a virtuous circle of rule making and exception finding, as in the following diagram:

The Virtuous Circle

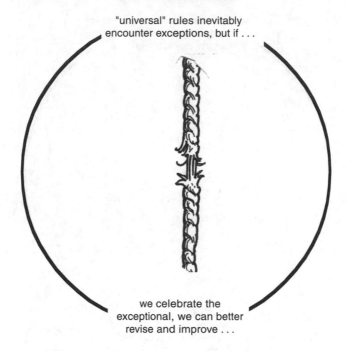

"universal" rules inevitably
encounter exceptions, but if . . .

we celebrate the
exceptional, we can better
revise and improve . . .

Among famous examples of how particularism can be integrated into universalism are (1) Anglo-American case law and (2) the case method taught at the Harvard Business School, which begins with particular cases before generalizing. Such virtuous circles are much easier to conceptualize than to put into effect. The fact is that it often is infuriating to promulgate a rule and then discover an exception. If you are a boss, you feel defied. If you are a scientist, you believe you have failed. If you are a moralist, you are aghast at such sinfulness. All too common, therefore, is the vicious circle shown here:

The Vicious Circle

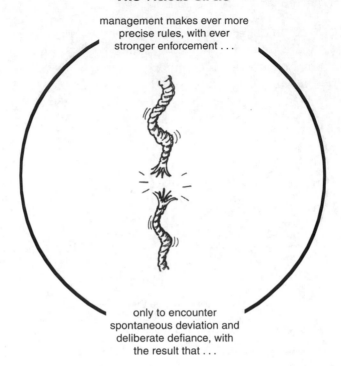

management makes ever more
precise rules, with ever
stronger enforcement . . .

only to encounter
spontaneous deviation and
deliberate defiance, with
the result that . . .

Once again "the string has broken," and the system is in run-away. Attempts to enforce rules escalate, as do deviance and defiance; these events only intensify rule enforcement as "the snake devours its own tail."

A recent incident at Motorola illustrates how a vicious circle was avoided at the last moment by a rule change. East Asian engineers were given a $2000 housing allowance so that they could live comfortably adjacent to the plant. One day a senior engineer had to be contacted urgently at home and was found to be living in a shack. He had spent his housing allowance on putting his siblings through school. The corporation's first instinct was to fire him—had he not deceived them and misallocated funds?—but its second thought was that he had put the money to better use than he would have by isolating himself in relative luxury as the "kept man" of a foreign corporation. Was thinking first of one's own family an "offense"? The rules were changed. Today you can use the allowance for your own purpose and to implement local values. The corporation learned from its environment about values different from personal affluence.

When a group changes its rules, we call this change *conceptual transformation*. There are several examples in this book of leaders who have learned from exceptions how to improve rules. In Chapter 3, Dilemma 5, Richard Branson of Virgin shows how a large organization worth over $3 billion, with its own rules of operation, can renew itself by spinning off numerous entrepreneurial ventures, each unique and particular. The trick is to let no unit grow too large and to quickly divide those which might do so. In Chapter 5 Philippe Bourguignon continues to protect the legacy that every Club Med vacation is a personal dream, a voyage into the discovery of an unfolding selfhood, with an *esprit* and an *ambience* that are unique and unrepeatable. Yet many of the elements that go into that holiday can and must be standardized, globalized, and systematized, generated in high volumes and at low cost—all ingredients of a universal logic. You can create fresh scenarios of satisfaction *out of* standardized inputs. It is their *combination* that is unique, not the elements themselves.

At LEGO (Chapter 6, Dilemma 3) Christian Majgaard faces the problem of how newly innovative companies that are allowed to break the entrenched rules and norms of LEGO's core culture can be integrated back into that core as success models embodying new rules. Only when these innovators are confident enough and successful enough are their exceptional virtues used to update and revise LEGO's traditional rules.

In Chapter 10, Dilemma 4, rules have been global and exceptions have been local. Yet Jim Morgan of Applied Materials has set up a system of transcultural learning in which a series of discoveries about local and exceptional circumstances are used to *test generalizations about universally applicable knowledge*. Does this principle apply in all places or only in some? How important are the exceptions? Might one of these exceptions become a new global rule, replacing existing rules? "Global versus local" is transcended by "glocalism," the process of modifying global rules by examining local exceptions.

In Chapter 13, Dilemma 4, Sergei Kiriyenko, onetime Russian premier, confronted a Russian economy of chronic cronyism, of collusion and special deals with particular customers who used the size of their indebtedness to gain concessions. He was at that time head of NORSI oil, a major state-owned refinery. Kiriyenko obliged all parties to negotiate new agreements with the new entity he had created from the bankrupt shell, but once agreements were forged, the parties had to live by what they had promised. The telephone crackled with threats, but Kiriyenko stuck to his guns. Renegotiation was possible after a stated interval, but in the meantime the rules applied to everyone. The Russian economy was getting its first taste of particular requirements encompassed within universal rules of contracts.

Measuring Intercultural Competence, Reconciling the Universal with the Particular: How We Did It and What We Found

We now turn to the measurement and strategic use of transcultural competence and the results achieved thus far. The results were first accumulated with our "old" questionnaire. In these investigations managers were given a straight choice between two conflicting values. For example, the issue of universalism versus particularism was measured by posing the following dilemma, which we refer to as question 1.

You are riding in a car driven by a close friend. He hits a pedestrian. You know he was going at least 35 miles an hour (mph) in an area of the city where the maximum speed is 20. There are no witnesses. His lawyer says that if you testify under oath that he was traveling only 20 mph, it may save him from serious consequences.

What right does your friend have to expect you to protect him?

Here the responding manager must either side with his friend or bear truthful witness in a court of law. There is no possibility of integrating opposites, no opportunity to display transcultural competence by reconciling this dilemma. In our conversations with managers who responded to this questionnaire, we kept encountering attempts to resolve the dilemma and some annoyance that we had pressed so stark a choice on them. We then designed a more discriminating questionnaire with five answers, not two. Two of the answers were the original polarized alternatives. One new answer was a compromise between the two values. The last two answers were alternative integrations: one that started with universalism and encompassed particularism and one that started with particularism and encompassed universalism. These answers are set out next:

a. There is a general obligation to tell the truth as a witness. I will not perjure myself before the court. Nor should any real friend expect this from me.
b. There is a general obligation to tell the truth in court, and I will do so, but I owe my friend an explanation and all the social and financial support I can organize.

c. My friend in trouble always comes first. I am not going to desert him before a court of strangers on the basis of an abstract principle.

d. My friend in trouble gets my support whatever his testimony, yet I would urge him to find in our friendship the strength to allow us both to tell the truth.

e. I will testify that my friend was going a little faster than allowed and say that it was difficult to read the speedometer.

The logic behind these positions follows the accompanying figures.

The Basic Cultural Template—Part One

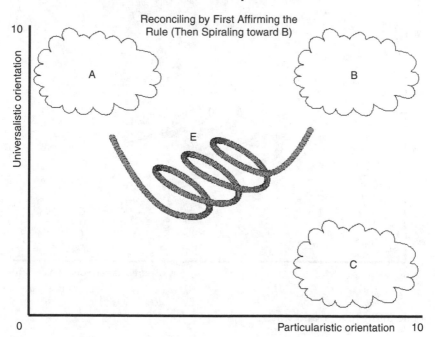

a. (1/10) This is a polarized response in which the law is affirmed but the friend is rejected (universalism excludes particularism).

b. (10/10) This is an integrated response in which first the rule is affirmed and then everything possible is done for the friend (universalism joined to particularism).

c. (10/1) This is a polarized response in which the friend is affirmed as an exception to the rule, which is then rejected (particularism excludes universalism).

d. (10/10) This is an integrated response in which exceptional friendship is affirmed and then joined to the rule of law (particularism is joined to universalism).

e. (5/5) This is a standoff or fudge in which both the rule of law and the principle of loyalty to friends are blunted (universalism compromised by particularism).

The Basic Cultural Template—Part Two

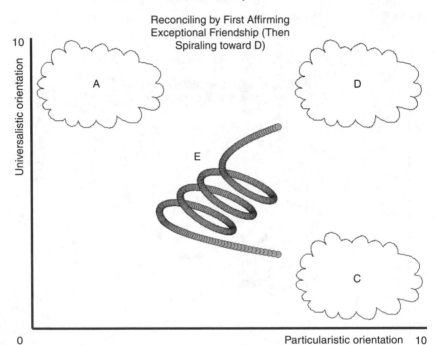

The underlying framework is as follows:

- Integrated responses (b) and (d) show more transcultural competence than do polarized responses (a) and (c) and a compromised response (e).
- American managers typically put universalism first (adopting the counterclockwise spiral) and East Asian and southern European managers typically put particularism first (adopting the clockwise spiral), but each can integrate that priority with its opposite.
- From this, it follows that there are at least two paths to integrity, not "one best way."

- There are, however, better ways and worse ways.
- Transcultural competence will anticipate and explain success in overseas postings and will correlate with 360-degree feedback ratings.

What We Found

The questionnaire based on these rationales has been administered to several groups: Executives with both extensive and limited experience of international management at Applied Materials and Ned Lloyd, Chinese "highflyers" working for a U.S. multinational, and trainees attending the Intercultural Communications Institute summer school in Portland, Oregon. What we found was that the capacity to reconcile rules and exceptions correlated positively and consistently with the capacity to reconcile several other dilemmas crucial to leadership and cultural effectiveness. Within Bombardier, the capacity to resolve dilemmas correlated positively with "promotions during the last three years," as opposed to lateral transfers and staying put.

Dimension 2. Self-Interest *versus* Group-Interest and Personal and Social Fulfillment Concern (Individualism) (Communitarianism)

The Sophisticated Stereotype

Here the contrast is between the freedom of the individual, in which personal fulfillment, enrichment, expression, and self-development are championed above all, and benefits accrue to the group, community, or corporation. There can be no doubt where America stands. Its population is formed by those who left the only community they had known to seek their fortune in the New World. Canada, the United States, Denmark, Switzerland, the Netherlands, Australia, and the United Kingdom head the national advocates of individualism, while India, Japan, Mexico, China, France, Brazil, and Singapore head the advocates of communitarianism.

In this matter, the United States stereotypes itself. Ever since Christian in Bunyan's *Pilgrim's Progress* shook off his pleading wife and child to journey alone to the Heavenly City, Americans have been making themselves, helping themselves, and accumulating on their own, lone rangers to the end. Did you ever see a Hollywood movie in which group opinion was proved right and the lone protagonist yielded to that view?

Yet the superior judgment of the one who stands alone has been vindicated a thousand times! It was Herman Melville who wrote,

> **Take a single man alone, and he seems a triumph, a grandeur or a woe. But take mankind in the mass and they seem for the most part a mob of unnecessary duplicates.**

The communitarian attitudes of rice-growing regions should come as no surprise. With fewer than a dozen people cooperating, it is impossible to survive. The self-aggrandizing schemes of warlords have brought China to starvation again and again. France progressed historically only when angry groups surged into the streets and manned barricades. The inspiration might have been individual, but the *force majeure* was communal. History shapes cultures.

Some Typical Misunderstandings

American plans to "motivate" employees in foreign cultures typically fall afoul of this crucial cultural difference. How many times has the "employee of the month" called in sick rather than face an envious peer group at work? Individual incentives can be unfair if other members of the group helped you succeed or if you believe that your supervisor deserves the credit for briefing and mentoring you so well.

There was a famous case of an error made in assembly work at Intel in Penang. A thousand units had to be reworked at great expense, yet the American boss could not discover who had made the error. The whole work group, even the plant director, took responsibility and apologized. They should have watched the worker more carefully, they explained, helped her more, trained her better. When a whole community is dedicated to higher productivity and quality, you may be wise to leave well enough alone. Communitarianism has its uses.

What Effective Leaders Know and Have Learned

The real limitation of sophisticated stereotypes is at its most obvious here. Of course Americans are individualists, but they also have created groups for a wider variety of purposes than in most other societies: the town meeting, the Community Chest, the protest group, the Skunk Works, the training group, teamworking, the support group, the political action committee, and so on. The main purpose of the group may be the advancement of personal interests, but it remains true that American individualism has important group expressions. Once again, the wealth-generating solutions lie not in values extolling groups or individuals but in interactions between these values.

In this book a large number of leaders have made artful combinations between individualism and communitarianism and between competitiveness and cooperation to create powerful learning systems. Richard Branson in Chapter 3, specializing, as Virgin does, in service organizations, looks first to the communities of his employees who serve the communities of customers; by taking back his company into private hands, he is able to moderate the demands of shareholders (himself) and take his gains in terms of growth, not dividends. A very similar strategy is pursued by Val Gooding of BUPA, Britain's premier private health insurer and provider (Chapter 8). Without shareholders, she is able to invest in staff, customer service, and rapid growth. This can be a crucial advantage for "caring organizations."

In Chapter 4, Dilemma 3, Martin Gillo deliberately fine-tuned the individualism of Advanced Micro Devices' American headquarters with East German communitarianism. He set up rewards for individuals who contributed to team success and gave bonuses to teams for giving the best support to the initiatives of individual members. Both cultures joined enthusiastically in a system that respected their values, even if each preferred an opposite aspect of the system. In Chapter 9 we see how Suez Lyonnaise des Eaux has captured an astonishing 52 percent of foreign-owned water and treatment systems by combining the energies released by privatization with a social responsibility that returns to the served community full ownership of and responsibility for its own municipal infrastructure after a 20-to-25-year overhaul. Rarely have private shareholder gain and responsibility for the integrity of a community been better combined.

Perhaps the boldest attempt to reconcile individualist and communitarian cultures, one that has been brilliantly successful, is that of Jim Morgan of Applied Materials (Chapter 10, Dilemma 2). Morgan turned author to write a pathbreaking book on Japanese business culture in the 1980s. The East Asian attitude toward electronics, microchips (the rice of industry), and computers was essentially communitarian. These technologies, contributing as they did to the community's industrial infrastructure in general, could not be allowed to fail and accordingly were nurtured by governments and banks. Jim realized early on that he had to give Applied Materials, Japan, the autonomy to locate itself at the heart of Japanese industrial policy, among the inner circles of industry. He has followed this policy in Korea, China, Singapore, and other major centers of communitarian consciousness. He has instituted an East-West dialogue at the apex of Applied Materials in which the new freedom of the electronic age converses with the priceless communitarian logic of accelerated learning for whole societies.

Finally, Stan Shih of Acer (Chapter 12, Dilemma 2) built on the communitarian family-based Chinese culture of Taiwan. His "Dragon Dream" had a traditional appeal to a Taiwanese community aspiring to be a force in the wider world community, but he was very well aware of the individualism of the Western world as well as the incipient individualism of the Chinese. Accordingly, he has made Acer a public, national company in most of the nations where it operates, with quotations on local stock exchanges. He also uses stock option plans for *all* employees so that they can share as individuals in the regional success of the company. Acer applies the ratio of individualism to communitarianism preferred by many of the cultures in which it operates.

It has been known for many years that giving incentives, sharing gains, and rewarding the whole group are more motivating for individual members than is trying to reward them directly. The virtuous circle looks like the following figure:

The Virtuous Circle

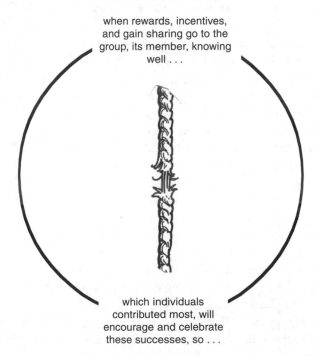

when rewards, incentives, and gain sharing go to the group, its member, knowing well . . .

which individuals contributed most, will encourage and celebrate these successes, so . . .

A group can make any of its members feel like a million dollars. There may be nothing more satisfying in the world than being a heroine or hero to those who know you best—and who would begrudge your subsequent promotion or pay raise once you had steered your group to fame and fortune?

The transculturally competent know that "individualism versus communitarianism" is a false dichotomy. The real art is to nurture individuals and individuals so that they serve groups, a process that Adam M. Brandenberger and Barry J. Nalebuff have called *co-opetition*.

An interesting example of this is Motorola's Total Customer Satisfaction competition. Teams that have "totally satisfied" their customers in any part of the world where Motorola operates gather together the evidence of their success and enter a worldwide competition in which they present their solutions on stage, together with the results achieved. These contests teach all members how to compete fiercely, but note that this competition is about cooperating with customers and fellow team members. Once again, this is "collaborative competing," or co-opetition (see the following diagram).

The Virtuous Circle

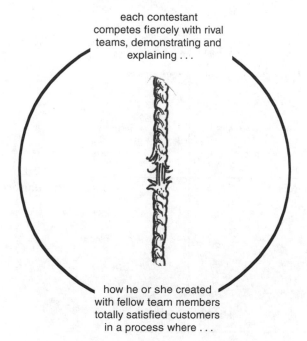

each contestant
competes fiercely with rival
teams, demonstrating and
explaining . . .

how he or she created
with fellow team members
totally satisfied customers
in a process where . . .

Among the advantages of this competition is that 800 or so winning solutions surface, to be studied and disseminated by Motorola University. Competing differentiates ideas; cooperating integrates them. Knowledgeable executives have finely differentiated, well-integrated strategic maps of their terrains.

The dimensions do not exist in isolation from each other. We get powerful insights into Russia's current predicament in Box 1–3.

Box 1-3

Russia's Agony

What is clear from Russia's scores on our first and second dimensions is that no viable system of social order currently exists. Civic order stems from two main influences: the combination of universalism with individualism, or "the legal harness of self-interest," and the combination of particularism with communitarianism, or "special deals for the socially responsible." If we cross our first two axes we find these two clusters.

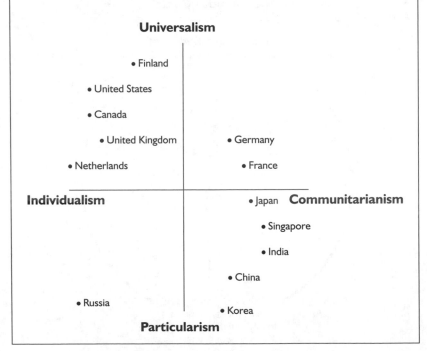

Measuring Transcultural Competence: Reconciling the Individual and the Group

We again turn to the measurement and strategic use of transcultural competence and the results achieved thus far. We repeatedly asked leaders to choose among five options. Two are unreconciled answers, one is a compromise, and two are reconciled answers.

Question 2. Jobs in Your Organization

Which of the following jobs is found most frequently in your organization?

a. A job that is part of an organization where everybody works together and where you do not get individual credit
b. A job that allows everybody to work independently and where individual credit is received on the basis of individual performance
c. A job where everybody works together in teams and where the teams constantly stimulate individual creativity
d. A job that allows everybody to work independently and where individual credit is given to the best team player
e. A job where neither too much individual creativity nor excessive "groupthink" is the norm

---

Answers (a) and (b) are unreconciled answers. Answer (e) is a compromise. Answer (c) is a reconciliation where we start with communitarianism, and answer (d) represents reconciliation that starts with individualism. We found that leaders who chose the latter two options were significantly more effective than were those who chose the other three alternatives.

Dimension 3. Preference for	versus	Preference for
Precise, Singular		Pervasive, Patterned
"Hard" Standards		"Soft" Processes
(Specificity)		(Diffusion)

The Sophisticated Stereotype

Here the contrast is between cultures that emphasize things, facts, statistics, units, atoms, analysis, and "hard" numbers and cultures that emphasize relations, patterns, configurations, connectedness, synthesis, and "soft" processes. These contrasting styles have been identified with the left and right brain hemispheres. We call them specificity and diffusion.

America's exaggerated specificity manifests itself in many forms, such as "keeping one's word" (as if there were only one!), "bullet points," piecework incentives, straight-line forecasts, bottom lines, financial ratios, and other attempted distillations of virtue. We urge each other to "get to the point" and "not beat around the bush." Specificity is increased by argument, by win-lose conflict that produces specific results, and by debates between the respective advocates.

Some Typical Misunderstandings

We remember the fury of a young Israeli engineering salesman who had beaten the three other salesmen, all Japanese, in his department. Indeed, he had sold more than all three put together while learning Japanese from his wife. When his Japanese boss gave him an "average" rating, he hit the ceiling. He appealed to the American headquarters of the company, which backed his position. His Japanese boss was furious. "You shoot me, I shoot you," the boss hissed. From an American and Israeli perspective this engineer's sales record said it all. Judged by specific criteria, he had done brilliantly. He had won the sales, worked longer hours, seen more customers, and not bothered his boss. Yet judged by diffuse criteria, he had failed. He had never informed his boss of his mounting success or allowed the boss to share in it. He had never passed intelligence or information to other salespersons or tried to improve the work process of the department. He had not contributed to relationships with his work colleagues at all.

Alfie Kohn recently compiled a long, sad dossier of what goes wrong with pay for performance. Many managers recognize these problems but are reluctant to give up on the idea that just as markets pull money and rewards toward successful enterprises, so should corporations. The problem with pay for performance is its exaggerated specificity. It assumes that superiors can know in advance how a task should be done, how difficult it is, and hence what pay should be attached to its performance, but increasingly, this is not possible. Work is too complex, too innovative, too subject to continuous improvement for superiors to know these things, much less to construct an elaborate system of rewards. Markets certainly do pay for success—this is their genius—but do not tell you in advance what you should do or how much you will gain by doing it! Markets are diffuse, chaotic processes with some very specific and measurable outcomes. Let us count, by all means, but not shrink reality to what can be counted.

What Effective Leaders Know and Have Learned

The answer lies, as before, between the preferences of business cultures, such as in the United States and the Netherlands, with predominant specificity and business cultures, such as Japan and Singapore, with predominant diffuseness. While Americans like to begin with forecasts, budgets, checklists, and plans and then start a process to hit those targets, East Asians typically value harmonious processes (*wa*) and the spontaneous flow of work and only later subject those processes to detailed feedback on specific indicators.

Some famous American gurus, among them W. Edwards Deming and Joseph Scanlon, had their ideas picked *over* in America but picked *up* and massively implemented in Japan and East Asia and then imported back into the United States. Why did this happen? Because both Deming and Scanlon placed spontaneous action and the free flow of ideas and industrial processes ahead of the feedback and specifics needed to monitor, guide, and reward them. Deming's cycle of act–plan–implement–check starts with spontaneous action. The Scanlon plan begins with the free flow of constructive ideas within workteams. Once they are implemented, their impact on the input-output ratio is calculated, and specific gains from the process are shared among group members. This is a much better "imitation of capitalism" than pay for performance because it sees that improvements are yet to be discovered and invented amid the "chaos" of work processes.

That employees are capable of self-organizing to form teams with their own flow and momentum is by now a truism. It could begin with a challenge or a definition of a problem by the sponsor of the team. Persons who care about this issue and have the skills and knowledge to address it select themselves or are selected by the regard of other volunteers. Note that the team is shaped by the profile of the problem and forms itself spontaneously to solve that problem.

Most of the leaders in this book developed ingenious ways to synergize diffuse and specific processes. Philippe Bourguignon of Club Med was determined to build a "power brand" (Chapter 5, Dilemma 2). This requires millions of impacts on the public of the Club Med brand via an accumulation of specific "sound bytes" and fleeting images in the media, all of which reinforce the brand through repetition. Yet at the same time, the brand stood for a vacation that was dreamlike, playful, experimental, and without precedent in the customer's experience, a seamless, diffuse pattern of intense enjoyment in which to reinvent oneself and rehearse new roles and different lifestyles. The specific brand stood for a cornucopia of novel experiences.

Val Gooding of BUPA, the British private health insurer and provider, realized that in health provision you have to go beyond specific medical crises in which you respond only after a diagnosis has been made. She instituted a policy of enhancing *wellness*, an extremely diffuse concept of living one of many healthy lifestyles while avoiding emergencies by means of careful screening (Chapter 9, Dilemma 4). Michael Dell of Dell Computers (Chapter 11, Dilemma 6) was one of the first to move beyond the supply of specific hardware or software to embrace process innovation via the Internet. Dell starts with why you want computers, what you want them for, and how you plan to mobilize information and then helps you with that whole diffuse process of knowledge management. Edgar Bronfman, chief executive officer of Seagram's, launched a major program to change the company's culture. He saw culture as a diffuse process to be negotiated between leader and employees. The leader managed the culture, and the culture produced hard, specific results. What leaders *cannot* do is order up results like items on a menu. Hence, Bronfman developed a dual scoreboard for his managers: They were rewarded for the specific results achieved *and* for exemplifying and managing the diffuse array of cultural values that guided the corporation and helped define excellence.

A major issue having to do with strategy (Chapter 6, Dilemma 3) is whether strategy is a specific, codified plan of action that is conceived in the abstract and then implemented by the staff or whether it is a diffuse set of local initiatives arising from the grass roots and providing vital clues to success. Hugo Levecke of ABN AMRO was able to show how powerful these two ideas are in combination. The organization learns by *first* appraising local initiatives and inquiring into their greater or lesser success and only *then* creating a specific strategy out of proven successful initiatives, generalizing from local to global gains.

Chicago psychologist Mihaly Csikszentmihali speaks of the *flow experience*, in which teams or single competitors have so closely matched their skills with the attainment of their goals that the boundaries seem to dissolve. They are their own challenge. The skier and the trail are one. The goal becomes a source of energy that speeds the team. Human beings and their teams, he says, are complex adaptive systems that can form seamless, purposeful wholes.

In highly effective organizations, diffuse, "chaotic," creative teams receive specific feedback on the success or failure of initiatives, managing, as it were, "on the edge of chaos." This is shown in the following diagram.

The Virtuous Circle

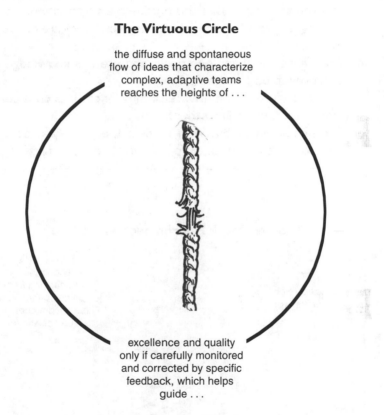

the diffuse and spontaneous
flow of ideas that characterize
complex, adaptive teams
reaches the heights of . . .

excellence and quality
only if carefully monitored
and corrected by specific
feedback, which helps
guide . . .

Measuring Transcultural Competence: Reconciling Specificity and Diffuseness

The 2500 managers who completed our transcultural questionnaire all considered five possible answers to the following ideas about the best work environment.

Question 3. The Best Work Environment

People have different opinions about how the work environment influences job performance.

Which of these alternatives best describes the work environment in your organization?

a. People you work with know you personally and accept the way you are both within and outside the organization.
b. Colleagues respect the work you do even if they are not your friends.
c. Colleagues know you personally and use this knowledge to improve job performance.
d. Colleagues take some private circumstances into consideration while disregarding others.
e. The people you work with respect the work you do and therefore are able to offer to help you in private matters.

The Best Work Environment—Part One

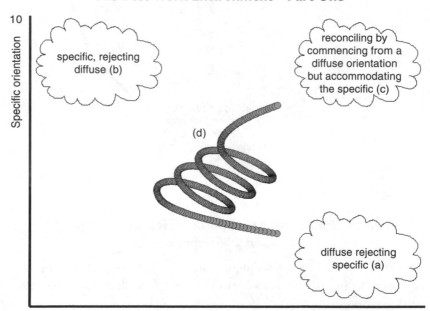

The Best Work Environment—Part Two

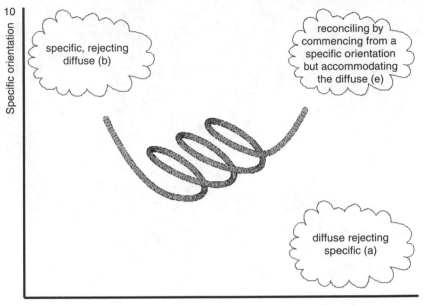

In the two preceding diagrams we see that the most effective work environments, (c) and (e), are those in which specific and diffuse sources of knowledge are combined—in either order.

This concludes the presentation of the first three dimensions. In each case the recognition of dilemmas and their reconciliation helped us and our leaders create a wider and more inclusive "integration of values." We submit that this integration, this bridging of diverse perspectives, is a vital aspect of creating wealth.

Chapter 2

Transcultural Competence: Learning to Lead by Through-Through Thinking and Acting, Part II

Fons Trompenaars and Charles Hampden-Turner

*I*N THIS CHAPTER we will consider our final four dimensions:

4. Emotions inhibited   Emotions expressed
    (neutral)   (affective)
5. Achieved status   Ascribed status
6. Inner-directed   Outer-directed
7. Sequential   Synchronous

Dimension 4. Emotions Inhibited *versus* Emotions Expressed (Neutral) (Affective)

The Sophisticated Stereotype

It is well known that cultures display emotions to greatly varying degrees. The fury of a Frenchman when you nearly collide with his car and the way he uses his whole body to express his rage is legendary. In contrast, one can be forgiven for imagining that Japanese executives have gone to sleep during a presentation. The posture of "half-eye" with the eyelids half closed can be galling to those who do not understand "respectful listening." Equally unnerving are the long silences that follow your statement. These might be read as "boredom," when in fact they are intended as evidence of thoughtful consideration. While the Japanese are highly neutral, the French, the Italians, and the Latin nations are more volatile and affective.

This dimension has more subtleties and variations than do most others because there is strong disagreement about what one should be neutral or affective *about*. Americans, for example, show up as moderately affective despite their Puritan origins of restraint in religious expression. They believe in showing enthusiasm for products, visions, missions, and projects but are less expressive to each other. They approve of positive emotion (enthusiasm) but not necessarily of negative emotion (anger or grief). They will talk *about* emotion ("I'm feeling angry") in a vaguely therapeutic manner but rarely explode or show physical signs of anger. The British use humor to release emotions and may begin a speech with a joke to relax the audience. The Germans and the Swiss may see this as unserious and frivolous. Japanese and Koreans reveal a desire for intimacy by getting drunk together; Germans prefer to bare their souls and share their philosophies of life. The patterns are extremely complex.

Some Typical Misunderstandings

> The Swiss can be quite serious, especially during work hours. Humor is for relaxing moments before or after the seminar. A Dutch presenter used a cartoon to "break the ice." Dead silence. He used a second cartoon. Again silence. Then a Swiss participant raised his hand and said, "Can we get on with the seminar, please?"
>
> The Dutch presenter tried to make a joke of the intervention: "You're a serious lot. Have you ever thought of going into banking?"
>
> Silence.
>
> *(continued)*

(continues)
   In the coffee break the senior Swiss manager approached the Dutch presenter: "We didn't want to embarrass you, Dr. Trompenaars, but in fact, the Swiss have been in banking for some time."

Note that both parties hung on tightly to their conviction that jokes were or were not appropriate in the seminar. Those who saw humor as inappropriate could not even recognize the attempt!

Often the same word triggers totally different associations. In a recent partnership negotiation the Japanese and American sides both vowed to be "sincere." By this the Americans meant outspoken, unreserved, and spontaneous, something the Japanese found insulting. By "sincere" the Japanese referred to genuine efforts to create a climate of politeness, etiquette, and gracious manners, a habit the Americans saw as "bull____." The meeting was a disaster.

What Effective Leaders Demonstrate

It is wise for a leader to make the greatest possible use of emotional range. There are wide variations in the fortunes of a company, and it is appropriate to have a mood that fits the occasion. As Robert Whittinton wrote of Sir Thomas More,

> **Where should we find a man of such wit, affability and lowliness? As time requireth, a man of marvelous mirth and pastimes, and sometimes of as sad gravity, as who say: A man for all seasons.**

In the Bible, we are told in Ecclesiastes,

> *To everything there is a season, and a time to every purpose under heaven.*
> *A time to be born and a time to die....*
> *A time to weep, and a time to laugh; a time to mourn, and a time to dance.*
> . . . .
> *A time to love, and a time to hate; a time of war, and a time of peace.*

An effective leader operates in two contrasting realms: calculated reasoning, which can require that emotions be temporarily suppressed, and a wisdom of the heart, which knows that emotional expression evokes a resonance that can heal, inspire, enthuse, comfort, and calm those present.

It is perfectly legitimate to postpone the expression of emotion until you are in a place or in a presence where it is appropriate to communicate it, but temporary *suppression* should not lead to *repression*, in which dangerous emotions are not admitted even to oneself. Persons with that tendency are likely to erupt into rage or grief, tremble uncontrollably, or act maliciously and destructively. An effective leader trusts his or her body to convey appropriate feelings and strives to make good sense of and logical deductions from those feelings. The mind includes the body and the messages it sends.

A number of the leaders in this book manage neutrality-affectivity particularly well. Richard Branson (Chapter 3) regards "*have fun*" as the surest recipe for an organization to serve its customers effectively. Good service should be a pleasure for those providing it, and in its absence, something is wrong. LEGO put the switch from neutrality to exuberance and excitement to clever use by charging customers *before* they went into Legoland Parks, while they were still in a calculative mode (Chapter 6, Dilemma 6), but the entrance fee gave families, especially children, free access to all the attractions so that they could let their excitement rip without clawing desperately at Mother's handbag for one more treat. There is a time to seek entrance and a time to enjoy having done so; the first should be sober, the second joyful.

Bang and Olufsen was a family firm when it got into trouble. The roots of its problem lay within the family, in a needlessly expensive lifestyle and a preference for product quality over what the market could afford (Chapter 7, Dilemma 3). Anders Knutsen was able to intervene and transform the company *both* because he was a son of the house who was trusted by the family *and* because he brought with him a cool, detached professionalism that understood the cost savings essential to the company. BUPA and Val Gooding (Chapter 9, Dilemma 1) had to combine the cerebral calculations of a smart insurance company that sees not people but trends, aggregates, and numbers with caring deeply about the one life that each customer has. When the customer calls for help after years of contributions, whether the company is "there" for him or her is a vital question. "I'm sick, I need you," says the customer, and the voice at the other end of the line will make or break that relationship through the swiftness, effectiveness, and empathy of the response.

For effective leaders, the virtuous circle of neutrality-affectivity reads as follows:

The Virtuous Circle

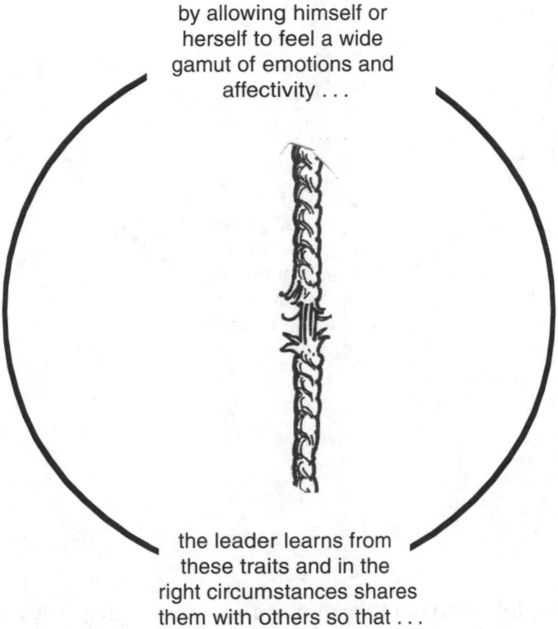

by allowing himself or
herself to feel a wide
gamut of emotions and
affectivity . . .

the leader learns from
these traits and in the
right circumstances shares
them with others so that . . .

We might pause to consider ways in which emotions are mishandled and leaders who are usually neutral may suddenly burst out with inappropriate emotion, uncontrollable anger, or self-pity. "You won't have Dick Nixon to kick around anymore" is a famous example from a leader whose emotions could not be trusted by himself or others and whose mental state was accurately rendered by "expletive deleted," a phrase that punctuates the Watergate tapes. This illustrates a vicious circle, as shown here:

The Vicious Circle

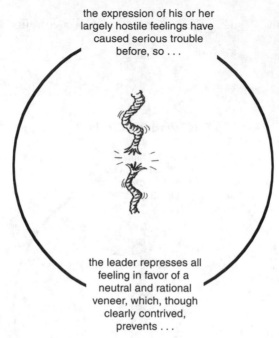

the expression of his or her
largely hostile feelings have
caused serious trouble
before, so . . .

the leader represses all
feeling in favor of a
neutral and rational
veneer, which, though
clearly contrived,
prevents . . .

It is such a leader from whom one hesitates to buy a secondhand car and who is nicknamed "Tricky."

Measuring Intercultural Competence: Reconciling Neutrality with Affectivity

We can measure the extent to which meanings and emotions have been reconciled by comparing two polarized strategies with two integrated strategies and a compromise. Emotions can be so strong that they obliterate thinking. Thoughts can be so calculated that they repress genuine feelings, but to think first and then let out the emotions at the right time, and to feel first and then think hard about how to express this feeling to the best effect are both pathways to integration.

Question 4. Upset at Work

In situations where you feel upset at work, which of the following behaviors are you most likely to adopt?

a. Express your upset overtly so that you can become rational again as soon as possible.
b. Express it overtly in a very moderate way so that your message gets across at least partially.
c. Keep it to yourself. Expressing upset overtly serves no purpose.
d. Keep it to yourself initially in order to find a more suitable moment to express yourself openly and in detail.
e. Express it immediately. A good working relationship depends on open, honest communication.

Question 4 (my answer)—(how others in my organization would answer)

We plot these answers on the following grid:

Grid Display

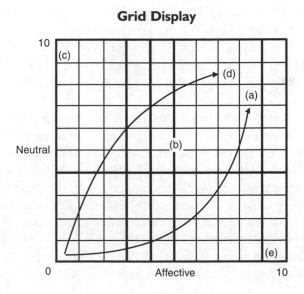

Dimension 5. Status Earned *versus* **Status Ascribed to a**
through Success **Person's Potential,**
and Track **e.g., Age, Family,**
Record **Education**
(Achievement) **(Ascription)**

The Sophisticated Stereotype

Here the contrast is between being esteemed for what you do and being esteemed for what you are. Status can be conferred almost exclusively on the basis of one's achievements. It also can be conferred on the basis of one's being or potential. We may therefore expect more of men, white people, the college educated (which includes past achievement), older people, well-connected people, and people from a good family or class. Persons assigned to certain roles (e.g., electrical engineer) may have higher status because the business or nation expects that their jobs are crucial to its future.

American culture tries to mock all unearned privileges and distinctions; witness the recent move against affirmative action. "Ragged Dick" in the Horatio Alger stories was an orphan and did not even have parents to thank for his achievements—only himself! Andrew Carnegie famously remarked that British lords, dukes, and earls had done nothing except be born of ancestors who had done "dirty deeds for kings." Yet ascribed status persists, and white males of northern European descent still enjoy higher status, even in America.

As we might have expected, Americans, Canadians, New Zealanders, and Australians, of immigrant nations all, have strong preferences for achievement. When you immigrate, you leave class and family associations behind. Few in the New World care that you came from a "prominent family in Kent." Norway, France, Sweden, Ireland, and the United Kingdom are also high in achievement orientation.

Among cultures *ascribing* status there are some with formidable records of economic growth in the recent past: Japan, Korea, Hong Kong, Taiwan, China, and Singapore. Are these cultures against achievement? Surely not. They approach it in a different way. They ascribe high status to those entrusted with "catching up with the West," who are given prestigious posts in key projects. The idea is that these persons will achieve as a consequence of the trust placed in them.

Achievement orientations assume that what is being tried is *worth* achieving, but this is not always true. Rising to the top of a criminal conspiracy engaged in racketeering is a doubtful achievement. An

American musical from the 1930s had a song entitled "You're the Top." The words have not stood the test of time:

> *You're Mrs. Sweeney*
> *You're Mussolini*
> *You're custard pie....*

There is something to be said for examining "achievements" critically to weed out fascist dictators.

Some Typical Misunderstandings

Individuals from societies in which people *achieve* status and those from societies that *ascribe* it are often at odds in first encounters. When Americans visit East Asia with a product or proposition, they usually "put their cards on the table" and automatically call it as they see it: This is the deal. These are the costs. This is the size of the likely opportunity. With profits on this scale, should we not reconcile our differences? All this is "achievement talk," and of course it is deeply offensive to cultures that ascribe status. What these cultures seek to know is, Who are you? Who are you related to and connected with? What is your background? What family do you come from? They also want to know whether you are inherently gracious, polite, and hospitable. By putting you in relaxed settings, they seek to establish trust. Many hours and even days may be spent on small talk, but the implications are not small. If you were pretending, you could not maintain the pretense. The scattered impressions would not be coherent. What, after all, is five days in a partnership lasting five years or more?

Attempts to get your partner excited about the product or the profit are deeply suspect. That is what con men do. They appeal to your greed and exploitiveness. A partner too concerned with gain is likely to cheat you. A partner you can trust cares more about his or her reputation, the status ascribed to him or her by colleagues. Pressure tactics are equally repellent. If the American partner really trusted us, he would respect our judgment and seek concurrence.

If we look more closely at this misunderstanding, we see that it is really a matter of priorities. Once Americans have decided to do business with someone and feel that a deal is in the offing, it is sensible to get to know the person, deepen the relationship, check his or her references. Once a Chinese or Japanese executive has gotten to know an American and deepened the relationship, it is time to turn to business. Each accidentally offends the other by getting this sequence "wrong."

The reason it is so important to learn from other cultures is that "pure achievement" and "pure ascription" are *both* apt to fail. The British pension industry is facing a pension misselling scandal in which tens of thousands of pensioners were induced to surrender their group plan for an individual portable pension with significantly lower benefits. The volume of this duplicity is a staggering £2 billion, with companies "named and shamed" by government watchdogs until they repay the difference. How could salespersons fan out across the country and talk luckless savers into a pension provision worse than the one they currently held? All too easily, we fear, because these sales staffs were being paid on commission only for what they achieved.

The signal this sends to employees is clear: "We care nothing for you as persons and will invest nothing in you personally. We will take a share in your performance." In other words, status ascribed 0 percent, status achieved 100 percent. What happened, of course, was that this attitude toward the sales staff was passed on by the staff to the customers: "We care nothing for you or your pension rights. You are there to help us achieve our sales targets." We must instead give status to simple humanity, to potentials capable of flowering in the future. If we think only of achieving, we risk trampling each other in the rush to succeed.

Pure ascribed status is similarly hazardous. Consider the loans made to relatives of President Suharto of Indonesia! No wonder the whole rotten edifice collapsed. Instead of money flowing toward success, it flowed from political crony to political crony.

Most companies in the world, by a very large margin, are still family owned. Even in publicly owned companies family concepts survive. One thinks of the Japanese terms *amai,* meaning "indulgent affection between mentor and subordinate," and *sempae-gohal,* meaning "brother–younger brother relationship." Training your workforce and mentoring workers represent an investment in their potential, a form of ascribed status. That people who care for and respect each other go on to achieve is a natural consequence. The larger training expenses of several East Asian cultures speak for themselves. Japanese auto-assembly plants in the United States give new workers 225 hours of training in the first six months; U.S. plants give 42 hours.

What Effective Leaders Know and Have Learned

The research findings in Box 1-1 should convince us that cultures that place ascribed status first are still capable of rapid economic growth. Even with the present troubles, East Asian growth rates are the highest recorded in the history of economics. The reason for this is that ascribing status and achieving status are complementary. If you want someone to achieve, show him or her initial respect. In America we keep stumbling over this fact, but "lean and mean" management too often ignores it. In the original Hawthorne experiment, Irish and Polish immigrant female workers were given the status of core-searchers with Elton Mayo and Fritz Roethlisberger from Harvard. Instead of just assembling telephone relays, they were invited to investigate how telephone relays might be better assembled, a totally transformed job description. The fact that they were withdrawn from the factory floor into a small group meant that they could affirm each other's identities. They began to achieve. As productivity climbed, the startled researchers treated them with even more respect, and their achievement climbed again as the virtuous circle took hold. What many dismiss as "the Hawthorne effect" is in fact a learning dynamic of great power and influence, as is shown in the following diagram.

The Virtuous Circle

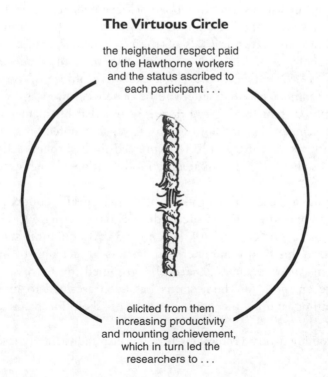

the heightened respect paid
to the Hawthorne workers
and the status ascribed to
each participant . . .

elicited from them
increasing productivity
and mounting achievement,
which in turn led the
researchers to . . .

The leaders in this book also showed great skill in handling the achieved-ascribed dimension and using it to learn with. Richard Branson (Chapter 3, Dilemma 1) starts by critiquing the industries in which he has decided to compete, that is, by ascribing defective status to them and ascribing to himself the reputation of a reformer of those industries and an underdog in challenging them. Unlike many reformers, he then actually *achieves* superior levels of performance and thus proves his original contention, using wide sympathy in the press and among customers to establish his case.

In Chapter 4, Dilemma 5, the issue is granting teams enough autonomy to *achieve* without diminishing the *ascribed* status of the senior manager who sponsors a team's efforts. Martin Gillo struggled with the need to have senior managers risk their senior positions by delegating resources and authority to problem-solving teams. When one of those teams was successful, the sponsor's authority was actually enhanced and the status ascribed to the team was used by it to achieve, and thus add to, the sponsor's reputation.

In Chapter 12, Dilemma 5, Stan Shih of Acer had to make sure *both* that managers and employees achieved *and* that others were prepared to mentor that achievement, to describe, judge, and celebrate excellence and in that respect rise above achievement to assure that the ends were worthwhile. You cannot have everyone achieve; some must judge and consecrate the goals of the achievement, and some must ascribe status to, and be seen to symbolize, the ends themselves. In Chapter 14, Dilemma 2, the chief executive officer of Seagram's, Edgar Bronfman, had to decide whether a new culture was created by his ascribing status, acting top down, or by what his managers were actually achieving, acting bottom up. He sensibly opted for a dialogue and synthesis so that the culture expressed itself through action, but he was also labeled and evaluated by his definition of what excellence constituted.

Koç was a successful family company in a Turkish context. Rahmi Koç, the son of the founder, succeeded his father at age 53, relatively late in his career (Chapter 19, Dilemma 5). Although his status was ascribed by his family membership, he was in fact sent to business school in America and was carefully groomed for succession. The pressure on those to whom status has been ascribed to live up to their billing and to the achievements of their forebears can be intense.

If you are a very visible heir to a Turkish industrial dynasty with tens of thousands of workers and associated charities dependent on your success, the spotlight is very much on your performance. The nation has given you high status and respect in the fervent hope that you will justify it by achieving on behalf of that nation. Status is intended to be a self-fulfilling prophecy.

A common experience for any consultant who uses interviewing as a method of inquiry is that many executives have rarely had the experience of being listened to and that when they are listened to their morale and competence grow before one's eyes. Royale Foote and colleagues tested the proposition that interviewing alone can boost productivity. In the Fairmont plant of Anheuser-Busch, they trained each level of supervisor to interview the level below, from the top of the organization down to the very bottom, which was represented by a tough Teamsters local. Interviews were focused not on work issues specifically but on whatever concerned the interviewee. There was no additional intervention. In the eight years of the interviewing process the Fairmont facility climbed from almost the worst plant in the network to by far the best on a scale of hard measures. Something as elementary as brewing, canning, and trucking rests squarely on the status and respect ascribed to each member of the organization.

No less a luminary than Douglas McGregor taught that the respect and confidence we have in one another expresses itself in subsequent achievement. He called this Theory Y. As Bernard Shaw wrote in *Pygmalion*, "It's the way she's treated that makes her a lady." No wonder the Pygmalion effect has been found in the workplace and the classroom. When teachers were told that a child would "spurt," the child did, although "spurters" actually were picked at random. It was the teacher's belief that spurred the child to achievement.

Measuring Intercultural Competence: Reconciling Achieved Status with Ascribed Status

There are two ways to integrate these values. You could argue that you must first decide *who* you are (ascribed status) if you are to go on to achieve in a way consistent with this, or you could decide that achieving at this and that is a good way of discovering who you are (achieved status) and what you were meant to stand for.

The following five responses were used to measure reconciliation versus polarization.

Question 5. What Is Important?

Which one of the following best describes your values?

The most important thing in life is

a. Getting things done, because in the long run it serves you best to think and act in a way that is consistent with the way you really are.
b. To be able to do things at some times and relax at others.
c. To think and act in a manner that is consistent with the way you really are, because in the long run you will achieve more.
d. Getting things done even if it interferes with the way you really are.
e. To think and act consistently with the way you really are even if you don't get things done.

Question 5 (my answer)—(how others in my organization would answer)

We plot these answers on the following grid:

Grid Display

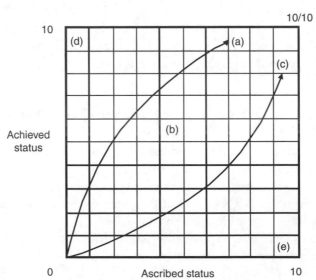

Dimension 6. Control and   *versus*   **Control and**
Effective Direction   **Effective Direction**
from Within   **from Outside**
(Inner-Directed)   **(Outer-Directed)**

The Sophisticated Stereotype

Here the question involves the source of virtue and direction. Is it inside each person, in the "soul," conscience, or integrity, or outside of a person, in the beauty and harmony of nature or the needs of families, friends, and customers? Is it virtuous "to be your own person" or "to respond to your environment"?

There are no prizes for guessing that Americans are inner directed (see Box 1-1). Americans tend to plan and then to make those plans work, to rely on ability rather than luck, and to prescribe taking control of one's life. The United States is joined in strong inner direction by Norway, New Zealand, Canada, Australia, and France. The latter country, we might note, combines communitarianism with inner direction, as in the group of fiercely convinced rebels who seized control of the nation's destiny. While inner direction is advocated by Judeo-Christian values, outer direction is sanctioned by Shintoism and Buddhism. Gods are believed to inhabit mountains, streams, storms, harvests, and winds. You mollify the gods by shaping attractive containers they will wish to inhabit.

In examining this bifurcation we cannot evade the truth that American pop culture celebrates and satirizes itself. We have Superman vying with planes and bullets and overwhelming natural forces. We have Frank Sinatra "doing it my way" and small children bearing arms against each other. *Fortune* magazine celebrates "America's Ten Toughest Bosses" despite their very brief tenures. Al Dunlap dresses in battle fatigues and ammunition belts to do an imitation of Rambo. Unfortunately, there are real casualties. When life imitates art, all concerned can escalate this process to absurd extremes. The flaw in celebrating inner direction is that for every boss "so tough that he tells you when to go to the bathroom" there have to be several American subordinates waiting to be told! This hardly improves effectiveness overall.

Some Typical Misunderstandings

No concept has ever taken American management theory by storm as powerfully as *strategy*. The metaphor is, of course, military, and it conjures up Alexander the Great's conquest of the known world. No concept better reflects the grip of inner directedness on the American

imagination. It is the genius and conviction of business leaders that justify their multimillion-dollar salaries. It is true that strategy can make
or break a business. People Express (PE) grew to a $2 billion corpora-
tion when Don Burr slashed the costs of flying. He took out galleys,
increased seats, sold tickets on board, and had passengers lift their own
baggage into larger lockers. This enabled him to slash prices and get
loadings (occupancy) above 80 percent, but strategy also defeated PE.
American Airlines and United used management yield software to predict how full their flights would be on the day of travel and slashed
fares to fill their planes. Their flexible fare cuts beat PE's rigid fare cuts.

The problem with brilliant inner-directed strategies is that they are
not confined to corporate headquarters. Intelligence is widely distributed, and the closer you get to the interface with the customer, the better
such strategies are informed. In a brilliant *Harvard Business Review* article
Henry Mintzberg argued that strategies typically emerge from the grass
roots of the corporation, where market changes begin. The problem with
strategy designed at the top (inner-directed strategy) is that top managers
are typically farthest from the field and the customers.

The danger is that their strategy will be abstract and largely alien-
ated from the culture of the corporation. At worst, the strategy will
command the impossible. At best, it will command something that the
grass roots of the organization has been doing for years without recognition. Top-down strategy says in effect, "I think, therefore you act." It
reserves for subordinates the role of putting their energies behind the
superior thoughts of their leaders. In fact, nearly everyone has a strategy,
and all of us want to think. This might help explain why outer-directed
Japanese carmakers still register 28 implemented suggestions per employee per year while inner-directed Western corporations register 1.8
at best. It is prestigious to be outer directed in Japanese and most East
Asian cultures; that is why superiors listen while subordinates exercise
initiatives as hundreds of suggestions and strategies emerge. If you are
really senior in a Japanese corporation, you hardly talk at all!

We are not, of course, claiming that outer direction is better. We do
not agree with Henry Mintzberg that emergent strategy obviates the
need for designed strategy or that it is worth holding debates between
their respective advocates. We believe that top management can create
grand strategies *out of* the initiatives that emerge from the grass roots.

What Effective Leaders Know and Have Learned

The metaphor that best integrates inner direction with outer direction
is the traditional jiujitsu artist. He carefully observes the outer-directed

momentum lurching toward him and deflects that person in the direction of his own choosing. Much of China, Japan, and East Asia tells the story of the Monkey King, who, unlike Superman, is physically weaker than other forces in its environment but is a lot more agile and clever. The trick is to harness your own aims to the external dynamisms and momentum of the market.

The leaders in this book have shown remarkable skills in attaching their own deliberate aims to the swirl of the external world. In Chapter 4, Dilemma 2, Martin Gillo helped build his "Fabulous Fab" by taking the high-risk, shoot-from-the-hip pragmatism of Advanced Micro Devices, with its inner-directed drive, and combining it with an East German love for rationalizing and analyzing external environments. The two groups optimized their "opposed" values to an extraordinary degree. Bang and Olufsen had suffered from a perilous imbalance almost from its founding. Product excellence was what the founders defined its mission to be, and if the external market disagreed, the market was simply wrong, consisting of a bunch of clods who failed to appreciate aesthetics and top quality (Chapter 7, Dilemma 1). The company was inner directed to an unaffordable degree. Its models were displayed in New York's Museum of Modern Art, but too few customers could afford them. Not until costs were brought under control and customers outside the company were accorded the respect due to them did the company transform itself and take off. Inner direction and outer direction must be fine-tuned if inner convictions are to receive external acclaim.

Michael Dell challenged the very categories of "inside Dell" and "outside Dell" (Chapter 11, Dilemma 1). Through the use of the Internet, Dell's "inner" deliberations were opened up to suppliers, subcontractors, and customers in an ongoing dialogue. Interested parties at any point in the network could gain access, and so parts suppliers could discover for themselves the company's inventory levels and take responsibility for making sure that customers never ran short and were supplied "just in time." Instead of ordering compliance, you share knowledge, and the other person responds. Knowledge accumulates whether its source is within Dell or comes from a partner.

Sergei Kiriyenko (Chapter 13, Dilemma 1), trying to revive Russia's NORSI, found himself trapped between unions and his managers, all demanding their "share" of nonexistent "earnings," and external creditors, tax authorities, and traditional recipients of NORSI's revenues. He obliged them all to negotiate with him and first favored those *inside* the organization, because he needed them to generate revenues; however, as soon as revenues were flowing, he paid off *external* demands.

Within two years the refinery was in the black, and Kiriyenko was famous and on his way to Moscow.

The transculturally competent leaders we have measured can integrate outer direction with inner direction. Typical of their thinking is the next virtuous circle:

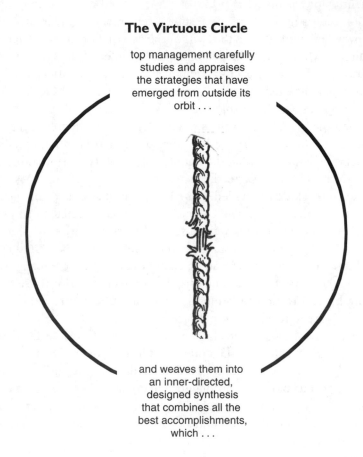

The Virtuous Circle

top management carefully
studies and appraises
the strategies that have
emerged from outside its
orbit . . .

and weaves them into
an inner-directed,
designed synthesis
that combines all the
best accomplishments,
which . . .

Mintzberg calls this *crafting* strategy, as occurs when clay rises spontaneously from the potter's wheel and hands lightly shape it.

Measuring Intercultural Competence: Reconciling Internal with External Loci of Control

We measure how inner directed versus outer directed a leader is by considering the relative merits of "push" and "pull" strategies. Should you allow customers to *pull* you in outer-directed fashion toward their wishes even when those wishes change, or should you *push* terms, conditions, and deliveries on a customer in an inner-directed fashion and, having won his or her agreement, carry through as promised? Following are the dilemma and some responses:

Question 6. Push or Pull?

Several consultants argued that you can achieve greater customer satisfaction and quicker delivery times by using a customer-focused *pull* strategy and that *push* strategies are outmoded. Several other consultants disagreed.

Which position is closest to your viewpoint?

a. A pull strategy is best because it lets the customer reset the deadline and allows resources to converge on the customer on cue. Remember, customers get behind schedule too and change their minds about the relative advantages of speed, quality, cost, and so on.

b. A push strategy is best because it commits the supplier and the customer to a joint schedule, with costs, quality, and specifications agreed on in advance. The customer can, of course, change his or her mind, but then the costs of altering the original schedule are calculable.

c. A combination of push and pull strategies is best so that the customer helps us decide when not to push our products and we tell the clients when we cannot meet their requests.

d. A push strategy is best because it commits the supplier and the customer to a joint schedule with costs, quality, and specifications agreed on in advance. If you do as you promised and do it in time, you cannot be faulted and your record speaks for itself.

e. A pull strategy is best because it lets the customer reset the deadline and allows resources to converge on the customer on cue. The customer wants it when she wants it, and pushing hard can get resources to her too early and at needless expense.

Question 23 (my answer)—(how others in my organization would answer)

The five possible answers are scored as shown in the accompanying diagram. Answers (a) and (b) are integrated, with outer-directed *pull* put first in the sequence in (a) and inner-directed *push* put first in the sequence in (b).

Grid Display

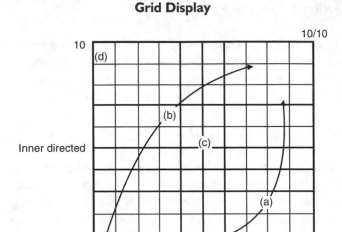

Answer (c) is a compromise; (d) and (e) are inner-directed and outer-directed polarities that brook no opposition from the conflicting principle. Answer (d), for example, is concerned with the supplier's not being "faulted," not with satisfying the customer.

Dimension 7. Time	*versus*	Time
Conceived of		Conceived of
as a "Race"		as a "Dance"
with Passing		with Circular
Increments		Iterations
(Sequential)		(Synchronous)

The Sophisticated Stereotype

The contrast is between two alternative conceptions of time: Time cannot really be seen or touched, and so culture looms large in its definition. *Time as a race* sees time as a sequence of passing increments. An aim of life becomes doing as much as possible within time limits. *Time as a dance* concentrates on timing, or synchronization, so that one moves in time with other persons or processes.

American managers take a sequential approach to time, in common with those in Brazil, Ireland, Belgium, Italy, and the Philippines. Japan and China take a mostly synchronous view, as do Hong Kong, Korea, Singapore, Sweden, and France. Orientation to time is part of America's self-satirical and stereotyped view of itself. There are time and motion studies, or "racing with the clock," as workers sang in *The Pajama Game*. Benjamin Franklin said, "Time is money," and so it is no wonder that Americans seek to "make a quick buck." Andrew Marvell, the Puritan poet, even chided his bashful mistress that "Time's winged chariot" was overtaking the slow pace of their love life.

America's time and motion studies have made a priceless contribution to the efficiencies of mass production, but so too have the Japanese conceptions of just-in-time and parallel processing. The former is clearly sequential, the latter synchronous. Before we consider how modern manufacturing combines these viewpoints, let us consider conflicts that arise from the clash of expectations.

Some Typical Misunderstandings

One of the authors was buying a book at the Singapore airport. The clerk took his credit card, wrapped the book, and proceeded to serve the next customer, with the card and the book still in the clerk's possession. When the purchaser objected, she explained quite reasonably that she was saving time. It would take several seconds for the credit card company to respond. When the credit had been cleared, she switched her attention back to the original purchaser. In practice, few cultures are as well balanced between concepts of time as Singapore is.

A more common experience is that sequential cultures regard synchronous cultures as "rude" because they typically run late and then overstay to "make it up to you." Synchronous people dislike waiting in line for service and often form a scrum. They also interrupt your work and are highly distractible, seemingly doing several things at the same time. Synchronous cultures may regard sequential cultures as "rude" because they respond not to the individual but to an "inner clock." They stride hurriedly from one place to the next, occasionally waving at you but never stopping, and are so immersed in their work that they ignore people. They seem to want to stand behind you or in front of you but not by your side. They refuse to abandon their plans in the face of unexpected meetings. Politeness makes them impatient.

Synchronous cultures have a logic of their own. You "give time" to people important to you, and if those people abound, you will be delayed. Top people deserve more scope to synchronize their face-to-face engagements; hence, they enter the room last, after the juniors have assembled. Synchronization often is symbolized by bowing, nodding, or making exclamations of assent. It is as if you were all on the same wavelength and practicing the coordination of your inputs. Pure sequentialism leads workers and employees to be machine timed and dehumanized, but purely synchronous cultures seem haphazard and inefficient, episodic, and lacking in purpose. Sequentialism is typically short term because deadlines need to be close by to have much of an effect; synchronous cultures may or may not be long term—if they lack direction, there is no long-term goal.

What Effective Leaders Know and Have Learned

We can identify transcultural competence by giving respondents an opportunity to integrate sequential with synchronous views of time and seeing whether they take this opportunity, because modern effective manufacturing practices must combine both concepts. Neither is sufficient by itself.

It is self-evident that you will complete a process sooner if you speed it up. The gains from synchronous thinking are less immediately obvious. One source of considerable timesaving is to take a sequence 80 yards long, divide it into four 20-yard sequences, work on them simultaneously, and then assemble the four parallel processes. No wonder the workers at AMD sing "Doing It Simultaneously."

What has happened historically is that costly sacrifices have been made to continuous-process machinery. These sacrifices symbolized speed. Sequential movement was what it was all about, and so cheap workers doing simple operations were hired to keep the machines moving. Other sacrifices were equally serious. The machines had to be buffered by large inventories of supplies and work in process. In some plants 80 percent of products were not worked on but remained in large piles tied up in such inventories.

Enter Taichi Ohno and the Toyota Production System. If you think synchronously as well as sequentially, the huge inventories and the semi-trained workers doing dumb, repetitive tasks are seen as limitations. Inventories are cut to a fraction by JIT (just-in-time), and you need multiskilled workers of considerable intelligence to ensure smooth synchronization among parallel processes. All this the West has known for a decade or more, but cultures are stubborn barriers to change.

There are few sequential-synchronous issues in this book, in part because we have not looked much at manufacturing. In the case of

LEGO's turnaround (Chapter 6, Dilemma 4), Christian Majgaard was particularly concerned that every stream of ideas meet its own "window of opportunity." The ideas themselves were neither right nor wrong; they had a *rendezvous* that shaped their destiny. Either they synchronized with the needs of the market, or the windows closed in their faces. It required good timing to dart through the window.

Stan Shih of Acer was also engaged with this issue, as explained in Chapter 12, Dilemma 6. He promulgated his "fast-food model" of computer production and marketing, even likening his company to McDonald's. Just as fast-food outlets concentrate on rapid sequences of high-quality components, they concentrate on getting them to customers in just the combinations ordered just in time, in Acer's case, three months from order to delivery. Shih reckons he borrowed speed from the West and timely delivery from his Taiwanese homegrown culture.

Reconciling a sequential concept of time with a synchronous concept of time can give you the advantages of both and the limitations of neither. Each corrects for the potential excesses of the other. Ever faster sequences with ever finer synchronization are what modern manufacturing is all about. The following virtuous circle illustrates this point:

The Virtuous Circle

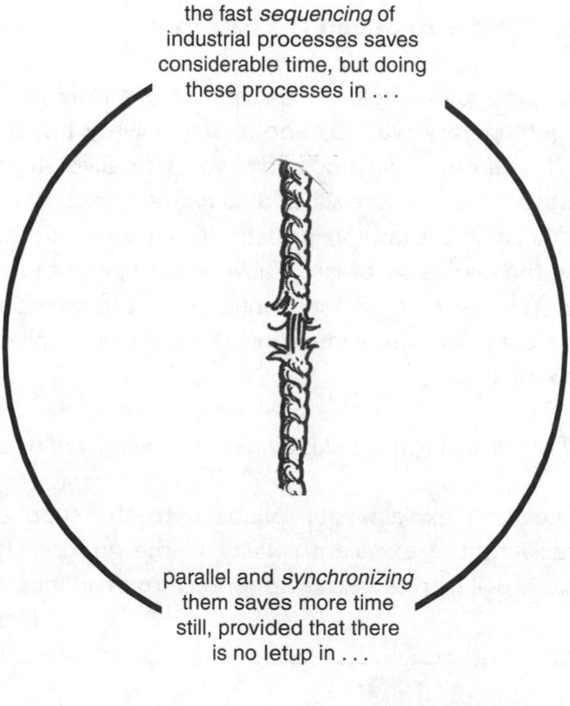

the fast *sequencing* of
industrial processes saves
considerable time, but doing
these processes in . . .

parallel and *synchronizing*
them saves more time
still, provided that there
is no letup in . . .

Roughly the same rules apply to reducing "time market." The traditional approach has been sequential, with "progress chasing" and a push strategy to get projects through faster. Advanced Micro Devices culled projects that were behind schedule by more than the permitted margin so that the remaining projects would "run for their lives."

A recent innovation at Motorola University has substituted a synchronous "pull strategy." This strategy adopts the deadline and the viewpoint of the customer and pulls resources, people, and products into the development process in the volumes needed to make the rendezvous with the customer. More resources will be needed for late projects, and fewer for those ahead of schedule. When customers themselves fall behind schedule, such delays can release resources needed elsewhere. Here just-in-time means "synchronization with the customer's latest deadline."

Measuring Intercultural Competence: Reconciling Sequential Time with Synchronous Time

In the following dilemma, a somewhat haphazard and synchronous fashion house is frustrating a sequential and time-conscious wholesaler.

Question 7. How to Speed Up Latecomers

As the manager of a wholesale distributor of a fashion company you are getting very worried about late delivery times to your clients. The summer did not allow you to deliver high-priced goods within a week of the scheduled delivery date, which is the accepted norm in the fashion industry. You have tried many ways of solving the problems of late delivery but have not made any progress. You are now also in conflict with the transport firm, because a contract was signed and the fashion supplier denies any responsibility.

Which of the following most closely describes what you would do?

a. You need to explain your problem to the supplier while appreciating the excellent quality of the goods. This most probably will lead to better adherence to deadlines.

(continued)

Question 7. *(continues)*

b. You need to order early and ask for the goods two or three weeks before you need to distribute them to the shops.
c. You need to recognize that the fashion business is highly dynamic, artistic, and in constant turbulence and accept the fact that sometimes goods will be early as well as late. What difference does another week make?
d. Your partners have a flexible-time mind-set, and you will not be able to change that. You need to talk to your clients to prepare them for a possible late delivery and give them a discount when it occurs. Separately, you need to negotiate a premium for punctual delivery.
e. You need to know the suppliers personally. Try to avoid problematic issues and during the visit emphasize how important it is for the clients to get on-time deliveries.

Question 7 (my answer)—(how others in my organization would answer)

In the following diagram we classify the responses (d) and (a) as integrated, (b) and (c) as polarized, and (e) as compromised.

Grid Display

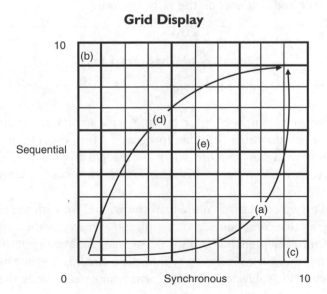

This concludes the discussion of all seven dimensions of difference.

The Seven Dimensions in American Pop Culture

The popular film *Armageddon* might well be viewed as having been constructed with the seven dimensions in mind.

In the film the mission is nothing less than to save humankind (universalism) from a giant meteorite. Two spaceships, the *Freedom* and the *Independent* (individualistic), are operated not by astronauts but by rugged roughneck oil drillers who will drill into the meteorite and explode a nuclear bomb. All this requires elaborate detail and precision (specificity), including placing a slingshot around the meteor. Luckily, their leader and his men are tough as hell. They never quit and (amazingly) have never failed (achievement), except of course in their social lives. They must drill in an incredibly hostile terrain of granite spikes, yet they prevail over nature (because they are inner directed). The film also features seven digital countdowns (sequential time), with time running out before spacecraft ascend and before nuclear bombs kill our heroes. Americans are affective, especially in this film, in which roughnecks shout, "I love you, man!" above the dust and din, and the characters are much given to domestic endearments on the edge of doom.

Summary of Chapters 1 and 2

Chapters 1 and 2 did the following:

1. We first contrasted rule making with exception finding and argued that they can be integrated. You use exceptions to improve rules and use rules to recognize what is genuinely exceptional. We call this learning *revising rules to accommodate exceptions.*
2. We then contrasted competitive individualism with the requirement that communities cooperate and argued that these qualities can be integrated. It is possible to compete at cooperating with customers or cooperating within the team. It is possible for communities to develop and at the same time to celebrate their out-

standing individual members. Competing helps us differentiate best practices; cooperating helps us disseminate and adopt those practices. We called this learning *co-opetition.*

3. We contrasted the preference for analyzing issues into specifics with the preference for synthesizing and elaborating issues into diffuse wholes, and we argued that these preferences can be integrated. You have to allow self-organizing knowledge, values, and team processes to flow diffusely and then supply detailed, specific feedback on their effectiveness. We called this learning *coevolution with corrective feedback.*

4. We contrasted *neutral* and *rational* with *affective* forms of expression, in which feelings are fully owned, and argued that these forms can be integrated. You cannot think about your emotions unless they are owned, expressed, and shared, but you also have to control yourself until the right moment and circumstances. We agree with Pascal that *the heart has its reasons.*

5. We contrasted two sources of experienced control: that from inside us, which is inner directed, and that from outside us, which is outer directed. Strategy, for example, can be designed from inside a company's top management, or it can emerge from the company's interface with customers, outside top management. We argued that these processes can be integrated. Top managers can use their inner resources to design and reshape the strategies emerging outside them that have already pleased customers. We called this *crafted strategy* in honor of Henry Mintzberg, who likened it to the rising of clay spontaneously from the rotating potter's wheel.

6. We contrasted status earned through achievement with status ascribed to the person's potential—for example, age and family—and argued that these statuses can be integrated. The more you respect people's potentials and the more you invest in training them, the more likely they are to reciprocate by achieving on behalf of the company. We called this *mentored achievement.*

7. Finally, we contrasted a sequential view of time as a race against the clock with a synchronous view of time as timing, as in a finely choreographed dance. We saw that these views can be integrated, as occurs when, by synchronizing processes just in time, you "shorten the racecourse" by way of parallel processing before combining the results in final assembly. We called this *flexible manufacturing,* or, in a market context, "pull strategy."

Not only do these seven integrations constitute transcultural competence, they represent a model for valuing in general, in which the preferences and stereotypes of a culture are relative while the need to integrate values is absolute and is essential to civic society as well as to the creation of wealth. The danger of stereotyped cultural imagery is that it hides this necessity. It follows that foreign cultures can arouse what is latent in our values to remind us that what is perhaps overemphasized in their culture is underemphasized in ours. We have the preferences of foreign cultures within our own, albeit in a weaker state.

Measuring Intercultural Competence: How We Did It and What Others Have Found

We administered our questionnaire to the Intercultural Communications Institute summer school near Portland, Oregon, and to several U.S. and European samples. The following trends are already evident:

There is a capacity to deal with and reconcile values in general. Respondents who reconcile dilemmas are likely to employ a similar logic across the board, as do "compromisers" and "polarizers."

Transcultural competence, as measured by our questionnaire, correlates strongly, consistently, and significantly with all of the following:

a. Extent of experience with international assignments.
b. Rating by superiors on "suitability for" and "success in" overseas postings and partnerships.
c. High positive evaluations via "360-degree feedback." Arguably, this reconciles equality and hierarchy, since the verdicts of peers, superiors, and subordinates are compared.

Moreover, there is a surprise: With the exception of Chinese "high-flyers" who recently have been influenced by American training, the transculturally competent do *not* put their own cultural stereotypes ahead of foreign values in a logical sequence. For example, American transcultural competents (TCs) are as likely to argue that good communities and teams generate outstanding individuals as they are to favor the reverse proposition. TCs can begin with the foreigner's sociotype and join it to their own. This probably reveals skill at negotiating and entering dialogue, where one shares an understanding of the other's position in the hope of reciprocity. It also may reveal a case-by-case adoption of foreign methods in which such skills are considered appropriate, along with curiosity about "the road less traveled" by one's own culture.

Finally, we would like to suggest that transcultural competence might be only the tip of the iceberg, representing the most visible manifestation of human diversity in general. The role of leaders and managers is increasingly to manage diversity per se, whatever its origins in culture, industry, discipline, socioeconomic group, or gender. If there is indeed a way of thinking that integrates values as opposed to "adding value," the implications are far reaching.

In Chapters 3 through 21 we show how our 21 leaders manage knowledge by integrating dilemmas and discuss these concepts in some detail. We refer again to the wider database in our summary in Chapter 22.

Chapter 3

A New Vision of Capitalism: Richard Branson, Virgin

Charles Hampden-Turner, Naomi Stubbe-de Groot, and Fons Trompenaars

*A*LMOST NO ONE has taken the art of being British to a higher level of popularity than Sir Richard Branson. The cultivation of a pleasing personality has been a British art form for centuries. The gentleman was traditionally "socially pleasing," although what pleases and what does not have changed dramatically since the 1960s, and Branson is very much a child of that era. Although the traditional gentleman, with his verbal fluency, formality, aloofness, strangled emotions, and chronic understatements, has been in decline for many years, the photogenic "media personality" has risen to replace him. Branson is very much the outrider of this new order, the celebrity of free enterprise. He turns his fascinations into businesses.

If British entrepreneurialism is being reborn, as many believe, Richard Branson is very much the role model of this new style and the symbol of this resurgent vitality. He is much more than a business leader famed for making money; he is the exponent of a new lifestyle in which business activity expresses the personality of its founder: irreverent, cheeky, ironic, enjoyable, and reformist. In a business environment whose exponents increasingly live in order to work Branson works in order to live, and he is seen by his culture as enjoying himself and expressing his personal convictions through his feats and adventures.

The Key Is Personality

In many of the subsequent chapters we will show how business leaders reconcile values, but we must first ask where these reconciliations are stored and how they are deployed. An important repository for reconciled values is the human personality. There is about the personality an inherent fascination. At its best it has surface and depth, changeability, and constancy. It can dazzle with its multiple facets yet impress with its underlying integrity. By turns sad and joyful, serious and humorous, tough and tender, idealistic and realistic, the personality has the peculiar power to bring unity to myriad aspects, what Joseph Campbell called "The Hero with a Thousand Faces."

To an extent almost unprecedented in world business the Virgin brand *is* the personality of Richard Branson. While Disney is symbolized by a giant mouse or duck, McDonald's by "Ronald," a red-haired clown, Shell by a scallop, and Michelin by a fat inflated man, Virgin is personified by the colorful, living personality of its chairman and founder.

There could be some danger in this policy. Personalities can come apart. Founders die. Masks can slip. Scandal may reveal that a person is not what she or he seems. Branson recently was forced to sue a biographer. The media profit when stars rise *and* when they fall, a process they aid and abet, but Branson seems able to charm even seasoned hacks, and his press is largely favorable. A pleasing personality is almost infinitely capacious. Branson has received repeated warnings from marketing men that his brand cannot stretch to so many diverse activities, yet are they right? When a company's image is contrived, its stretch is limited. Would you want Ronald McDonald to fly you across the Atlantic? Would you entrust your savings to Mickey Mouse? A living personality as versatile as Branson's, however, can brand all Virgin's 200 companies, from bridal shops, to cola, to condoms, to MGM cinemas, to insurance, to pensions, trains, books, and music.

The Search for Moral Enterprise

The now-conventional view is that Margaret Thatcher ended Britain's "hate affair" with business enterprise. Whereas the British were once ashamed of "trade," they now demand more profits than other cultures do. There is some truth in this, but no culture changes so completely or so fast. The British still believe that business enterprise needs redemption—witness the popularity of the business writer Charles Handy, who has profiled Branson on moral grounds. Shareholders in Britain are among the most demanding, yet admiration is withheld from profit providers. "Rip-off Britain" is still a common accusation. Alan Mitchell, another business writer, said of Branson, "Somehow his values and style allay our nagging doubts about the morality of modern capitalism's means and ends."

The secret of Sir Richard's popularity is his knight-errant attitude toward consumers. The Virgin on his shield blesses not his personal enrichment but the creation of wealth for the larger society by improving service to consumers. He turns business enterprise into *moral* enterprise. He began by backing new countercultural stars in the music industry. He beat British Airways on quality of service and tweaked its tail in court. When the AIDS crisis struck, he supplied cut-rate condoms. He even offered to run the national lottery at no profit, thereby maximizing revenues for good causes. He challenged the pension industry with cheaper products offering higher yields and entered the insurance industry with Virgin Direct, which cut out selling and brokerage costs. He has set up an Internet company to import cars cheaply from the Continent, where prices are generally lower. Finally, he plans to use his "lightships," airships illuminated from within, to detect and destroy land mines, redeeming a pledge to the late Princess Diana.

Branson's appeal is, however, not exclusively to the post-1950s generations. There is something traditional in his derring-do reminiscent of *The Boy's Own Paper*. He broke the world record for crossing the Atlantic in a speedboat and tried to circumnavigate the earth in a hot-air balloon, at some risk to his life. All this harks back to the age of intrepid explorers, to Scott of the Antarctic, to Sir Richard Burton, and even farther back, to Sir Francis Drake. No wonder one poll of youth culture discovered that Branson was among the very few people trusted by respondents to rewrite the Ten Commandments!

The Use of Irony and Humor

What makes Branson such an elusive target for critics and competitors is that he does not take himself seriously. He makes far better fun of himself than satirists have succeeded in doing. Irony and humor in the personality have a very important bearing on the capacity to reconcile dilemmas. It takes a sense of irony to acknowledge dilemmas in the first place. Hitler, Stalin, and Mussolini, for example, were all notoriously humorless.

Arthur Koestler pointed out that laughter arises from an accidental collision between two frames of thought that connect incongruously. The "punch line" surprises you and produces a "ha ha" reflex. Take, for example, e.e. cummings's quip, "She was a good cook as cooks go, and as cooks go, she went." You rarely laugh if the joke is familiar. While laughter is not the *reconciliation* of contrasting ideas, it often greets their *juxtaposition*. Because you must juxtapose ideas if you are ever to reconcile them, irony and humor can be regarded as *approaches* to reconciling values, necessary but not sufficient conditions. Branson's tongue-in-cheek "virginity" may therefore be a vital clue to his leadership skills in reconciliation. He tells wonderful stories on himself (see Box 3–1).

This style is a quintessentially British way of releasing tension and disarming critics. For example, Branson called his first flight from Gatwick in June 1984 "the Maiden Voyager," changed from "the Maidenhead" at the last minute. The plane was packed with celebrities, notably English cricketers Ian Botham and Viv Richards, and the crossing was one long party hosted by "the Grinning Pullover" himself. Branson's motto is "Do Business, Have Fun." He thinks nothing of dressing up in drag and serving his own customers in flight. "Fun is at the core of the way I like to do business," he explains. "It has informed everything I have done from the outset. More than any other element, fun is the secret of Virgin's success. I am aware that [this] goes against the grain of convention."

Box 3–1

"I Puffed Out My Chest . . ."

Richard Branson had just won his libel action against British Airways and was being lionized by the British media. To escape the photographs and applause he took his family to Majorca for a vacation.

"I was lying by the side of the pool one morning, reading all the press cuttings about Virgin which had been faxed over to me and trying not to let everything go to my head, when a young couple came up to me. They coughed nervously to attract my attention. 'Excuse me,' they said, proffering a camera. 'Would

(continued)

Box 3–1 *(continues)*

you mind? We'd love a photograph.' I smiled at them. 'Of course not,' I beamed, standing up and grinning. I brushed back my hair. 'Where do you want to take it?' 'Just here would be nice,' they said. I went and stood with my back to the swimming pool, puffed out my chest and pushed back my hair. 'About here?' I asked them. To my surprise, they were looking confused. They whispered together. Instead of pointing the camera at me, I realised they were holding it out towards me. 'Sorry,' the husband said. 'We were hoping that you could take our photograph. I'm Edward and this is my wife Araminta. What's your name?' "

Source: *Losing My Virginity: Richard Branson, The Autobiography.* London: Virgin Publishing, 1999.

When Branson launched his first flight from Heathrow in July 1991, he posed for press pictures in front of British Airways's proud model of the Concorde outside Terminals 1–3. He wore a pirate outfit and had draped a banner proclaiming "Virgin Territory" in front of the Concorde. Nearly every British newspaper and newscast featured the publicity coup. Lord King, the chairman of British Airways (BA), who had originated the "pirate" epithet, was reportedly so furious that he broke his own sound barrier. Branson's "Virgin Bride" chain of bridal shops is clearly tongue in cheek. How many brides are still virgins on their wedding day? He invites them to share the joke.

We will now consider six important dilemmas that Branson has reconciled. These are not simply the dilemmas of one company; they are in most cases the dilemmas of conducting business in the United Kingdom and of appealing to its consumers, media, and establishment. The dilemmas are as follows:

1. Making money versus critiquing and reforming the economic system
2. Gains for shareholders versus gains for employees and customers
3. Specific aims versus diffuse contexts
4. Fierce haggling versus benign branding
5. Large established business versus everlasting entrepreneurialism
6. The victorious antagonist versus the proverbial underdog

Dilemma 1: Making Money versus Critiquing and Reforming the Economic System

Ever since Adam Smith poured scorn on the idea that businessmen might serve the public interest consciously, making money has been regarded as an act of personal aggrandizement, connected to public benefit only through the inadvertence of the invisible hand.

"I have never known much good done by those affected to deal in the public," sneered Smith, taking a sideswipe at his patron, the duke of Buccleuch. "It is an affection indeed not very common among merchants, and very few words need be employed in dissuading them from it." Quite so; this is the kind of businessperson with whom we are all too familiar, and this attitude helps explain British ambivalence toward wealth creation in general.

Branson is demonstrably different. He campaigned against corporal punishment and "fagging" (younger boys acting as servants to older boys) while a schoolboy. Those battles have been won. He marched on the U.S. embassy in London to protest the Vietnam War. He founded the nonprofit Student Advisory Center because his girlfriend could not get an abortion. The center published *The Student Magazine.* This publication came to the rescue of a student on whom the police had planted drugs, and in retaliation they prosecuted the journal under a nineteenth-century law forbidding any published reference to venereal disease. Branson was fined £7. He was prosecuted again in 1971 by Her Majesty's Customs and Excise for selling cheap Jimi Hendrix records that had been diverted from an export consignment. He spent one miserable night in prison with a filthy blanket and recalled his mother's adage that one's most precious asset is one's reputation. He repaid the excise due on the records and escaped conviction, but he has guarded his reputation ever since. He says of this incident, "Undoubtedly that created one of my values. I have told myself I would never enjoy being accountable to anyone else or not being in control of my own destiny."

Earlier that year the postal strike had forced Branson to switch from mail order to his first record shop in Oxford Street. This was his first step into the music business, in which he promoted artists whom the music establishment had shut out. Among his successful discoveries in the ensuing years were the Sex Pistols, Boy George, and Mike Oldfield. He considered the two major record retailers at that time, W H Smith and John Menzies, to be stuffy and hostile to new styles of music.

By 1978 he was opening nightclubs where many of his studio performers gave live concerts. In 1984 Branson challenged BA's near monopoly of the British-based airline business, flying from Gatwick with Virgin Atlantic Airways and Virgin Cargo. He remarked, "I see something done badly which I know could be done better, like the airline. No one was offering their customers a decent service. I was sure that whoever did so would not only have a successful company but change the whole industry."

In 1989, in the face of the growing AIDS crisis, Branson marketed Mates condoms, a challenge to Durex and considerably cheaper. His hilarious commercials, in which a salesgirl in the drugstore shouts a query from a shy purchaser so that the whole shop hears, were accompanied by public service messages on the multiple chances of getting AIDS from the partners of each partner. All the profits were donated to AIDS charities.

In 1990 Virgin Lightships, using helium, was formed. The initial purpose of the aircraft is advertising. In 1992 Branson alleged "dirty tricks" by BA against Virgin Atlantic passengers who were being poached and misinformed about alleged "cancellations" of Virgin flights.

In 1993 Branson won a libel suit against BA, which had claimed that his allegations were invented for purposes of self-publicity, forcing BA's chairman, Lord King, to make a public apology. Damages and costs reached a record £5 million ($8 million). Virgin Atlantic was voted *Executive Travel*'s airline of the year for the third year running.

In 1994 Branson took on Coca-Cola and Pepsi-Cola with Virgin Cola, going against all marketing advice about the entrenched positions of those giants. In 1995, in the middle of the long-running pension misselling scandal, in which Britain's major pension businesses were forced to repay more than £1 billion to purchasers they had misled, Branson launched Virgin Direct Personal Financial Service. In the same year, amid growing complaints that Hollywood had a stranglehold on movie distribution through the ownership of movie houses, Branson bought MGM and promised to give independent producers a better chance.

In 1996, when an ailing conservative government broke up British Rail and sold off the pieces, Branson started Virgin Rail Group. This is often cited as his one major mistake in judgment. The rolling stock was obsolescent, and the track was in very poor condition—a situation that only Railtrack, another company, could remedy. Virgin is among the poorest performers in the whole industry, a problem likely to persist until new rolling stock arrives and Railtrack gets around to Virgin's part of the network. In the same year he launched Virgin Brides, a chain of retail bridal shops; Virgin Express, a short-haul airline; and Virgin Net, an Internet service provider that soon offered free access.

In 1997 Branson launched Virgin Direct, an alternative telephonic and Internet banking service and a response to persistent press reports of stealthy increases in bank charges by the major clearing banks. In 1998 Branson won a libel action against G-Tech's Guy Snowdon, who had sued Branson for telling the media that Snowden had offered him a bribe to withdraw from the competition to run Britain's national lottery. G-Tech was the prime contractor for Camelot, the successful bidder. Branson's bid was finally unsuccessful in highly mysterious circumstances, though he greatly reduced the profits of the operator by submitting a not-for-profit bid.

In 1999 Branson announced a £4 billion ($6.5 billion) investment in high-speed tilting trains for Virgin Rail and launched Virgin Mobile with protections against radio waves affecting the brain. In February 2000 Virgin announced an Internet-based car-buying service designed to combat the exorbitant prices of new cars in the United Kingdom, which were 18 to 30 percent above those of cars of the identical make on the European continent. He hopes to use this competition to get British car prices down.

In March 2000 Virgin announced that its lightships service, using remote mine-sensing equipment developed by the Ministry of Defense, was planning a major clearance of millions of unexploded mines, which were bankrupting farmers in thousands of acres of the world's war zones.

All these examples share a single theme:

- There is an injustice, an abuse of power, a scandal, an overcharge, or an important need not being met.
- Branson allows the press, the politicians, and the public to do most of the moralizing.
- What he does is offer a lower-price, higher-quality alternative, thereby becoming the consumer's champion and the media's darling. If customers want to avoid being ripped off, they should switch to his brand, which is increasingly identified with Branson's personal integrity, so much so that he jokingly suggests he should call himself "Brandson."

The dilemma that Virgin has so artfully reconciled is illustrated in the following diagram:

Dilemma 1: The Reforming Millionaire

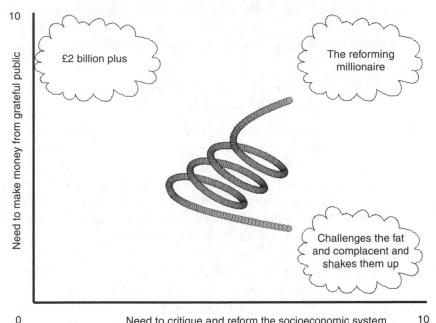

Branson is frank about his strategy: "I can't walk past a fat, complacent business without wanting to shake it up a bit." When he entered the personal pension (PEP) market, he sold £400 million in the first year and £1 billion in the second: "If you go for big, fat, lazy brand leaders, it is often easy to offer better value for money."

"Life insurance?" everyone snorted upon hearing the idea. "People *hate* life insurance. It's a terrible industry." "Exactly," he said, "It's got potential."

Branson has certainly grown rich. His personal fortune is estimated at over £2 billion, yet his riches have been gained by rescuing customers from "fat and complacent" overlords. He has a critic's view of most British businesses. Instinctively, he felt that the world of financial services was shrouded in mystery and rip-offs and that there must be room for Virgin to offer a jargon-free alternative with no hidden catches. "Apart from a few exceptions," he says, "postwar Britain has bred a domestic commercial culture that is anticompetitive, cartel based, and patriarchal."

He explains that one should never go into an industry with the sole purpose of making money. One has to believe passionately that it is possible to change the industry, to turn it on its head, to make sure that it will never be the same again with the right people; with that conviction, anything is possible. "Whenever I see people getting a bad deal," he observes, "I want to step in and do something about it. Of course, this is not pure altruism—there's profit to be made, too."

Dilemma 2: Gains for Shareholders versus Gains for Employees and Customers

Richard Branson has very cleverly adjusted a serious imbalance in Great Britain's economic system, at least as far as Virgin companies are concerned. After going partially public in 1986, he and his managers bought back the stock in 1988, making Virgin once again a private company. This was done in part to evade the grip of institutional shareholders and the heavy emphasis that the financial interests nicknamed "the City of London" put on the rights of shareholders. One result of the dominance of Britain's financial sector over the rest of the economy is that the pound is kept strong, interest rates stay high, and profits are squeezed out of industries, often at the expense of employees and customers. Hence, Britain remains, compared with the European Union nations, an arena of low wages, high prices, and high profits, with interest rates for the pound sterling considerably above those for the euro.

Branson believes that customers are very important and that you cannot reward them if the morale of your employees is low. Hence, satisfied employees are a precondition for satisfying customers, which in turn is a precondition for making profits. If external shareholders are pressuring you for the lion's share of trading surpluses, it is hard to avoid the erosion of employee and customer interests. Once Virgin was converted back to a private company, Branson could spend his profits as he wished, and he wished to benefit *all* stakeholders, not just himself. He explains his view: "Virgin staff are not mere hired hands. They are not managerial pawns in some gigantic chess game. They are entrepreneurs in their own right."

You look after people because at least some of them will invent your future. As Branson puts it, "I get the best people. I ask questions, and then I say, 'Let's have some fun.'" It is simply not possible to enjoy yourself if your job or career is under threat. Virgin is fueled by exuberance; for that, employees must be happy and secure. "Staff should come first," he says. "If it means making £5 million less, then that's the right decision to make."

Branson believes in a "share the wealth" philosophy that the City would not tolerate, but *how* he shares it is ingenious. There are two levels of shareholding: in the group as a whole and in the individual business units. Branson is generous with the shares of each unit, but 60 percent of the shares of the whole group is still in his own hands and is likely to remain there. That way, he controls the relative shares of all stakeholders, and the clamor to harvest profits and squeeze other resources cannot grow so far as to wreck the system. The dilemma is illustrated in the accompanying figure.

Dilemma 2: Stakeholders United

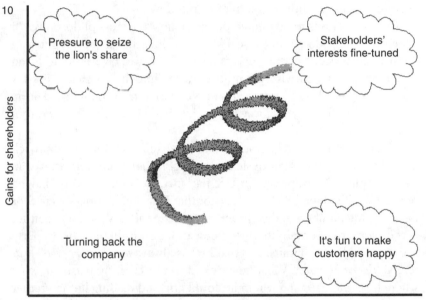

Branson's assumption is that *it is fun to make customers happy.* You do not have to bribe employees to do this, but you *do* need to sustain the morale and enthusiasm they bring to their work and their clients. If any one kind of stakeholder gets too much, tensions will grow and the common purpose will suffer. Virgin has pledged to give consumers a better deal, and this goal is endangered by siphoning off jointly generated funds. "But the difference is that I'm prepared to share more of the profit with the customer so that we're both better off," Branson explains.

Dilemma 3: Specific Aims versus Diffuse Contexts

One of the major dimensions discussed in Chapter 1 was the dilemma of specific versus diffuse criteria for judgment. Some cultures are "bean counters." They ask, "What is the bottom line? Cut the crap and give me the *results!* Give me the facts and *only* the facts. Get to the point." Other cultures are broad and inclusive in what they deem important. People work to improve their relationships with peers, superiors, subordinates, contractors, and customers. Through such relationships, they learn. Indeed, information is stored in rich networks of knowledge. Concepts such as morale, ambience, atmosphere, goodwill, fun, and esprit de corps are diffuse and hard to pin down.

Branson refuses to be pinned down to any "business philosophy." "I generally won't do so, because I don't believe it can be taught as a recipe," he says. That Branson associates hard work with being loved may have originated with his mother, who thought up challenges for him and would drop him by car some distance from home so that he would have to find his own way back. She also taught him the secrets of contributing to a family.

There is another interesting reason why Richard Branson's approach is so diffuse: He has been dyslexic since childhood and left Stowe, an English "public" (i.e., private in U.S. parlance) school, at age 16, having repeatedly failed mathematics. It is not that Branson ignores specifics or fails to value numbers and contract terms. After all, a Virgin bank either gets its sums right or fails its customers; either a Virgin plane is properly serviced, or disaster awaits. It is that he has always *needed other people to do the specifics on his behalf.* What he excelled in was creating trust, knowing whom he could trust and whom he could not, and reading human rather than written characters. His critical weaknesses could be overcome only by high levels of social intelligence. That he had problems double-checking his accountant's figures made it all the more important for him to know that person so well as to be able to deduce that he would not be cheated.

Branson has to be diffuse for other reasons too. Work cannot be fun unless you invest it with all or most of your personality, humor, gaiety, romance, and social life. Satisfying customers means reading their thoughts and needs—realizing that an airline passenger is exhausted and wants a quick snack before the longest possible sleep, could do with a back massage to relax him, or needs a cough drop to ease an itchy throat. Branson also believes that people *define* themselves through their tastes in films, music, travel, vacations, and so on. Service must be broad enough to cater to such self-definitions.

Branson's early attempts to create diffuse systems of service sometimes went too far. His early West End music store was designed for people to hang out in, chatting with the staff, trying out records, and sitting and listening to the latest music, but he had reckoned without some of the parasitic characteristics of the hippie culture of that time. People were using the store to party and to listen, but not to buy. Branson solved the problem in his own gentle way. A doorman reminded each visitor that this was a shop, not a pad. If no one bought, the shop would have to close. Sales, which had dropped to a quarter of those in the opening week, picked up again, and the Virgin chain of music stores—later Megastores—prospered. Branson is well known for elaborating rather than streamlining services. His multiplex cinema chains make clever use of the heavy human traffic around movie houses, and his plans for railway stations on Virgin lines would turn them into small shopping centers like the ones in Japan.

Virgin Atlantic (VA) beats BA and other carriers year after year in the standard of its service, as judged by travelers' associations and journals—especially its service in upper class and premium economy. Branson learned early on to look at "the big picture." He was unable to raise $10 million to put videos in every seat back, but he *was* able to raise $4 billion for 10 Boeing 747-400s, which had the videos thrown in as an inducement. That's diffuse thinking!

One of VA's few rivals is Singapore Airlines, with its diffuse East Asian custom of caring for the whole person and catering to the total experience of travel. Somewhat surprisingly, Singapore Airlines has purchased 49 percent of Virgin Atlantic, uniting two of the world's most diffuse, elegant, and sophisticated airline services. In the joint venture with Singapore Airlines, an East Asian tradition has merged with a British one. The combination is well epitomized by Raffles, Singapore's famous English colonial hotel and restaurant. Business class on Singapore Airlines is called "Raffles Class." So long as a corporation is willing to pay for it, the British executive likes to be treated as if he were dining in his London club or country estate. Style may be valued over substance. Fiddling with money to pay for each drink or headset is regarded as vulgar. Service is, ideally, seamless. That Branson has captured the diffuse ambience of East Asian and British service and epitomized it in upper class is beyond question.

Virgin Atlantic is also very effective at getting you to and from your aircraft. If you live within a 60-mile radius of London, Virgin's limousine service brings you to Heathrow or Gatwick, and another limousine picks you up at your destination. A driver for Virgin told the author, who asked whether wages were good, "To be honest, no, but the passengers flying Virgin Atlantic are so thrilled with the service level that they always give very good tips. Therefore, it's okay that our basic salary is not that high. And I always have happy people in my limousine." Finding yourself in the safe hands of a driver who knows your destination when your body clock has passed midnight is an agreeable and restful way to reach America.

Diffuse social processes are also essential in order for Branson and his top managers to *learn as they go*. We might ask how a music shop and recording studio boss expects to run an airline, much less an insurer, a bank, a lottery, a railway, a cinema chain, nightclubs, hotels, real estate, a condom supplier, and a chain of bridal shops (there are many, many more). The answer is that Virgin enters joint ventures with people who have mastered the specifics of those industries, hires the needed experts, and funds a proposal that includes those specific resources and people as parts of the project. Branson dissents from the "stick to your knitting" school. If you sell records in shops but do not know the Internet, that will ruin you. You need to be well dispersed.

In an important sense Branson is forever trying to complete the education interrupted at age 16 by taking a series of "learning journeys" into new industries and magical mystery tours into unknown territories. He avoids high-tech or science-based industries, where success cannot be learned from social interactions alone, and sets up diffuse communication patterns in which experts can teach him the specifics while he teaches the experts how to learn from the diffusely spread network of employees and customers. You learn faster from those you respect, from those you trust, and from those you treat as equals. His affable, easygoing style is the key to learning as you go. As he puts it, "What I like most of all is to learn. When I feel that I've learned what there is to know about telecommunications, or airlines, or cosmetics, then I move on to something else. It's like being at university, which I never went to, and taking crash courses."

Several observers have noted how well women and minorities do at Virgin and how relatively numerous they are, but Branson declines to moralize about this or even proclaim the statistics. You "have fun" meeting lots of different people. Of course, Virgin would be culturally diverse in the same way that its consumers are. Is variety not the spice of life?

For Branson the rules of sociability link all his businesses: "If you know how to motivate and deal with people, it doesn't matter if you are taking on the airline industry, the soft drinks industry, or the film industry. The same rules apply."

What makes Virgin one coherent company despite all the disparate tasks it undertakes is an underlying social intelligence that builds information-rich contexts in which all concerned learn fast, as is illustrated in the accompanying diagram.

Dilemma 3: Specific Aims versus Diffuse Contexts

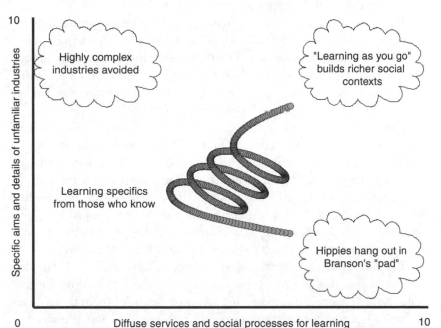

Dilemma 3: Specific Aims versus Diffuse Contexts

- Highly complex industries avoided
- "Learning as you go" builds richer social contexts
- Learning specifics from those who know
- Hippies hang out in Branson's "pad"

y-axis: Specific aims and details of unfamiliar industries (0 to 10)
x-axis: Diffuse services and social processes for learning (0 to 10)

Dilemma 4: Fierce Haggling versus Benign Branding

Many people cannot stomach the seeming contradictions of Richard Branson's personality. Perhaps he only *pretends* to be nice, and inches beneath the surface there is a ruthless workaholic and scheming self-publicist who can bring even BA to its knees. Many people, social scientists among them, are threatened by any hint of anomaly. Economists, especially, deem people to be *essentially* self-seeking and profit maximizing, with a false veneer of altruistic and social concern muddying the clear waters of causation. In this reading Branson is all facade, with a machinating mind behind a false front.

Much is made of Branson's love of haggling. He enters joint venture negotiations with little but his grin and his pullover and emerges with the best of the deal. Tim Jackson, in *Virgin King,* refers to Branson's "street-trader's aptitude for negotiation, knowing exactly when to talk and when to stay silent, when to press his counterpart on a point and when simply to walk away." According to Des Dearlove, "Charisma and affable charm belie a calculating business brain." These affable attributes "are complemented by an appetite for haggling that would put a Turkish carpet salesman to shame." Branson also has a propensity to renegotiate contracts when relationships have changed. Does any of this throw doubt on his reputation as a nice guy?

For those writing this book a haggling competitor and a benign brander are wholly compatible. An effective personality changes with the circumstances. An Olympic wrestling champion strains every sinew against a strong opponent but does not go home and tie his wife, children, and neighbors into knots. "For all things, there is a season." Why would Branson *not* haggle with competitors and woo customers?

Indeed, if we look more closely, his benign branding is what makes his haggling so effective. Norwich Union (NU) gave him the secrets of the life insurance industry, while he gave NU a brand far better than its own. "Goodwill" and "brand recognition" being notoriously difficult to value, Branson would be failing in his job if he were not brash about his brand's advantages. After negotiating with him you realize just how formidable is that brand, which is coextensive with his personality. He and it are utterly persuasive, and so of course he comes out on top.

Branson calls this "reputational branding." He explains: "I'd like people to feel that most of their needs in life can be filled by Virgin. The absolutely critical thing is that we must never let them down." He points to Japan, where corporations such as Mitsubishi and Yamaha are seen as benefiting the Japanese culture and people, whether by banking or by supplying pianos, cars, or motorbikes. The reputation is for fair dealing, consumer service, and high-quality employment opportunities. These are attributes not of manufactured things such as "Speedy" Alka-Seltzer but of effective social processes. Ninety-six percent of Britons are aware of the Virgin brand, one of the highest recognition scores recorded. Thirty-eight percent reported that they "liked and trusted" the name and were therefore more likely to buy the products.

Virgin seeks to provide "a lifetime relationship" of service and trust. Will Whitehorn, director of corporate affairs, has expressed it well: "At Virgin we know what the brand means, and when we put our brand name on something, we're making a promise. It's a promise we've always kept and always will.... Virgin sticks to its principles and keeps its promises."

The reputation that Virgin promotes and keeps is that the company will be all of the following:

- Genuine and enjoyable
- Contemporary and different
- A consumers' champion
- First class at a business-class price

Armed with this world-class reputation, Branson is in a very strong position when it comes to haggling. When his opponents find their reputations tarnished by their own ruthlessness, it proves how much more they need Virgin than Virgin needs them. "You need *us*...." No wonder Branson grins. As Dearlove puts it, "Nice guys finish first."

Branson's use of benign haggling is illustrated in the accompanying diagram.

Dilemma 4: Benign Haggling

Those who have spent their lives in big corporations often are surprised when they confront a market trader. They have traveled so far from the actual coal mine that its cheery, grubby countenance is a rude shock. It occurs to them too late that they have sold their expertise at a bargain price.

Dilemma 5: Large Established Business versus Everlasting Entrepreneurialism

One reason Richard Branson has so much fun is that he is *both* the founder-owner of a large, established business *and* an everlasting entrepreneur, always starting enterprises, renewing himself, and exploring new territories. How is it possible to have the best of two worlds—to maintain a schoolboy's enthusiasm for fresh experiences while presiding over a business empire? Why does he not become stuffy, pompous, staid, and arrogant like so many others with early achievements behind them?

One reason can be found in the organizational structure of Virgin. It is simultaneously large and small. The network is large, but the headquarters is small, barely 20 people, and most of the business units are small also, although not all of them. Sir Richard clearly identifies with the start-ups and new ventures in his portfolio. It is this that imparts a Peter Pan quality to his character and style. He is always renewing himself, always starting again from scratch, and he has the openness and humility of a novice in strange environments, an approach that is genuine, not contrived. He really *has* to discover new vistas, *has* to listen to people who know a certain field.

Branson no longer dreams up projects by himself. His conviction that employees are entrepreneurs is not posturing. He receives 50 proposals *a week* from within and outside his network and is obliged to pass up 90 percent of them. His major energies and his enthusiasm are reserved for these new departures, and he will see them safely off the ground and into the air before turning his interest to newer launches: "I immerse myself in them [new ventures] for three months [and] then back off." He subsequently looks in on going concerns once or twice a year.

"The idea for Virgin Bride came from a flight attendant from Virgin Atlantic. After a single conversation she was set to work in the new company, and the first Virgin Bride retail outlet opened its doors in 1996," stated Branson.

All these projects are run on a profit-sharing basis by those who dreamed them up and are passionate about the realization of their ideals. Branson poses questions, points out obstacles, identifies pitfalls, helps locate the experts, and then sets the project free to "have fun" and go for it.

He might start a new business because an older one is getting too big. With a hundred or fewer people, first names are the rule, and groups are capable of a spontaneous self-organization made possible by the knowledge persons have of each other's skills and attributes. But where a business grows above such numbers, bureaucracy sets in, rules must be instituted, procedures must be followed, and the division of labor segments employees into mental compartments.

Branson struggles to prevent the onset of business formality by keeping units small and quick on their feet. Small airlines or train companies may not be economically feasible, but the units that compete most effectively—for example, the cabin staff aboard an airliner—*are* small enough to take a spontaneous interest in passengers and care for them. It is a cabin crew that enjoys *one another* that can bring enjoyment and genuine hospitality to passengers. Branson explains: "Every time a business gets too big, we start another one. Keeping things small means keeping things personal; keeping things personal means keeping the people that really matter." He clearly wants personalities to develop and bloom under his aegis, and that is why he favors start-ups. It is interesting to note what he does *not* do: grow by acquisition or seize, dismantle, and sell off large bureaucracies.

Des Dearlove has called Virgin "the Atomized Empire"—an empire broken down into chunks made manageable by face-to-face relationships. The company eschews office blocks and prefers to locate itself in one-time residential blocks around Holland Park, in Regency houses with ample space for conviviality. Such housing encourages the integrity and identity of each business unit. Each business has its own board of directors and substantial independence.

Sir Richard is nonetheless constantly on the lookout for new combinations of strategy. For this reason business units are also *clustered* according to the markets they serve. A trading drinks cluster includes branded vodka and cola. A travel cluster includes two airlines, aviation services, and a travel company. A new idea by any one business unit in a cluster could require the cooperation of another unit. For example, travel magazines on Virgin trains might feature tourist destinations owned or serviced by Virgin, helping to create a network of care for tourists. Joint ventures within clusters are encouraged. Creativity requires new combinations.

In fact, it is new ideas and exciting ventures that catalyze the Virgin network. Out of seeming chaos comes a spontaneous tendency for people to self-organize around ideas that excite them. It is in this way that new order keeps emerging from a party atmosphere and Virgin's "aimless" socialization generates new projects. Bureaucratic order always faces backward to past production processes. The trick is to generate a new order appropriate to the novel task envisaged. Improvisation and quick adaptability are the keys. New processes must be invented to deliver novel products and services. This is illustrated in the accompanying diagram.

Dilemma 5: Creative Microcosms in a Large Network

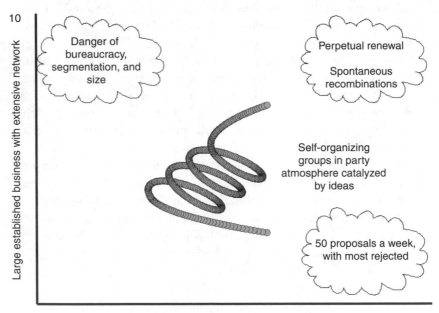

The overall effect is rather like splashing water onto a tangle of live wires: Sparks leap across connections, flames flare up, the possibilities of new circuits are realized, power jumps across gaps, everything crackles with new energy, and a mess takes on new meaning.

Dilemma 6: The Victorious Antagonist versus the Proverbial Underdog

Sir Richard Branson is a fighter, and many are the businesses that have regretted taking him on, but he has escaped the reputation of a bruiser or a vexatious litigant by choosing his opponents carefully and by setting the scenes of his confrontations so that he is clearly the underdog, likely to attract public sympathy. If he wins, he wins, but even if he loses (as in his failure in the bid to organize the national lottery), he wins sympathy and (in this case) the jury's verdict against Guy Snowden of G-Tech. Richard is the boy "who picks on someone bigger than himself." Whatever the outcome, his reputation is intact. Branson's skill at "underdogism" revealed itself at age 13 (Box 3–2).

Box 3–2

Saved from Suicide

Richard Branson was such an unpromising student that he had to be sent to "a crammers" (a school specializing in getting backward students through exams). Unable to recognize dyslexia, the headmaster beat him instead. Young Richard succeeded in attracting the headmaster's daughter, Charlotte, age 18, but was caught climbing out of the bedroom window and was summoned before the headmaster, who promptly expelled him, telling his parents to take him out of the school the next day.

"That evening, unable to think of any other way to escape the wrath of my parents, I wrote a suicide note saying that I was unable to cope with the shame of my expulsion. I wrote on the envelope that it was not to be opened until the following day but then gave it to a boy who I knew was far too nosy not to open it immediately.

"Very, very slowly, I left the building and walked through the school grounds towards the cliffs. When I saw a crowd of teachers and boys beginning to run after me, I slowed down enough

(continued)

Box 3–2 *(continues)*

for them to catch me up. They managed to drag me back from the cliff and the expulsion was overturned.

"My parents were surprisingly relaxed about the whole episode. My father even seemed quite impressed that Charlotte was 'a very pretty girl.' "

Source: *Losing My Virginity: Richard Branson, The Autobiography.* London: Virgin Publishing, 1999.

He has taken on Coca-Cola, Pepsi-Cola, the giant clearing banks, the pension industry, the U.S. gambling industry, BA's 95 percent of British-originated airline traffic, the automobile cartel (which used Britain's right-hand drive to overprice domestic vehicles), and the closed system of movie distribution. Under normal circumstances these big boys would swat Virgin like a pesky fly. Distributors of Coke have huge muscle that has sent a long series of would-be interlopers packing. These are simple products, and they stay on top by controlling shelf space, slashing prices, and crushing rivals.

What appears to have happened is that Virgin's big competitors prefer to leave Branson with a small foothold rather than drive him out because attacking Branson can be a public-relations disaster. He is brilliant at using the press to his own advantage. He disguised himself as a can of Virgin Cola at Shinjuku Station Square in Japan. A BA plane that landed in Kuwait a few minutes after the Iraqis invaded stranded itself, its passengers, and its crew. It was Branson who sent one of his planes to get the people out. BA drops you in it; Virgin organizes your escape. It was a public-relations triumph.

So was the coup against Pepsi. "When Pepsi recently spent $500 million telling the world that its cans had turned blue, Virgin announced with a grin that it too had introduced new cans, which would turn blue on their expiration date. We got a huge amount of publicity and didn't pay a penny for it," according to James Kydd, marketing director of Virgin Cola. Virgin hitches rides on other companies' expenditures by re-framing their expensive publicity.

Big bureaucracies are hopeless at public relations. Spokespersons read prepared statements in a flat monotone with the script shaking in their hands, as if they expected their lies to blow up in their faces. The text has been written by a committee dominated by lawyers and designed to admit nothing while tediously espousing public virtues. Once accused, top managers in large bureaucracies look to exculpate themselves and defend their own positions, with rival leaks to the press and crumbling credibility for the company as a whole.

All these symptoms afflicted BA's defense of Branson's libel action against the airline. The public had to choose between, on the one hand the honest indignation of one man, in alliance with investigative journalists, speaking off the cuff in response to late-breaking news, and, on the other hand, the denials, protestations, and contrivances of public-relations consultants and political fixers rearranging screens around the scandal. Having misled the public, BA officials were reduced to disowning the acts of their subordinates and offering Branson £11 million if he agreed never again to mention the sorry affair. (He refused.) The jury's award of £500,000 to Branson and £110,000 to Virgin Atlantic was the highest in the history of uncontested libel settlements in the United Kingdom. *Branson gave it all to his employees!*

Lord King was forced to retire prematurely and departed, glowering at the media, like a villain in a Victorian melodrama, cursing his disgrace. It was game, set, and match to the spontaneous powers of personality over the artificiality of contrived stratagems. Sir Richard the Lionhearted had won again.

Several commentators have suggested that Branson's artlessness is in fact high art. Tim Jackson and Des Dearlove have both proposed that his motto should be *Ars est celare artem:* "Art lies in concealing art." This seems unnecessarily cynical. To have a highly developed personality and reveal it spontaneously is not a stratagem; it is simply a matter of being yourself before others, striving always to reconcile but, when that is impossible, pointing out your anger at the dissembling of opponents and asking witnesses to choose between your testimonies. Some people can trust their own reactions and do not need to rehearse their moral positions. Others hire an army of advisers to dress them up before the battle in armor so heavy and cumbersome that it weighs them down and forces on them absurdities of posture.

There is also public sympathy for the wronged individual confronting a collectivized assailant, part of Dilemma 2 in Chapter 1. Branson does, to be sure, head a large organization, but before public opinion he is a man alone facing servants of power—a personality against an institution. In individualistic cultures such as the United Kingdom and North America, the individual is going to win the public relations war every time. It is part of our folklore that groups conspire against individuals.

Dilemma 6: The Victorious Underdog

In the preceding chart Branson starts from his underdog position and uses the sympathy generated to win his fights against compromised corporations in David-and-Goliath battles.

Now that we have looked at the six dilemmas that Richard Branson has successfully reconciled, what can we learn from his potent example? We can draw six important conclusions, one from each dilemma he has confronted:

1. Social criticism answered by social remedy is salable in a "moral marketplace." A world in which we can offer our convictions and lifestyles for public approval could change the face of capitalism and bring new meaning and motivation to work.

2. There may be a limit to the level of profits shareholders can demand from business enterprises. By remaining a private company, Virgin appears to have redressed the imbalance between investors on the one hand and employees and consumers on the other.

3. As we move into a service economy ever richer in information, Branson's diffuse style of management, in which employees

learn as they go, appears to produce ever greater effectiveness. We must learn to cater not to numbers and bottom lines but to whole people in whole scenarios of satisfaction. Has it taken a dyslexic school dropout to show us the way?

4. "Brandson" is a fascinating example of the fusion between a brand and a human personality, with all the stretch, versatility, humanity, humor, and tenacity that a living person can bring to a corporate logo. A brand as a promise made by a company to its customers—a promise that can include an extraordinary variety of businesses—is a new and profound phenomenon.

5. Equally important is the idea that a company can perpetually renew itself and avoid growing up into a segmented, soulless bureaucracy of roles and statuses instead of a team of people. Virgin shows that entrepreneurialism need never end, that we can remain forever curious, open, impulsive, and exploratory— and thus forever young.

6. Traditionally, business has supported the top dogs and the powers that be. Even the great dictators had business on their side. Branson has shown the viability and great strength of becoming a champion of consumers, an advocate of the underdog, and a proponent of a better deal for the public. If we learn these lessons, we can transform capitalism profoundly and vastly increase its powers of social provision. Perhaps Branson has started a revolution in the form of capitalism. Are we on the threshold of "buying" the social character of product- and service-related organizations? Could the Internet be used to monitor the conduct and responsibility of moral enterprises? Has Branson started something that will have momentous consequences?

Chapter 4

Creating a Hyperculture: Martin Gillo, Advanced Micro Devices

Charles Hampden-Turner

*W*HAT DOES IT take for a firm to stake its future on a huge, groundbreaking decision? Clearly, it requires a convinced and passionate chief executive officer (CEO) with a daring vision and the stamina to see the project through its tribulations to success. Fortunately, Advanced Micro Devices (AMD) had that kind of CEO in Jerry Sanders, plus a courageous board of directors that backed him on this important strategic decision. It also requires a team of top managers to support the CEO. Among these people are key players whose hands are on the levers crucial to the company's strategy. This chapter focuses on the account of one such key player. At the time of this writing, the story is still in progress.

Advanced Micro Devices, a large U.S. chip maker, made an audacious move when it decided in 1995 to pursue CEO Jerry Sanders's vision to build a mega-fab (factory) in the region of Dresden in the former East Germany for producing state-of-the-art microprocessors at least equivalent, and in a number of ways superior, to those of Intel. To convey a sense of the degree of AMD's courage, at the time the product was not yet defined, the processes for manufacturing were not yet spelled out, suppliers were still developing the production machinery, the company had no experience in manufacturing chips outside the United States, the employees would be totally new, and East Germany faced the challenge of an inferior infrastructure compared with that of the West.

Funding was very attractive, as is usual for this kind of investment around the world, and so the key issues quickly became the people questions. Would it be prudent for the company to risk so much on this challenge? AMD has always defined itself by the motto "People come first; products and profits will follow." Here was an opportunity to put that commitment to the ultimate test. Would the formula work in this context? Could an American high-tech firm carry its approach to the deepest parts of East Germany and win? Could the Silicon Valley spirit of passion, time pressure, and doing the impossible with a limited number of people be brought to life in a region that had to live for decades under a communist system? What about the work ethic? Would the West German executives try to show the East how to win in the Western way? How would the different cultures work with each other? Here three cultures were going to come together: U.S., West German, and East German. There are significant differences between the latter two. In fact, our research database shows that there are larger differences between East German and West German cultures than between West German and other European cultures.

The project could become a smashing success if it unleashed needs long latent in the East German workforce but not yet given expression. It also could be a disaster—a snake pit of resentments. When the first explorations of the viability of this program were made, the company approached Martin Gillo, its director of human relations (HR) for Europe, with an avalanche of questions. There were many skeptics at the outset.

In our opinion Gillo is an example of someone who contributes to success by recognizing that when it comes to people solutions, *where one places the leverage point* is often more important to the outcome than is the magnitude of the force applied. A principle of minimalism is present in reconciling dilemmas. If you really understand the force fields, it may take only a nudge to create a virtuous circle. Martin Gillo was a fortunate find for AMD. He had spent half his life in Europe and half in the

United States. German by origin, he had studied and taught at U.S. universities before moving into HR in the consulting and management fields. He had contributed nine years at AMD's headquarters in California as HR director before spending 10 years as AMD's head of HR in Geneva.

Some teased him at the outset that Dresden couldn't be done successfully. As it turns out, the more he studied the situation and the dynamics of the region, the more he became one of the key supporters of the project, and he got ever more involved, becoming one of four managing directors (*Geschäftsführer*) of Dresden AMD and moving to Dresden in 1999.

That said, an American, Jack Saltich, whose excellent leadership during the first three years of the project was crucial to its eventual success, managed the project. Saltich and Gillo were two of the four general managers. Hans Deppe, head of operations and slated to become CEO for Dresden, and Jim Doran, the expatriate CEO for Dresden at the time of this writing, are the others.

Gillo was well placed to help unify the three cultures of AMD Dresden. His case is different in another regard. Nearly all the leaders featured in this book had no knowledge of dilemma theory. Their ways of thinking were their own. But Gillo had studied our earlier work and had appeared with us on occasion to explain its use. He had used it in earlier years to help AMD's European organization understand its opportunities for marketing with cross-cultural synergies. We have consulted with the AMD Europe marketing organization and also briefly with AMD in Dresden and Austin to help present the ideas of cultural dilemmas and their resolution.

That Gillo used some of our ideas detracts in no way from his accomplishments. Dilemma theory is not a set formula. It is not a technique that can be applied with guaranteed results. Rather, it is a way of organizing and utilizing one's own judgments and is useless unless those judgments are sound. Gillo also is a longtime enthusiast of the work of University of Chicago psychologist Mihaly Csikszentmihalyi, who advocates the creation of *flow states* in personal life and in the workplace—states of total group engagement in the task to be solved so that the boundaries between task and solution collapse in an experience of transcendence, or a flow state. We share his enthusiasm for these concepts and assisted Gillo in using them.

The Dresden location benefited from some crucial advantages. Most obvious were the sizable grants offered by the German state government for locating in this area. Also significant was the fact that East Germany's former communist government had designated Dresden as the center of microelectronics for the whole German Democratic Republic (GDR). Indeed, much of the former Eastern Europe has a well-educated professional class and a numerate and literate workforce yet seriously deficient industries.

It is crucial to grasp the fact that the perceived East German "backwardness" under the communist regime was by no means uniform. For example, the University of Dresden had been specializing in high technology for 30 years before reunification and was an established center of excellence. The educational part of the communist blueprint had always worked better than the industrial part, and the theory had outshone the practice. In fact, one could argue that in some crucial respects East Germany was ahead of West Germany. In technical education the former GDR awarded degrees for highly skilled manual labor and had a long-term apprenticeship program aimed at placing people in high-technology jobs (e.g., *Halbleitertechniker,* or semiconductor technician, a craft that was eliminated because it did not exist in West Germany). Ed Crump, a German-speaking U.S. AMD HR executive, considered the local technical high schools to be superior to the community college system in California. Given the chronic level of unemployment in Saxony when AMD began to hire, there were *very* well educated employees lined up to take advantage of the opportunity to work for the company.

The local *Bundesland* (state government) was heavily committed and invested financially, politically, and psychologically in the success of this Fab. At stake was the whole vision of "Silicon Saxony" as a microelectronics cluster. If AMD (and Siemens nearby) succeeded, other multinational companies (MNCs) would probably follow, and Saxony might recapture the wealth and magnificence of its past. The phoenix would rise from the ashes.

The deal to move to Dresden was hammered out between Jerry Sanders, founder and chairman of AMD, and Professor of Economics Kurt Biedenkopf, the popular and visionary governor of Saxony. At the outset the deal was not widely popular in AMD. There were strong opinions about Germans, communists, and German laws on unions, work councils, and codetermination. With Siemens already there, doubts were expressed about timing. The decision had been struggled with intensely. Under Governor Biedenkopf's leadership, however, the ministries of labor and economics had been combined so that all industrial partners cooperated in one ministry at the highest levels of government to reindustrialize the region. Although Germany is a country of laws and countless regulations, AMD never lost a day's work having to wait for a permit. All the permits applied for were delivered punctually. The workforce proved flexible and highly motivated, out to demonstrate that Saxony was world class. Saxony is very much a source of the Protestant work ethic. The elector of Saxony was the first German prince to endorse Martin Luther's Reformation, and the state was at the core of the Reformation down the centuries.

A word should be said about the critical dimensions of a fabrication plant for microchips. Manufacture of the chips consists of large, highly automated processes with extremely exacting standards of quality. Modern transistors are made of layers, some of which are only a dozen atoms in thickness. The key measure of success is the "yield," that is, the percentage of silicon not wasted during the production process. Yields typically are low when operations first start, but they ramp upward over time in a steep learning curve.

Profit and loss depend crucially on this rising curve. A plant with a disappointing yield can lose millions of dollars a week and exhaust its energies on breaking even. A plant with a yield rising quickly to record levels is not just a feat of intercultural competence but a highly profitable outcome for the company. In such circumstances misunderstandings, breakdowns in communication, and mutual resentment between those of different national cultures or between managers and workers are potentially catastrophic in their consequences. A series of fine balances is easy to upset by any dissatisfied party. Harmonious working requires the fine-tuning of all efforts. The overall process is extremely delicate and vulnerable to disturbances. The business is hostage to the continued high quality of cross-cultural communications.

Given the well-known but often denied or "repressed" antagonism between "Ossis" and "Weissis" and given the varying approaches to business of Americans and Germans, the whole project had to be considered hazardous. Might AMD be bled dry by interpersonal conflicts carried out thousands of miles from the United States in a language it did not speak? Jerry Sanders had put his reputation and the company on the line. However, if AMD succeeded, it would have the invaluable experience of a highly successful foreign operation under its belt. The stakes were very high.

The Dilemmas Martin Gillo Perceived

Our interviews with Gillo elicited the following major dilemmas confronting the Dresden Fab:

1. Neither one culture nor the other dominates: the creation of hyperculture
2. Beyond reason and pragmatism
3. Beyond individualism and communitarianism
4. Learning from errors and corrections
5. Skill versus challenge: the flow experience
6. Sponsoring the empowered team

We will now consider each of these six dilemmas in turn, but first an important word of introduction to the case study that follows: When talking about differences between groups, cultures, and peoples, we must remember that we can talk only about trends and about quantitative, not qualitative, differences between them. There will be many Germans who act and think in some respects more "typically American" than "typically German," just as there will be many Americans who think and act in some respects more "typically German" than "typically American." The reader needs to keep this in mind or be at risk of seeing only a world of stereotypical caricatures in black and white, not the real-life world of shades of gray. Yet when we are dealing with cultural differences, we are dealing *only* in shades. Having said that, we are ready to explore this case study's ideas for creating a hyperculture.

Dilemma 1. Neither One Culture Nor the Other Dominates: The Creation of a Hyperculture

From the very beginning the AMD team realized that trying to import and impose AMD's American culture on Dresden would be a mistake. In no way can one culture reproduce another exactly, even if it wants to—and it rarely does. A large number of German engineers visited the existing Fabs in Austin and facilities in California. This was done not to indoctrinate them but to provide various models of operation and give them the feel of an operational Fab. Two hundred fifty Germans visited American operations, and most loved it. It was a whole new world of self-organizing systems. Their right to organize themselves when they got home was not questioned.

America retains its tradition of openness and hospitality to strangers. Several German visitors were moved to tears by the genuine welcome they got. Not that the visit was free of misunderstandings: When the Germans presented their annual vacation plans upon their arrival, as German law and custom decree, this action was misconstrued! Here they were, on their first day on the job, already thinking about vacations.

The numbers alone show why American culture could not be imposed. The Dresden Fab would soon be 98 percent German—90 percent East German. You can command people up to a point, but not their culture, their shared mental programming. Even the German employees were "singing" at times from "different sheets"; many of the senior managers were West German, while virtually all the workers and some of the managers were East German. Our research shows that cultural differences between West Germany and East Germany are *at least* as wide as those between other European countries. Many East Germans saw Americans as examples of best practices, open-mindedness, optimism, and can-do conviction. Many West Germans expected an American company to adopt their views on how to succeed with people in all of Germany.

It was for this reason that Gillo proposed early on that Dresden AMD should cocreate a new *hyperculture* of its own. The company would borrow and synthesize from the cultures of America, East Germany, and West Germany. It would copy no one culture but would distill that which was best in each of them and most relevant to the task at hand. This was a crucial decision because it prevented each of the cultures from having to defend itself or insist on its own ways. The sterile jousts between Ossis and Wessis or between U.S. culture and German culture were broken up and sidelined. The truth was that the work to be performed jointly was in advance of, and more complex than, that which any culture had yet achieved anywhere. The new Fab would exceed the performances of all AMD's current Fabs because it included all the latest technology. It was also dedicated to producing the six-copper-layer K-7 chip (entered in the market under the AMD Athlon brand name) to within a tolerance of 0.18 micron, a feat never before accomplished.

The hyperculture was organized around a task like no other and of necessity had to be unique. It followed that although several national cultures could contribute to a solution, no single culture owned it. A hyperculture is precisely tuned to its corporate objective and exists in order to excel. The dilemma looks like this:

Dilemma I: Creating a Hyperculture

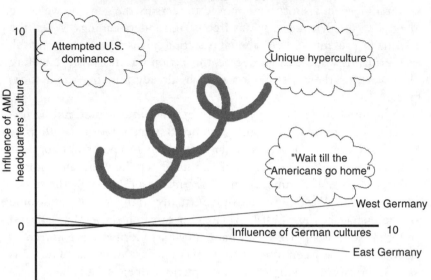

Creating a hyperculture was not without its tribulations. When some Germans felt unhappy, they would say, "Wait till the Americans go home!" The 10 percent U.S. presence in Dresden during the preparatory phase quickly dwindled to 2 percent or lower. Long before that the American influence could be squeezed out. Its dominance had to fade with time and with the preference of Californians and Texans for their own patch.

Dilemma 2. Beyond Reason and Pragmatism

A famous German-American dilemma is the distinction between solving problems by reasoning and logical insight and solving them by empiricism and pragmatism. We picked this up ourselves when interviewing German engineers recently sent to Austin, Texas, who were still sensitive to culture shock.

Here was the situation as seen through some German eyes:

- The Americans were very often in team meetings discussing this or that initiative.
- The Americans kept changing tack and trying something new instead of sticking to agreed avenues of inquiry.
- The Americans rarely spent any time alone *thinking through* their problems and coming to rational conclusions.

- On some occasions for which German engineers had carefully prepared their positions and were ready to present them, the objectives had been changed again and their efforts had been wasted.
- If Americans did not joke, kid around, and change their minds so often, work could finish at a reasonable hour. It was a question of discipline and keeping to schedules. German engineers had their families to consider, who were having to deal with strange environments and were often lonely at school because of language barriers.

The tension here, according to Gillo, is between *high-risk pragmatism,* favored by Americans, and *lower-risk rationalism,* favored by Germans. From the German point of view the Americans "shoot from the hip" without taking careful aim; German engineers, by contrast, coming as they do from expert cultures, like to solve problems by rational and cerebral means. In extreme cases Americans even criticize German engineers for "paralysis by analysis." You don't have forever to find solutions when definitions of problems are changing quickly. However, the dilemma is not that simple, nor are Germans or Americans so homogeneous. What surprised Gillo initially was that East Germans were in this respect closer to Americans than to West Germans, although the reasons for that were intriguing.

Because of the decades of extremely limited resources in the old GDR and the frequently unreliable delivery of necessary supplies, and because prices for electronic goods had been fixed arbitrarily in Moscow, often at unrealistic levels aimed at exploiting the Warsaw Pact countries (the old Eastern Bloc), East Germans had learned to improvise, to substitute cheaper components at the last minute, and generally to scramble to remain solvent. The joke about centralized planning was that it spawned local improvisation on a massive scale because the plans were so rigid. In any event, many of the East Germans took to the American pragmatic style as if they had been born to it. Sudden changes of tack were what they were used to, and they suffered much less than West Germans did when parameters were changed suddenly. Moreover, it gave them equal footing with their West German peers. This was a "new game," and everyone came to it afresh.

We must nonetheless take care not to put rationality down. It saves us from reinventing the wheel. German engineers learned much by analyzing the operation of American Fabs. Without analysis, the Dresden Fab could not have done as well as it did.

The value that the AMD Dresden team strove to endorse was *systematic experimentation*. The *systematic* part was designed to appeal to German rationality, and the *experimental* part to American (and East German) pragmatism (and improvisation). The dilemma is set out in the following diagram:

Dilemma 2: Reason versus Pragmatism

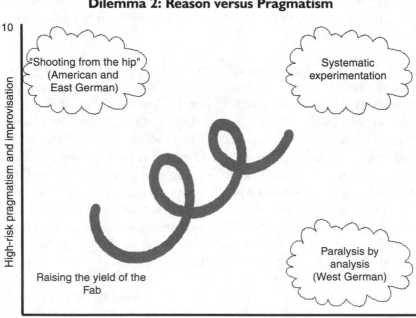

Systematic experimentation is monitored by raising the yield of the Fab progressively. What works pragmatically is retained; what fails is discarded. Rationality remains crucial in providing insights into what works and what does not. This holds true even more for painstaking systematic experimentation.

Dilemma 3. Beyond Individualism and Communitarianism

One dimension on which the former West Germany and East Germany still disagree is the relative salience of individualism versus group orientation. While much of the former Eastern Bloc now claims to be more individualistic than Americans and extols the ideology of the

West, many East Germans still reject the "arrogance" of the West Germans and their perceived tendency toward consumerism and superiority, according to Wolfgang Wagner's research. The courage it took to survive the oppression of the Stasi (secret police) and the high price of resistance are rarely honored in the new Germany. The East retains a solidarity based on suffering that few in the West wish to understand or appreciate. Martin Gillo likes to cite recent surveys comparing Wessis with Ossis that showed that West Germans embrace a form of individualism while East Germans identify with the common good (Box 4–1).

Box 4-1

Individualism versus Common Good

	West Germans	East Germans
Description	Are more oriented toward individualist and pluralist community of interests; decision making through dissent, conflict, and compromise	Are community and group oriented and are disappointed by individualistic Western society; decision making through consensus about the common good
Advantages	All the individuals can find happiness in their own ways	More cohesion, clarity, and dependability
Characterize themselves as	Independent, casual, lonely, uptight, pleasure oriented	Overwhelmed by change, group dependent, family oriented
Characterize others as	Bourgeois, kind, trusting, narrow-minded	Independent, arrogant, cynical

Source: Wolfgang Wagner, *Kulturschock Deutschland*. Hamburg: Rotbuch Verlag, 1996.

The descriptions in this box give the flavor of the East Germans' mood of resentment toward their Western compatriots and other outsiders. "How shall we deal with such differences?" asks Gillo. He rejects cultural colonialism ("Follow us"), the melting pot ("fondue"), and tolerance (the cultural mosaic) because in all these cases there is no genuine engagement between the integrity of one culture and that of the other. "Follow us" ignores the East German culture. "Fondue" opts for one sticky mass. Tolerance follows the discredited policy of separate but equal, a result that almost never eventuates because the weaker of the separated cultures wilts.

The AMD team's answer was *cultural symbiosis*, or *synergy*, a process by which West German culture, East German culture, and American culture could combine their preferences. The resulting symbiosis is individualistic because the United States and West Germany are involved yet communitarian because East German employees constitute the large majority of the participants. Both values are joined together at higher levels of intensity, not in a fondue mix but by catalytic conversion to higher levels of energy and power.

"We go through five steps," explains Gillo:

1. Recognize that the cultures are legitimately different.
2. Respect those differences; there is no "right" or "wrong."
3. Locate the cultural differences on a dual axis, as illustrated in the following figure.

Dilemma 3: Individualism versus Communitarianism

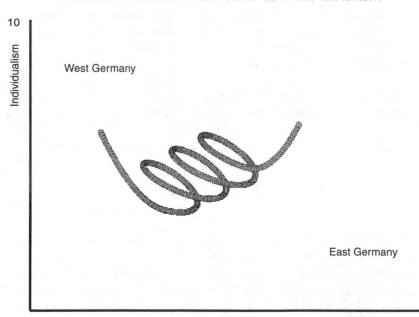

4. Caricature both extremes to make them unacceptable: "Look out for no. 1" (individualism) and "Only society counts" (group orientation).
5. "Symbiotize" (as one might call it) both values; that is, strengthen one value *through* the other. For example, a symbiotic combination of East and West helps create the climate of a communitarian culture in which the groups work extremely closely together *and* the individuals are encouraged to take initiatives and risks for the best interests of themselves *and the group*. Communitarianism has been described in the United States in recent years by writers such as Amitai Etzioni, the author of *The Third Way to a Good Society* (London: Demos, 2000).

"The truth is, individualism and a group orientation are complementary, not opposed, provided that we can fine-tune them," Gillo says. "The group can, if it so desires, nurture individuality, whereupon the individuals so formed contribute to that group, all the more effectively because of their independence of judgment and opinion." But you cannot just announce this philosophy and hope that it sticks. You have to treat employees according to its tenets. You have to reward individuals *as* individuals for their support for the team, *and* you can also give them a bonus as a team for supporting and championing the initiatives of the individual members. Between them, these rewards encourage individuals to improve teams and encourage teams to develop individuals.

In this overall dynamic each culture tends to see its preferred value. East Germans tend to prefer the "descending arc" on the right. West Germans and Americans tend to prefer the "ascending arc" on the left. What all cultures should be able to recognize, whichever arc they prefer, is that the *entire cycle* is necessary to enhance both individualism and communitarianism in symbiosis.

A second dynamic is to let individuals or groups compete in friendly rivalry until a team emerges that can cooperate around the winning formula. For example, one team's initiatives might produce a better yield than do another's, but most crucial is the capacity of the whole community to adopt those winning initiatives. The ideal is *collaborative competition*. To achieve that ideal, once again we stigmatize the extremes: "tooth and claw" is corrupted individualism, and "cozy collusion" is corrupted communitarianism.

Note that the term *co-opetition* had to be coined recently to convey a type of symbiosis that dictionaries still do not acknowledge. Only the

Japanese, to our knowledge, have an accepted term for "cooperating while competing."

Gillo does not confine his concept of symbiosis to these two values alone but sees golden opportunities for the reconciliation of numerous dilemmas. We now turn to three more of these.

Dilemma 4. Learning from Errors and Corrections

Let us look more closely at the unique challenges of building a proto-type Fab. You cannot rely on reason because it is not possible to get a clear definition of all of the problems to be solved. Reasoning assumes the preexistence of a logical solution to a definable problem, but building a Fab is less a definable problem than a nest of interdependent problems, each of which affects and changes the definitions of the others. You have to start somewhere, but depending on this choice, the remaining problems rearrange themselves spontaneously. One bottle-neck once removed, for example, creates several more. The task itself constantly evolves along with those who perform it, a process Gillo calls *coevolution,* in which we change the environment, which in turn throws up fresh challenges to be met. It is less the survival of the fittest than the survival of the *fittingest.* We keep reengaging the environment in ways that increase the yield; however, this improvement quickly changes the competitive environment and triggers the need for never-ending virtuous cycles of improvements. This is not unlike an *error-correcting system* in which you zero in on improving yields through *successive approximations* to ever-increasing levels of expected quality. W. Edwards Deming made this process famous.

Yet conventional wisdom tells us that errors are somehow "evil" and must be extirpated, while corrections are "good." Good must conquer evil to create a world that is perfect and free of contaminants. The problems with this view are that it makes learning from our mistakes almost impossible and that it assumes that what is best can always be known before we act.

Conventional morality is a serious impediment to the discovery of better ways by trial, error, and continuous improvement. Building a K7/AMD Athlon Fab is not like searching for the Holy Grail, where the object is ideally "out there," to be found in all its perfection. Rather, a high-yield Fab is the culmination of thousands of continuing trials that successively improve on earlier attempts. "Error" is not a devil; it records what was once good enough but now is surpassed because we are aiming higher. The dilemma looks like this:

Dilemma 4: Error, Correction, and Coevolution

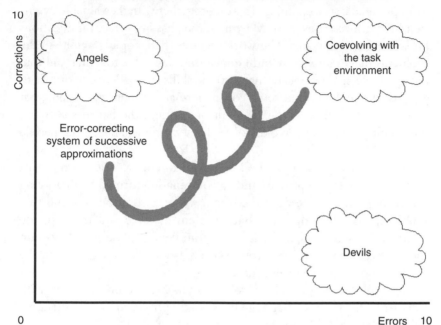

Included in the coevolution are all the cultures involved, plus the remaining resistance to a heightened yield contained within the environment of the whole Fab. Persons, tools, tasks, and work environments evolve together.

Dilemma 5. Skill versus Challenge: The Flow Experience

As was mentioned earlier, for many years Gillo has been fascinated by the results of over 25 years of research by Mihaly Csikszentmihalyi, especially his description of flow states. Even before moving to Dresden Gillo had published his own in-house pamphlets to promote the idea of a continuous flowing engagement with the task at hand, one that learners find all-absorbing and intensely stimulating. (The original research was into the state of happiness itself.)

Flow states, sometimes called *peak experiences,* occur when the team (which could consist of one person) confronts a problem that almost exactly matches its combined potentials and skill sets so that, provided that these potentials can realize themselves, the solution is (just) within the team's reach. The intensity of pleasure comes from stretching toward and reaching new levels of attainment, discovering strengths within the team that were formerly aspirations, and overcoming additional barriers to attainment. Csikszentmihalyi's work, together with the valuable extensions of the Swiss consultant Martin Gerber, has important ramifications for self-organizing teams. The work suggests that people gravitate to the problems they want solved and believe they can solve together and that those people spontaneously match their skills to challenges not just to get past the problems but to discover more about themselves and what they can accomplish. At the moment of triumph the barriers between the problem and the people dissolve. They *are* the challenge the people have met.

The word *solution* holds the key to this dilemma. The word means both "the answer to a puzzle" and "a combination formed by dissolving something into a more fluid medium." When a solution is found to a problem, the hard edges of that problem dissolve and the separate identities of skills and challenges are transcended. The one flows into the other like an onrushing stream of energy as the team rides on the momentum in a surge of excitement.

We took Martin's insights into flow dynamics, combined them with a dual-axis diagram of challenge versus skill proposed by Csikszentmihalyi and created the following image:

Dilemma 5: Skill versus Challenge

Where challenge (the vertical axis) is greater than skill (the horizontal axis), you get anxiety; where skill is greater than challenge, you get boredom (bottom right); but where skill engages challenge to realize its ideal and actualize the person, you get a *whoosh* of excitement and a flow experience (top right). All of a sudden the skills and the challenge that were formerly in conflict (the first seeking to surmount the second) are suddenly one, so that the very strength of the challenge testifies to the skills developed. These moments of ecstatic attainment can be fleeting, as when we look back nostalgically, say, "Then we were happy," and wonder how we can recapture that feeling.

Dilemma 6. Sponsoring the Empowered Team

Progress is not equal on all the dilemmas facing AMD in Dresden. Work still needs to be done, in Gillo's estimation, on the process of sponsoring groups or teams to empower them. "Group sponsorship" needs to be defined.

Dennis Roemig, working on team effectiveness in AMD's U.S. manufacturing plants, coined the phrase *semiautonomous team*. His research found that such teams were a lot more effective than either totally autonomous teams or closely supervised teams. (We shall see why in a moment.) So successful was the team approach that had been used in Texas and California that it was defined as a nonnegotiable aspect of operations at the new Dresden Fab. Teams are vital because problems have grown in complexity beyond the expertise of single professionals and even beyond the mandate of top managers. Managers may know there is a problem, know it must be solved, and know the solution when they see it, but they do *not* know exactly what has to be done to solve the problem or improve the yield. Problems in a mega-Fab need to be *discovered*, and it takes a team to do this and to work out the remedy as quickly as possible.

It is sponsorship of a team by a leader that renders the group semiautonomous. The sponsor describes the problem to be solved, allows the group to form spontaneously around the problem profile, and makes sure all the required skill sets are present. The sponsor then delegates authority to the group and gives it the needed resources. Finally, the sponsor sets the group free to complete its task.

However, this "freedom" is a question of degree. The team must report back in weeks or months, and so that autonomy is measurable by the *time interval between supervisions.* If the team is left alone for months, the autonomy is great and the risk is high. The team might go off course and waste time and money. If the team is left alone only for days and is seeded with the leader's spies, the autonomy is low and so is the risk, and so also is the likelihood of the team's coming up with anything remotely innovative or significant.

Dilemma 6: Sponsoring Empowered Teams

In the preceding diagram note that Gillo has added a third dimension: time. It was he who wrote to us some years ago to insist that *all* dilemmas were resolved over time.

The authority of the sponsor is on the vertical axis, and the empowerment of the team is on the horizontal axis. If the sponsor hangs on to authority for dear life, the team remains on a short leash, a captive of its leader's doubt and distrust (top left), but if the team is *totally* autonomous, it could deviate from, misinterpret, or defy its sponsor's charge and use its newfound power to bind its sponsor to developments that are neither sought nor intended (bottom right). After all, the team has the delegated authority and the resources given to it and *could* diminish both. In this event the sponsor's authority is seriously weakened.

Alternatively, the charge could be so clear, the problem so important, and the team so motivated and in such a flow state that the sponsor's problem is solved, and this solution, along with part of the credit, goes back as a gift from the empowered team (top right). In this event all concerned are better off. The sponsor's judgment and authority are vindicated and enhanced. The team's morale is sky-high, and its power and influence are enhanced. The semiautonomous nature of the team is indicated by the gaps between the loops. How often must the team check back with its sponsor? Too often or too seldom can both do damage, but "just right" makes the team a strong investigative arm of its sponsor, an invaluable way of uncovering new facts and testing propositions.

The problem in this case could be with traditional German culture, East and West, which places the sponsor's expertise above the team's initiative in the organization's hierarchy. Sometimes German sponsors are less willing than American ones to delegate authority to teams and trust them to develop capacities for problem solving. Yet given the nature of new fabrication plants, delegating may be the only way. Sponsors rarely know the answer for which the team is searching, and it would be a waste of the team's time and effort if they did.

The Dresden team does everything possible to preserve and develop "natural work groups," that is, groups that have learned and experimented together and in whose relationships much crucial information is stored. Gradually these natural groupings are growing in their reputation for discovery and problem solving. In the continuing coevolution of natural work groups it could turn out that they benefit from constitutionlike protective boundaries and explicit role clarifications for the groups and their sponsors. The same could also apply to the owners and to the internal as well as the external customers of the problems to be solved. Of all the dilemmas, the last one is turning out to be the most stubborn.

How Has the Dresden Fab Fared?

We cannot give figures for AMD's yield at the Dresden Fab (they are commercially confidential), yet the signs of significant success are everywhere. As of this writing, the 0.18-micron copper version of the AMD Athlon microprocessor is the most ambitious and most advanced in AMD's worldwide operations. Gene Conner, a senior vice president of AMD, pronounced Dresden "the most successful start-up in the history of the company." Learning curves by which yields climb can be steep and rapid or shallow and slow. The Dresden learning curve was the steepest and fastest among all the start-ups of AMD's Fabs. That the Fab we have been discussing was a mega-Fab employing a thousand people to produce a chip of unprecedented complexity and sophistication merely made the feat more remarkable. That Dresden was chosen to produce the AMD Athlon was an occasion for regional rejoicing, a triumph not just for the plant but for Saxony, where ancient castles were selling for $1 if the owner would restore and properly maintain them.

Gillo comments: "We now run two day shifts and two night shifts. The plant never sleeps. At 3:00 A.M. several engineers will still be there. This is their baby. Employees have rights to unionization and a works council under German law. So far these have not been organized. I like to think this is in some part because we look after everyone's needs. We all share the great adventure of improving the world's most advanced Fab. We want to hear everyone's voice. We are determined to give their opinions and cultures the weight that is due to them. We are a *partnership-oriented* company indeed."

Chapter 5

—◆—

Remedy for a Turnaround: Philippe Bourguignon, Club Med

Fons Trompenaars and Charles Hampden-Turner

*I*T IS A particular pleasure to write about Club Med because one of us (FT) has taken his wife and family to its village resorts at least 10 times. To study the company is to begin to understand the intensity of our enjoyment, but we are not simply indulging ourselves here. Club Med caters to an international clientele with a prodigious mix of international staff. Vacationing is the world's fastest-growing industry, and within that industry, which is the best-known brand? Club Med.

While at least one of the authors is a Club Med fan, capable of playing the fool at the club's nightly evenings by dancing in a tutu or otherwise frolicking, the recently interrupted success of the company has a serious side as well. Our experiences of Club Med's French stylishness; its easy camaraderie; its well-trained staff, seemingly also on vacation while eating, dancing, and flirting with the guests; the sports; the buffet; and the free wine among the gregarious mix of nationalities are unforgettable. We even thrived on those hand-waving sing-alongs ("Hands up! Gimme, gimme, your heart!").

Yet all these fond memories might have been nonrenewable if not for Philippe Bourguignon. Until 1997 he had been busy trying to turn around the fortunes of Euro-Disney. Even while he was thus engaged, the fortunes of Club Med were ebbing as it descended further into financial trouble, with annual losses of $200 million, until in February of that year Bourguignon was asked to take the helm. It was said at the time that the Gulf crisis had hit hard at the company's "villages," several of which were too close to the fighting. But the real problems were more endemic to the system.

Radical action was needed to stop the losses, and Bourguignon had to move fast. Among other things, he closed 8 of Club Med's 116 sites and renovated 70 others. He imposed high-quality standards on the remaining sites. Before we can understand the subtleties of his many strategic moves, we have to look at the history of Club Med and the troubles into which the company had descended by early 1997.

Early Brilliance That Lost Its Way

Club Med was founded in 1950 by a Belgian, Gerard Blitz, a former Olympic water-polo competitor. He was soon joined in partnership by a Frenchman, the recently deceased Gilbert Trigano, who as a member of the French Communist party saw Club Med as breaking down class barriers. That summer they introduced their "all-inclusive vacation," consisting of a military-surplus tent village in Alcudia, Majorca. The concept of the club was born in a prewar context where people had to learn to live together in mutual trust again. This package holiday was a major innovation for its time but is now so common that we rarely inquire into its origins. In 1954 the first concrete apartments were built in Greece, followed by the first winter village, in Leysin, Switzerland. The company was years ahead of its time. It pioneered exclusive hotel and resort facilities as well as the concept of "club membership" with accompanying brand loyalty. Today Club Med has 116 resorts, or "villages," plus 11 villas across the world, and serves 1.6 million vacationers a year from 40 different countries, largely in the winter and the summer. It also features a three-mast cruise ship, the *Club Med 2*, which was launched in 1992.

The company's extraordinary success can be traced to key features of French culture and its capacity to combine values not previously integrated by its competitors. The all-inclusive package differed from those of its more standardized competitors by combining freedom and choice for the vacationer with prearranged bookings and accommodations and extensive opportunities for conviviality and generosity.

The club goes out of its way to attract families while providing an opportunity for parents and children to be separately entertained and relieved from each other's company for periods of time, including relief from the parental chores of cooking, housekeeping, and baby-sitting. The club also reconciles the improvisation and informality of camping with the luxury of good food, wine, and entertainment. Blitz refers to this as "a strange cocktail of chateau life and wild life."

Blitz intended his company to restore the values that had been lost in modern tourism: "Adventure is dead, and solitude is dying in inter-linked systems of tourism. The individual doesn't like promiscuity but needs a community. Therefore, we offer him flexible vacations to which he can adhere himself at any moment or avoid." The village provides a "base camp" from which those seeking solitude and adventure can roam with or without guidance and companions.

Gilbert Trigano claimed that Club Med was designed deliberately to straddle "the contradictions of French life," to make up for what was lacking in work life: "Vacations result in a kind of liberation that enriches the rest of the year. The club has crossed some borders by giving serious people the right to be ridiculous and to try out almost anything. Therefore, the villages were initially designed to respond to typical French contradictions: sophistication versus back to nature, individualism versus cama-raderie, a mix of sports, sensuality, culture, and exotically strange decors, a yearly escape from the barriers and tensions of society in a utopian brotherhood. As the company's own history puts it, Club Med members "spent their days frolicking in the Mediterranean Sea and their nights sleeping under army surplus tents supplied by the Trigano family."

France, as our research shows, is perhaps the most communitarian nation in Western Europe, and to a great extent Club Med celebrates this fact. Each table accommodates eight people, room enough for your own family and one you have met during the day. Every evening there is live entertainment that brings families together and in which the audi-ence can participate. But during the day different people can follow any of dozens of sporting or adventure activities, with special interests of particular family members catered to and supervised within "clubs."

Now, it would not be French unless the conviviality had real style and panache. *Les gentils organisateurs* ("the gracious organizers," or GOs) set an example of social grace, hospitality, and exuberant spirits, mak-ing sure that everyone is included who wants to be and usually helping to provide the evening *spectacle*. On Friday evenings the GOs help arrange *spectacles* featuring the children of *les gentils membres* ("the gra-cious members," or GMs), who don colorful costumes to perform for their parental audience the numbers they have rehearsed. You pay up front, and everything else flows and bubbles with the wine as spontaneous communities self-organize to have fun and exhibit their talents to each other.

We can summarize the reasons for Club Med's initial success by listing the dilemmas it helped reconcile:

DILEMMA	RESOLVED BY
1. Many separate bookings versus one shared experience	The all-inclusive, all-paid holiday
2. Preorganized holiday versus adventure and autonomy	Individuals explore around their base camp
3. Attract the family versus give members a rest from each other	"Clubs" in which children have separate daytime activities and evening reunions
4. Improvisation and informality versus luxury of food and entertainment	"Cocktail of chateau life and wild life"
5. The individual's solitude versus the need for community	Attach or detach yourself at will
6. Serious people versus the liberation to have fun and enjoy losing oneself	*Spectacle* and camaraderie
7. Sophistication versus back to nature	The noble savage (Jean-Jacques Rousseau)
8. Exotic decor versus barriers and tensions of society	Utopian brotherhood of mutual self-expression
9. Guests as audience versus guests as entertainers (especially children)	Freedom to do what you want when and where you want
10. International diversity versus *les gentils organisateurs*	GMs celebrate their common humanity through GOs

In the preceding table we have tried to supply a resolution or reconciliation for each contradiction; most were provided by the two founders, but some by us and one by Jean-Jacques Rousseau. France is perhaps the only country in the world where "contradictions"—what we call dilemmas—have intellectual status as recognized societal phenomena.

So What Went Wrong?

Given this feat of *bonhomie,* it seems surprising that Club Med could get into trouble. Yet success is in the details, and even as the GOs and GMs were celebrating each other, certain crucial details began to slip.

The trouble began as early as 1993. Club Med's prodigious growth had overstrained as well as obscured its antiquated management structure. It had become intoxicated by its self-celebrations week after week and was not keeping track of costs or logistics. What Bourguignon called the *spirale infernale* ("vicious circle") was kicked off by a series of uncontrollable accidents and worsened during the 1993 global recession. The company's downward spiral had begun. Meanwhile, some holidaymakers copied Club Med's concept and took some market share from it. Combine these factors with bad management leading to a series of expensive, faulty investments and a decreasing number of innovations, and it explains higher prices and lower perceived quality. One of the core values of Club Med, "generosity," was not affected by the downturn best expressed by lower occupancy rates. No company survives for long under these conditions, but maladministration drove Club Med farther under. Resorts were not profit centers, and several had lost money without anyone's being aware of it or of opening too early in the season or not early enough and closing too early or too late.

Moreover, hospitality had been increased with no awareness of diminishing returns. Forty different sporting activities were too many, requiring too many experts in each sport and smaller membership in clubs. The food and wine expenditure had escalated too far. Too many GMs were aging friends of the founders' families, with an average age of 50-plus. Club Med's strengths had been extended to the point of weakness and indulgence. In the meantime the rest of the tourist industry was catching up, and Club Med was soon seen as too expensive. It responded to lower bookings with higher prices, and the downward spiral intensified.

Philippe Bourguignon Takes Charge

Bourguignon took charge in early 1997 and started by making a tour of the villages around the world. On his first day he showed up in a village in Africa rather than in the more established life of the headquarters in Paris La Villette. He was very clear in his objective: to find out why the club was hitting bad weather financially. "It is typical of Bourguignon that he refused the best bungalow in our village on the Ivory Coast, which I, as *chef de village,* had dedicated to our new president," says Vincenzo Del'Zingaro, one of the 100 *chefs de village,* or site managers, of Club Med. "Bourguignon loves luxury, but his job was to find out how local sites were operating. Therefore, he wanted a standard bungalow. When I asked him how he was doing the morning after a terrible night of storms, he said it was okay except for the water on his floor and the fact that the water in the shower didn't rise beyond room temperature. But he was very factual about it and just suggested that he had had bad luck. Even when, the next day, his new bungalow was unexpectedly surrounded by nudists from the neighboring hotel, he just responded by saying that it was quite an interesting experience."

By the end of his tour in July 1997 Bourguignon had a pretty good idea of the mess his company was in. The annual report for 1997 listed the weaknesses he had uncovered, and it was typical of his straightforward behavior that he pulled no punches. The brand had not responded to the entry of new players. Prices were too high, driven by failures in cost containment. Excessive choices at each village diluted the experience of sharing as well as pushing up costs. Villages should specialize more instead of offering everything. Many villages were shoddy and in disrepair. Lack of investment had taken a toll. Finally, the communications system among villages and to headquarters was deficient.

Bourguignon was faced with a powerful, formerly successful club culture proud of its history and pioneering tourist attractions. So many of those traditions were valuable and right that he did not want to attack them. How could this unique way of serving and satisfying people make money again?

Behind every great strength lies a potential weakness. Those who excel at lavish hospitality and gentle sociability are rarely the best accountants or "number crunchers." Bourguignon set about analyzing the profits and losses for every individual village and resort and discovered monumental waste. He closed 11 losing resorts in Greece, Ireland, and Switzerland and sold off a cruise liner, *CM1.* He built 10 new resorts, renovated 70, and extended opening and closing times to increase the overall room capacity until every week was profitable in itself. He adjusted prices to reflect demand through a simplified price policy, a reduction in the number of advertising promotions to improve the discount factor, and the implementation of yield management.

He kept the *chefs de village* and replaced some GOs as heads of departments and country managers in headquarters functions with colleagues he had known at Euro-Disney, Accor, and other companies such as PepsiCo and Danone, but the test was always performance and an understanding of culture, not favoritism. A delicate touch was required to create a renewed management team of 49 new managers out of 86, combining new skills with existing talents. Bourguignon emphasized and celebrated the mission that had made Club Med great. You entertain people with their children in a variety of activities, including sports, and give them excellent accommodations and food in a beautiful site with charming and entertaining hosts.

As an outsider and a turnaround specialist who earned his spurs at Euro-Disney, Bourguignon could be more drastic about severing old relationships. One European GO observed: "In a French company you need to be a relative outsider to be able to take tough measures like closing a site or asking people with 20 years of experience to leave because they are unwilling to change. Previous management couldn't do this. They were too much attached to existing relationships and traditions."

Bourguignon was clear that Club Med's values were not wrong per se but had in many cases been taken so far that they were hurting, not helping, the organization:

"All companies have strengths that are weaknesses if you take them too far. The club's strengths are its unique formula, in which GOs eat, play sports, create shows, and dance with GMs. [The club] offers a vast variety of sports, some 60 in total, which we keep extending. We are the largest sports institute in the world. We are located in some of the loveliest places, and our miniclubs for kids are a great success, as is our cuisine. This triangle of GO, GM, and site in an atmosphere of generosity and living together needed to be reassessed and rebuilt in an affordable way.... But all these were also expensive and came at the cost of other luxuries and attentions, at higher-than-necessary prices. Headquarters was too large. Relationships to headquarters were too hierarchical. We needed to empower villages by giving them information on how they were doing and the authority to act. Every unit is now a self-conscious center that knows the costs of its activities and can estimate their value."

Before his first year was over Bourguignon had coined a new watchword: *Être-Re,* or "Re-New." Club Med's traditional values would not be abandoned but would be renewed in their attractiveness and impact on customers. Renewal had four strategic axes, all built on past accomplishments:

1. *Re-Focus* the product by renovating villages and featuring this strategy in a marketing campaign.
2. *Re-Store* the brand and the product as the all-inclusive vacation with a brand entity aligned with its perception.
3. *Re-Gain* price competitiveness: reevaluate price policies by more closely tracking and responding to peaks and troughs in demand.
4. *Rationalize* management and organization—the way operations are done in headquarters and in each site—in a way that takes advantage of what is common to all sites and hence emphasizes what is unique and special to each site.

In implementing these strategies Bourguignon employed the famous French axiom *Plus ça change, plus c'est la même chose* as "We change it all, we keep it all," or literally, "Everything changes yet remains the same." He wanted Club Med as an idea and a set of values redefined in changed circumstances.

We will now examine these four strategic thrusts and consider what dilemmas they addressed and how those dilemmas were reconciled.

1. The Dilemma of Refocusing: The Unique, Seamless, Personalized Vacation versus the Reliable, Affordable, Segmented, Standardized Global Product

The need to refocus comes from the fact that the unique personalized vacation presided over by GOs who get to know you well and concentrate on creating an unforgettable experience is not enough. This meant that more effectiveness had to be created. The worst that could have been done would have been to offer a little bit of everything. That is like offering nothing. The *Re-Focus* program was aimed at "an increased offering by focusing on what you offer." This was done on all levels: sports, food, shows, and so on, with all the operational risks that come along with it. Less lyrical issues such as occupancy rates and how to improve them must be considered at the same time. You cannot be "gentle" only with those who turn up. They will not turn up if they do not expect the standard of service they seek at an affordable cost. Little inexpensive things that create a "personal touch" include details such as memorizing a person's first name and a previous occasion on which the GO met the GM. This is what refocusing is all about.

Bourguignon has concentrated his offering into four categories instead of six levels of luxury. He created this arrangement by renovating 70 of the 100 villages and classifying them all. The two main markets are young couples and families, with the latter generally wanting more luxury and services than the former. Quality control also has been brought to the subject of sports and *spectacles* (evening shows). Top tennis professionals are available at some sites, are featured in marketing, and help bring sports specialists at the villages up to scratch.

Club Med had always emphasized the life and pleasures of the body to the exclusion of those of the mind. Starting in North America, summer forums were held in which writers, intellectuals, artists, and agents of change could discuss weighty topics such as globalization, cultural diversity, and literature. One purpose was to drive a stake into Club Med's reputation as a swinger's paradise. The plethora of clubs "swinging" in alarming ways for people with esoteric tastes had made this market inaccessible and potentially dangerous for Club Med.

Bourguignon wanted an appeal much broader than hedonism, with multiple themes to enlighten the human spirit: "People can come to Club Med to rediscover their body, to rejuvenate their minds, their families, their friendships, themselves. So far I am pleased with the results of the preliminary efforts in this area. A classical music series at a Portuguese resort in 1999 helped boost attendance in June, a low season. Likewise, a Christmas festival at a Moroccan resort in November of the same year helped the company lure vacationers in what are usually seen as the resort's slowest months."

Club Med has also professionalized its *spectacles*. There is now a creative center where shows are devised and produced by professionals with the help of village impresarios, who are inspired to higher standards. The original shows varied from brilliant improvisation to amateurism. Costumes, scripts, scenarios, and new ideas (from kids' fashion shows to Asterix the Gaul) are offered to participants, who can borrow whatever is most relevant to their village and type of customer. The creative team has been so successful that Club Med is thinking of turning it into a business in its own right and offering shows to impresarios and organizers of parties and festivities.

An important aspect of Re-Focusing is improving access to the company among would-be vacationers. Information technology (IT) systems that work out travel itineraries for customers, along with rental cars and other amenities, replace work done previously by travel agents, with the company getting commissions. This arrangement allows for a total view of each customer's plans and renews the concept of inclusivity. Early in the year 2000 Bourguignon launched Club Med On Line, allowing customers to make on-line bookings as well as setting out the sheer range of choices available, along with comments by other customers on the attractions they sampled.

The Web site will also feature services linked to Club Med offerings, such as fitness, sports activities, music, and film, along with such branded Club Med products as sun wear, swimming costumes, luggage, skin care products, and perfume. To integrate these products with vacation scenes, distribution agreements with Carrefour, a large retailer, will feature these products in the context of vacation themes and offerings.

Says Bourguignon: "Club Med needs to refine the art of placing immaterial experiences above the bits and pieces of the material world. The wholeness of experience with its *esprit* and stylishness is vital. What fills empty beds is not concentration on each separate bed but an overall impression of dreamlike intensity and sensual satisfaction. With ever-advancing living standards, the separate elements of luxury and good living are available to more and more people. What is often missing and is more elusive is the integration of these elements into a diffuse sense of satisfaction, a *savoir vivre*. We no longer manage villages, but a shared spirit, a seamless scenario of satisfactions, an *ambience* or atmosphere, as Planet Hollywood or Starbucks Cafe started doing for restaurants and bars, but more discriminating, less harsh, and augmented by food and wine.

"Our new city sites in Club Med World allow us to create 'menus' of city attractions, restaurants, cinemas, museums, lectures, libraries, and stores concerning which we are the guides, the gourmets, and the connoisseurs, arranging transport, dinner, theater, coffee, brandy, and a safe return, a flawless series of fulfillments.... But all this would be prohibitively expensive if we did not boost density, volume, and throughput. So many customers choose our favorite haunts and consume the same sights and sounds that we achieve volume. In one sense the experiences and products we line up are global objects, but when synthesized with the help of choosy customers, they are transformed into novel blends of experience in which the client participates. We operate on these two levels simultaneously, a reliable world of high-standard objects and replicated services and an exotic world of unique personal experiences organized around each customer."

The dilemma of the unique, seamless, personalized vacation versus the reliable, affordable, segmented, standardized global product is set out in the following graph:

Dilemma 1: The Global Ingredients of a Personal Dream

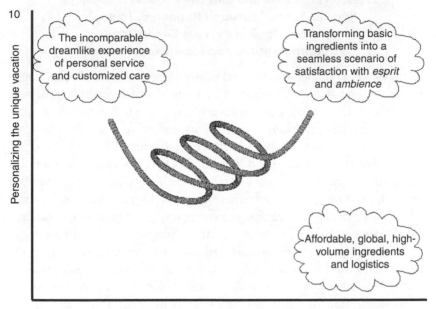

Note that the specific ingredients that go into the making of these diffuse experiences (Dimension 4 in Chapter 2) can coexist simultaneously at different levels of analysis. They are each a part of a whole.

Club Med's tradition belongs at the top left of the chart. As a vendor of incomparable experiences it has to find renewal in a fiercely competitive world of superficial impacts. What Bourguignon has done is move toward the bottom right, segmenting the market, reducing vacations to the standardized units out of which they are constructed, and offering affordable high-volume sales of these units.

However, he has not abandoned Club Med's founding values. These standard ingredients are used to create an *esprit* and an *ambience* that represent a transformation of those ingredients into seamless scenarios of satisfaction. He has pushed down the costs of the parts while elaborating the value and the luxuriousness of the whole.

2. Restoring the Brand and the Product: Building a "Power Brand" through Repeated, Multiple Itemized Impacts versus Dream Play, Experimentation, and New Experiences

Club Med is a branded service, and Bourguignon saw it as his challenge to restore and renew the brand. The brand had become blurred and ambivalent. Club Med was appreciated for its guest orientation yet increasingly was criticized for its prices and poor plant. Its physical assets were run down. "When I started my job with Club Med," he says, "what I found was exciting and frustrating. On the positive side I inherited a strong brand with huge awareness and a huge international presence. But the image was somewhere between blurred and ambivalent. There was a strong culture that was extremely guest oriented, but there were operational inefficiencies and the physical assets had been run down. Over the years our guests had built up expectations that were integrated into the brand of Club Med. Over the years we have seen a wider gap developing between the brand, its identity, and perception."

One criterion for judging a brand is its authenticity. Is it revealing the company honestly, or is the impression false and contrived? Bourguignon decided on the theme of *regeneration*. Club Med was being reborn so that customers could be reborn in unforgettable milieus. Regeneration was a theme capable of being shared by the company and its customers. If customers were regenerated, the company would arise. In Bourguignon's words, "We want to make the brand breathe again, and we want it associated with regeneration. We want people to renew, to rejuvenate, and to recharge. We want Club Med to be the place where people rediscover their minds and their bodies, where they reacquaint themselves with families and friends."

When people are briefly and intensely thrown together with strangers for a limited time in highly unusual environments, an opportunity is created to experiment with new identities, to offer and confirm new strengths, and to live out dreams that the work world has suppressed. If your new capacities are confirmed by intimate companions, it can lead to permanent change—to the regeneration of underused aspects of your personal repertory.

Historically, Club Med had undermarketed itself. It had an aura and an atmosphere, but there were too few salable products attached. Its reputation was seriously underutilized. "We have enormous brand awareness, with scores of 80 percent spontaneous awareness in France, Australia, and Brazil," Bourguignon points out, "while we are only a

$1.6 billion–turnover business. Where awareness is high and sales are low, there are fantastic opportunities. We need to become a *power brand*. Nike does not sell just shoes. Disney sells more than Mickey. Club Med is a better way of life."

It is for this reason that Club Med is busy expanding its range of products associated with vacations. All the villages now carry branded produce. There are advertising partnerships and joint campaigns with Coca-Cola and Konica. In America, Club Med features the family and family values. Aquarius, a discount subsidiary of Club Med, has been reintegrated into the single brand. The total environments that Club Med consists of can be used to encompass other products, such as the BMX bikes used to climb walls and for trick cycling generally. Club Med is busy wrapping its own logo around some of the most enjoyable pursuits it can devise. It is increasingly a backdrop for other distinguished products.

As you might expect from a man who once ran Euro-Disney, Bourguignon sees endless repetition and multiple impacts as essential to the creation of a power brand. Yet such brands can have hidden depths and elusive qualities that invite further exploration. You can recognize a brand while still wanting to discover the experiences it stands for. Bourguignon summarizes his rebranding as follows: "We need to approach this from a broad historical perspective. Man is not just *Homo faber* ('man the worker'), but *Homo ludens* ('man the player'). Free time allows you to 'play' at what you might be, a person with new physical, emotional, and intellectual resources.

"The leisure industry has become the largest industry in the world. In 1998, 290 million European tourists traveled abroad, spending $225 billion. In the year 2020 there will be 1.6 billion tourists leaving their country to enjoy a vacation, three times as many as today. Tourism and travel represent an economic power that is bigger in Japan than the economy represented by electronics and bigger than the automobile industry in the United States. Our business is responding to large sociological developments during this century; a society of consumers has become the information society, and a mass society has become a society of diverse individuals with myriad pursuits. A society oriented by norms and rules has become groups of players rehearsing new roles for themselves. A society built on exclusion has become a society seeking connection around chosen themes of interest.

"We have to be more than dreamers; we have to dream of *new realities*, new forms of fulfillment that we can then try out in everyday life. We need to regenerate old talents and find new ones. We are no longer enjoying ourselves on the side; we are bringing new enjoyment to our *being* in this world. These are the values we must integrate into our brand.

"Add to that that we have to develop a worldwide power brand integrating universal values with a Club Med product that still has many local perceptions. For example, it is seen as rather expensive in the Netherlands, focused on the family in the United Kingdom, but rather adult in Germany and Belgium. Our regeneration needs to be focused on the integration of these varieties of orientations."

It is difficult to diagram such a rich and nuanced philosophy without simplifying it, but here is our best effort:

Dilemma 2: Rejuvenating Customers and the Brand

If hammering on about happiness were all Club Med did, it would end up as just so much noise, signifying little but its own bangs and crashes. But creating worlds of pure fantasy for short ersatz "honeymoons" will soon be lost in a world of inquiry and serious information. The dream will fade in the routines of daily work. What *can* be of lasting significance is *serious* play—playing to learn about yourself, rehearsing undiscovered aspects of yourself among new friends, dreaming and then realizing those dreams, and rejuvenating yourself. Club Med wants no less for its brand than it wants for its customers. Whenever people rediscover their own powers through play, the brand is reinforced.

3. Reevaluating Price Policies

If you have an experience that is basically pleasurable, the more people who pass through it, the better the word-of-mouth advertising. If you have high investments in plant and equipment or fixed costs, you need increased utilization of those premises. If you have a slow season such as Christmas or late autumn, you need to invent and create reasons for coming to you during those times. Stage a major event or engage a sports hero.

Club Med found that boosting off-peak occupancy increased the demand for expensive peak occupancy too. There was a "halo effect." It paid to drop prices as long as you were not losing money. Thus, a 30 percent off-season cut at the Moroccan resort of Al Hoceima pushed up peak bookings by 38 percent and sales for that village by 73 percent over the year.

In many resorts seasons were extended by charging less and featuring new attractions. With cheaper last-minute Internet transportation, spare places could be filled. In making each village a profit center, the local management soon learned how to match demand with supply and use its assets more intensively. Another strategy was to win a greater proportion of the vacationer's total outlay, gaining increased shares of air travel, car rental, equipment purchase, branded Club Med products, and fees for joining clubs affiliated with Club Med.

There is no real dilemma here except perhaps the well-known crossed axes of supply and demand, which are elementary economics. But we must not underestimate the extent to which this dream-selling company had lost touch with economics until Philippe Bourguignon and his tough-minded controller, Henri Giscard d'Estaing, reengaged with market forces and decentralized responsibility for that engagement.

4. Rationalizing What Is Common to Appreciate What Is Unique

Philippe Bourguignon's success at Euro-Disney inevitably led to his being stereotyped in France as "too American," as sacrificing people for profits. He had spent some years in the United States earlier on, and his rescue of Disney's highly mechanized and globalized amusements was seen as one more example of the American invasion of French culture, this time aided and abetted by a Frenchman. Some would have preferred Euro-Disney to fail.

Bourguignon introduced process reengineering into Club Med, putting 500 GOs through a process not known for its gentleness. He modernized the global reservation systems and supplied all sites with up-to-date financial data. That he rationalized the system from top to bottom is undeniable, but does this of necessity militate against human concerns or detract from a sensuous experience? Bourguignon would argue that to rationalize what is amenable to rationality allows you to concentrate on and appreciate the uniqueness of what Club Med provides—and there are plenty of those unique characteristics. First of all there was a significant discrepancy between the actual functioning of people and sites and their creative reporting. This was due partly to the fact that the Club had an oral tradition, not a written one. Many creations of the mind are possible that can't be written down. Add to this the fact that the typical *chef de village* acts like an "artist" rather than a manager. He likes to be creative and would rather "reinvent the wheel" than adopt a solution provided by an outsider. Finally, the complexity that arises from operating as an international firm in both Western and non-Western countries created quite a challenge for Bourguignon.

We can see this most clearly in the area where his reasons impinge on people: human resources. He insisted that the age of distribution must be rebalanced. The organizers were much older than most of the customers. He wanted more mobility between sites so that the staff would learn faster. He wanted new kinds of expertise to keep pace with what customers wanted to learn, and he wanted those at a site to be held accountable for its operations. They could ask for help, but that too was their responsibility.

Above all, the staff had to professionalize. Experts in sports had to have recognized competitive ability. Those in the arts had to have respect in their fields. Those looking after kids had to be competent, all-around generalists. All GOs of any kind are assessed by customers and peers.

Evaluation of a kind had long been practiced, but rather than being a "balanced scorecard," it was perilously unbalanced. The *chefs de village* had long competed fiercely in the quality of food, wine, *spectacles*, costumes, and the fireworks let off at the end of the week at great expense. Each chef wanted to win the village oscar, an election based on the votes of GMs.

Such was the rivalry that best practices were not shared or learned, nor were scripts revealed or ideas discussed. Villages did not want other villages to beat them, and individual ambitions were pursued at the expense of the wider company. Outstanding performances and the reasons for them were village secrets. In effect, competition had gotten the better of cooperation and learning together.

Bourguignon rebalanced the scorecard by measuring *both* customer acclaim *and* the performance by *chefs* in regard to targets, budgets, and profits. In frantic attempts to win, *chefs* had earlier squandered money on food, wine, fireworks, and *spectacles*. The new scorecard demanded that they delight customers *while* making profits for the company; they had to integrate these objectives to win the contest. Each *chef* is evaluated on these opposing measures of effectiveness. Pay was also reorganized to more closely reflect performance, and the success of a unit or village became the measure of the leader's success.

Bourguignon is not happy with the accusation of being "American." He believes that France needs American disciplines, just as America needs French aesthetic appreciation and sensuous satisfactions:

"I am not an American but French, and proud, for example, of the changes we have made in Euro-Disney. I am not trying out an Americanized version of Club Med, but if being rigorous and professional is American, then I am American. Club Méditerranée is not and will never be a reflection of American culture. It has values that are strongly embedded in all its key processes. After the Second World War the club represented freedom and the lowering of social thresholds—later, freedom and the release from old *moeurs* [customs]. Today it represents the freedom to rediscover and redefine yourself. It stands for the family and the community, both still stronger in France than elsewhere.

"Take McDonald's; whether you like it or not, it is the number-one restaurant in France. If an organization has so much success, it is because these restaurants are clean, hygienic, and without problems, which is not the case in many French bistros. The day when the French bistros, while keeping the ambience that has accounted for their success, become clean, that formula can be exported to the States. This would be the best way to react to our fear of the world becoming Americanized."

The dilemma diagram that follows represents Bourguignon's view that America and France share between them the reasons for Club Med's newfound organizational effectiveness. You cannot exclusively be rational or exclusively constitute unique experiences; you have to confront this contradiction and reconcile it.

Dilemma 3: Franco-American Effectiveness

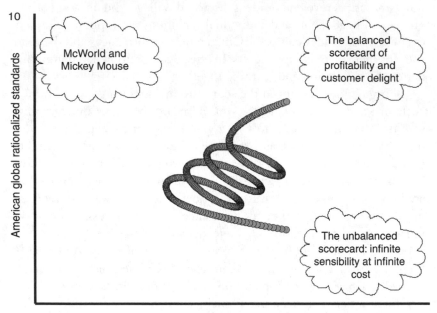

McWorld and Mickey Mouse

The balanced scorecard of profitability and customer delight

The unbalanced scorecard: infinite sensibility at infinite cost

American global rationalized standards

Incomparable French uniqueness and sensibility

No European wants a "hamburgerized" McWorld or Mickey Mouse entertainment (1/10). Those things can occur when global rationality seeks to be an icon for all possible tastes. On the other hand, French indulgence in being unique and incomparable gets you in trouble, too. The improvised bistro is no match for McDonald's, even in France. When every *chef* has to excel at lavish hospitality, costs go through the roof. It was the scorecard balanced between profitability and customer delight that helped turn Club Med around and symbolized Franco-American organizational effectiveness.

Indeed, the company has prospered under its new leadership. Occupancy rose to 73.5 percent in the 1999 financial year, up from 66.9 percent in 1996. Other results have also improved markedly.

In fiscal year 1999 attendance rose 5 percent to almost 1.6 million. The company earned $39 million, against $26 million in 1998 and losses of $130 and $215 million in 1996 and 1997, respectively. In 1999 sales went up again, reaching $1.5 billion. Perhaps Club Med is now positioned as a brand rather than an experience, but the company wants to revolutionize the leisure industry in the new millennium just as it did 50 years ago. "We have a global concept, with global clients," says Bourguignon. "No other company is developed internationally as we are, and nobody is looking at leisure time in a global way."

Sadly, the remaining founder quit, lamenting that the spirit and soul of the organization were gone. We believe rather that the spirit and soul were *qualified* by some apparently contradictory values that actually strengthened them. One of us (FT) went back to Club Med last summer and lost whatever remained of his dignity and reserve!

Chapter 6

———•———

Recapturing the True Mission: Christian Majgaard, LEGO

Dick Devos and Charles Hampden-Turner

LEGO, THE DANISH supplier of children's construction toys, recently faced some difficult choices. Was it selling to children or to their parents? The answer was "both." Were the children just playing or learning? "Both." Should the idea be to supply children with implementable construction kits so that the kids would become in essence part of the assembly process? Or was the point to stimulate children to create something unique, as one does with vocabulary? Was the company in the plastic bricks business, or was it a promoter of intelligent and constructive play in general? Again the answers were "both." The task of being constructive may *start* with plastic bricks, but it goes beyond such materials into the creation of an integrity on which the future of the company depends. LEGO is an assembler of customer satisfactions, and the broader this synthesis, the greater the prosperity and success of the company.

One of us (DD) went to Schiphol Airport in June 1999 to meet Christian Majgaard, the member of LEGO's group executive team personally responsible for global branding and business development.

Majgaard looked relaxed and cheerful. He was traveling from Billund, the small town where LEGO was founded in 1932, to an international executive conference in Nice, where he had been invited to expound on LEGO's heroic saga of innovation. He and the author spent most of the day conversing and produced the origins of the account that follows.

LEGO had recently survived a rough passage. Majgaard, who worked closely with Kjeld Kirk Kristiansen, the chief executive officer (CEO), was on the front line. Kristiansen and other team members had forged the World Wide Fitness Programme, which was designed to weather the storms they faced. The year 1998 had brought the collapse of Southeast Asian markets, followed by the Russian market, resulting in a loss after taxes of DKr 194 million (194 million Danish kroner, or over $24 million).

It was this crisis that convinced the company it was carrying too much "ballast," which prevented the timely changes of direction and the speed necessary to escape episodes of turbulence. It was time to ask the crucial questions with which this chapter began: What did LEGO stand for? What kinds of innovation would renew its brand image and recapture the meaning the company had long had for children and their parents? The values for which LEGO stood were eternal, but new ways had to be found to realize them, using modern media and materials.

Majgaard and the author found an easy rapport and a shared appreciation of the values that had made LEGO. Those values did not just join interviewer and interviewee; they had helped LEGO's executive team surmount the recent crisis. The values are lived out in the actions of team members, all of whom know the following words:

LEGO Vision
The LEGO name shall become universally known and shall be associated with the following concepts:

IDEA	EXUBERANCE	VALUES
Creativity	Enthusiasm	Quality
Imagination	Spontaneity	Caring
Unlimited	Self-expression	Development
Discovery	Unreservedness	Innovation
Constructiveness		Consistency

LEGO is also distinguished by what it has avoided—war toys inconsistent with peaceful construction—and what it includes—5 billion compatible LEGO bricks with none unusable.

Mission and Scope
Children are our vital concern. Our basic business concept and the foundation for all LEGO products and activities is that we take children and their needs seriously. As a dependable partner for parents, it is our mission to stimulate children's imagination and creativity and to encourage children to explore, experience, and express their own world, a world without limits. As a quality leader, we will do this by offering creative, developmental, and enjoyable play and learning materials, experiences, and brand values, all bearing the LEGO logo, to children all over the world. By the year 2005, we want the LEGO brand to be the most powerful brand in the world among families with children (measured among brands with children as a part of their target group).

Today the LEGO Group is a family-owned and -managed business employing 9000 people and selling products in more than 130 countries. LEGO is the clear leader in the construction-toy sector. In addition to the core business (LEGO bricks), LEGO has developed the following new categories:

- LEGOLAND parks: development and operation of family parks (Denmark, United Kingdom, United States, Germany)
- LEGO lifestyle products: license agreements for clothes, watches, and other compatible products
- LEGO media products: software, music, video, books, and films for children

LEGO has decided to globalize geographically and strategically within a single global marketing strategy. According to this strategy, quality is more important than speed, and the notion of quality—the conviction of what LEGO stands for—has to come from LEGO people themselves in dialogue with the executive team. Kjeld Kirk Kristiansen believes that success will come from this redefinition of core values.

The History of LEGO's Innovation

Before we reengage with current issues, it will be useful to chronicle LEGO's history.

- 1932: The Depression forces a change in the nature of the business. Formerly serving the agriculture industry with carpentry and joinery work, the company switches to wooden toys made by hand.
- 1934: The name LEGO is chosen; it comes from two Danish words, *Leg Godt,* meaning "play well"; later it is discovered that in Latin it means "I study" or "I put together." Core value and ambition of the company: "Only the best is good enough."
- 1942: The LEGO factory is burned, but production of wooden toys is resumed.
- 1947: Plastics and injection molding are adopted. Plastic toys are produced.
- 1949: The first plastic brick is manufactured.
- 1955: The LEGO system of play is instituted.
- 1958: The quality of the LEGO brick is improved, with tubes placed inside the brick.
- 1960: Fire guts the LEGO warehouse with wooden toys. The company makes a strategic choice to produce plastic toys only.
- 1963: A new type of plastic replaces the old plastic.
- 1968: LEGOLAND Billund, the first family park, opens to the public.
- 1974: LEGO figures are a hit with both boys and girls.
- 1979: Kjeld Kirk Kristiansen is appointed president and CEO of LEGO A/S.
- 1995: Kjeld Kirk Kristiansen's father dies.
- 1996: LEGO goes on the Internet and the first family park outside Denmark is opened.
- 1997: Computer games, software, and the LEGO MindStorms learning center are featured.
- 1998: License agreements are reached with Lucasfilm/Star Wars and Walt Disney Company. The Next Generation Forum is created.

From this historical overview, we can glean the following insights:

- Enabling technologies have played a major role in LEGO's development (1947, 1963, 1996, and 1997).
- Crises have had a major impact on the company [1932, 1960, and 1998 (a loss-making year)].
- Visionary leadership leads to decisive moves (1932, 1934, 1955, 1958, 1960, 1968, 1996, 1997, and 1998), including the idea of a system (1955) in which the child is active.

It is in this context of brands, markets, products, ideas, people, and relations that Christian Majgaard and his colleagues have revitalized the tradition of innovation.

Christian Majgaard's View of Strategic Innovation

Christian Majgaard has been championing strategic innovation at LEGO for eight years. Most of the new initiatives, including the Fitness Programme, bear the stamp of his way of thinking. During his daylong stopover in Amsterdam, he explained to the interviewer the five main themes with which he was struggling:

1. How can the business system be restructured to realize ideas?
2. How can we form teams with a diverse mix of members?
3. How can we achieve distance from yet gain an understanding of the core business?
4. How can we seize each idea's fleeting window of opportunity?
5. How can we ensure that all new departures and innovative projects eventually are welcomed by and integrated with the core of the company?

1. How Can the Business System Be Restructured to Realize Ideas?

"The problem is not the availability of new ideas," says Majgaard. "We have plenty of ideas. Nor is the problem getting funds to develop those ideas. The problem is, and always has been, that the business system can get in the way of good ideas being realized. I have learned that the person who has the idea should be given the resources, the people, and the freedom to develop it into a viable product. It can be fatal to split the idea from its implementation. The board often comes up with ideas, and because of the influence and status of its members, the idea gets implemented, but by persons other than the originator; this leads to the idea and its underlying assumptions not being properly challenged and critiqued.

"A case in point 10 years ago was the idea to create small indoor entertainment centers of less than 8000 square meters, unaffected by seasonal climate and attractive to commercial partners in the same mall or complex. But when we searched world markets for an example of a small, profitable entertainment center, we could not find a single one! Still, we were reluctant to give up on an idea coming from the board level, and so we hired consultants. It was one of them who explained that entertainment centers were where children were left off. When adults sought adventure jointly with their children, they typically went *out* into the wider environment.

"Hence, this idea would violate one of the key principles of LEGO: that children and adults are joined by constructive appreciation. It had taken us an inordinate amount of time to turn down a nonviable idea, which, as it turned out, originated in Australia and had everything to do with a local initiative to upgrade shopping malls. I learned not to separate ideas from their originators.

"But our time investigating entertainment centers and theme parks was not wasted: We discovered that those who charged a sizable entrance fee did much better than those who charged for each separate ride or amusement. Why was this? We came up with two possible answers:

- When you pay up front, you act when the excitement of children and adults is at its height, and once you are inside, everything is free. You can stop calculating. You do not have to say no to excited children or let them bankrupt you, and there is no restraint on their enjoyment.
- When you pay extra for each attraction, the conflict between adults and children is exacerbated, and resentment at the company that has driven your children to 'extravagance' is keen. Adults are caught between guilt and unaffordable outlays and cannot control their spending.

"Anyway, this caused us to change the pricing policy at our new Billund theme park. Suddenly receipts soared, and what we had regarded as a mainly promotional activity became an important new concept. The family park is now in four countries, and we have plans to expand globally.

"What I learned was that the business system must facilitate, not impede, the flow and refinement of ideas so that they can be realized."

2. How Can We Form Teams with a Diverse Mix of Members?

"When you have too similar persons on a team, the knowledge the team has is limited," says Majgaard. On a team, opposites are needed. Six people in a group is optimal, with both genders and various nationalities and backgrounds represented. In strategic innovation projects people from the new industry and people from the original company should work together. That's the hard part: How can you make a group of people like that work together effectively?

The key is to realize that if people are different, they have more to say to each other—have information to communicate that is more likely to be novel and illuminating. Of course, *dis*agreement is more likely, too. Thus, one must use process theories, group dynamics, and anything that facilitates interaction.

Giving people a superordinate goal that contributes to a shared "win" is very important. A common destiny also helps bind together a team with diverse talents, and is smart to include younger people who have a reputation to make rather than to protect. Perhaps most important is a shared passion for turning a common vision into a powerful reality to gain ownership of an important initiative.

3. How Can We Achieve Distance from yet Gain an Understanding of the Core Business?

"The older the core business, the less likely it is to be able to reinvent itself," opines Majgaard. The business is too brittle for new life to emerge. Strategic innovators often condemn these aging cores. What is needed is greater understanding. Only then will we know what to do. An organization with a long history has established rules that protect its core values: "Do this and you will succeed. Don't do that or that; we tried them once, and they failed." These prohibitions accumulate with time until the core is left with a severely limited number of possible moves.

Reinventing yourself may require doing something prohibited, and so the core stagnates. We are not talking about good or bad people but about entrenched belief systems, many of them not consciously examined. As with driving a car in the United Kingdom, you have to concentrate hard on not moving instinctively to the right-hand side of the road. Because it is painful to change ingrained habits and responses, you can innovate successfully only if you can achieve some distance from the belief system of the traditional core of the corporation.

However, being "distant" from beliefs that stifle innovation is not enough: You also have to understand why the traditional core thinks and believes as it does. You have to understand this because in the end you are one company. You have achieved distance in order to *serve* the core, not abandon it.

4. How Can We Seize Each Idea's Fleeting Window of Opportunity?

Ideas are not good or bad in themselves. They are practicable under certain circumstances, but when those circumstances change, they are no longer practicable. For many ideas there exist windows of opportunity that can open and close quite quickly, and so timing is everything. An idea can fail because it is too early to try it—the creator is ahead of the market. Or the idea may fail because it is too late: The competitors have moved, costs are rising, and diminishing returns have set in. This is why speed is important and timing is all-important. You have to keep learning so that when the window opens fleetingly, you are ready to jump. Those who thought up the idea may not be the right people to train others or to pounce. Those who pounce successfully may not be the right people to exploit the opportunity and push for the big numbers.

If the opportunity turns into a sizable one and you find yourself in a race to meet demand, you will need your core organization.

5. How Can We Ensure That All New Departures and Innovative Projects Eventually Are Welcomed by and Integrated with the Core of the Company?

We have already seen that innovative strategies must maintain their distance from the company's traditions if they are to escape being caught in thickets of prohibition (theme 3). But sooner or later innovative business units initially separated from the old core need to be integrated with it to restore a sense of a single company. Some units had a prolonged separation (LEGO family parks), and some were integrated quickly (LEGO software). It helps if the success of the unit is spectacular. LEGO software generated net sales of 500 million DKr, and the core was proud of it. But some early integrations, such as robots, approached the core because they needed its financial support. Thus, integration is not a "must" in the short term, but it is a question of the health and survival of the innovative unit.

What is more important is that the entrepreneurs in the innovative units be treated as the heroes they are. All too easily do the old core and the old values gang up on the newer ones. Some very balanced old-timers say disparaging things about new initiatives. If the success has been spectacular, there is rarely any opposition, but new projects that need support to be genuinely successful can have trouble finding it, and that leads to cruel disappointment. "I'm fighting for the future," these innovators say. "Why can't they see this?" Successful innovators should be offered a promotion and public recognition. That sends powerful signals about their entrepreneurial qualities. We have to make the core not just tolerant of but enthusiastic about strategic innovation.

Dilemmas at the Heart of the Five Themes

Each of Majgaard's five themes is for us a key dilemma that has to be reconciled if LEGO is to grow and prosper:

- Theme 1 is the dilemma of *the ideal versus the real:* How can the business system help realize the ideas generated by employees?
- Theme 2 is the dilemma of *diversity versus harmony among team members:* Are members sufficiently different from each other that novel information is processed but sufficiently unified to turn that novelty into solutions?
- Theme 3 is the dilemma of *distance* from the traditional core of the company and one's *relationship* to that core. Paradoxically, you

can contribute more to LEGO's core if you are independent of its toils.

- Theme 4 is the dilemma of *originating* ideas and *seizing the opportunity*, often fleeting, to implement them. The key is timing. Every good idea has a brief window of opportunity, which then closes in your face. You can be too early or too late.
- Theme 5 is the *creation of innovative strategies versus the integration of their instigators into the core culture of the company.* Innovation will soon dry up unless LEGO's best entrepreneurs find honor and reputation within the company.

There is in fact one more fascinating dilemma, which we may introduce as a footnote to theme 1: In exchanging satisfaction for payment, should *payment precede satisfaction* or should *payment accompany the choice of each event?*

Can Any of the Seven Dimensions Help Illuminate LEGO's Dilemmas?

In Chapters 1 and 2 we introduced the seven dilemmas, or dimensions, we use to research various national business cultures. Are there any connections between the themes or dilemmas Christian Majgaard defined and our own dilemmas? We hope to show that added insights are achieved by connecting LEGO's definitions to ours.

Theme 1
LEGO's Model: The Ideal versus the Real
Our Model: The Individual versus the Community

Majgaard pointed out that there was no problem finding enough individuals to generate enough ideas. The problem lay with the "business system" or community, which had to translate those ideas into the reality of viable products and services. Not infrequently the community or system would impede the realization of good ideas, especially when they came from senior people. Juniors were expected to implement the ideas.

This dilemma could be diagrammed as follows:

Dilemma 1: The Path to Realization

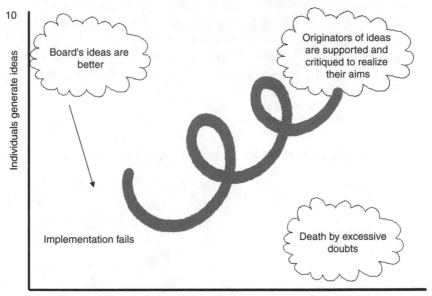

From the diagram we can see that while ideas originate with individuals, it is *not* a good idea simply to pass the ideas down for subordinates to implement. Subordinates are inhibited in their criticism, and consultants have to be hired to legitimize skepticism. Instead, the originator must work *with* critics, implementors, and builders of working prototypes to help debug the idea whenever that is necessary. (This is why the helix periodically winds back toward the individual originator.) Furthermore, it is unwise to give higher status to the idea than to its implementors; if you do that, defective ideas will persist to disappoint their backers. Realization is at least as important as idealization, and the two must be reconciled (at the top right of the diagram). You must also beware of testing ideas to destruction (bottom right).

Theme 2
LEGO's Model: Diversity versus Unity in Teams
Our Model: Competing as Individuals versus
Cooperating as a Community

Here we have once again used our second dimension, individualism versus communitarianism, but in a slightly different form: competing versus cooperating. If we combine these dimensions with Majgaard's insight that the membership of teams must be *diverse*, consisting of people whose values and talents are opposite, yet these teams must achieve a *unity* of purpose and shared solutions, we can diagram the dilemma as follows (once again we have two polarized failures but also the potential for coming up with a solution that has benefited from diverse viewpoints and novel inputs):

Dilemma 2: The Search for a Unity of Diversities

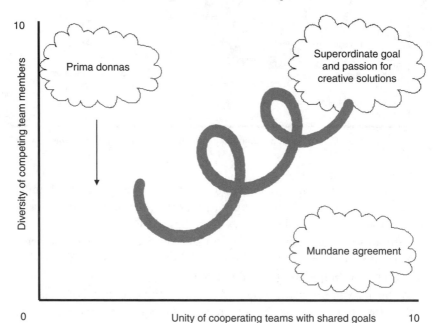

The problem with having highly diverse, competing individuals is that they may behave like prima donnas, singing their own praises. The problem with emphasizing unity and team spirit above all else is that diverse and novel inputs can be squeezed out.

Majgaard's reconciliation, which we heartily endorse, is to make the superordinate goal so exciting and the process of creating new shared realities so passionate and enjoyable that diverse members overcome their differences to realize a unity of diversities that makes the solution far more valuable.

Theme 3
LEGO's Model: Distance (from Core) versus Relationship (to Core)
Our Model: Particular Exceptions versus Entrenched Rules

Here, we may recall, Majgaard argued that strategic innovation had to maintain a distance from the core of the company; otherwise it might find itself impeded and opposed. Later it might be able to reestablish relationships and might have some very significant innovations to bring to LEGO.

Majgaard also explained how this impedance occurred and how we could come to understand it without hurling accusations. Over time a residue of entrenched rules accumulates around the core of the company, things that once failed and therefore are not permitted. Those at a distance from the core see many exceptional opportunities and particular chances to succeed, but those closer to the core have a learned inability to break old rules. They regard the history of the company as teaching universal prohibitions against certain avenues of exploration. The dilemma looks like this:

Dilemma 3: The Return of the Exile

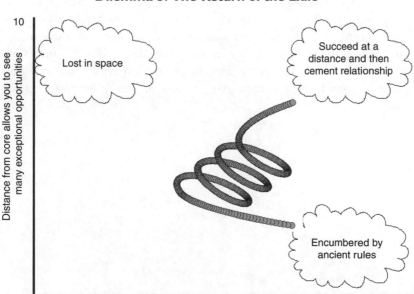

The distance can be too large (lost in space) or too small (encumbered by ancient rules). What you have to do is "exile" the innovator and the idea temporarily, as when Jesus went into the wilderness or Odysseus went on his odyssey, and then return them either with notable success or with elements of success. What exile gives you is freedom from the prohibitions that have petrified the core.

Theme 4
LEGO's Model: Ideas versus Fleeting Opportunity
Our Model: Time Sequences versus
Timely Synchronizations

Majgaard argued that all good ideas had a fleeting window of opportunity allowing for their realization. It was a question of preparing and educating yourself and then pouncing at the opportune moment. We have a similar concept: time as a sequence of events versus time as seized moments of opportunity, a timely synchronization of the ideal and the real. Only when the window opens do you dart through it.

Events rush past you in sequences, and you need to pounce when there is a *rendezvous* between idea and opportunity. Mistime your leap, and the chance is gone forever, with a new product or technology replacing the one you had in mind. Business is unforgiving. You can actually *change reality* in your own favor if your intervention is timely, but if you mistime your intervention, the windows close in your face or events pass you by, as the following diagram shows:

Dilemma 4: Leaping through the Windows

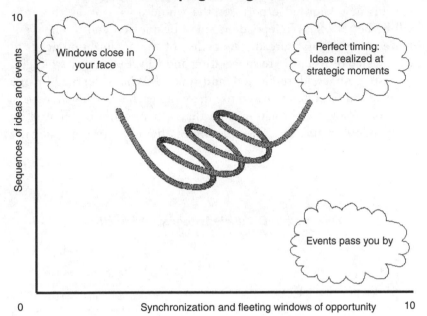

The helix starts with a sequence of ideas and events but requires that the best of those ideas be realized precisely at strategic moments so that you "leap through the window of opportunity."

Theme 5
LEGO's Model: Strategic Innovations versus Integration with the Core of the Corporation
Our Model: Specific Initiatives versus Diffuse Relationships

Majgaard mentioned that innovative business units that had kept their distance would later need to reintegrate with the core of LEGO. Unless this was done so that successful entrepreneurs could receive the honor due to them, the core values were unlikely to change quickly enough. We have combined this insight with our own dimension of specific versus diffuse phenomena. LEGO could have many specific successes via business units created for a particular purpose, but unless this new knowledge perfuses the whole organization, the units will be better off as independent small businesses, and the new enlightenment will not spread. The center of the organization needs to learn which of its units are succeeding and why. In this way strategies are tested, reviewed, replicated, and revised. What is learned by one business unit is communicated to all, giving each a much wider spectrum of strategic information than that which would be enjoyed by independent businesses. The dilemma is depicted in the following diagram:

Dilemma 5: Diffusely Integrated Specifics

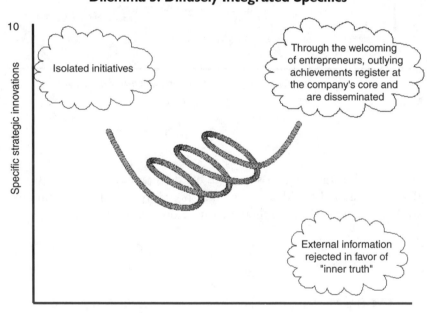

At the top left even successful initiatives remain isolated. At the bottom right all units are welcome but must abandon ideas and information that do not fit. Only at the top right are many specific innovations registered, compared, and celebrated and then communicated to the entire company, which becomes the champion of entrepreneurialism.

Theme 6
LEGO's Model: Pay as You Go versus Pay Up Front
Our Model: Affective versus Neutral

This was originally a subissue of theme 1, but it is important enough to receive special treatment. LEGOLAND Parks transformed its balance sheet by moving from pay as you go to pay up front, or, as we would say, by getting the neutral calculation out of the way at the beginning and leaving the children free to be as affective and exuberant as they wish and sample every amusement available. With payment up front, parents do not need to limit their children's enjoyment; they do not have to face the painful dilemma of either overspending in response to a clamorous child or refusing that child. The calculated decision to spend a certain amount on getting in can be made in a neutral environment, and after admission, pleasure can run riot and vindicate the original decision by exploiting it to the utmost. The dilemma looks like this:

Dilemma 6: Calculated Enjoyment

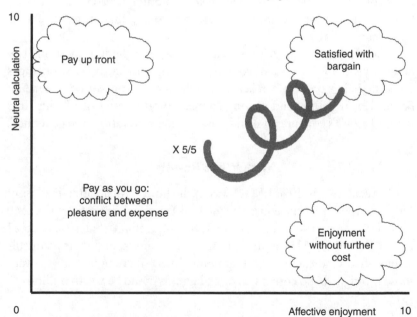

When you pay up front (top left), you make a neutral calculation without being pressured because the children have not yet sampled the

treat. You then move rightward along the affective enjoyment axis, and as the children rush joyfully about, you become satisfied with the bargain you paid for.

In the middle of the diagram, next to the X, we see the fate of "pay as you go," in which your children's exuberance costs you and their excitement cuts holes in your pocket. The greater the children's pleasure is, the higher the parents' costs become. LEGO's mission to enrich parent-child interaction is frustrated.

The pay-up-front solution closely models LEGO's celebration of unlimited imagination and creativity, spontaneous enthusiasm, and lack of reserve, all of consistent quality and innovativeness. Once their parents have paid, children should get to express their exuberance without hindrance.

Which Is Where We Began . . .

We began this chapter by asking how LEGO reconciled parents and children, play and learning, solutions suggested to children and solutions found by children. We also asked whether LEGO was a plastic bricks company or a company dedicated to intelligent, constructive, and creative play.

LEGO's latest strategic moves have answered the last question. The company is in the business of constructive play, with putting plastic bricks together being one form taken by such play. Using software, reading books, viewing films, and playing games are other ways of playing. It is within LEGO's core purpose and mission that innovations are generated.

With What Results?

Let us recall that in 1998 LEGO was in the hole, with an after-tax loss of DKr 194 million. By the end of 1999 LEGO was back in profit by DKr 560 million (after restructuring costs of DKr 700 million). Sales were up 22 percent. Christian Majgaard, Kjeld Kirk Kristiansen, and their team colleagues had vindicated their judgments. Every incremental step toward those top right-hand corners on our diagrams could be worth millions.

Postscript

On January 30, 2000, LEGO was voted "Toy of the Millennium" in a poll of international retailers and consumers. It beat the teddy bear and the Barbie doll to win the prize.

—◆—

Chapter 7

The Balance between Market and Product: Anders Knutsen, Bang and Olufsen

Fons Trompenaars and Charles Hampden-Turner

*I*N THIS CHAPTER we will examine another feat
of leadership. Anders Knutsen assumed the leadership of Bang and
Olufsen (B&O), the Danish audiovisual company, at a point of severe
crisis. He rescued a tradition of immaculate design and engineering so
"perfect" that fewer and fewer people could afford it! It started with a
bang. It nearly ended in a whimper, but thanks to Knutsen, the Bang is
now bigger than ever.

From a Whimper to a Bang

When someone creates and invents a new product, the market is in his or
her mind's eye. The person thinks, I love this product I have made, and
others will soon come to appreciate its beauty and quality. That is a sup-
position that sometimes comes true but often does not. The creator can
be too subtle or too aesthetic for the customers "out there," and finer
sensibilities do not come cheap. Customers are expected to pay for ineffable qualities they do not understand and cannot fully appreciate.

This had long been the trouble with B&O. When we inquired among potential customers, they told us they "loved its looks and sound" and were keen to buy a product "when I can afford it." In 1972, when the company sent its catalogue to the Museum of Modern Art in New York City, no fewer than seven of its products were chosen for the museum's permanent collection of modern design. It was a great tribute in a way, but as one customer put it, "I can always visit a gallery for something as beautiful as this. I want something that plays music to high standards, not an artwork."

Products Emphasized, Markets Neglected

B&O began in 1925, when two young engineers met in Quistrup. Svend Olufsen and Peter Bang were intrigued by a new radio that Peter had obtained in the United States. Their second factory was blown up by the retreating Germans in 1945, but it was reassembled by volunteer Danish citizens in the weeks that followed, and the company became a symbol of Denmark's postwar resurgence.

In those days Peter Bang was the creative technologist and Svend Olufsen was the extroverted salesperson. It may be significant that Olufsen died as early as 1949 while Bang lived another eight years. In any event, technical prowess gained ascendancy over marketing, and so it continued. Among B&O's "firsts" were giant Loudspeak Cars—perhaps an extravagance, but in many respects the company was consistently ahead of its time, creating the first fully transistorized radio (in 1964), advanced movie projectors, the Beocord 844, and the wire recorder, the forerunner of tape recorders. As early as 1957 B&O launched the first stereo pickup for music recording.

All monies the company made were immediately reinvested in more product development. After Olufsen died, Bang brought in a financial specialist to "fight the fires" that were distracting him from the "real" business of new products. P. H. Jensen kept the company solvent, but sales and marketing were no longer among the firm's strengths. After Peter's death Jens Bang, his son, took charge of product planning until 1984, working with the brilliant freelance designers Jacob Jensen and David Lewis; thus was created the elegant synthesis between design and high-fidelity performance for which B&O is famous. A synthesis is, however, only as commercially viable as its weakest link, and in the process of celebrating two forms of product excellence, the customers' needs and preferences for lower prices started to be ignored. The delights of modern art had captured the company's imagination, but how many affluent music lovers are also connoisseurs of modern design and want to gaze at their equipment?

B&O's problem was symbolized by the creation of System 6000, a quadraphonic high-fidelity music system. There was only one flaw: No one had made any records to play on it. In those days there were seven corporate identity components: authenticity, auto visuality, credibility, domesticity, essentiality, individuality, and inventiveness. All were characteristics of the product. The cheapest product with those sterling characteristics cost $2500. Outside Denmark the sales staff was in despair at such prohibitive prices.

Neglect of the Market Leads to Crisis

Senior managers had developed expensive habits during the 1980s, believing that an aristocracy of good taste entitled them to aristocratic lifestyles paid for by the few who could afford their products. However, it was not simply that B&O headquarters was divided from the humbler people of Struer, a village of 14,000 in Jutland; rather, research and development (R&D) was divided from marketing and sales, and finance was a separate kingdom. The principal casualty was logistics. It took so long to get spare parts that many customers gave up and switched to other systems.

Anders Knutsen realized that he had little time. Upon taking over leadership in July 1991, he proposed emergency action. The company was facing the prospect of accelerating losses in the near future. His plan was to focus on the following:

1. Growth and profit
2. The most important strategic opportunities that produced growth and profit
3. A reduction in service and maintenance activity by rendering it almost unnecessary
4. The identification and prioritizing of activities that produced a surplus

These items were emergency actions, but they did not blind Knutsen to the deeper underlying problem, which was the disconnection of sales and marketing both from R&D and from production. His "butterfly model" saw these opposite wings of the organization as being in urgent need of coordination and reconciliation. Of the two wings, the product side had long been dominant. "We knew we had a great product," Knutsen explained, "but we did not always have a market for it. We knew we were creative, but could we afford the costs and the subsequent price? This company had to think numbers and business *without* losing its creative traditions. The right brain had to be reattached to the left, or the whole would suffer."

Early attempts at cutting costs by shutting down noncore activities such as cables did not restore profitability on the scale intended. Knutsen launched a plan called "Break-Point az" to restore harmony between the feelings of customers and the undoubted excellence of design and technology without losing either one. It was this balance that found favor with markets.

Professionalism or Family Membership?

The Break-Point program was very ambitious. It had to be. Costs had to come down radically. Of the 3300 employees at the Struer headquarters in late 1992, only 2100 were left by the end of 1993. Seven hundred people lost their jobs in a small town in which B&O was the principal employer.

Anders Knutsen explained that he was able to do this because he had convinced so many people of the necessity of doing so and because the management team backed him to the hilt, but interviews among colleagues revealed that he was able to perform so unpleasant a duty because he was seen as "a son of the house." The son of a company foreman working in Vejledalen, he had joined B&O as an economist and had directed the radio factory in Skive before a succession of promotions to chief executive officer (CEO). He had never behaved like the "aristocrats" who had pushed the company's costs sky high in the 1980s. For years he had owned a rusty Citroen and then an aging Alfa Romeo. This frugality and his friendships at all levels of the organization saw him through.

B&O could have brought in an outside professional hatchet man with no ties to those he fired, but there almost certainly would have been strikes, and quite probably B&O would not have been Danish anymore. It was *how* Knutsen managed this difficult downsizing that was the secret of Break-Point's success. He described the crisis with frankness and courage and then outlined the remedy so that everyone could follow the logic to its culmination. The objective was to save the company and its contribution to audiovisual excellence. The price was steep, but surely it was worth paying, given the alternative.

Knutsen was helped considerably by the steadfastness of the five-man board of management, which supported him publicly and energetically. Each member agreed to play a role in communicating the solution, and they all kept their promises. There was near unanimity on what had to be done to survive. At the end of what was a traumatic experience for everyone, the workers erected a portrait of Anders Knutsen in their factory. It was their tribute to a truth teller, the person who respected them sufficiently to put them in touch with reality. Per Thygesen Poulsen, a local journalist, marveled at the event and wrote about it.

Although Knutsen was an economics graduate, one does not readily impress the people of Jutland with higher degrees. What impressed them was his honesty, realism, long-established concern with keeping down costs (now seen to be vindicated by events), and encouragement of workers' development and creativity (which had always been combined with a tough negotiation stance on wages). Now that the company was running out of money, he was the man of the hour.

From Technology Push to Market Pull

The second major challenge was to develop an understanding of the market and the patterns of demand before aligning B&O's products with them. "We had to teach people how to think in business terms without sacrificing their pride in their creativity and their products," Knutsen recalled. "Beauty, style, and technical superiority were everything. No one had been paying attention to development costs or commercial success." The product had taken the place of the persons who were supposed to lead. Knutsen regarded this imbalance as so serious that he made himself the head of marketing and sales until an internationally experienced vice president could be found. In this way he was able to discover facts that the company had long ignored. By the time Ebbe Pelle Jacobsen had been hired from IKEA, Knutsen believed that he had diagnosed the problem. Jacobsen agreed and was able to give us the following account.

"B&O thought communication was a one-way process and that its customers were dealers, not consumers. Of course, the dealers were passing on our arrogant treatment to the final customers." Knutsen had discovered that dealers used the B&O aura to upgrade the image of their dealerships while putting most of their energy into selling rival products better suited to the market, including Philips, Daewoo, Sony, and Grundig. These products appeared reasonably priced compared to B&O's expensive, upmarket offerings. "There was a radical disconnection between the product and the market," Anders recalls. "It was as if we communicated to the product and not with the people."

In the mid-1980s B&O moved out of stand-alone products and into integrated systems. It made sense visually and acoustically to use B&O for all system elements, but it meant that customers had to abandon many existing purchases and start again, and it meant pricing systems from $2500 upward. Many younger buyers were put off accumulating the elements of a B&O system over time and were faced with an unrealistic price threshold.

The first move was to change the distribution channels. B&O actually reduced the number of dealers from 3200 to 2200 in the European Union (EU), yet sales climbed from $250 million to $400 million in six years. B&O did not insist on exclusive dealerships, but it did insist on certain sales staff members being dedicated to its products so that they could listen to and learn from the firm's customers. The substitution of dialogue for monologue revealed the extent to which B&O's values were shared and how that sharing could be increased.

B&O also defined carefully the niche in the market to which it was appealing and the customer segments it aimed to reach; then it made sure the message was consistent internationally. It also introduced a computerized system of direct ordering through its own shops, with a guaranteed delivery date so that customers could essentially build their own system, using a wide range of alternative B&O components.

Technical Excellence and the Emotional Climate

The third and last major challenge that Anders Knutsen saw himself as confronting was technical excellence and the emotional appeal of products. This was a subtle and diffuse concept. Beautiful audiovisual information had to be conveyed on instruments worthy of their content in the same way that the instruments of an orchestra carry the spirit and express the feeling of the composer. "Time is in our favor," Knutsen believed. "The world is flooded with discount junk products that strive to become classics; products with emotional value will be strongly placed in our 'throw away' culture." In the history of B&O both technical excellence and emotional climate had been important, more so than sales or marketing, but even those leading values had not been reconciled or harmonized. First one was dominant, then the other, and their fight for dominance had made the product that resulted unaffordable.

Knutsen extended "Idealand," a nonlocalized space where engineers, music lovers, designers, and others, both within R&D and outside the company in the community of experts, could engage in a dialogue that would stimulate and balance ideas. Another balance is between the audio and the visual, which come together in digital sound pictures.

Carl Henrik Jeppesen, a senior colleague, explains: "We send development teams, usually to the United States, to study what sounds and sights are being made and consumed. They go to concerts, music halls, discotheques. You need someone to champion the original sound picture and the emotions generated from it and someone to champion the technologies of recording and playing those sound pictures. It is this creative clash between the artists and the engineers that gives you optimal integration. In the old days one competence would dominate the others, but no more. There came the day when Anders Knutsen and his team refused to sponsor a prototype product because the costs were out of line. That was a real shock for all of us. It had never happened here!

"With Break-Point the culture changed dramatically, but values were retained and began to strengthen one another. In one sense the B&O secret is integrated seamlessness—every part of the system has to work with every other part—and now this became true of our values as well.

"We now test our products with our customers, and if they like a product, sales start at once, with a projected product life of 10 years. We position ourselves in the market in a way that confirms or fails to confirm the hypotheses developed in Idealand. Idealand is not a private muse but a testing laboratory for viable ideas, a set of hypotheses to which our customers say yes or no."

Analyzing B&O's Dilemmas

According to the information we received, B&O faced three major dilemmas, which it defined as follows:

a. The disconnection of sales and marketing both from R&D and from production and the elevation of the latter functions to a dominant position so that commercial marketing considerations were largely ignored
b. The prospect of laying off almost a third of the company's workforce at headquarters without violating the culture and family spirit that made B&O such a friendly and creative community
c. The reconciliation and integrity of two important traditions: an aesthetic and emotional commitment to the beauty of sights and sounds recorded and played and an engineering and technological commitment to brilliant solutions

B&O would not have survived the Break-Point of 1993 without solving the first two dilemmas, and it would not have turned around into substantial growth and profitability without reconciling all three. We will try to diagram all three dilemmas. As in Chapter 2, we will compare the client's model with our model and use both to try to deepen the insights obtained.

Dilemma I

The Client's Model: Research,   *versus*   **Market, Sales,**
Development,   **and Customers**
and Production
       Our Model: Inner-Directed   *versus*   **Outer-Directed**
Individuality   **Community**

The company had all the classic symptoms of technology push by inner-directed, individualistic, genius entrepreneurs who built a company that celebrated their notable strengths and downplayed what, after the death of Olufsen, they lacked. Neglected were the market, sales, customers, service, and effective distribution—everything that lay outside the select criteria of "brilliant professionals" in the wider community. From those elements B&O took little or no direction. The dilemma can be diagrammed as follows:

Dilemma I: Market Orientations

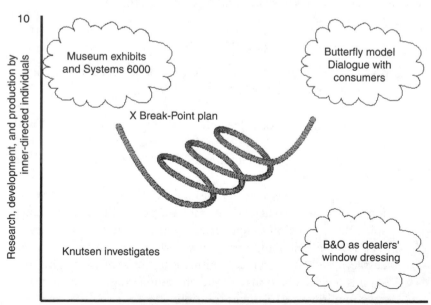

In the preceding grid the museum-type exhibits and System 6000, built without any records to play on it, are two symptoms of excessive emphasis on the vertical axis at the expense of the horizontal axis. The Break-Point plan is the culmination of this chronic imbalance as B&O faces a cash-flow crisis. Knutsen realized that he had to move toward the marketing "horn" of the dilemma, or the horizontal axis. He appointed himself marketing director pro tem and discovered that distributors were using B&O's reputation for quality as window dressing to sell rival products. His answer was the butterfly model, with products and marketing to the final consumer as two coordinated "wings" of the same operation. Having fewer but more dedicated distributors facilitated dialogue with the consumers and the company. Consumers could order directly from retail outlets, building up a modular system over time.

Dilemma 2

The Client's Model:	**The Ethos of a Family with Trusted Parents and the Resilience to Face Common Adversity**	*versus*	**The Ethos of Cool Professionalism and Realistic Commercial Decision Making**
Our Model:	**Affectivity and Concern for Particular People's Hardships**	*versus*	**Neutrality and the Application of Universal Accounting Principles**

Our model combines our dimension 4, affectivity versus neutrality, with our dimension 1, universalism versus particularism. As before, the combination of the client's model and ours deepens an understanding of the dynamics.

B&O was a relatively small family-owned company that loomed very large in the small town of Struer. It had many of the advantages of a family—friendliness, a human scale, and generativity—and some of the disadvantages—expensive lifestyles for a privileged few, traditional prejudices against outsiders, and "poor relations" who were largely ignored, such as sales and marketing. Charismatic leaders tended to deemphasize those activities which did not interest them or in which they were not proficient. There was a desperate need for business realism, for economic calculations independent of family feeling, and for someone to face the facts, however unwelcome to the community those facts were. The accompanying diagram gives the picture:

Dilemma 2: The Trusted Family versus the Indifference of Cold Logic

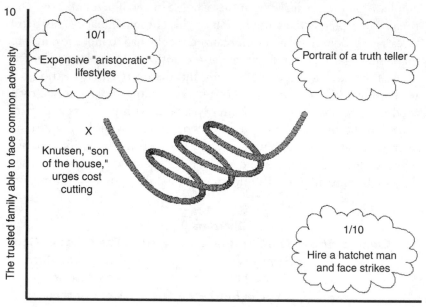

When the Break-Point plan was launched in 1993, B&O was close to the X in the diagram and was suffering from years of inattention to cost control. If the company had swung to the opposite extreme and hired an outside hatchet man to ax employees, strikes and protests would surely have erupted and claims to be a family of employees would have been forever forfeited. It was crucial that the cost cutter be associated with the family—not necessarily a relative but a metaphorical "son of the house." Despite the cruel circumstances in which over 900 people had to go, this necessity was explained with such honesty and such shared pain that Anders was seen as the rescuer he was, not as an executioner or an itinerant hatchet man. The cost cutting was done by the "family," in the context of the family, to save the family. It was because the employees understood the need for surgery that a portrait of Anders was erected in the factory. The workers might have hated the medicine, but they appreciated the cure and admired the person who had shared the truth with them.

Dilemma 3

Client's Model:	**An Aesthetic and Emotional Commitment to the Beauty of Sights and Sounds, Recorded and Played**	*versus*	**An Engineering and Technological Commitment to Brilliant Scientific Solutions**
Our Model:	**Particularism of Art**	*versus*	**Universalism of Science**
	Diffuseness of Experience	*versus*	**Specificity of Solution**
	Affective	*versus*	**Neutral**

The client's model actually touches on three of our dimensions: the diffuse and affective experiences of particular art forms and the specific neutrality of scientific and universal solutions. B&O had two strong traditions that were often at odds with each other tilting the balance of power now this way and now that. On the vertical axis of the diagram of this dilemma that follows we have the engineering commitment to *specific scientific solutions,* on the horizontal axis the aesthetic and emotional commitment to *music* and *visual art forms:*

Dilemma 3: Two Strong Traditions

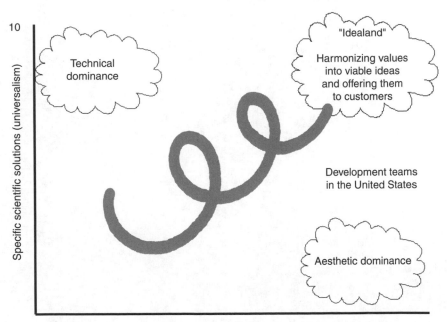

To counterbalance the strong influence of scientifically oriented R&D, teams were sent to the United States and elsewhere to try to capture the ineffable qualities of new sounds and sights so that they could be rendered faithfully. You have to love what you are trying to reproduce in high fidelity in order to convey the genuine experience. It is in Idealand that various values meet, clash, and achieve a final harmony. Each group champions its own values until they find inclusion in a larger system and a more creative synthesis watched over by a *principle of parsimony* that seeks to cut costs to the bone. The synthesis of values must be spare, rich, elegant, and "price wise."

Through the kind of thinking portrayed in this chapter, B&O was able to turn around from a company in very serious financial trouble to a profitable niche supplier showing strong growth and quality leadership in the international industry.

Chapter 8

————◆————

Private Enterprise, Public Service: Gérard Mestrallet, Suez Lyonnaise des Eaux

**Fons Trompenaars, Peter Prud'homme,
and Charles Hampden-Turner**

THERE IS AN ongoing public debate about what private enterprise can and cannot do about the limits of privatization and whether "public goods" such as clean water and sanitation can be entrusted to profit-making enterprises. A ringing endorsement of the capacity of private enterprise to dedicate itself to public goals is provided by Gérard Mestrallet, who built upon the achievement of Jérome Monod, the long-time leader of Lyonnaise des Eaux. Monod pioneered the internationalizing of water distribution and treatment. Mestrallet's grand vision is of a transcultural "one-stop" provider of utility systems and infrastructure, now including, in addition to water, electricity, gas, and telecommunications. This was a classic meeting of minds. The provision of water and other basic necessities is an issue of geopolitical significance.

Gérard Mestrallet has the academic pedigree of much of the French industrial elite. A graduate of the Grand École Polytechnique and the École Nationale d'Administration, he began his career in 1978 in the Treasury Department of the French Ministry of Economic Affairs and Finance, typifying the close intellectual ties between the public and private sectors in France. Among his mentors was Jacques Delors. In exchange for the lifelong status guaranteed by elite schooling, individuals dedicate themselves to serving the broader community beyond France. Yet Mestrallet is of modest origins: His father was a *patissier-traiteur* in Montmartre in Paris. He is a scholar who has made good.

This capacity to adapt to new environments led him, after he joined Compagnie de Suez in 1984, from the post of senior vice president of the Société Générale de Belgique to the position of its chief executive officer (CEO) in 1995. After the merger with Lyonnaise des Eaux (LDE), in which he and Jérome Monod were the prime movers, Mestrallet became head of the merged company, Suez Lyonnaise des Eaux (SLDE), in 1997. The global ambition of this new group was immediately recognized by the international press. Lyonnaise des Eaux had already had a 50 percent world share of foreign-managed water companies. "SLDE's new mission is to conquer the world," commented *The Times* in April 1997.

Favorable press comment also greeted Mestrallet's early years at the helm of the new group. *Le Nouvel Économiste* named him the French "Manager of the Year 1998." From 1994 to 1999, with the addition of Lyonnaise des Eaux, group turnover at Suez rose from $15 billion to $35 billion. Martine Aubry, writing in the same journal, observed: "With the speed of light, the CEO of SLDE has completed his mission: transforming two companies into one coherent industrial group with global ambitions." A reported compliment to Mestrallet was overheard at a public ceremony: "You know where you want to go, but you make certain not to travel alone." It is this capacity to bring people with him on ambitious journeys that captured public attention. Mestrallet gave to the whole company a strong industrial focus and a genuine service strategy. His vision, although Europe-based, is broadly multicultural.

Joining the Histories of Two Venerable Companies

The merger could not have been a success without respect being paid to the quite different yet equally distinguished histories of the two companies, each more than a century old. We see their histories side by side on SLDE's Web site. Suez was the former Suez Canal Company, founded in 1858 to build the Suez Canal, joining the Mediterranean to the Indian Ocean. Lyonnaise des Eaux et de l'Éclairage (Water and Lighting) was founded in 1880 to distribute water, gas, and, later, electricity. Both companies internationalized early, Suez from its inception and Lyonnaise from 1914 onward, largely in French colonies. Both were used to long-term time horizons in the provision of infrastructure. Typical of this approach was the 25- to 30-year contract for the building, operating, and management of utility systems, which would then revert to local control and ownership. These concessions originally were made by French or colonial administrations to the company concerned, but the vision of returning a vastly improved infrastructure system to independent communities was postcolonial in its inspiration and a charter for the freedom of developing nations.

The vision has proved immensely popular, and, aided by French diplomacy, LDE especially has dwarfed its international competitors. It was a vision worthy of Jérome Monod. Public health and low infant mortality rates are important foundations for economic takeoff and social development. LDE would put an end to cholera, typhoid, and other diseases caused by polluted water supplies. It would train an echelon of indigenous professionals to operate and maintain the system and then depart. A private company would help developing people help themselves and leave their destiny in their own hands. This is an undertaking that cannot simply be shifted from one location to a cheaper one, like electronics manufacturing. You are committed to that locality for a generation, and inevitably, you lose some and win some. Yet you are not free of competition simply by virtue of having a long-term contract; the instability of local politics is a constant threat, and you must justify your performance to critics. It was Jérome Monod who wrote in 1999: "You cannot live without a grand vision, and only those who see the invisible can realize the impossible."

Mestrallet's challenge has been to translate that overarching vision and timeless quality into clear goals that stockholders can grasp and monitor periodically. His success can be gauged by a June 16, 1999, headline in *The Financial Times:* "Utilities Group Has Crystal Clear Aims." His five-year objectives were bold and unambiguous: The water business was to become a world leader not just in market share but in profitability. To that end, he acquired Calgon in the United States in 1999, that country's third-largest water-conditioning company, and just two weeks later acquired Nalco Chemical, the biggest water-treatment company, which turned SLDE into the world's number-one water conditioner. For SITA, the waste-management unit of SLDE, the objective was to double its sales, an aim that was accomplished within a year by means of the acquisition of all the units of Browning Ferries Industries outside the United States. This made SITA the world leader outside North America. In the same year Mestrallet gained full control of Tractebel, its Belgian electricity and gas subsidiary, and was therefore in position to use it as a launch vehicle for acquisitions in the energy industry.

Mestrallet is personally very gentle, courteous, and unassuming. His *courtoisie* is much remarked on, but it covers a steely determination and an unswerving pursuit of the goals he has set for his group. A veritable Boy Scout in his demeanor and charmingly intelligent, he nonetheless is unswerving in the pursuit of objectives. He told his senior staff: "The road we have chosen is hard and passionate. Therefore, let's internalize Leonardo da Vinci's beautiful motto: obstinate rigor." Here is a list of what Mestrallet sees as his major challenges:

- "Globalization," or more precisely, building a transnational corporation that is global in scope but rooted in every region
- Meeting the variety of requests from countries at every stage of development
- Creating new, up-to-date forms of urbanization and basic infrastructures for multiple utilities
- Deregulation of public monopolies in the supply of, for example, water and energy to create new opportunities for industrial customers
- Privatization of public utilities, opening them up to world financial investment and increased capital
- New ways of safeguarding the environment and monitoring its quality
- Combining constancy of purpose with the capacity to make quantum leaps in technology and service, with the aim of strengthening the whole

Dilemma 1. The Search for Complementarity

Mestrallet's first task was to get two very different companies to work in tandem. This was not easy. Both companies were old and effective operators with deeply ingrained habits for achieving success that had strongly affected their cultures. Neither had reason to defer to the other in the area of its own expertise.

Lyonnaise des Eaux was a well-regarded national number two in local public services, desperately in need of capital to develop its infrastructure. Suez was strong in the finances Lyonnaise needed. Despite such complementarities, the cultures were very different. LDE was oriented toward projects and led by engineering. The concession model necessitated a 20- to 25-year commitment to build, maintain, and operate water and sewage treatment facilities and pipelines in far-flung locations, with the municipality as a customer. LDE was mostly intuitive in its assessment because of the large number of uncontrollable variables in regions far from headquarters. The company also depended substantially on relationships of trust and confidence between local officials and French engineers on the ground. Foreigners assuming command, however temporary, of local water supplies is a potentially tense issue. That which falls from the heavens on a community is surely that community's own. LDE's triumph had been one of diplomacy—its own and that of the French government. Such skills were highly localized and decentralized, with no two problems alike and with few safe generalizations possible about the best practice.

In contrast, Suez was a highly capital-intensive company with a financially oriented culture. It had knowledge and skills in banking and financial services, in evaluating profit and risk, and in structuring finance and raising money at a low cost. Mestrallet's first move was to sell off all noncore activities, including the making of pâté de foie gras and the extending of consumer credit. He also divested Suez of companies in other financial services, concentrating on capital investment in, and the operating of, water, waste, and energy activities. The aim was to make a 14 percent return on global investments.

LDE's search for complementarity is captured in the following diagram:

Dilemma 1: The Search for Complementarity

- Y-axis: Orientation toward profit and global shareholders (0 to 10)
- X-axis: Orientation toward market share and local stakeholders (0 to 10)

Suez culture
Capital-intensive
Commercial–managerial
Calculated risk
Shorter-term payoff

SLDE culture
Rapid global expansion and regional extension through better capital resources profitably invested

Lyonnaise des Eaux culture
Diplomatic skill
Engineering projects
Endemic uncertainties
Long-term commitment

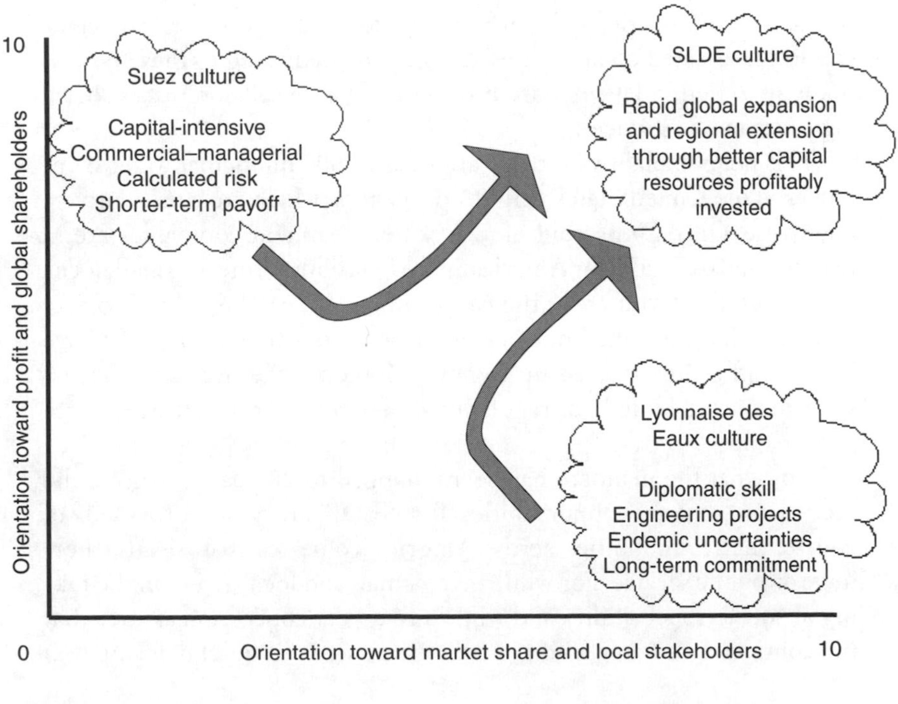

LDE's ability to open up ever more varied opportunities around the globe had been enhanced immeasurably by cheaper and more plentiful capital. Jérome Monod was traveling more widely. Commitments to stakeholders can be longer and larger when the company is well financed and profitable. When you are putting in energy pipelines, you can leave room for water, and vice versa. With good management you need to install those infrastructures only once.

Dilemma 2. Socially Responsible Privatization

It was Margaret Thatcher who first beat the drums for Europe-wide privatization, yet paradoxically, it was the French who were the best positioned to take advantage of this. Why? Because for many French managers the proper conduct of private enterprise has never excluded a sense of public duty and social obligation to the wider community. In Chapter 1 we saw that French managers, to a greater extent than most other Europeans or Americans, have seen in business the opportunity "continuously to take care of the needs of your fellow man."

It follows that privatization, as practiced by French companies in general and by SLDE in particular, is less likely to lead to local communities' being taken advantage of and more likely to be seen as an opportunity to care creatively. Fresh water supplies and the proper treatment of waste have historically been responsible for doubling life expectancies in the affected communities. A company dedicated to these tasks is not easy to find in laissez-faire economies, where self-interest is sovereign over public services.

This helps explain why there are over 55,000 municipal water companies in the United States, only 15 percent of which are run by private enterprise. Only 9.0 percent of U.S. water treatment companies are in private hands. Clearly, for Americans "responsibility" means small, local, and nonprofit. If you are *of* the community, you can be trusted to take care of it, but unelected out-of-town operators who go for profit have been insufficiently trusted up to now. Moreover, the five-year concessions mandated by federal regulations were too short to attract private investment.

Now that the mandate has been changed to 20 years or more, the race is on, and the opportunities for SLDE are vast—provided, of course, that communities across America come to trust SLDE's heritage of public service. For while being small and local assists in the taking of social responsibility and while a five-year concession assures that the contractor can do nothing much wrong without quickly losing that concession, the system was chronically inefficient, lacked economies of scale, and afforded disincentives to investment.

Today the opportunity for SLDE to be locally responsible *and* a big, efficient investor is too good to miss. "The company sees a great opportunity in the fragmented U.S. market," explained Mestrallet. Here is a chance to show that privatization is not just technically and economically superior but also matches the concern for local communities shown by contractors on a short leash, forever lobbying for the renewals of their five-year concessions. SLDE is targeting big cities in which its professionalism is appreciated. It has projects going in Atlanta, Indianapolis, Gary, Milwaukee, and San Antonio, among others, and the comments have been favorable: "SLDE's tap water may not yet taste like Perrier, but it is just as French."

However, deregulation is not purely a matter of gain: It pushes down prices and puts profitability under pressure. For this reason, "we need Monod's talents to develop all corners of the planet, from Casablanca to Djakarta. Here the desperate need is for drinkable water."

The dilemma of socially responsible privatization and deregulation can be diagrammed as follows:

Dilemma 2: Socially Responsible Privatization and Deregulaiton

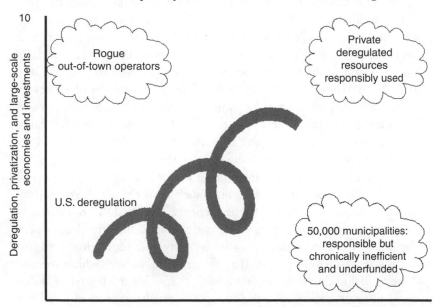

In a world where political controls over corporations are weakening and utility companies are "natural monopolies," it becomes increasingly important not to abuse this power and behave like a rogue operator. Deregulation has perhaps started a stampede, but it will take dedication to customers and communities to avoid injuring them in this stampede.

The future of privatization is *not* necessarily secure. Much will depend on how private companies conduct themselves. Some developed nations have declined to take this path; the Netherlands, for example, where water is an issue of national survival, argues that private companies push for "cheap solutions" that leave out less prosperous citizens. The United Kingdom has had occasion to criticize its privatized water companies severely, and there is some dismay over foreign ownership. Privatized electricity companies in the United Kingdom treat their large users very well, their small users far worse. Norway has suffered large price fluctuations, with price rises during droughts, because of the domination of hydroelectric power.

The idea of making a profit from rain and rivers still sticks in many voters' throats despite the value and technical challenges of water treatment. France is nationalistic about water and about privatization involving foreigners. It also has a long tradition of government influence in industrial affairs. SLDE may find its foreign operations curbed if its base country does not become more hospitable to foreign investment in its infrastructure; nor is France privatizing fast enough, according to Mestrallet: "In France, we are losing time now. It takes too long to privatize important industries. Just look around you. We cannot maintain this idea that France can be a small laboratory apart from the rest of the world. Of course, we must preserve our unique history and traditions, but we cannot be blind to developments around us. There is a real risk of a 'back to public service' spirit if private companies make too much money while contributing too little to communities. *Le Mal Français*, with its state-influenced rigidities, its suspicion of flexibility and initiative, and its tendency to politicize all decisions, is still a threat to us."

All these factors make it even more important that SLDE commit itself to the communities and municipalities it serves. If the tide turns against privatization, there is still a chance that SLDE could be regarded as an exception and a future model, one of the few global operators that serve their customers with honesty and dedication, creating an oasis in a spiritual desert. It is this kind of caring, which Jérome Monod's vision described as "invisible," that Gérard Mestrallet is determined to demonstrate in the company's results. It is to this dedication that we now turn.

Dilemma 3. Enriching Shareholders versus Sustaining the Poor, the Underdeveloped, and the Environment

One might ask how SDLE can *afford* to pursue social goals except at some cost to its shareholders, who might object to this use of their money. One answer is the very large gain from network-accelerated returns. Much fuss is currently made over the economic advantages of the Internet and the huge share prices for unprofitable companies, but investors know that networks can produce accelerating rather than diminishing returns. This is the case because every additional member of a growing network lowers the costs of serving all the existing customers. By simultaneously expanding the service base and lowering per-unit prices, a utility precipitates a virtuous circle, with ever more customers at ever lower per-unit costs, which in turn gives access to ever more customers, even the very poor. SLDE's policy is to *share these gains with the communities it serves,* all of which have produced "net gains." The Internet is only the latest of several networks.

For example, in Buenos Aires the state utility company was widely unpopular and financially troubled, and it reached too few people. SLDE invested $1 billion and reached 1.6 million more people, with upgraded equipment, and it did all this without raising water rates! In Santiago, Chile, the company worked with the government to provide "water stamps" so that even the poorest people became paying customers and were involved in consultations about better service. Finally, popular participation and suggestions elicited from poor customers in La Paz, Bolivia, led to costs being cut by two-thirds.

Mestrallet likes to make Monod's caring more visible, just as he likes to make strategic objectives clear. To that end he created an ethics charter and employs an in-house deontologist (a practitioner of the branch of ethics concerned with duty, obligation, and good intentions, much influenced by Immanuel Kant.) The values embodied by the company include professionalism, partnership, esprit de corps, respect for the environment, and the creation of genuine value.

The impact of these ethical practices must be viewed in the context of taking over inefficient, overstaffed, and sometimes corrupt municipal services; upgrading these services over 20 years or more; and then returning them to the local control of trained, professional, indigenous managers and workers. In these circumstances the following ethical principles guide policy:

- Fire as few people as you can and try to get unions on your side and acting responsibly.

- When downsizing and layoffs are unavoidable, demonstrate as soon as possible the improvements in service and the impact on public health that arise from them. Write measurable improvements in water quality into the contract and extend services wherever you can to get costs down. Sponsor surveys of public health so that improvements are publicized and preventable illnesses are seen to become less common.
- Build long-term partnerships by improving efficiency and holding or lowering prices to the customer. Hence, in Budapest raising prices at less than the level of inflation, which is a net lowering of prices, is written into the contract. Efficiency includes energy saving so that customers' key appliances use less energy.
- Focus especially on poorer people, their employment, and their access to water, electricity, and other utilities.
- Assist the environment through recycling and separation of glass, tin, and so on, from other wastes, with rewards for the apprehension of illegal dumpers.
- Learn to respond to dire emergencies. For example, during the destructive storms in France in 1999 SLDE staff rode to the rescue of many communities cut off from water and electricity. Mobile water treatment units were installed, and individuals and small and medium-size enterprises were helped to get through local electricity distribution emergencies.

An important insight into the success of these policies comes out of the dilemma theory we have been using. Why, for example, does it benefit SLDE to persuade customers to save water and energy? Conventional economic thinking would scoff at this strategy. After all, you are *selling* energy, and so the more customers who use and pay for energy, the more money you make. Why save energy at all? Shouldn't your shareholders be angry? Why provide water for the poor, who are "uneconomical" to serve? These might indeed have been the attitudes of municipal water and electricity authorities in underdeveloped economies, which SDLE replaces temporarily, but if we look at the situation as a values *system*, the reasons for social responsibility become clear. If you lower energy costs for a pizza maker with two ovens, he or she can cut costs and use the proceeds to buy a third oven, which consumes the electricity you supply in greater quantities than before. You are better off, the pizza maker is better off, and more customers are served. If you pipe clean water to poor people and collect in payment "water stamps" that the government cashes, those people will no longer dig up the pipes and sell them, no longer have to sit up all night with a cholera-stricken child, and no longer absent themselves from work because of illness. Again, *everyone* is better off and lives longer.

The same is true of sustaining the environment. It is not the fittest who survive but the *fittingest.* The unit of survival is the person *plus* the environment. They survive together or not at all. In the end, those who pay for pollution are the poor, pushed into the dirtiest corners of the urban sprawl and picking over the piles of trash.

In short, joining people to networks for the supply of such mass utilities as water, electricity, gas, telephone, and telecommunications produces network economies that are *shareable among all parties,* including shareholders and stakeholders. Such networks create the infrastructure for economic takeoff and accelerating returns to that community. The dilemma is reconciled as in the following diagram:

Dilemma 3: Enriching Shareholders versus Sustaining the Poor and the Environment

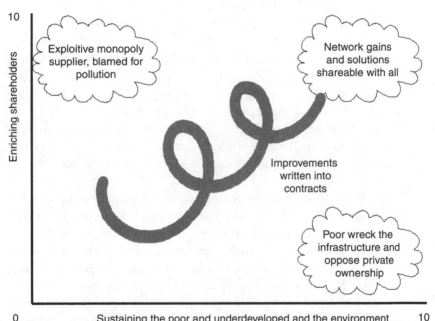

At the top left we have the monopoly supplier, like some of SLDE's U.S.-based competitors, widely blamed for environmental pollution. At the bottom right we see that infrastructure actually may be destroyed by people too poor to pay their rates. What is necessary are gains and solutions for the whole national and regional network. These can be paid for only if all citizens participate, because a whole network can be sabotaged by a desperate minority. As Monod put it: "We are world leaders only when we help solve problems on a world scale: like the future of Lake Aral now crippled by salination." Mestrallet agrees: "To be a world leader, you must think about the problems of humanity, about making the desert bloom, [and] about how to treat water in large urban agglomerates."

For this reason SDLE sees environmental organizations as its partners, not its enemies. It installed a Water Resources Advisory Committee that was established in February 2000. The committee consists of a group of international experts who brainstorm major water resource issues. The committee will be consulted on social and environmental issues raised by major SLDE projects as well as on basic principles related to public-private partnerships, and it will be asked to help in providing answers to water-supply problems. The committee includes experts in water-resource issues throughout the world: Europe, Asia, Africa, and North and South America.

A "laboratory" for trying out new ideas is Casablanca, where SDLE has a multiutility concession. The project includes the inspection of systems, the improvement of network efficiency, the reduction of electricity use and water wastage, and the cleaning of 50 kilometers of piping every month. Since taking over the responsibility for sewerage in Casablanca, SLDE has made protecting the city's population a key priority. Part of the project has been a major stormwater-drain infrastructure, because regular flooding used to disrupt city life. SDLE also has sponsored Aquassistance, an association of volunteers trained to deal with floods.

Since 1994 Aquassistance has intervened in many stricken countries. Along with the Water Resources Advisory Committee, SLDE published an environmental charter in which the company pledges to universalize best practices, optimize energy use, control carbon dioxide emissions, guarantee potable water, recycle household waste, and train disadvantaged communities to collect and reuse wastewater.

This is why SDLE is expanding rapidly around the globe. China has been a market since the late 1970s. Its huge population has urgent needs for water treatment and infrastructure. As recently as September 1999 SLDE signed a deal to build and operate a $23 million water-purification facility in Shanghai and a $28 million incineration plant in the Pudong zone. There is a $20 *billion* water and sewerage network for Buenos Aires and a $3 billion multiutility project for Casablanca. Contracts have been won in Manila, Budapest, Jakarta, La Paz, and Pots-dam. SLDE is cooperating with Vivendi to bid jointly for the $1 billion water-system privatization in Rio de Janeiro, and in a consortiumwide project for Santiago various utilities cooperate on installation costs.

To the extent that developing nations have an effective networked infrastructure sustaining their health, rapid economic development is that much more likely. To the extent that the poor and the environment are included in a program of sustainable development, all citizens will contribute to common objectives and all forms of "development" will coincide.

Dilemma 4. Differentiated versus Integrated Service Provider

Providing added value through multiservice, multiutility offerings challenges SLDE to establish synergy between its three main businesses: energy, water, and waste services. According to Mestrallet, "Our very ambitious strategy is possible only because there is complementarity among our diverse activities. Clients are on the same terrain, and our partners are often cities, states [nations], and regions. We all manage complex sets of activities, frequently buying companies that are privatized, and we are all in a large number of cases the project managers for the public service. We are all in the same business: delivering basic necessities to our customers' doorsteps. The future is in one-shop service: water, electricity, gas, heating, cable services, and the collection and treatment of solid waste and wastewater."

The added value comes not just from applying the same concept to the different services. SLDE's capacity to design, finance, build, and manage can be used to offer unique integrated services such as combining the activities in "waste" and "energy" in "waste to energy" projects and combining the activities in "energy" and "water" in desalination technology. Integrated service providing is especially relevant for "late-developing" nations or regions. One advantage of being a late-developing nation or region is that the utility infrastructure is new and can be built from scratch. Instead of having water pipes here, gas pipes there, telephone wires overhead, and sewage everywhere, it makes sense to build a multiutility pipeline and distribution system with all utilities in single channels, laid side by side, often under large curbstones that need only be lifted to avoid the necessity of digging up the roadway to make serial repairs.

While such combinations are ideal, they are quite rare. One example of an "ideal" multiutility system is SLDE's concession in Casablanca, where the firm is installing water, energy, sewerage, and telecommunications simultaneously. The problem with extolling such opportunities is that they seldom recur; what is needed is a viable model for more common patterns of customer demand. The multiutility pipeline is an "engineer's dream," but most engineers working for SLDE have to alter their course and do something else that the customers want. Nonetheless, the search for integration is strategically important: For example, when running a desalination plant, you generate steam, and it makes sense to use that steam for heating or for generating electricity. Such dual functions are more economical than are separated functions. If you are laying pipelines anyway, billing customers anyway, treating water anyway, it typically pays to integrate those activities so that you treat water *and* supply it *and* supply electricity or steam from the process.

Attractive though the multiutility concept is, it applies largely to the downstream delivery of services. Electricity still has to be generated, water still has to be treated, and these activities usually are separate, specialized functions that require very different technologies. Upstream integration is relatively rare. Even the process of generation is changing. Mestrallet explains: "We are moving from a centralized energy-generation system to an increasingly decentralized one with smaller and smaller plants. At the same time gas-fired turbines are growing smaller, too. Today we can supply a hospital with its own 10-megawatt turbine. Soon individual gas-fired turbines will be sold to personal clients."

These trends intensify the differentiation of the company, which provides different utilities, on different scales, in different places. The most common situations are utility systems in chronic disrepair, which need overhaul, extension, and proper maintenance but *not* rebuilding from scratch. Accordingly, SLDE faces every variety of system in greater or lesser crisis and has to call on a wide repertory of skills. Perhaps more relevant to the integration of this variety is SLDE's small but growing telecommunications business. This is much more than an additional service, an extra cable, or sharing the same trench. SLDE is in a position to include telecommunications in its multiutility offerings in order to turn a vision of "total housing service" into reality. In January 2000 Mestrallet announced that SLDE would accelerate its communication activities: cable services, the Internet, satellite television, terrestrial television, and mobile phones, including applying for a mobile telephone license for the new UMTS norm, which supports convergence with the Internet. "Our cable activities are full of promise," he says. "To connect just Paris on the Internet through our cables is a jump start. Many investments can be gained back by these great new e-commerce times. There progressively develops a demand for bytes. Digital quality is part of an explosive growth. Next to that, we are extending our services on the cable, including speeding up the Internet by a factor of 1000 compared to the telephone. Here also we manage the infrastructure."

This initiative in communication is not just helping SLDE create value for its shareholders; it also can help SLDE get closer to its final customers: Call centers and e-commerce implementation will create advantages in offering new services and billing. In addition, the initiative can help SLDE reconcile the dilemma between differentiation and integration of its services. All this gets the company much closer to its final customers via home information systems that switch on, switch off, monitor, and economize on the utilities entering a house. Mestrallet's phrase "one-stop service" has two meanings: "one stop" for the ultimate household customers, who can get a simple readout of how all their utilities are performing, and "one stop" for SLDE's distributor customers out in the regions, who require only one major contractor to advise on and provide many different utilities in just the proportions required by the situation. "One stop" means that SLDE can do it all: You need only one consultation and one contract. We can diagram the dilemma as follows:

Dilemma 4: Differentiated versus Integrated Services

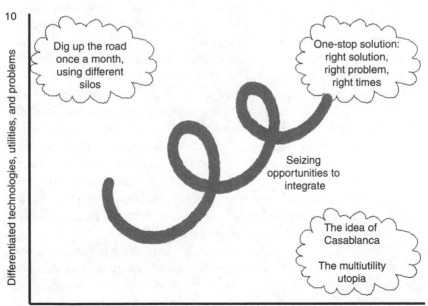

At the top left we have the typically overdifferentiated approach, with "chimneys" or "silos," the digging up of the road once a month to fix faults, and the blocking of traffic for half a year. It is hard to overcome this situation because it is typical of many urban centers in the West, where utilities have been installed by accretion over time and some of the systems date from the turn of the last century. The tabula rasa of a city such as Casablanca, where it is feasible to start from scratch and build an ideal up-to-date system, is not so much wrong as rare, too rare to act as a model for most of the company. By far the most common situation is that in which each region has its own unique problem yet the solution draws from SLDE's wide skill base and resource base. In Budapest, for example, 99 percent of the population gets piped water, but water quality has deteriorated. In parts of Latin America there is no infrastructure where poor people live. In many cities the municipalities are the employers of last resort, hiring the relatives of politicians. What is needed here is professionalization and training. You stop once to consult with SLDE, which will provide for your particular situation.

Dilemma 5. Globalism versus Multinationalism: The Ideal of Transnationalism

SLDE is very much in a race to globalize. Already it has concessions for over 50 percent of the world's foreign-owned water companies—although that accounts for only 4.0 percent of all such companies, and so the race has barely started. SLDE has made a fast start. Mestrallet emphasizes this: "Essentially, I believe that internationalization is our next important challenge . . . the process has only just started. It does not make sense to stop water, waste, or energy development at borders. All these businesses will change their shape. Unfortunately, the French do not have a strong tradition of needing foreigners and tend to stay within home markets. Even so, we have managed to move from 50 percent of turnover being French in the early 1990s to 73 percent being foreign today. Tractabel, our energy company, is number three in the world among independent suppliers, although it too is homegrown, with 95 percent of the Belgian electricity market."

Mestrallet's vision is of a transnational organization in which any one of 100 countries in which SLDE operates could inspire the rest, much as Casablanca's multiutility model is an inspiration to those installing an infrastructure for the first time. Local solutions might remain local, but they could also lead to powerful global generalizations.

Mestrallet announced in 1998 that he wanted to develop the organization according to the transnational model: "We need to take advantage of our Franco-Belgian base, equally shared in terms of business. We are in the process of building a truly transnational organization with multicenters of excellence—for example, in Paris and Brussels. We need to be able to have the possibility of having a financial center in Brussels and Hong Kong, while research and development and legal services are seated in Paris. However, it is impossible to be active in 100 countries or so without having a strong home base in France and Belgium—or, rather, Europe. In our business being international is significantly more than just a process of exporting. If we enter a new market, in most cases a nation-state, we do this for 20 or 30 years. Every franc of nondomestic business is generated outside of France by people who are locally distributing water or electricity or who manage waste. We need a much larger time horizon than many other industries do. We need to have a very fundamental knowledge of the economic workings of a country as well as its sociopolitical and cultural life. In our business we can't take a power plant or the network of water pipes on our back and leave a city or country. We are condemned to the physical place, and so we had better do a good job. Because we can't easily pack our bags, we do our best to develop long-term relationships and have a great assimilation with local partners. Both in water and in electricity we have to face local authorities and laws. Once you decide to codevelop a region that is politically unstable, you have to combine a long-term view with a tremendous amount of political and social risk taking. We are coresponsible for creating the wealth of a country or region. Therefore, we need to have a total integration of our and our clients' interests. We are not able to abandon any of our countries. Furthermore, it is impossible to organize ourselves as a multiregional company. We need to be there locally. The main dilemma is to be present globally anywhere in the world, but nowhere in particular. Our base is European, but our growth potential is elsewhere. And we need to deal with former local monopolies in many cases, if not all. We need to understand the country's culture."

Mestrallet clearly tries to build on SLDE's traditional strength of an informal, pragmatic approach: building contacts, networking, forging unique political and personal relationships with municipalities and governments at various levels, and fostering the culture of understanding what the party is. As he said in a speech in 1998, "The development of the French model of outsourcing is an answer to the present world situation." The French particularistic approach can definitely be a strength in comparison with, for instance, that of American companies, which tend to see the civil service as inferior to them and don't build long-term relationships. However, the informal and pragmatic approach also can turn into a weakness. The group spirit in SLDE at the operational level is very much based on a personal network of French expatriates. This monocultural and often monolingual group is good at sharing and exchanging knowledge in an informal way and at encouraging an entre-preneurial spirit and networking. However, this strength often goes together with a weakness in formal planning and decision making. Glob-alization inevitably requires more formal control.

If SLDE is multinational by necessity, working on the ground in the context of scores of long relationships with foreign regions, what needs more emphasis is linking these sites with a transnational learning sys-tem in which up to a hundred contracts and concessions are monitored and studied for the lessons they will yield for each other and for the sys-tem as a whole. But there is an additional way to globalize effectively. Next to local public authorities, industrial clients are becoming more important for SLDE, if only because developing with global industrial clients will help SLDE globalize itself. You follow an industrial client from operating site to operating site throughout the world so that all plants, for example, benefit from recycling systems, waste disposal, and incineration, wherever in the world the plants are located. In short, you use the globalism of client companies to expand your own operations.

Industrial outsourcing is rapidly becoming a new market, combin-ing storage, transportation, treatment structures and control over con-sumption. SLDE is well positioned for these types of activities because of its combination of urban water services, industrial water services, turnkey project engineering, and huge opportunities to sell electricity to industrial clients after deregulation. SLDE applies this model to waste management with its industrial customer. Waste-management systems for a car company are highly specialized. You typically must get into the production processes if less waste is to be generated and much of what remains is to be recycled. The similarity of these types of expertise helps SLDE integrate itself as one company with bodies of core competence available at all sites. Essentially, such learning is part of the partnership with Ford, a form of coevolution in which manufacturing skills and waste-control skills develop together. Once these skills are learned, the client company would be foolish not to apply them at all its plants.

The dilemma of how to be multinational and regional but also global and centralized is reconciled in the following diagram:

Dilemma 5: Globalism versus Multinationalism

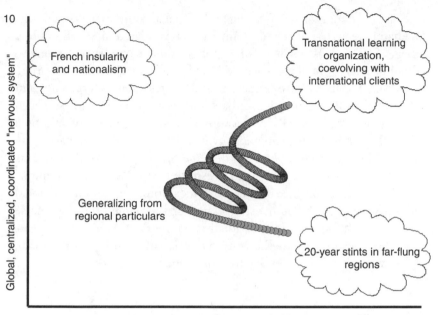

Mestrallet has forced himself to overcome French insularity (at the top left) and uses the far-flung regional concessions in foreign lands and the many information points, sending news of greater or lesser success to the company's "central nervous system" in Paris and Brussels. It is from there that well-informed strategies arise.

Being committed to a regional site for at least 20 years challenges SLDE to learn. The ideal of transnationalism allows any country in the international network to influence others. A solution in San Antonio could have vital lessons for 30 other sites around the world. Resources needed in Jakarta might have to come from a dozen other sites. In addition, the company is learning and coevolving with its international customers in developing methods of production that are more friendly to the environment. This alone could win contracts in several other regions. SLDE made huge steps in building further on the transnational model in 1999 and 2000 as part of the integration of Nalco and Tractebel. Chicago was designated as the global center for water-treatment activities, and Brussels as the global center for energy activities. Mestrallet made an effort toward putting global project teams together for projects at one location (e.g., in Berlin and in Casablanca) and toward knowledge management.

The need for global marketing and global account management immediately leads to the next dilemma, which is related to SLDE's public image. SLDE does not have one global brand name at the moment, although such a brand name would help in building a global reputation. However, SLDE has strong local brand names such as Tractebel and Electrabel in Belgium and Lyonnaise des Eaux (water business), Elyo (energy business), and SITA (waste business) in France. It would be a pity to lose these brand names and even a risk for the French market situation: Having SLDE operate under one brand name would make its presence in France too dominant. Mestrallet says: "We face a dilemma: We risk having to balance between our local interests and international interests for years." The question whether the name Suez Lyonnaise des Eaux is sufficiently international is often asked. Mestrallet replies: "On the question of whether our name is sufficiently international, no—I think that it is necessary to think about an evolution."

Conclusion

Suez Lyonnaise des Eaux is in many ways an extraordinary case, emphasizing not just the "social responsibilities" of private enterprise but the international communal *advantage* of using private finance and technology to solve environmental and social problems on a world scale. What is required is a level of leadership that approaches world statesmanship and vision. These are the legacies of Jérome Monod and Gérard Mestrallet. They have taken their French heritage of civic and municipal responsibility for public resources and extended it around the globe. They have given new meaning to privatization. They have provided networked infrastructures that lay the foundations for economic takeoff.

The ambition of Suez Lyonnaise des Eaux is to become the world leader in businesses that are at the heart of humankind's essential needs: energy, water, waste services, and communication. Mestrallet's great passions are a reflection of SLDE itself. SLDE is a company that delivers basic necessities to the customer's doorstep; Mestrallet, as a youngster, wanted to become a farmer, being attracted by the great forces the earth exerts. His second major hobby still is horseback riding. Mestrallet's great passion is a reflection of SLDE in that it aspires to be close to the basics of life. "The most important [thing] is that I work for the interest of my company," he says, "but my real happiness is my family and friends. Today, obviously my passion is my work, but tomorrow I could start anywhere else. One day without any doubt I will return to the earth, and I will take care of my horses. I will become a farmer—not a gentleman farmer like now, a real one."

Chapter 9

—◆—

Leading One Life:
Val Gooding,
British United
Provident Association

Charles Hampden-Turner

VAL GOODING HAS been chief executive of
BUPA, the British United Provident Association, since 1998. BUPA is
the United Kingdom's largest private health insurer and provider, with
around 40 percent of the private health insurance market, or nearly 3
million members. It is the second largest employer of nurses and medical staff, after the National Health Service, Britain's giant state-
sponsored medical system, free at the point of delivery and paid for
from tax revenues. BUPA's interests extend to home care, health screening, fitness, occupational health products, and a private medical insurance business overseas.

Val Gooding, who is married with two children, came to BUPA after
a distinguished career with British Airways (BA). As head of cabin service from 1989 to 1992 she was involved in BA's famous transformation
in customer service, in which cabin staff engaged customers in "*moments
of truth,*" according to a philosophy first enunciated by Jan Carlzon of
Scandinavian Airlines. (We shall explore the significance of these
"moments" later and trace their impact on Gooding's leadership.) She
rose from this position to head of marketing (1992–1993), then to the

director of business units (1993–1994), and finally to director of the Asian Pacific region of BA. At BUPA she was briefly managing director UK before becoming chief executive in 1998.

Gooding appears to have been something of a late developer. In a recent graduation speech she identified with the tortoise in the fable of the tortoise and the hare. She did not spring spectacularly from her school starting gates, but she did make solid, steady, impressive progress in corporate settings. It was, then, with quiet satisfaction, that at one point in her career she assumed a leading role in an organization that had refused her a place as a student intern some years earlier. That people do much of their learning and development at work has been both her own experience and her credo as chief executive officer (CEO).

Asked about the major dilemmas she faced as BUPA's new leader, Gooding identified the following major issues:

1. An effective insurer versus the carer for the one life customers have
2. The quality of business systems versus the degree of staff's caring and morale
3. Free universal provision versus allocation of resources by free markets
4. Responses to medical crises versus wellness as preventive medicine
5. Nationally based services versus globally expanded services
6. For-profit status versus nonprofit status

She would have to grapple successfully with these issues or see her efforts undone by cross-pressures in the business environment. This chapter will describe, in a paraphrase of Gooding's own words, the dilemmas BUPA faced and how she resolved them.

Dilemma 1. An Effective Insurer versus the Carer for the One Life Customers Have

In some respects Gooding's background in BA was an excellent preparation for BUPA, and she was grateful for what she learned there, but in one important respect BUPA turned out to be very different from an airline service. Its biggest business is health insurance, although it also provides direct care to patients in acute-care hospitals and to elderly residents in nursing homes. In the insurance part of the business BUPA is guided to a certain extent by actuaries, by aggregates, and by statistical projections of likely future demands on services. Above all, an insurance culture is averse to risk. It tends to think of customers as claimants—people trying to get money out of the company—and of course, it does have to be legal and contractual in its orientation. Members have paid exactly so much money for exactly so much coverage, and the company cannot afford to go beyond those stipulations if it is to be fair to all of its customers.

Like so many insurers, BUPA tends to be internally focused on its own procedures, numbers, rules, and limits. Its millions of customers are viewed in general as trends and probabilities, not so much as particular people with one life that is infinitely precious to each person. Gooding noticed early on that BUPA missed the "little" things, things that on closer inspection were not little at all. When she looked at how BUPA answered customer complaints, there was courtesy, often under trying conditions, but there was also a culture of self-justification. It was as if BUPA had to be right about everything all the time and had to convince the complainant of this. It was as if the smallest admission of error would be used in evidence against it. BUPA needed claimants to endorse the way *it* thought instead of understanding them.

Also, BUPA was oddly cold and formal in its manner. Gooding had not read "Thank you for your letter of 15 inst." for more than 10 years before joining BUPA. She insisted on a change in the whole style. It was not possible to give key staff members the kinds of financial bonuses they could get elsewhere, and so it was all the more important to create a culture like no other: BUPA, despite being an insurer and having to think like one, identifies with the one life each member has.

Another key strategy arose from BA's seminars for cabin crew and the importance of Carlzon's "moments of truth" concept. This concept held that most passengers interacted with the cabin crew for only about 20 to 50 seconds throughout a long-haul flight but that from such fragments of interaction they drew conclusions of wide generality about the airline. The moments might be very brief and specific, but the truth inferred from them was sweeping and all embracing. Yet the truth about an airline is of minor consequence compared with the truth about a medical service on which a person's health and life depend. According to Gooding, it is a moment of truth when you have been paying out premiums for years to BUPA and suddenly you need the company to reciprocate. How does the person on the other end of the telephone behave? Is he or she immediately and authentically concerned with *you* or concerned mainly with the company's categories and rules—with how it should conceive of you in the abstract? Are those people trying to save your life or reduce their costs? Now that *you* need *them*, are they warm, welcoming, considerate, moving with the same alacrity as when they accepted your premium?

Those first 30 seconds on the telephone are not just moments of truth but moments when you calculate your survival chances, when you thank heaven for BUPA or curse the day you heard of it. BUPA makes its reputation in those moments—good or bad. BUPA has to create a culture acutely conscious of the one life on the other end of the line.

Of course, Gooding *tells* people this, but it is not enough just to tell them; she models the behavior she wants others to show: servant leadership, consisting of doing it yourself, serving others as you would have them serve the customer. She tries to model nonarrogance, noncomplacency, dissatisfaction with progress thus far, and a willingness to learn from one's environment by listening.

She judges that she needs to be there when those moments of truth are happening. Accordingly, she attends surgical operations (as do the other senior managers), talks to patients before and afterward, visits call centers, takes calls herself, and talks with those constantly on the front line with anxious inquirers. She used to hear some skeptical comments: "She won't keep *that* up for long" and "New brooms sweep clean." But she has been at it for four years now and has no intention of stopping. And staff members remember. "I saw you at Staines Hospital," they tell her. She does it for herself, too, to remind herself what all this is about: that 3 million people have placed their lives in BUPA's hands and the company has to be there for them.

BUPA has a new training program called Leading One Life. It's not like other programs. Participants do not go through it like sheep being dipped and having some substance deposited on them. Instead, it inquires of participants, "*Who are you* as a person? What are you outside work? Is there any part of that 'outside' you that you could bring to the workplace, to members and their concerns?" The more of themselves and the more of their personal experiences they can bring to the workplace, the more they care and the more ways they have of caring.

Early on in the program the participants form groups that self-organize around the central concerns of the members. "How can we be of more help and enjoy that experience? What are the recent high points, and how can there be more of them?" they ask. They share the zest of being able to do more for customers, of being there for them, of finding just the right words, of sheer gratitude for their own health and good fortune and the feeling of having lent their strength, experience, and adulthood to others.

These teams also come up with practical suggestions and solutions, such as a special *health line* for those facing bypass surgery. On the line were people who had specialized in the operation and would patiently explain the preparations, the procedures, the aftermath, and the odds of surviving. There is another specialized line for breast cancer, with an experienced nurse. Customers are extremely appreciative of these developments. Any person or team can write up a suggestion and be financially and socially rewarded when that suggestion is implemented. In sum, no set formulas or prepared spiels are going to train you to deal with people whose health and lives are unexpectedly threatened. What is required is nothing less than the totality of your personal experience and all the compassion you can muster from within yourself.

We are now in a position to diagram the first of Gooding's dilemmas:

Dilemma 1: An Effective Insurer versus the Carer for the One Life Customers Have

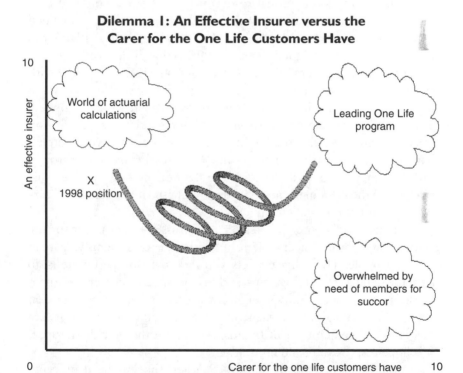

Note this important point: BUPA *remains an insurer,* with the disciplines and categories of an insurer. You cannot evade this reality, but you can treat members in life-threatening situations as suffering human beings, not as claimants shaking you down. This need of members for succor, potentially overwhelming for carers, is another level of reality—a pit of despair that most insurers keep away from if they can. It requires "emotional muscles" to move from where BUPA was in 1998, at the top left of the diagram, toward that pit to help those in crises.

The Leading One Life program and policy *rely* on a sound insurance basis and then use those strengths and resources to reach out to members in peril. It is scary to try but wonderfully satisfying to succeed, to be the voice at the end of the line that made everything happen. This helps explain why the Leading One Life program is not a "data drop" but the elicitation of the carer's powers to be fully present for others.

Dilemma 2. The Quality of Business Systems versus the Degree of Staff's Caring and Morale

There is simply no emotional reservoir to invest in frightened customers, no patience or understanding, if those qualities have not been received by service staff. In the mid-1990s staff morale at BUPA was poor. When Gooding took over in 1998, it had improved, but not enough. Certainly there were too few emotional riches to share with the members. Gooding saw at once that increasing staff morale was a top priority, yet her view of the problem was typically tough-minded. She saw staff morale as not simply a "human relations thing": You treat other people with the kindness and consideration you yourself have received, but it is not that simple. Professionals work through the tools they use, and if the tools are neither the best nor the most relevant to the customer's needs, then even with an abundance of caring, one cannot do an adequate job.

Imagine a call center. The caller is distressed—that is par for the course—and you are eager to help, but without good systems you are in serious trouble. The caller expects you to know who he or she is, to have the details at your fingertips, and to have speedy answers to urgent questions about such things as eligibility, costs, and appointments. Can you imagine trying to help when you have poor equipment or software that answers the questions of the insurer but not those of the insured? It is hopeless, stressful, and infuriating.

Gooding learned this lesson at BA when she was head of cabin crews. Her section fought for and finally won the right to upgrade the galleys on long-haul flights. It meant taking out a couple of business-class seats, so one can imagine the opposition to that move! But it had a phenomenal effect on the morale of the cabin crew. Pushing a trolley with a bad wheel or handling hot food in painfully confined spaces can destroy one's morale. Workers will believe nothing you say if you leave them to suffer with defective equipment. What Gooding found true at BA proved even truer at BUPA. The staff members are trained professionals whose equipment is bound up with their pride and identity. If that equipment does not work properly or takes the staff away from its customers instead of helping to focus on them, morale is going to drain away and the number of complaints will rise. If the software is not right, if you can't get the customer's history and situation right there in front of you while the customer is begging for answers in a voice strangled by anxiety and panic, can you imagine how awful the staff person feels, how helpless and angry? If the screen does not contain plain English, if it does not address the question the member is asking but is full of in-house jargon, helpfulness is impeded. There was a need to change training, software, and even hardware.

In its state-of-the-art call centers at Staines and at Salford Quays BUPA now has a "calming room" to which staff members can retreat after highly stressful calls. BUPA trains its staff to recognize the stress in a caller's voice and bring it down. The company has invested heavily in the environment of call centers: soft fabrics to dull noise, curved desks arranged in clusters so that team members can call on one another for help, and specialist resource people and help lines that can be relied on. Managers are right there in the center to provide help and guidance, not in privileged corner offices where they can hide away. There are restful, muted color schemes, a gym, a staff restaurant, and recreational facilities. Whatever horror stories one has heard about call centers do not apply at BUPA. Help is available in depth and so if staff members get distressed or must go away to find answers, there is backup.

BUPA monitors service carefully: Eighty percent of calls are answered by the fifth ring—that is, in 20 seconds. BUPA learns, especially from its corporate clients, how service can become better. When an institution deals with individuals with their own worries, there is no time for feedback or suggestions about improvements, but corporate clients tell the firm exactly where it succeeds and where it fails.

All this upgrading of the tools BUPA works with has been expensive but absolutely necessary to staff morale and to the credibility of the One Life programs. "If you are not going to back your people up, talk about care is so much rhetoric. And now we are getting the results," says Gooding. Her second dilemma is reminiscent of the sociotechnical systems described by Eric Trist and Fred Emery. You cannot, they argued, consider technical systems in isolation from social systems, and you must always bear in mind the social meanings and implications of technology. If the equipment in use says "only profit counts" or "let the cabin staff suffer," conflicts between systems doom even the best intentions and the advocates of each system are frustrated. The dilemma looks like this:

Dilemma 2: The Quality of Business Systems versus the Degree of Staff's Caring

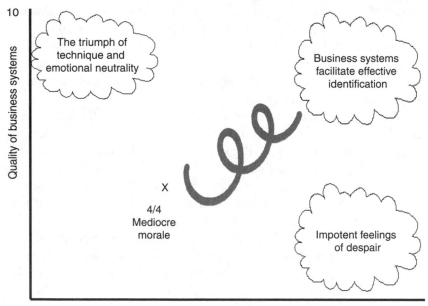

At the top left we have the triumph of technique and emotional neutrality, a trap into which several giant insurers have fallen. At the lower right there is plenty of identification, but it gives rise to impotent rage and despair because poor technology cripples the capacity to care for members effectively. In 1998 the authors located BUPA roughly at the X, lacking up-to-date equipment and with insufficient feeling reaching members in trouble.

Gooding's move was to invest in more customer-relevant technology, which allowed more identification to be expressed, symbolized by the virtuous helix moving upward and to the right toward a reconciliation in which business systems facilitate effecting identification.

This achievement has to be measurable. Gooding not only thinks in terms of offsetting measurements, she speaks of a "balanced scorecard" where gains on both axes can be monitored. BUPA measures levels of complaints and then follows up to see how the complaints were dealt with. BUPA measures health outcomes: how hospitals and surgeons have fared in curing patients, how patients benefited from surgery and how quick their recovery was, how their initial calls were dealt with, how swift appointments and diagnoses were and how soon intervention followed, and how well the patients were prepared for their treatments by those who counseled them. But the key is never to rest content, always to ask how you can do better, and never to be deflected from the task of continuous improvement.

Dilemma 3. Free Universal Provision versus Allocation of Resources by Free Markets

Everything BUPA does is in the shadow of its huge state-owned neighbor, Britain's National Health Service (NHS), financed out of general tax revenues and dedicated to free universal provision at the point of delivery. Neither Conservative nor Labour governments choose to envisage the failure of the United Kingdom's most ambitious social experiment. Cradle-to-grave entitlement to medical care is programmed into the British political psyche. Inevitably, the perceived effectiveness of the NHS and the extra tax revenues pumped into it under pressure from voters as elections approach affect the decision to take on medical insurance. If the NHS were a perfect provider, medical insurance would be unnecessary. BUPA thus relies to a certain extent on the shortcomings of the state system. Under Margaret Thatcher, herself privately insured, BUPA grew apace, but the private medical insurance market never really recovered after the recession of the early 1990s.

BUPA has to decide whether there is a future for private health care. At the moment the market is flat in numbers but slightly up in value. BUPA's future is very much tied in with that of the NHS. Gooding believes it is up to BUPA to make the market grow by offering what the NHS and other insurers do not provide. The difficulty is that BUPA benefits from the shortcomings of the NHS—especially its long waiting lists—and so people see BUPA as an alternative and hence as "opposed" to the NHS. The company cannot help being an alternative model to which people turn when the NHS is criticized, but it does not behave in a rivalrous way, and it does everything possible to help and supplement the NHS.

In Gooding's view, BUPA acts as a valuable adjunct in several ways. When elderly people in "acute" beds are not acute anymore but are not ready to be sent home because no one is available to look after them, BUPA can provide facilities for care and convalescence that free up emergency beds. BUPA is also in a strong position to shorten NHS waiting lists, especially for routine procedures such as eye surgery for cataracts. Cataracts are progressively disabling; a patient can experience significant loss of vision while on the waiting list for a relatively simple operation. BUPA's actuaries worry about such offers of help, since cataracts are one of the main reasons people turn to it, and so BUPA is relieving a problem that could win it many members. But Gooding is personally determined to show that BUPA *complements* the NHS, whose service would cost British taxpayers "one hell of a lot more but for the 7 million people who use private health insurance" and make no claims on the NHS.

What handicaps BUPA is that the NHS is fragmented into local hospital trusts. As a result, BUPA has many local ad hoc arrangements with various trust hospitals, but there is no national policy that would entrust it with key support functions. BUPA would love to pilot NHS policies and spearhead its innovations, but there is no central decision making in that area.

BUPA has certainly undertaken some important initiatives. At the Bristol Royal Infirmary patients recover from heart surgery at a nearby rehabilitation unit run by BUPA and are joined by outpatients further on the road to recovery, who attend weekly physiotherapy sessions. A similar arrangement is in operation at the East Surrey NHS hospital at Redhill; patients recuperate in a nearby BUPA facility. BUPA also takes the lead when it comes to elder care: More than 70 percent of the residents in BUPA homes are state-funded, and some would certainly have to be in NHS hospitals but for BUPA's skilled carers. In Cambridge BUPA has a joint venture with Addenbrooke's Hospital to provide an additional magnetic resonance imaging scanner for both NHS and BUPA patients. Training has been offered to radiographers working for the NHS in other hospitals. There are many such examples, but they are scattered, and they depend on the not always positive attitudes of trust hospitals. The private sector as a whole contributes £240 million to NHS pay beds and local authorities.

Gooding appears to be of two minds about whether the NHS might render private medical insurance obsolete or vice versa. One of the main arguments in favor of the NHS becoming obsolete is that massive investments, far greater than tax revenues allow, will be attracted to the health field, by people becoming more used to the idea that they must provide for some of their own personal and social needs. One way this might happen could be piecemeal, with failing hospitals (like failing schools) turned around by private-sector intervention. Another way is to privatize the provision side, with more and more private services brought in. Yet another route is to give employers incentives to provide health insurance, to make private health insurance tax deductible, or to provide insurance out of savings.

Why might the NHS, for all its fame and political support, be unable to continue providing comprehensive health care? For one reason: Demand rises faster than resources. Resources are finite, but demand is infinite. Already the NHS is dependent on the private health-care market to ease an otherwise intolerable burden. Gooding points out that the private health-care market is small (in the United Kingdom) in comparison with the NHS. Six and a half million people, or 11 percent of the population, commit themselves to private health by taking out medical insurance. It is worth noting, however, that the private sector carries out 20 percent of all heart operations and 30 percent of all hip replacements in the United Kingdom. Without it, the NHS would have to perform another half a million surgical operations a year.

The mood of voters about paying higher taxes has not been favorable, and British state health care is inferior in its outcomes to that of most developed countries in Europe, where people pay more for their health care. Although Britain is pledged to close this gap, whether it can do so without losing votes through tax hikes is highly problematic. One way or the other, the private sector is likely to have to provide the answers.

Another important consideration, discussed later under Dilemma 4, is that health services under pressure are obliged to focus more and more on crisis medicine, accidents and emergencies, and life-threatening illnesses. Everything else must wait. But exclusively emergency medicine is not good medicine, since it fails to catch preventable conditions early and help patients keep from falling ill in the first place. It is not even economical on its own terms, since the dangerously ill are expensive to treat.

Although Gooding is unsure about whether the future belongs to private medicine, currently in a 10-year lull, or to the NHS, plagued by hostile media and party politics, she has few doubts about BUPA's best strategy: to *complement* NHS services wherever possible and to join with that service in a *partnership to raise overall standards.* This is one of the key gains from competition: Standards rise and, with them, public and political expectations. That was the gist of BUPA's submission to the House of Commons Health Committee in January 1999. BUPA sought to raise quality, extend regulation and monitoring, and create clinical indicators of quality. It offered to contribute to the measurement of outcomes.

There is an underlying method in these proposals that might do more than anything else to assure the future of private health care: BUPA and other private health suppliers are in a position to use these outcomes to award contracts to health-care professionals or to withhold the contracts from them, depending on the monitored quality of their services. This has always been the secret of free markets: They reallocate funds from the least successful to the most successful. With information about outcomes, BUPA can learn who is best and what works best and move its support in the direction of those activities.

Dilemma 3 is described next. Val Gooding notes that BUPA confronts "one of the most famous mandatory health insurance systems in the world and one that has been emulated by a number of other countries.... It is a service in demand, more demand than it can cope with." The very existence of BUPA and other insurers is, to those who extol the NHS, a reproach and a means of siphoning off the will to maintain universal coverage.

The dilemma looks like this:

Dilemma 3: Free Universal Provision versus Allocation of Resources by Free Markets

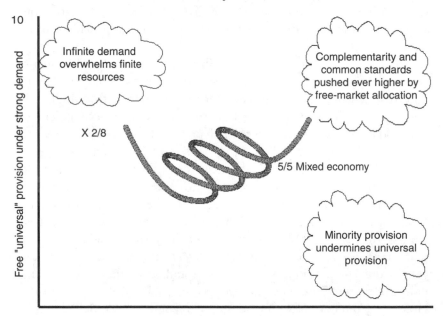

As of now, BUPA is about where the X is, with very high demand on the NHS and a relatively small, flat market for private care, where the reallocation of resources to the more competent is working on a modest scale. Gooding's strategy of complementing NHS services wherever possible and cooperating on nationally monitored standards is the "level playing field" on which BUPA hopes to excel and to start to move resources toward successful outcomes (upper right).

The fear, of course, is that good medical service will be available only to the wealthy, who will be influential enough to make a mockery of universal provision by voting down taxes. Somewhere in the middle is the mixed economy, which, unless it learns from its own indicators, will muddle through as a compromise solution. Whether private medical insurance proves more effective and learns faster than state-sponsored medicine depends crucially on which system can best keep people well. It is to this issue that we now turn.

Dilemma 4. Responses to Medical Crises versus Wellness as Preventive Medicine

The greater the strain on the NHS becomes, the more likely the state-sponsored system is to fall back on "crisis medicine." Those under immediate threat, whose plight can be readily publicized by the media, are bound to receive the bulk of public resources. Increasingly, the system will be geared toward forestalling scandals and avoiding the expensive litigation that scandals bring. It makes sense, after all, to use limited resources for the most urgent cases.

There are other strong forces pushing toward crisis medicine. Generally speaking, medicine is rewarding to practitioners who are the most specialized and the most professionally qualified. Disease is interesting in a way that health is not. In a system full of doctors but without paying customers, crises get more attention than does routine care. Crises evoke "heroic" interventions in a male-dominated profession and are part of the struggle of life against death in which doctors are the field marshals.

Another good reason for crisis medicine is that it maintains the power of doctors in any conflict or dispute. If lives are at stake, the doctor's authority is supreme. If patients are flat on their backs while doctors are steady on their feet, not much argument can ensue. *Patient* comes from the Latin *pati,* "to suffer." Our roles are to suffer patiently;

the doctors' is to decide. Recent scandals, especially at the Bristol Royal Infirmary, where many children died during high-risk operations, could not have occurred without this tradition of absolute command during crises. Crisis intervention also maintains medical specialization, since one part of the body usually gives way first. Unfortunately, good overall health is not subdivided: A cure in one specialty will often cause symptoms handled by another, and you start to make the rounds of hospital departments.

The problem with focusing more on crisis medicine is that you lose sight of one of the mainstays of a healthy, long, and zestful life, which is to *avoid getting ill in the first place* and, if possible, avoid going to the hospital, where disease entities inevitably congregate. It is for this reason that BUPA puts prime emphasis on *wellness*. Val Gooding explains that there is only one way out of this bind (posed by finite resources and infinite demand): People must take responsibility for their own health and lifestyles. By "take responsibility" she does not mean only "take out medical insurance," although that is obviously vital to BUPA. She also means taking responsibility for how you live—your diet, exercise, stress levels, and way of work—and doing the same for those you love. BUPA is actively committed to wellness. This is not just a state of wholeness involving mind, body, and environment; wellness is independence of living, a personal commitment to remaining able to make your own choices.

Of course, wellness is an elusive term. Ill people have stereotypical diagnostic symptoms that easily lend themselves to classification. In contrast, the ways of wellness are many and varied. Those who dare to describe them are easily dismissed as quacks. Those ways are influenced by fashion—like most lifestyles—and easy to discredit as fashions change. The invocation of holistic health means that many different variables are included, and so precision tends to suffer. BUPA's *Guide to Healthy Living* resembles a magazine supplement. Health consciousness can, in other hands, become narcissistic and self-indulgent.

From all these objections, however, there can be salvaged a central truth: Health grows out of personal commitments through yourself to others, especially family members and coworkers. In short, health is a *stance*, not just a safety net, a demand, an entitlement guaranteed by the government—not even just a restorative to be used when your lifestyle has let you down. Health begins, paradoxically, with a determination *not* to suffer patiently but instead to engage, while on your feet, those who can help prevent illness in the first place. It is there that BUPA is strong and the NHS is woefully weak. Indeed, in a curious way, a crisis bureaucracy *needs* you to be helpless. Instead of rewarding those who rise above their condition, systems based on welfare psychology tend to punish such fitness. Hence, a seven-year-old amputee and sufferer from meningitis hopped on his remaining leg with such cheerfulness and energy that he was nominated for a Child of Courage award, yet the child benefits agency stopped his mobility allowance, leaving his single mother without a car to supervise his hopping. Welfare and crisis systems have difficulty working *with* the process of recovery rather than against it. The system affords incentives to prolong crises.

BUPA started its sixth business unit, Wellness, in 1999 to provide services to both personal and corporate customers. The unit combined a new acquisition, Barbican Healthcare, with BUPA's existing health screening and occupational health activities, providing health assessments and screening at over 50 medical facilities around the United Kingdom. Up-to-date screening devices include a bone-density scanner to detect early signs of osteoporosis (in which bones become brittle and break easily), the cardiorespiratory exercise bike test, and a resting electrocardiography machine. Over 60,000 people have had problems detected in time for early treatment.

It is perhaps in the corporate sector that the greatest opportunities lie. It should not be too difficult to prove that employees who share a vision, an exciting strategy, or a superordinate goal have better reasons for reporting to work every day and work more creatively as a result. Health is above all a state of mind. Those who can locate themselves in a context of meaning that transcends their own lives have that much more to live for.

You can start modestly with occupational health and then add, one by one, the variables that make a difference. You might well end up with a corporation, not unlike BUPA, in which case the model you seek to build is already within you. You begin with "saving on absenteeism" and end with the meanings of work itself, and the more meanings you find, the healthier and more effective the workplace becomes.

The two axes of Dilemma 4 are *responses to medical crises* and *wellness as preventive medicine*. Britain is currently biased toward responding to crises—hence the location of the X.

Dilemma 4: Responses to Medical Crises versus Wellness as Preventive Medicine

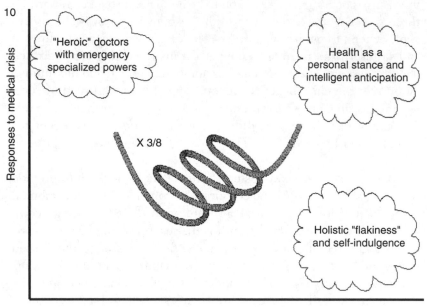

It is important, when moving from BUPA's position at the top left, not to fall into the trap of health fads or that of believing that your mental state can "conquer" all illness. The right response to crises, which we all face before we die, is intelligent anticipation of inevitable failings. You do not ignore crises; you act to preclude and delay them. That is why the helix is counterclockwise: first prevention and then a timely response that prevents the worst. Health is a stance that invites your body to sustain you until necessary activities are complete.

Dilemma 5. Nationally Based Services versus Globally Expanded Services

A final reason that either the personal or the group insurance model might prevail is that the world of medicine, although slower to global-ize than other industries, is at last doing so. While the NHS concen-trates on its mandate to serve British citizens and tourists at a price, BUPA is engaged in some 180 countries around the world. It can mobi-lize world resources at the behest of its members, and many of those members are foreigners to the United Kingdom.

Gooding is articulate on this subject: "Globalization is upon us. There are giant health insurers 'out there,' and before too long our members will be able to purchase their operations anywhere, while the members of other insurers will buy them from us. Already there are people flying to India for cataract operations, because even with the airfare, it costs less. Waiting lists are shorter in France, and British patients could attempt to make appointments there. When the Internet gets properly utilized, there will be a giant market for various procedures, and Europe, which outspends the United Kingdom on health, is sure to attract many customers."

She goes on to say that BUPA is importing more nurses from overseas, and once again, it has the advantage of its existing foreign contacts and operations. The weakness of the NHS is in ancillary staff and those able to look after the frail, not necessarily the ill. BUPA hopes to be able to remedy skill shortages by importing key staff in various fields.

BUPA International recently undertook an £8.5 million relaunch, including a Web site with on-line price quotations and with enrollment and claims forms for brokers. Bill Ward, general manager of BUPA International, made the following pedge: "Wherever you are in the world, whatever time of day, we are seven seconds away, and we will deliver on our promise. If you're in trouble, we will get you out."

BUPA now has 4 million customers worldwide and assesses 4000 requests a week from 180 countries. Much of the international coverage is done through multinational businesses concerned about getting expatriates home in emergencies. Even so, there are 115 nationalities among BUPA members, and there are many foreign companies with activities in the United Kingdom. Since 1989 BUPA has owned Sanitas in Spain, with 830,000 insurance customers and a capacity for 135,000 accident-and-emergency admissions. A joint venture with the Primal Group in Mumbai (Bombay) runs a health-care services clinic in that city. There is an insurance joint venture with the Nazer Group in Saudi Arabia, and BUPA health-insurance companies exist in Thailand and Hong Kong.

Crucial to a global health system is "telematics," the means for communicating medical information between countries and hospitals and for obtaining readouts of members' medical histories. Telematics will allow procedures to be carried out safely in many parts of the world and will bring prices down through competitive tendering. If it plays its cards right, BUPA should be able to capitalize on some of these opportunities.

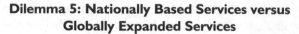

Dilemma 5: Nationally Based Services versus Globally Expanded Services

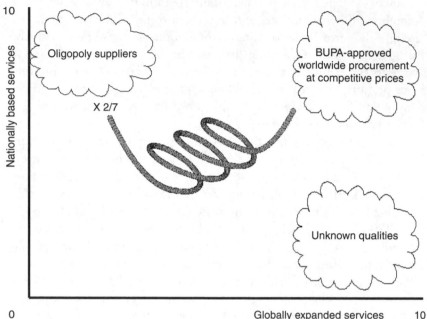

The problem is the relatively few (oligopolistic) suppliers for highly specialized British-based procedures. Hence, in the diagram of Dilemma 5, we have located BUPA as of 1998 at the X. The strategy, as the authors understand it, is to expand services globally while avoiding the purchase of items of unknown quality by means of rating procedures available on the Internet and by approving only the best and most reliable suppliers. Competition should make prices fall, and members could be offered the most appropriate procedures.

Dilemma 6. For-Profit Status versus Nonprofit Status

There is much ongoing speculation about whether "care" should or even could be effectively delivered by those seeking to make profits from it—profits that match the rising returns increasingly common in the British stock market. Should a "care home" yield a 25 percent profit to shareholders and have to compete with high-tech stocks and Internet companies "to make a killing"? When the customer is very old and frail or when investments in facilities take several years to pay off, some other corporate form would seem preferable to the shareholder-driven private company. For this reason BUPA has no shareholders but is a *provident association,* an interesting hybrid of for-profit and nonprofit status. It differs from a for-profit company by having no shareholders to demand their cut as a price for not raiding the company. But this condition does not mean that surpluses are not generated and cannot be reinvested in making the company more provident. In fact, BUPA is well positioned to acquire other companies in part *because* it has no shareholders to pay off and can use *all* of its surplus to expand and acquire. Nor is there any reason why BUPA cannot feature profitability or surpluses among its principal goals. Unlike the members of mutual societies, BUPA's members are not its owners, and so the company is free to invest where it chooses. Gooding regards provident status as a strong advantage, at least if she can furnish the stimulus for growth and risk that would otherwise come from shareholders. She explains that her problem has been how to get the sense of urgency and constant striving for improvement that shareholders often bring. BUPA can plow everything it earns into new investments, provided that the will is there and that the firm is determined to proceed along commercial lines. That is where she deems her predecessor so valuable. It did not always make him popular, but he turned BUPA into an organization that aimed to generate surpluses in order to succeed and expand.

In a provident association the customer is unambiguously the top priority, and because it takes high staff morale to keep customers happy, employees become the means of satisfying customers. Furthermore, a provident association can invest for the long term; BUPA has made investments in upgrading equipment and call centers that will take 10 years to justify themselves. Most stock companies, having impatient shareholders, cannot do that, which is why several in the elder care businesses recently quit. The short-term pressures on them were simply too great.

It takes time to build a genuine reputation for caring, but as a provident association, BUPA can afford to take the time to win customers and make that caring pay. But it's not all plain sailing: Provident companies can be laid-back, lazy, risk averse, and self-congratulatory about their noble intentions. BUPA's board has to take the role usually played by shareholders: to set targets, provide incentives, and get people to stretch their capacities. Yet Gooding can't do it with stock options, because BUPA has no stock. Therefore, she has to create a culture second to none, a place where people want to stay and to which they choose to give their working lives.

The dilemma looks like this:

Dilemma 6: For-Profit Status versus Nonprofit Status

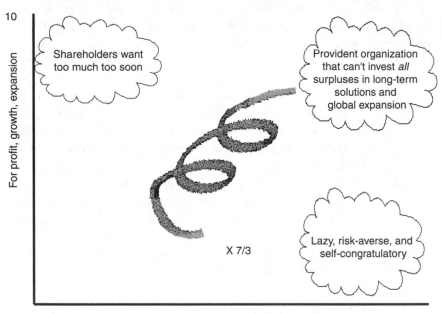

Gooding has taken BUPA from roughly the vicinity of the X, as a company that is somewhat risk averse and too noble of intention to try hard to succeed, into being a company eager to grow as fast as its success allows, with no need to pause for private enrichment, but dedicated to worldwide customers and willing to invest in its long-term welfare. It is a vision of capitalism serving social ends in which the human meaning of the work is its own reward and all join in celebrating the one life we have in common.

Sadly, Val Gooding is the only woman leader with a chapter in this book. Women leaders will not, in the authors' view, ever "make it" by being exclusively kind, gentle, and compassionate. Business is too predatory. But they will and can succeed by reconciling hard and soft, by possessing and expressing an iron will, and by exerting a relentless push to care deeply and sincerely for their customers. Val Gooding has toughened her compassion with hoops of steel, and she has brought closer the day when "nice gals finish first."

With What Results?

The 1990s was a mixed decade for BUPA, but since Gooding's arrival, things have been looking up. By 1999 the company had turned a profit, staff morale had soared, and BUPA had hit the acquisition trail. The firm's newspaper, *BUPA TODAY,* carried the following editorial written by Val Gooding:

"We have seen the first-quarter results for 2000, and we are on course to meet the challenging targets we have set for this year.... Profits are up, and there is no dividend to be paid. I was able to tell the annual general meeting that through the hard work of our people, all BUPA business units are doing well in their markets."

Chapter 10

———◆———

Pioneering the New Organization: Jim Morgan, Applied Materials

Fons Trompenaars, Peter Prud'homme, Jae Ho Park, and Charles Hampden-Turner

*F*ONS TROMPENAARS WAS fortunate enough to be invited to the Applied Materials Quarterly Global Management Meeting in Palo Alto, California, in 1997. Applied Materials is the world's largest manufacturer of semiconductor-producing equipment, the machines that make the circuits. It is also the most transcultural company we have ever encountered, a microcosm of world cultures. The authors have a broad experience of American "global" companies; many are American at the core and foreign only at the fringes. Even when group photographs are taken, the foreigners gravitate to the edges of the picture; the beards and darker countenances surround the paler center. Here, however, everything was different. The core management team spoke English in a variety of accents. President Dan Mayden was an Israeli scientist. Chairman Jim Morgan was an American business executive. Korean and Japanese officials were prominent. In all, the top 50 managers represented 30 different nations.

We sought an interview with Jim Morgan, chairman and chief executive officer (CEO). We wanted to know what it feels like to bestride such a high degree of global diversity. How does one lead such a mosaic of nations, such a cosmopolitan mix of talent? What he had to tell us is described under the following heads:

1. The history of Applied Materials
2. The transcultural reach of Applied Materials
3. What Applied Materials learned from East Asian cultures and the resulting core values
4. A value-driven corporation
5. Reconciling seven paradoxes
   a. Errors and corrections
   b. Extensive participation with satisfied customers: quick decisions and high efficiency
   c. Excellent technology and effective production outcomes
   d. Local fit and global reach
   e. Stable continuity and flexible change
   f. Growing bigger yet remaining small
   g. Leaping up and diving down

The History of Applied Materials

Think about it—Applied Materials touches almost everyone's life. Every time you log on to a personal computer (PC), surf the Internet, send an e-mail, or make a call on a cell phone, you use technology made possible by Applied Materials' chip-making equipment. Applied Materials makes the systems that make the chips that make the products that change the world; that's why the company says, "The Information Age Starts Here."

When Applied Materials was founded in 1967 in Santa Clara, California, it started with five employees and a little over $100,000. Companies in the budding semiconductor industry preferred to build their own manufacturing equipment in-house and treated their systems as proprietary, and so Applied Materials started by supplying them with materials and components for their homegrown systems. The problem with those systems, however, was that no two were alike—or performed alike—yet in semiconductor manufacturing uniformity and reliability are essential. Seizing the opportunity, the founders of Applied Materials began offering turnkey chip-making systems with performance guarantees based on rigorous testing in the company's laboratory. That led to more standardization of the manufacturing process, revolutionizing the semiconductor industry.

The strategy paid off. By 1972 the company was shipping systems to every major semiconductor manufacturer in the open markets of the world. That year, with sales of $6.3 million and 155 employees, Applied Materials, Inc., made its first public stock offering.

During the 1970s Applied Materials continued to broaden its markets and diversify its product line, stretching its resources dangerously thin. As the new CEO of the company in 1977, James C. Morgan refocused Applied Materials on its core business: semiconductor manufacturing equipment. The timing was just right.

In 1980 Dr. Dan Maydan joined the company from the prestigious AT&T Bell Laboratories. Following him were Drs. Sasson Somekh and David N. K. Wang. This trio developed and commercialized many successful innovations, beginning with the Precision Etch 8100 and 8300 Hexode Etcher. In 1987 the company marked its twentieth anniversary with what industry observers hailed as "the most successful product introduction in the history of the semiconductor equipment industry": the first of the Precision 5000 series of single-wafer, multichamber processing systems. In 1989 Applied Materials reported annual revenues of over $500 million, and in 1990 the company broke into the ranks of the Fortune 500. On March 3, 1993, the first-built Precision 5000 was inducted into the Smithsonian Institution's permanent collection of Information Age technology, next to the first transistor and the first semiconductor chip.

In 1992 Applied Materials became the top manufacturer of semiconductor equipment in the world, and it has held that position ever since. In support of manufacturing efforts, the Austin Volume Manufacturing Center became the volume manufacturing site for the company. With over 1 million square feet of dedicated manufacturing space, the site produces nearly 90 percent of the company's products. In further recognition of the company and its leadership, James C. Morgan, chairman and CEO, was the recipient of the 1996 National Medal of Technology, America's highest honor for technological innovation, awarded by the President of the United States.

Distinction is also given to the company through frequent rankings as a well-managed organization and an employer of choice. *Fortune* magazine rates Applied Materials as one of America's most admired companies as well as one of the 50 best companies for the employment of Asians, blacks, and Hispanics. *Fortune* also highlights Applied Materials as one of the 100 best companies to work for in America. Today the company's worldwide sales, service, manufacturing, and technology-development capabilities remain unrivaled in the semiconductor-equipment industry. Forecasts indicate that the markets it serves will continue to develop in the new millennium. Applied Materials is positioned to grow right along with those markets.

The Transcultural Reach of Applied Materials

In addition to corporate facilities in Santa Clara, Applied Materials maintains research, development, and manufacturing centers in the United States, Israel, Europe, and Japan as well as technology centers in South Korea and Taiwan. To support a growing worldwide customer base, sales and service offices are located in the United States, Europe, Israel, Japan, South Korea, Taiwan, Singapore, and the People's Republic of China.

In 1997 Applied Materials entered the metrology and inspection market by acquiring Opal, Inc., and Orbot Instruments in Israel and integrated them into its Process Diagnostics and Control Group. AKT in Japan (formerly a joint venture with Komatsu), which produces fabrication systems for flat-panel displays, has been fully owned by Applied Materials since 1999. Applied Materials employs 13,000 people worldwide in more than 95 locations in 14 countries. Financial highlights for fiscal year 1998 showed net orders of $3.1 billion, revenue of $4.0 billion, net income of $230.9 million, and ongoing net income of $437 million. Investment in research, development, and engineering in 1998 was $643.9 million.

Applied Materials' 1998 worldwide sales demonstrate its global capability: Sales in North America yielded 38 percent of its revenue; Japan, 17 percent; Taiwan, 20 percent; Europe, 16 percent; South Korea, 4 percent; and Asia-Pacific (China and Singapore), 5 percent.

What Applied Materials Learned from East Asian Cultures and the Resulting Core Values

The first foreign market Applied Materials engaged with and learned from was Japan. At the time Japan was the major threat to U.S. economic hegemony, at once the culture most different from that of America and the most successful culture among those of East Asia. Since the 1980s the threat from Japan has been somewhat lessened, but that from the Chinese diaspora (Singapore, Hong Kong, Malaysia, Taiwan, etc.) has become considerably greater. Morgan is not just a CEO but an author. He wrote *Cracking the Japanese Market* in 1991 with his son Jeff Morgan and has since switched his focus to the burgeoning economies of East Asia generally.

Globalizing ideally should start with those cultures most *unlike* your own. If a U.S. company can "crack" the way those cultures think, despite the fact that their views are virtually the logical opposites of its own, differences found in Europe, the Indian subcontinent, Latin America, and the Middle East are unlikely to shake the company's composure. Japan, a culture the early Jesuit missionaries deemed "devilish" because of its contrariness to their own views, is an acid test of cross-cultural sophistication. If you make it in Japan, much of the rest of the world will hold fewer challenges in comparison.

Scores obtained by using the TH-T data base for the United States, Canada, and Northwestern Europe on the one hand and for Japan, Singapore, Hong Kong, China, and Malaysia on the other hand are summarized in Box 1-1 in Chapter 1 for all seven of our dimensions detailed in Chapters 1 and 2. It can be seen at a glance that the scores for most of the world fall between the scores of the United States and those of Japan. To "crack Japan" was not simply to come to terms with America's foremost competitor but to span some of the widest cultural divergences on record.

Morgan's book is perhaps the most insightful account of Japan written by a working foreign executive. He likens the Japanese market to the fugu, or blowfish, a delicacy served at only a few select restaurants that have been licensed by the government to prepare the fish for eating. The reason for this is that the blowfish has poison-secreting glands that must be removed carefully before cooking and serving. If you do not know the fish well, you can do yourself great harm. If you know and understand it, you derive great benefit. Morgan sees fugu as a metaphor for the impact of Japanese culture on American corporations.

"Fugu can be used as a symbol for the Japanese market," he explains. "When approached properly, it is a market that offers great opportunity for wealth, but approached improperly and without care, a venture in Japan can prove ruinous." Applied Materials' Japanese adventure began as early as 1979. In those early days it was a relatively small company ($42.6 million in sales), the first wholly foreign-owned company to secure funding from the Japanese Development Bank. But once the company was in, the momentum was unstoppable: Applied Materials rode the wave of Japan's 1980s economic miracle, leading the huge expansion of the electronics sector, which spearheaded and underpinned that nation's prodigious record of growth.

Finding himself at the very center of Japan's catch-up strategy, playing a crucial part in the effectiveness of chip manufacturers nationally, Morgan received a crash course in what it meant to be an insider:

working within government "guidance" in producing chips, "the rice of industry," to the highest possible specification in order to create "mechatronics," the fusion of mechanical engineering with electrical engineering. Morgan learned, for example, that instead of the customer "coming first" or being "always right," *the customer was God.* Morgan had a bond of trust and service not just with specified chip producers but with *their* customers and with Japanese chip users as a whole. As a typical "horizontal technology" (a technology cutting across the economy as a whole and used in many industries), chips constituted the infrastructure of the economy itself, the yeast in the rapid rise of the economic cake.

Morgan observes: "The Japanese use the word *anshin* (trust from the heart) to describe the type of relationship they want to have with their suppliers and business partners.... Vendors are loyal to their customer, and in return they receive loyalty back. Japanese customers are much more demanding in terms of expectations of quality, service, and delivery schedules. The relationship is an ongoing process of problem solving and opportunity creation. What the Japanese look for in a supplier is the strength of the company that makes its personal history and track record." Whereas in the United States a customer typically will run suppliers against each other and create a relationship with the winner, in Japan you first create the relationship and then pressure your partner to turn in a winning performance. This pattern is common in East Asia, Southern Europe, and Latin America.

Morgan explains how Applied Materials used its Japanese experience to cement relations around the world: "We have since used the relationship model to build relationships with other customers throughout the world. Applied Materials has been successful by globalizing what we've learned from competing in Japan." Applied Materials also learned from its Japanese experiences to improve its relationships with its own suppliers. Part of this is the notion that it is the customer's responsibility to help the supplier achieve excellence. The Trompenaars Hampden-Turner group responsible for this book has benefited from Applied Materials' relationship philosophy. Morgan is thinking of a new book called *Cracking the Asian Market,* detailing how the lessons learned in Japan can be applied more widely, especially in China's huge market.

South Korea was another crucial lesson for Morgan and for Applied Materials. In some respects South Korea outdoes Japanese expectations. For example, South Koreans expect discounts from list prices for their own "particular" company, a variation of universalism (same price for everyone) versus particularism (special price for friends). Koreans also expect free service and training support until the machines supplied are being used effectively. If you have not factored these costs into your initial offer, you are in trouble. Applied Materials Korea (AMK) sold only two or three machines during its initial sales pitch, but it sold hundreds once it had figured out how to offer discounts and give support. Between them, just two South Korean companies—Hyundai and Samsung—produce 40 percent of all DRAMs sold on world markets. It pays more to get close to them than to anyone else! South Korea's export of semiconductors has passed $20 billion, and semiconductors are its single biggest export product.

In East Asia relationships last a lifetime, and when a local economy is in trouble, you discover who your friends really are. During the Japanese recession of 1985–1986 employees of Applied Materials Japan (AMJ) were assigned to more prospering regions of the globe instead of being laid off or dismissed. In the Korean recession of 1998 this pattern was repeated; furthermore, Young I. Lee, president of AMK, avoided many layoffs by increasing training and development budgets. A time of slack demand was an opportunity to learn as well as to bounce back from the recession with renewed vigor.

It did not take long for Morgan to discover that foreign companies in East Asia, especially firms from the West, had a reputation as fair-weather friends, and so he determined that Applied Materials would be different. Semiconductors are not a product for on-again, off-again investment. East Asians continue to produce these products even during times of loss, because electronics undergirds industry in general and renders more profitable any product with an advanced chip inside it. East Asian economies therefore continue to make semiconductors for the leverage this gives to all their industries and do not insist that every product pay for itself.

Applied Materials' work is therefore essential to these entire economies, and it is crucial that the company be seen as a rock of reliability and a steadfast ally of Korea, Japan, Singapore, and the other Asian Tigers, as well as of the companies actually involved. Morgan hates to see them making chips at a loss and tries to reward their persistence by steadily increasing quality and decreasing costs. He can make these heroic efforts because the mutuality of commitments is so strong: "We try to do a good job so that they do not feel the pressure to [manufacture at no profit]. That's why we put so much emphasis on being a local company and a loyal friend, a committed supplier who hangs in there in good times and bad. With our global view, our low cost structure, and our breadth of technical understanding, we can really help them."

A Value-Driven Corporation

Morgan sees the company as being driven by values, certain attributes that grow stronger over time and are subject to continuous increase, and by paradoxes requiring resolution, which we will address in the next section. Here we will deal with the values that power Applied Materials' global success.

Applied Materials, Morgan insists, must *demonstrate world-class performance in everything it does.* But that is possible only if Applied Materials *keeps very close to the customer,* who defines what its "performance" must accomplish and whether it has been delivered. A final value is *practicing mutual trust and respect* in a world of multiple sources of expertise. Applied Materials has to be good so that its customers can produce superlative products, allowing the industries using those semiconductors to succeed. Applied Materials' own success depends on the success of those it supplies, on the success of the customer's customer's customer. Mutual trust and respect integrate the improving performances of all suppliers and customers, who succeed in combination, not separately. Applied Materials strives continuously to adopt the principle of carefully listening to one another trying to understand different perspectives.

The aim of the Total Solutions approach is to provide a "total solution" to the customer's problems—one that can then be used by the customer to focus on its own customers: "We strive to walk the talk of these values every day in our Total Solutions approach, to systematically meet our customers' needs worldwide. In 1998 our team focused like a laser beam on leveraging every one of our assets to the benefit of our customers, through Total Solutions. At Applied Materials, Total Solutions is expressed in our innovation, product line breadth, equipment productivity, human and intellectual capital, and global service and support."

Asked what characteristics his company would need in the twenty-first century, Morgan answered at length: "In the twenty-first century and the evolving Internet economy, leadership companies will have to develop a core set of success characteristics to survive and win. Let's consider some of these elements. First, you will have to be global. Applied Materials led the way in going global because we realized early on that the Information Age has no borders. This revolution is about borders and walls falling down to allow the free flow of ideas, people, and capital. So while many companies, including some much larger than us, are just now grappling with globalization and all that that entails, we've been global for decades.

"Second, you must be lean and fast. The accelerating pace of change, particularly in our industry, and the unpredictability of markets mean there is less time for correcting errors and no time for hesitation; because narrow windows of opportunity are open only briefly, you can't let yourself be too heavy to squeeze through.

"Third, in the Internet economy you must be knowledge based. This means unlocking and using all the knowledge that resides within your team and your global organization. At Applied Materials we're working full time to connect all the centers of excellence we've already developed—in product, support, and regional organizations. Further, we are linking to our customers and our suppliers to help them and help Applied Materials. The goal is to build an Internet-fast knowledge organization that uses all its global knowledge to meet customer needs.

"This leads me to a subject I'm going to be talking about in this millennium. As we change the world and the world changes around us—as change accelerates and markets move faster—our products must move from imagination to production in ever-shorter time frames. In the Internet economy of the twenty-first century business success will depend on a company's ability to demonstrate leadership in times of change—the ability to thrive on unceasing waves of change and the ability to both manage and capitalize on rapid change. The new global economy offers both unparalleled market opportunity and risk. As Asia's boom and gloom have shown us, the global market can be rich and volatile. Driven by the instant information of the Internet, the global economy rewards speed, resilience, and, most of all, courage. In this new world where capital, information, and goods flow almost friction-free, the old rules of the physical economy apply less and less.

"Leadership companies in the fast new global economy will need to compete on speed, innovation, and differentiation. Those organizations which can't keep up, and which aren't creative, will have to compete primarily on cost. The upending of the old physical economy means that many economies that once competed from regional strongholds or on brand loyalty will find themselves in a commodity gulag. Meanwhile, fast innovators will rewrite the rules. To avoid this pit, leadership companies will work to ensure that they are high-change companies in high-change industries. In the fast new economy now being born you will want to work for, partner with, and invest in companies with the ability to change, adapt, and grow—leveraging their fundamental strengths to take advantage of new opportunities. These companies will succeed because they have clear vision, a focused mission, shared values, an ability to deal with dilemmas and paradoxes, and a sense of unfolding history."

It is to these paradoxes and dilemmas that we now turn.

Reconciling Seven Paradoxes

Errors and Corrections

In a world where speed is crucial, you cannot wait to get everything right the first time. Fast learning involves pouncing on mistakes and improving fast. It involves reclassifying what was acceptable last month as unacceptable this month and doing better. Errors never go away, because the bar keeps rising and because you keep trying new things to see what works better. Another reason for being close to "godlike" customers is that you need their feedback to improve rapidly.

The successful corporation of the twenty-first century, according to Morgan, "will foster a culture that is resilient in the face of setbacks, [a quality that] also rewards success. They encourage taking risks and forgive failure, because mistakes will be inevitable in the new world. People will require emotional intelligence to survive disappointment and then rally quickly in the face of tough times. In a market of ideas, some will work spectacularly and some won't. It takes courage to live with your mistakes so as to transcend them and move on, learning as you go."

This dilemma can be diagrammed as follows:

Dilemma 1: Learning Fast through Mistakes

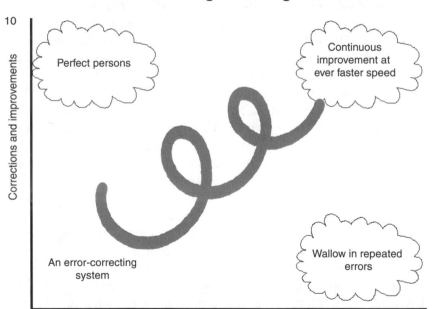

W. Edwards Deming, an American consultant whose ideas have been largely vindicated by Japanese auto manufacturers, showed how to set up error-correcting systems of continuous improvement and ever-rising standards. Every error is an opportunity to improve rather than the cause of shame or disgrace. People must be empowered to monitor and improve themselves, reflecting on their work and rethinking it. No one can be a perfect person (upper left in the diagram) the first time around, and there is insufficient time even to attempt this. At the same time, you should not wallow in repeated errors (lower right). The idea is *not* to avoid making the same mistake twice but to *learn*. We tend to learn fastest by making smaller and smaller mistakes, successively approximating to an ideal. This process is not without pain and emotional tensions are strong, but beyond this tension lies the capacity to improve continuously and even to redefine improvement.

Extensive Participation with Satisfied Customers: Quick Decisions and High Efficiency

The ideal of rapid decision making has an almost military flavor. When danger abounds, when emotions run high, when panic is a potential hazard, the clear voice of authority from field headquarters helps turn an army into a fighting weapon. There is no time for debate or hesitation. If decisions are delayed for even a matter of seconds, the day may be lost. Controversy is tantamount to indecision. Argument, in its power to sap morale, can amount to treachery.

Fortunately or unfortunately, the design and supply of machines for making semiconductors are on a level of complexity much higher than that of most battlefields. Moreover, those at the top do not have all the necessary information and have goals more elusive than winning at the expense of an opponent. They have to create multiple winners, not force losses on an adversary. You cannot help someone else "win" unless you know what that person's problems are and what his or her customers' problems are. The Total Solutions emphasized by Morgan are for the satisfaction of multiple players. Inevitably, those players must be consulted widely and must participate in decisions. So how do you make quick decisions while consulting and participating widely with interested parties? How do you maintain outstanding efficiency while satisfying multiple customers?

It certainly is not easy, but it is possible. The first point to grasp is that although customers have many varied concerns, the same themes recur: They *all* need to be as efficient and cost containing as they can.

Morgan explains: "We work for some of the best companies in the world: Intel, Samsung, IBM, and so on. Companies like these are increasingly looking to us to take a more active role in the totality of the manufacturing process because they trust us. With our global capabilities and their global reach, they continue to offer us more and more opportunities."

Applied Materials' industry is changing as the twenty-first century dawns: "First, chip making is increasingly process intensive: more circuits, more layers, more fabrication steps. As the semiconductor industry evolves toward future generations of smaller devices, using new materials such as copper and larger wafer sizes, our customers will demand that we provide a broader set of innovative solutions that add increased value. Worldwide, chip demand is growing, and so more Fabs are being built. One of the top priorities for chipmakers—our customers—is to maximize the return on their existing capital investments and contain operating costs. Applied Materials is committed to leading the way—and rightly so."

That particular solutions have been devised for other customers makes all of Applied Materials' customers concerned about staying abreast of developments. To lead or even survive in chip making, you must have up-to-date fabrication equipment at least as good as that of your competitors': "Because Applied Materials has the largest number of installed systems in the world, it represents a global standard of which customers dare not fall short. In an industry where the sale of a hundred systems is a major milestone, we recently celebrated the installation of the five-thousandth Precision 5000 system. Applied Materials systems reside in virtually every production Fab in the world."

Customers have a huge stake in the equipment already installed in their fabs: "Therefore, we are making an all-out commitment to protecting our customers' sizable investment in our family of advanced products.... Perhaps the most significant issue our industry [is facing] is the changing relationship between chipmakers and equipment makers. Given the scale of their opportunity and the speed at which they must perform, our customers are increasingly focusing on their core capabilities as their key source of advantage. They bear down on chip design, architecture, and engineering, and they look to us for solutions in the manufacturing process. Our history shows that over time customers have asked equipment companies to take responsibility for more and more aspects of the chip-making process, thus increasing our market. And today we see that trend accelerating. In effect, we are becoming process partners in the business of chip making.

"This is the most fundamental and important shift in the past 30 years of our industry. With the pressures they are under to perform and compete, chipmakers today can afford—and should expect—no less than total solutions from their process partners. First, provide a set of unique process solutions. Second, make systems that work reliably and back them up around the world. Third, design compatible products that work together and can be integrated. Fourth, invest mightily in leading-edge capabilities to keep solving new customer problems. In short, Total Solution products are unique, cost effective, compatible, and, increasingly, integratable. And they are fully supported on a worldwide basis for maximum uptime performance. We have been the first to recognize what our customers need in this most dynamic, demanding, and fluid of markets—and the first to offer solutions to them."

The dilemma or paradox that Morgan is describing can be diagrammed as follows:

Dilemma 2: Organizing the Race

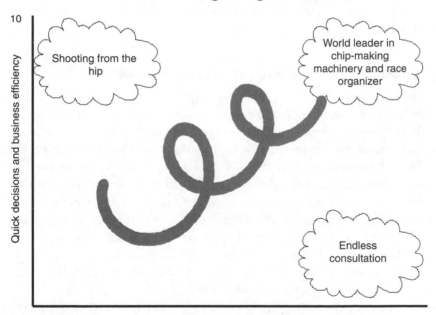

Applied Materials moves from consulting widely among top world competitors to designing Total Solutions that will upgrade the chip-making race in general. Because of its ready access to the most creative chip designers in the world, the company has unprecedented and unmatched levels of knowledge about how global competition is shaping up—about who is winning and why. You cannot create a machine for fabricating a superchip without knowing its design, purpose, and performance. Hence, Applied Materials has a grandstand view of the race for global supremacy in different forms of chip making. It is in the position of a coach helping most of the contestants in a race and is even virtually the race organizer who provides the contestants with their equipment. It is as if many competing vehicles in the Grand Prix or Indy 500 had the same constructor and were competing for her time and attention. Applied Materials is in a *very* strong position.

Its high level of extensive participation is what informs the company's swift decision making and upgrades the efficiency of its machines. Because chips can be designed for cheaper and higher-quality manufacturing, Applied Materials soon becomes an expert on design and a consultant on manufacturability. The real secret of combining participation with decision making and combining consultation with efficiency is *leadership*. Having consulted widely, you discover who and what is best and learn that key performance standards, which you make your own, lead the industry.

Excellent Technology and Effective Production Outcomes

From a strictly legal point of view Applied Materials supplies the technologies of manufacturing to customer specifications. If customers misuse, misunderstand, or misapply that technology, thereby failing to derive the full benefit from it, that could be considered *their* lookout, but Applied Materials does not operate that way. Its responsibility does not end with world-class technology or even a conceptual solution. It ends when customers can use their new equipment to the limit of its powers. Applied Materials has completed its success only when the customer has achieved a successful production outcome and the Fab is up and running with a record high yield (the proportion of silicon not wasted). This is necessary because billion-dollar Fabs are involved that are capable of catastrophic loss or soaring success. Because chips are the intelligence in several hundred varieties of product, it might well be that nothing less than national economic priorities and strategies are at stake. If the chip fails, so does "the food chain" for countless products. Chips are a "catalytic" technology, the secret ingredient that transforms a product's value by rendering it responsive to its environment and capable of communicating information.

It is necessary to distinguish product innovation from process innovation. If a product is innovative, it may have to be manufactured in a new way, and that can vitiate its value, but even if the *product* is not new, an innovative way of *manufacturing* it can create a substantial cost advantage. Process innovation involving a reduction in the number of manufacturing steps is one of East Asia's principal advantages. Applied Materials concentrates on Total Solutions that actually work in situ. As Morgan puts it, "Our customers have voted for our solutions by making us the leader in etch, metallization, thermal processes, chemical mechanical polishing, and installed base support services and by supporting our efforts in emerging markets. In our industry it takes quite a while to develop a new technology, and we are trusted for that persistence by our customer partners in business. Applied Materials' success is very much based on our ability to translate these developments into operations, and we have been better able than many of our competitors to commercialize it."

The dilemma that is resolved here can be diagrammed as follows:

Dilemma 3: Responsibility for Outcomes

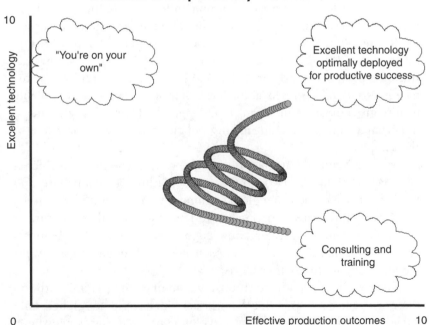

We see from the diagram that it is not enough to supply superb equipment that operates to specifications: You and your customer assume joint responsibility for how well that equipment works and the outcome it achieves. The customer has to be able to exploit innovation, not just be in receipt of it, and making the whole system operational is an aim to which Applied Materials is dedicated.

This is similar to the specificity-diffusion distinction introduced in Chapter 1. The excellence of the machinery has been specified in advance, and the machinery either meets or fails to meet those specifications. But *actually making the machinery work* is a much broader, more diffuse process that includes person-machine interfaces and effective human adaptation to new work routines. Customers feel genuinely supported when Applied Materials' acceptance of responsibility extends to jointly determined outcomes.

Local Fit and Global Reach

How does Applied Materials succeed in constantly extending its global reach while simultaneously improving its local fit? Can a company be sufficiently diverse to solve each region's particular problems and at the same time pursue a global strategy of offering the best to all comers? One answer is to have powerful regional influences. Young I. Lee, head of Applied Materials Korea, showed his courage early in life by crossing the demilitarized zone (DMZ) between North and South Korea on his own as a young man. Very much a national celebrity, he has attracted top talent to work for AMK. AM Japan has been similarly fortunate in attracting strong local leadership, which is not always available to foreign companies in Japan. It is Applied Materials' key strategic importance in regional chip-making policies that attracts top talent to the company.

Applied Materials' attitude toward the various countries in which it is engaged is that every country has something to contribute and lessons to teach to the wider global community. You learn "chip making as infrastructure transformation" from East Asia as well as the pursuit by whole nations of greater knowledge intensity—an old Mandarin value. (China had a civil service chosen *on merit*, through written examinations, four centuries after Christ.)

The Israeli semiconductor industry is among the most innovative in the world, and so what is "local" to Israel today could be "global" only a few years from now. Every new development has to start somewhere, and it is through this diversity of "somewheres" that Applied Materials keeps ahead of its competitors and in touch with new departures. With the acquisition of Opal and Orbot in 1996, Applied Materials gained direct access to Israeli research and development (R&D). Morgan observed: "We learned so much in Japan and now apply it in all other, much less complex corners of our business. I think Israel comes in a good second in complexity."

Imitating Japan and Korea does not mean that America has gotten it wrong; it means that there may be one strategy for early-developing, pioneer economies such as Britain and the United States and quite another for a late-developing, catch-up economy. Certainly, semiconductors and electronics are major targets for catch-up economies. Applied Materials' aim is to be effective in the circumstances faced by different kinds of economies, using different strategies for fast economic development. The chip world is in a "learning race" mentored by Applied Materials.

We asked Morgan how he had developed his broad cultural tastes and appreciation for diversity. "It might have to do with my early managerial and business exposure," he answered. "I was working as a manager in the seasonal food and agriculture business. I had to supervise people twice my age, and I learned two important lessons. First, never judge people on their age, gender, or racial background, only on how they add value. Second, look at how individuals fit into larger teams. Complementarity is of the utmost importance. That is perhaps why I have a management team of so much diversity. I learned how to make tough decisions when being young, around those crucial issues."

This brings us to a crucial issue in reconciling globalism and localism. Slogans are not enough. "Act locally, think globally" is a cliche by now, as Morgan sees it. You can talk "glocal," but talk by itself will not conjure the synthesis of globalism with localism into reality. What is needed are *transnational teams* that knit together local contributions and global trends. The importance of teams is that they place diverse people in close, face-to-face relationships. It follows that resolving conflicts on a team—say, between American and Japanese members—is a dress rehearsal for resolving conflicts between the two companies. The diversity within the team gives vital clues to the diversity between the companies, and because team members have a track record for successful cooperation, they usually can provide clues to what has gone wrong and find agreed-upon solutions to problems. The relationship at the very top of Applied Materials between President Dan Mayden, an Israeli, and CEO Jim Morgan, an American, is international in itself.

A cross-cultural team is at its best a microcosm of the diversity within the company. If the team can reconcile its own conflicts, there is at least a chance that it can mediate successfully in more attenuated relationships between remote sites. The team also symbolizes the fact that agreement is possible when people take the trouble to get to know each other—in other words, cultural conflicts are the result of ignorance and misconceptions, not an everlasting chasm between values. A transcultural team also admits all concerned to the status of "insider." There are no outcasts. It is of considerable significance that the cross-cultural team is *at the top* of the organization, an example to all the subordinates.

The dilemma looks like this:

Dilemma 4: Generalizing Local Discoveries

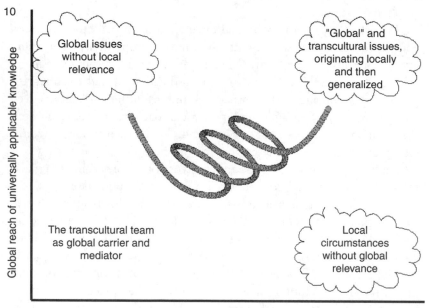

Morgan emphasizes the importance both of local circumstances that cannot be generalized (lower right in the diagram) and of global issues without relevance to local circumstances (upper left). But once one has categorized both of these, there remain issues that originated in particular localities yet can now be globalized as well as global issues that are still underexploited in particular localities. No doubt all customers are different, but not all customers are equally effective and successful. Applied Materials is in the enviable position of being able to discover the difference that makes the difference and to inform everyone who still wants to learn. Every culture wants to succeed in its own way, but these "ways" do not all lead to the best results. Applied Materials helps various cultures "keep score" and discover the strengths as well as the weaknesses of their cultural values. No wonder so many different accents are found at the heart of Allied Materials (an observation made in the introduction to this book).

Stable Continuity and Flexible Change

Morgan understands that, paradoxically, you must change if you want to remain the same and must pursue a stable continuity of core values if you want to experience continuous change. He elaborates on this theme: "In our business, change is a strategic weapon and change management is a survival imperative. The world that Applied Materials envisioned decades ago is now coming to pass—perhaps even faster than we imagined. While other, much larger, richer, more famous companies sweat through implementing change programs to deal with the coming new world, anticipating and preparing for change is already deeply wired into our culture, our thinking, and our strategies. Ours is a dynamic business, and that's the way it has to be. We're on the cutting edge. The semiconductor chip market has always been fast moving, and we've come to expect changes. We thrive on them. At Applied Materials we believe that change is the medium of opportunity."

In other respects, however, Applied Materials has to remain true to its core beliefs: always close to the customer, always technologically efficient, always learning from mistakes, and always practicing mutual trust and respect. Indeed, the more Applied Materials changes in some respects, the more it must remain the same in others.

Morgan believes that he knows the trajectories of change: more Fabs, more complexity, more responsibility for the supplier of manufacturing equipment. But some linear projections will not extrapolate as planned, and that is when you have to be flexible—to take Asian booms and busts in stride and hang in there with your customers. The more clear and definite your conjectures are, the more vivid and memorable is any refutation. Just as you learn from mistakes, you learn when your expectations do not pan out and must be revised. To be true to your own values through turbulent times is to keep your nerve and not go into shock. Cultures without values to which to be true are disintegrated by external change. Change is a great opportunity only to people and companies that know who or what they are and what they stand for.

We can diagram Morgan's fifth paradox as follows:

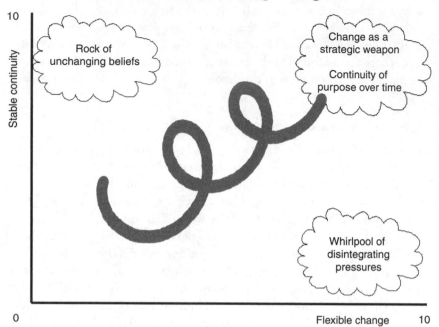

By steering between the rock of unchanging beliefs (upper left in the diagram) and the whirlpool of disintegrating pressures (lower right), Applied Materials uses change as a strategic weapon, maintaining a continuity of purpose over time and changing to preserve that continuity.

Growing Bigger yet Remaining Small

This is an industry in which size is a definite advantage. Morgan made the point clear: "In this industry you need to be big because you need a large amount of cash for R&D in order to be able to continuously introduce leading products, you need global service capability, you need to have an extensive product line, including full process modules, and so on. At the same time you need to be small to meet the customers' demands: be easy to deal with, be flexible, work with customers on their needs as if we were a small enterprise, be fast to react, and be able to deliver single systems as well. Because we are big *and* small, we have the capability for rapid introduction of leading products. Our message to the industry is clear: Applied Materials is the Total Solutions company.

With suites of interactive products covering six of the eight essential manufacturing steps, with a global support and service infrastructure, and with pacesetting investment in research, development, and engineering, Applied Materials is the leader in delivering total solutions worldwide—and we intend to remain so."

This fusion of bigness and smallness is achieved by means of *modularity*. The totality of Applied Materials' offerings can be broken down into modules, each one a Total Solution. Customers interface with a relatively small local supplier, of human scale, who can offer whatever module or combination of modules a particular customer wants. It is because Applied Materials has so many solutions to call on, through its sheer size, that it can customize offerings locally and behave like a small, friendly job shop to create just the solution that has been asked for. Customizing solution allows each business unit to exercise a high degree of autonomy: to have Koreans serving Koreans or Israelis serving Israelis while being able to draw on a global network of accumulated know-how.

The sixth dilemma looks like this:

Dilemma 6: Small Modules, Large Combinations

"Can giants learn to dance?" asks Rosabeth Moss Kanter, or are they doomed to trample on intimate, one-to-one, small-scale relationships? Perhaps this is the wrong question. The trick is create your "giant" out of hundreds of modules, each viable in its own right yet capable of joining with others in customized combinations. In this way you enjoy vast economies of scale and a wide variety of solutions while being able to get the best-fitting solutions to the customer in a personalized way. That small is beautiful is a common experience. We want service that is of human scale, but small by itself can be insignificant in global commerce. We want right-sized solutions from a corporation big enough to customize itself globally.

Leaping Up and Diving Down

We come finally to Jim Morgan's distinctive "porpoise-style" leadership. Is this also the reconciliation of a dilemma or paradox? It is. The most admired of Morgan's leadership traits is his strategic foresight and long-term planning abilities, but he is also capable of rapid tactical shifts and is the master of the moment. It is the combination of these traits that has stimulated rapid growth. "We are always among the first to enter and invest in potential new markets, which reflect our long-term business strategy," Morgan comments. "I respond to short-term crises not by throwing money at the problem but by asking, What business advantage to the firm can arise from this crisis? Where should we be positioned at the end of it?"

Morgan tries to take a "big-picture" view of the industry, looking from above and seeing far ahead. While doing this, he delegates responsibility downward and empowers his staff to act in his absence. Yet he also makes periodic plunges into the detailed workings of the company and examines key issues up close. This is less to check up on his subordinates than to learn (or reacquaint himself with) the fine details of the operation. "I have confidence in myself and our product," he says. "Hence, I feel comfortable delegating responsibility and empowering [my] staff... but this does not mean that I wash my hands of day-to-day minutiae and never examine [anything] up close. I ask many questions and look carefully at whether standards are being maintained. What I don't do is tell my staff how they should perform or operate. Rather, I look at the results, on occasion 'with a microscope.' It is this mix of a long, large view and short, sharp examinations that leads me to form generalizations that work on the ground in many concrete instances. I call this the porpoise style: diving into the business to stay close before gaining height once more. You can get a lot done in a hurry."

We can use this porpoise analogy to summarize all seven paradoxes, since Morgan is explaining to us how he moves in sequence up and down between two contrasting sets of values. (See the accompanying figure.)

X axis (a) Correcting (b) Quick deciding (c) Excellent technology (d) Global reach
(e) Continuity (f) Growing bigger

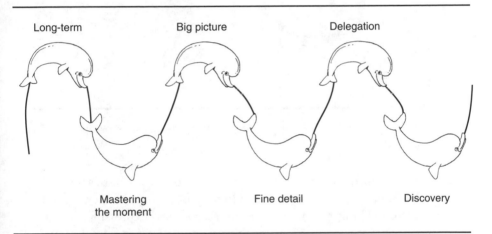

Long-term   Big picture   Delegation

Mastering   Fine detail   Discovery
the moment

Y axis (a) Erring (b) Participating (c) Effective outcomes (d) Local fit
(e) Flexible change (f) Remaining small

On the x axis, the vertical one in most of our diagrams, we see that Applied Materials corrects quickly, decides fast, excels in its technology, and so on; on the y axis, the horizontal one in most of our diagrams, we see that Applied Materials errs, participates, jointly seeks successful outcomes with customers, and so on. Jim Morgan, adopting a porpoise style, jumps and dives from one axis to the other.

We can, of course, express this dilemma in the same style as the other six:

Dilemma 7: Leaping and Diving

By constantly moving between the two axes, Morgan escapes both control freakery and having his head in the clouds. Indeed, the porpoise pattern of bobbing up and down is another way of expressing the virtuous circles or helices we have been using throughout this book. A frequency wave is a rolling circle.

Applied Materials exemplifies the unexpected 1990s renaissance of U.S. business. If the twentieth century was the American century, the twenty-first century is apparently going America's way, too. Morgan's company has shown its readiness to learn from Japan and East Asia faster than those regions have learned from the United States. This is a triumph of transcultural competence as well as of technology. Morgan has encompassed East Asian values in a more inclusive whole and has mastered this novel synthesis.

Chapter 11

———◆———

The Internet as an Environment for Business Ecosystems: Michael Dell, Dell Computers

Maarten Nijhoff Asser and Charles Hampden-Turner

THE COMPUTER INDUSTRY stands at the summit of the new "information economy." The future belongs to the enterprises that can receive, organize, distribute, and utilize information most effectively and swiftly.

As James F. Moore has pointed out, we have moved beyond competition and cooperation to the creation of business ecosystems—whole economic communities of interacting organizations and individuals. Informational goods and services are produced *by* and *for* ecosystem members. The most effective strategy is to position yourself near the center of the web or ecosystem and make your enterprise indispensable to its major transactions. As the ecosystem develops, its principal modes of transaction grow with it, often faster than the ecosystem itself grows. Wherever an enterprise is a node in a system, every new member increases nodal transactions, which grow exponentially. Thus, the tenth member of a group produces nine additional relationships, all of which may pass through the nodal enterprise. The quantum leap "beyond competition" looks like this:

Dilemma 1: The Emergence of Business Ecosystems

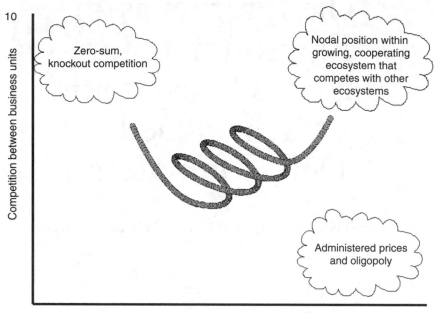

Note that competition and cooperation have jumped to a higher level of complexity. Whereas employees once cooperated *within* the firm to compete against those *outside* the firm, now the companies composing an ecosystem cooperate *within* that ecosystem to compete against *outside* ecosystems, which could even include replacements for the computer—not an impossible scenario. But unless such a challenge takes place, the computer industry will remain a powerful and burgeoning ecosystem. If we compare computer ownership with that of telephones and consider how much more versatile the computer is and its possible links with telephones, we see that computers could still grow massively, especially with the cost of millions of instructions per second (MIPS) falling year after year and Intel and Apple charging around half a dollar for each million instructions of capacity.

Also crucial is the convergence of telecommunications and content—for example, entertainment, education, business, and news—all of which will need computers to store a wealth of information. But the biggest catalyst for the spread of the computer is the Internet and the World Wide Web, which currently require computers to receive, store, and communicate information.

Michael Dell, the Successful Late Starter

Michael Dell took on the giants of the computer industry after making a late start and succeeded so spectacularly that Dell is now the world's number-two computer firm in terms of global sales. The company's growth has indeed been phenomenal even by the standards of a mercurial industry. It is a major player in a major market, and we shall show how it embraced fundamentally different rules of operation in order to flourish in a quickly changing marketplace. We shall examine Dell's approach to the new global economy in the light of the dimensions of culture and values and show how Dell brought about a grand reconciliation of seemingly opposing values to harness the true power of the new economy.

Short History of Dell Computer Corporation

Michael Dell founded Dell Computer Corporation in 1984 with $1000 of start-up capital and an idea unprecedented in the computer industry: bypassing the middleman and selling directly to the consumer. This was dubbed the Dell Direct Model. The idea caught on. Dell Computer Corporation is now one of the top vendors of personal computers. In 15 years company sales grew from $6 million to $25 billion. Dell now has sales offices in 33 countries and sells its products in 170 countries. It has manufacturing centers in the United States, the United Kingdom, Ireland, Malaysia, China, and Brazil. By 1995 shares of Dell stock, originally priced at $8.50 in 1984, were selling for $100.

The fundamental competitive advantages of the Dell Direct Model were enhanced by the advent of the Internet. In 1996 Dell customers were able to buy a Dell computer on the Internet. By 1997 company sales on the Internet reached $1 million per day. Also in 1997 Dell shipped its ten-millionth computer, and the per-share value of its common stock reached $1000 on a presplit basis. By 1999 sales on the Internet had reached $30 million per day, representing 40 percent of overall revenue.

Michael Dell is chairman and chief executive officer (CEO) of the company he founded. When the company was added to the Fortune 500 list in 1992, he became the youngest CEO of a company ever to earn such a ranking. His strong belief in the power of information technology to improve productivity and change entrenched methods of working has been the driving force behind the company. He realized early on that information was capable of changing the economic models of the new global era, and he was one of the first to latch on to the power of the Internet.

Dell's Direct Business Model

Because Michael Dell came late to the computer industry fray, he *had* to do something entirely different, something that would distinguish him from competitors and get around the fact that distributors were so stuffed full with rival products that to dislodge the major brands was an apparently insuperable task. It was not simply that channels of distribution were blocked; the seas of information, service, and support surrounding computing technology were ever more expansive. Even if distributors could make room for Dell products physically, could they absorb the additional information, service, and support; master it; and pass it on?

Michael Dell decided to bypass distributors entirely. He would sell directly to customers, establishing a unique advantage over other computer vendors and creating his own ecosystem apart from theirs. Direct selling had some crucial advantages:

- Manufacturing to order would minimize the capital sunk into inventory, especially obsolete inventory that had become unsellable as a consequence of technological advances.
- Speaking directly with customers instead of using intermediaries brought information on changing customer needs to the company more quickly and with greater clarity and urgency. It became possible to learn at first hand the strategic aims of major corporate customers.
- With inventory turning over every six days, innovative technologies can be introduced very swiftly, along with needed refinements to new models. The quicker this feedback loop, the finer the adjustments to the details of customer requirements.
- A process of *mass customization* became possible by which standard components were assembled in the unique configurations that customers demanded. In this way, economies of scope were combined with economies of scale.
- The model of direct selling received a welcome and powerful boost from the Internet, which was first used to sell a Dell computer in June 1996. Today there are more than 40,000 customized home pages, called Premier Pages, especially for corporate customers. These pages contain not only the details of customized

configurations and instructions but also a total record of past and current transactions between Dell and the customer.

* One consequence of this direct link is that Dell becomes privy to far more information about its customers than would otherwise be the case. When configuring a customized package, you can serve the customer better by knowing why it is wanted and how it will be used.

Dell's Dilemmas

We hope to show that Michael Dell has brilliantly and intuitively solved several crucial dilemmas facing the computer industry. It is the quality of his reconciliations that has elevated the company to its present powerful number-two position in global sales. We will consider the following dilemmas, numbered starting with 2 because the first problem—how to break into the business at all—was solved by Dell's Direct Business Model and its creation of an ecosystem:

2. Broad spectrum versus deep relationships
3. Porter's dilemma: low-cost products versus premium products
4. Face-to-face selling versus Internet selling
5. Uniting inner and outer
6. Virtual integration of product and process
7. Premier Pages: the bridge between gift and sale

Let us consider dilemmas 2 to 7 in turn.

Dilemma 2. A Broad Spectrum of Customers versus Deep, Personalized Customer Relationships

This dilemma was exacerbated by Michael Dell's youth, which made him the latecomer in a maturing industry in which he faced the prospect of pushing into a crowded field full of existing attachments, some of long duration. Could Dell push entrenched competitors out of their dugouts? That turned out to be unnecessary, because the Direct Selling Model had the advantage of being simultaneously very broad and deep, personal, and customized. The conventional wisdom is that you can aim either for many customers broadly distributed across the field or for just a few clients with complex problems and specialized needs who desire deep ongoing service relationships. The first strategy is cheap but rather superficial. The second strategy is intimate and personal but typically niche-oriented and expensive because of the detailed attention necessary. The dilemma looks like this:

Dilemma 2: Broad Spectrum versus Deep Relationships

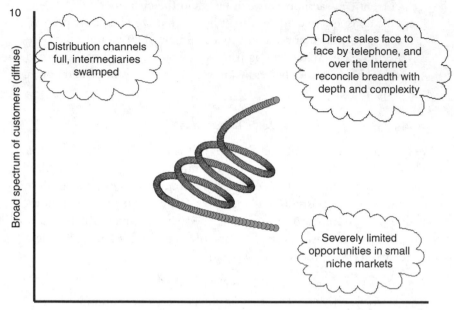

The genius of direct selling on the Internet is that you reach an ever-increasing spectrum of customers *and* can use the Net to give personalized, detailed, information-rich services to each of those customers. As long as you assume that distributors are necessary, you are stuck with the fact that existing channels are full and that no intermediary's brain is capacious enough to hold the details and information about several rival products and their accompanying instructions.

It is only when you let go of the whole idea of using distributors that the processes of direct selling on the Internet commend themselves. The Internet is uniquely suited to information-rich products, which can be embedded in an ongoing community of discussants and can be woven around with dialogues on details and special opportunities. You can serve the whole spectrum of Net users *and* go deeply into specific problems. This dilemma is close to Dilemma 3 of our seven-dimensional model described in Chapter 1, the dilemma or dimension of specificity-diffusion. You can get down to each customer's problems in *specific* detail, *and* you can serve a *diffuse* array or spectrum.

Dilemma 3. Porter's Dilemma: Low-Cost Products versus Premium Products

Michael Porter's two "generic" (meaning "of their own kind") strategies are of very special interest to Michael Dell. Porter claimed that these strategies were exclusive: *Either* you went for low-cost products *or* you tried to give the product a special premium that would make it unlike competitors' products and so earn higher returns. Dell sounds skeptical about Porter's warning that if you try both strategies, you can muddy the consumers' perceptions and achieve neither aim effectively: "I believe that Dell has continued to grow at three times the market rate by doing both. We have provided the lowest overall cost to our customers, and since our cost structure is less than half of our competitors', we can sustain our advantage in pricing.

"We have also offered superior service based on our differentiated, direct customer relationships. Further, I believe the Internet era gives Dell the opportunity not only to sustain its costs and service advantages but also to extend them."

Dell's premium, customized direct service is not only of higher quality and more complex, it is cheaper at the same time, transcending "Porter's dilemma." One important reason Dell can do both is that it orders its components in mass quantities from its suppliers, achieving economies of scale, and also codesigns its computers with its intended customers so that all those cheap components are assembled in unique, customized configurations.

Joe Pine has called this process *mass customization;* it was introduced by the Japanese automobile industry and has been widely imitated. Through the delivery of components "just in time" to a central assembly line, 30 to 40 varieties of automobile can come off at the end of the assembly line with little loss of speed or momentum. Information systems devise each configuration in advance, and components are dispatched to make a synchronized rendezvous with the vehicle in the process of assembly. This can be diagrammed as follows:

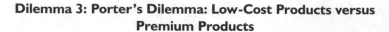

Dilemma 3: Porter's Dilemma: Low-Cost Products versus Premium Products

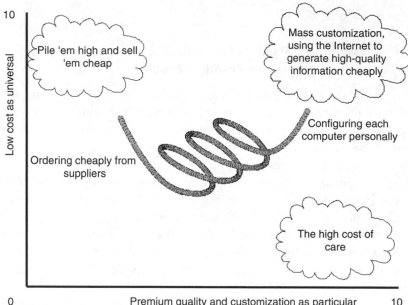

How does Dell deliver high-quality service cost-effectively, reconciling Porter's dilemma and steering between pile 'em high...(top left in the diagram) and the high cost of care (bottom right)? First, there are no distributors' margins to pay. Second, information via the Internet grows cheaper per instruction per day. Third, an economy of scale makes components cheap, while economies of scope allow every detail of every customer to be attended to on-line. What made customized service so expensive originally was the labor intensity of personal visits and the ensuing face time. Problem solving over the Net is considerably cheaper. Furthermore, the Net has helped Dell's service become much more sophisticated as it connects customers directly to a technician after special intelligence embedded on the computer motherboard has self-diagnosed—either ruled out or identified—common problems. At Dell, this service is known as *e-support*.

In any event, compared with major competitors that use distributors, Dell is *both* competitive on cost *and* more customized. Note that there are elements of universalism-particularism (Dimension 1 in Chapter 1) in this dilemma. Low cost has a universal appeal, one that works only if all units on offer are substantially similar members of a universe. By contrast, premium products appeal to particular and unique sets of requirements. At Dell Computers the two have been powerfully combined. Essentially, Dell has created (and now dominates) its own ecosystem, one that competes with the ecosystem of companies that use distributors. The distributors are a bottleneck that Dell has cleverly eliminated. Without these bottlenecks, information flows more freely and grows to greater and greater complexity. Dell's competitive advantage lies in its being more capable of managing knowledge than are rival ecosystems. First it orders components en masse and more cheaply from suppliers; then it uses the Net's mastery of details to customize each sale at highly competitive prices.

Dilemma 4. Face-to-Face Selling versus Internet Selling

The Direct Business Model preceded the use of the Internet by several years, and so the almost limitless opportunities supplied by the Net came as a very welcome surprise and challenged Dell's capacity for quick adaptation. Dell's sales force initially felt threatened by the Internet. Because the Internet was capable of creating dynamic and complete customer-client relationships, down to the purchasing of a computer, sales teams felt that their role in the era of the Internet would be drastically minimized. Field-based account managers, who "own" customer relations, were especially sensitive to how the Internet could supplant their role.

Dell management knew it had to educate its sales force to work with the Internet and seize a new kind of initiative. The Internet was an inevitable and incredible development. Rather than fight it, sales representatives would need to know how to use the power of speeded-up information channels to gather better information and further enhance valuable customer relationships—and so Dell invested heavily in education and training. He explains: "Not only did we teach them to use the Net, we jointly invented ways to make them more effective by managing more relationships while providing value-added services for the customer as well."

The most crucial change was to start valuing and rewarding the communication of knowledge rather than the mere registering of sales. It is not that sales are unimportant but rather that knowledge applied successfully to customers is the origin of *subsequent* sales. The first is prior to the second. Under the original face-to-face system in the industry, knowledge of customers' needs tended to get hoarded by the local agent and the field office. Sharing this information with others puts your office at a competitive disadvantage. You reported your sales, not the *reasons* for them or the changing *patterns* of customer demand discovered in your territory. Knowledge was considered proprietary. After all, you had visited the customer personally and gained choice insights into how computers might be used to advance a new strategy. Such knowledge is hard earned.

Sales teams were instead rewarded for entering this knowledge on electronic forms that were accessible by all other sales teams. The more potentially valuable this information was, the more the team was rewarded. For example, a new use of software could spread rapidly through particular industries. If Dell was alerted from the moment this process started, it could help spearhead the new trend elsewhere. Also, customers usually are not confined to single sales regions. Knowing that District 7 of Company X has tried a new approach successfully allows you to spread the same system to all company sites. In these and many other ways, knowledge of what customers are strategizing about can be systematically computerized.

Sales representatives soon stopped seeing the Internet as an adversary. They found that the Internet could be a source of highly qualified leads, as a result of which they could close a deal with fewer calls and have greater reach within existing accounts. Rather than being intimidated by the competition provided by the Internet, they could use the Internet to add a dynamic dimension to unique customer relationships. Michael Dell explains: "We wanted the Internet to become a key part of our entire business system. We wanted to make the Internet the first point of contact for every customer and prospect.... Our information technology perspective was—and still is—to reduce obstacles to the origin and flow of information and to simplify the systems in an effort to maximize our processes."

Brushing aside fears that employees would make "improper" use of the Net, Dell encouraged browsing and information collecting. You could make much better use of face time if you were properly briefed on a computer before a meeting and kept careful track of the success of previous initiatives: "If you are preoccupied with the ways in which your staff might abuse technology, you're going to miss out on the benefits while your competitors run away with the future. For us, the issue wasn't whether people would waste time on the Internet but whether they would use the Internet *enough*. Not to become completely familiar with a transformative business tool like the Internet is just foolish— especially when it is an integral part of the company's strategy and competitive advantage."

The dilemma Dell solved was to make personal, face-to-face knowledge, which had earlier been confined to and hoarded by single sales agents, into highly relevant *networked knowledge* in which the deep, personal insights of local agents become the potential inspiration for the entire community. The dilemma is set out in the following diagram:

Dilemma 4: Face-to-Face Selling versus Internet Selling

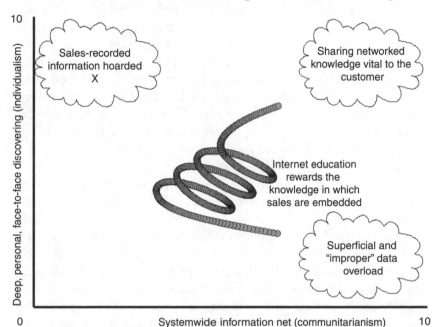

At the top left we have the old competitive system where agents compete on sales but refuse to share their secrets. At the bottom right we have Internet overload of superficial and even "improper" data. Dell was unafraid of this, because his people had much important information to communicate and he was rewarding them for communicating it. Thanks to Internet training and education and the emphasis given to the knowledge contexts in which sales occurred, Dell has succeeded in *sharing networked knowledge*, all of which was vital to at least one customer and could be generalizable to some or all other customers. E-relations (electronic relationships) do not substitute for personal relationships, but recording what was communicated, agreed on, and planned enables later understandings to be built on earlier ones.

We may note in passing that this dilemma is a variation and special case of individualism-communitarianism. The Internet makes possible cheap communal links earlier undreamed of. It gives an entire community access to the vital knowledge of a single member.

Dilemma 5. Uniting Inner and Outer

Of crucial importance to Michael Dell was bringing the "outside" of the company into the "inside" and letting the inside go out. He observed: "One of the things that makes the Internet so exciting is that it brings the outside in. In today's marketplace you cannot afford to become insulated in your own activities." It is a characteristic of modern business that information increasingly is stored in relationships—but *where* are these relationships located? Dell's relationship with an automobile systems supplier is neither inside Dell nor inside that supplier but is carried via electronic impulses between the two. It is simultaneously accessible by interested parties from any point in the system. It is everywhere yet nowhere in particular.

What the Internet can do is host an entire ecosystem of suppliers, customers, partners, and subcontractors. Instead of ordering spare parts from its suppliers, Dell allows its suppliers to discover for themselves the current state of inventories and how many units new orders from customers will draw down those inventories. This is done to make sure that Dell never runs out of components while simultaneously minimizing its carrying costs. Suppliers have the information to deliver "just in time," exactly as their supply contracts specify. All elements in the ecosystem adjust themselves in coevolutionary patterns of mutuality. According to Michael Dell, "By virtually integrating with our suppliers in this way, we literally bring them into our business, and because our entire production is built to customer order, it requires dynamic and tight inventory control. By working virtually with our company, we challenge our suppliers to reach new heights of quality and efficiency. This improves their process and their inventory control, which creates greater value for them, as well as for us and our customers."

Instead of Dell telling partners, suppliers, and subcontractors what to do, it provides and shares with them the knowledge on which those instructions would have been based. The partner can then combine sources of information to make even more intelligent decisions. The ideal is to cooperate seamlessly—to use knowledge from the whole system to enable each node to behave autonomously. Dell manages this cooperation with a high degree of sophistication. Metrics of supplier-partner performance are agreed on jointly every year and can be reviewed through Dell's secure Web portal for suppliers. Through this portal, each major supplier has in essence its own equivalent of the customer Premier Page. The portal also allows suppliers to link into Dell's procurement orders, factory flow, and other useful sources of information.

Moreover, new levels of mutual understanding and greater joint intelligence are achieved when you and your partners share the same bodies of information and can follow each other's reasoning. Everyone has the same "inside information" and can draw the attention of either party to something the other may have missed. The dilemma looks like this:

Dilemma 5: Uniting Inner and Outer

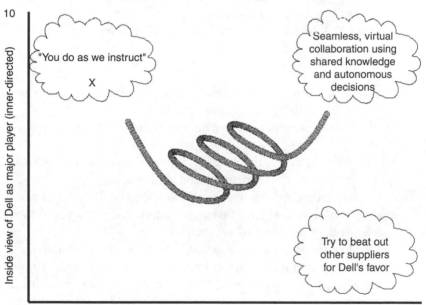

Economic value in this model stems from speed, effectiveness, and complexity. Instead of arguing about who is right or wrong, each party cites the information that informed its decision. In this way you share mental models, get across to the minds of other players, and make decisions that have been mutually qualified by the players.

Dilemma 6. Virtual Integration of Product and Process

The computer industry initially organized itself along vertically integrated lines. This was the ticket to creating maximum value and establishing a sustainable scale of operation. Suppliers were not well established, and computer companies had to design and manufacture their own products and components. Proprietary technology and physical assets and products could be priced at a premium. In these initial stages product differentiation was a key to competitive advantage in the marketplace. But as the industry matured, product differentiation gave way to process innovation. Dell came to the conclusion that a successful company would have to move from vertical integration to virtual integration to survive and succeed.

Michael Dell argued for virtual integration along the following lines:

1. Seek to establish direct relationships that close the gap between customers, manufacturers, and suppliers.
2. Place yourself strategically in an ecosystem of cooperating players.
3. Discover and define the value you intend to add and then focus on that distinctive competence and contribution.
4. Choose and help develop partners who are equally good at what *they* do. Make them part of a single system that measures its own effectiveness with agreed-on metrics.
5. Think of the Internet not as an add-on but as the environment in which you operate, an integral part of Dell's strategy. Only then can you achieve virtual integration and surpass more traditional companies.

The Dell Direct Model was the basis of this virtual integration, allowing customers to make purchasing decisions that were better informed, more involved, and more elaborately detailed and specified. It integrates physical with virtual assets to configure the whole better.

The changing shape of the computer industry and its transition from vertically integrated products to virtually integrated networks is illustrated in the following diagram:

Dilemma 6: Virtual Integration of Product and Process

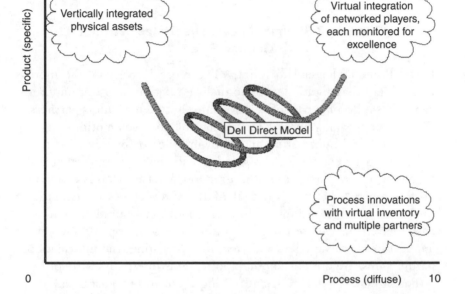

The traditional part of the computer industry is stuck at the top left of the diagram, maintaining necessary coherence through vertical integration, in which the computer maker "does everything." Dell used its Direct Model to develop several process innovations that created a novel *virtual integration* of key suppliers, manufacturers, and component specialists, each selected for excellence and each connected to the Internet ecosystem. The entire system is self-evaluating and self-monitoring, and all parts jointly agree on the metrics by which the system will assess its own integrated performance. Note that Dell is still a supplier of computer hardware—specific products that customers buy in greater or lesser quantities. But these products are embedded in information about strategic aims and purposes. You buy a Dell computer because it is an effective means to your ends. Virtual integration is about understanding those ends and customizing and deploying the products appropriately.

Michael Dell's dilemma or challenge in creating virtual integration is similar in some respects to the third dimension in Chapter 1: specificity versus diffusion. Products such as computers and their components are specific, but the oceans of information in which they swim are diffuse. You have to understand the ocean currents if you are to move your own hardware.

Dilemma 7. Premier Pages: The Bridge between Gift and Sale

It was Romeo who said to Juliet, "The more I give you, the more I have." This has always been true of love relationships, but only recently has it become true of relationships between business partners. We are not speaking here of wellsprings of positive emotions but of sharing seminal information and allowing the combinations of that information to create new knowledge and new synergies that are usable by all the parties to the interaction. Michael Dell is eloquent on this topic: "The real potential of the Internet lies in its ability to transform relationships within the traditional supplier-vendor-customer chain. We are using the Internet to share openly our own applications with suppliers and customers, creating true information partnerships. We are developing applications internally, with an Internet browser at the front end giving them to our customers and suppliers."

Dell computers are an integral part of the information and knowledge communicated as well as a means of storing, receiving, retrieving, and sending knowledge, and so the more this knowledge is "given away," the more necessary it becomes to purchase the computers to which the knowledge refers and by which it is organized. Several Internet entrepreneurs made their fortunes by giving away programs, browsers, or tools and asking users to make a donation if they found the gift useful. Their subsequent enrichment was largely or entirely the result of voluntary reciprocity. Similarly, if Dell supplies you with vital information, buying the company's computers is a rational response and a way to keep that information coming.

Instead of arguing whether this is "really" a gift or "really" a sale, we need to understand that cogenerating knowledge on the Internet transcends this dichotomy and that gifts and sales facilitate one another. The bridge that Michael Dell has built between Dell, its customers, its suppliers, its partners, and its subcontractors is the Premier Pages, password-protected Web pages that serve the special information needs of business customers and technology partners. There are over 40,000 Premier Pages, and they serve as a dynamic interface for customers and partners to access relevant information. For a corporate customer this could include information on global accounting, preapproved pricing and configurations, technical white papers, product road maps, and so on. At the click of a mouse, the corporate client has immediate access to a complete picture of its purchasing channels. For a particular client this could be the number of computer systems bought at its European operation, details of standing orders, or preapproved configurations and discounts. Of course, customers have to be willing to share information with Dell and its suppliers in order to benefit from better-informed relationships. Many purchasing departments are secretive by habit, but they learn that being more transparent can lead to more attractive and better-customized deals.

What Dell does is model the transparency it seeks from others and wait for them to reciprocate so that confidences are mutual. Michael Dell explains: "Driving change in your own organization is hard enough; driving change in other organizations is nearly impossible. But we believed, and still believe, that the Internet will become as pervasive as the phone. We knew it was too important to our business, and potentially to our customers' businesses, to wait for them to figure it out for themselves. What teaches parties to reveal more about themselves is experience: The more that is known about your needs, the better others can serve you."

The value of Premier Pages soon became evident. Companies no longer had to work through purchasing channels every time they needed to purchase a computer. Dell made a point of having this kind of information up and ready from the very beginning. Dell's Premier Pages have resulted in massive savings, and companies have told Dell that they are saving millions of dollars by ordering their products and getting support in this way.

Michael Dell is persuasive about the economies achieved: "Early on Ford Motor Company estimated that it saved $2 million in initial procurement costs by placing orders through its Premier Page, and Shell Oil saved 15 percent of its total purchasing cost. Premier Pages also allow us to deliver critical service and support information directly to our customers, based on the specific products they buy and use. This information is drawn from the same databases our own technicians and engineers use. This doesn't necessarily result in major cost savings for Dell, but it has resulted in significant cost savings for our customers, enriching their relationship with Dell."

Premier Pages are also a bridge to research and development between Dell and its partners: "The Internet is changing the way we work with our technology partners. We are moving to truly collaborative research and development models, using the Internet to share information openly and work together in real time. We can also engage our customers in our product development, giving them the same level of access to critical information that our own people have. For example, we were able to develop and introduce an award-winning line of notebook computers, using the Internet to keep a common set of notes by engineers in the United States and Asia. By making the same information available to critical partners, we were able to close the information loop. A traditional, vertically integrated company would have spent months, if not years, designing parts and building them."

Dell has built supplier Web pages for its top 20 suppliers, covering 90 percent of its procurement needs. These pages allow Dell's suppliers to provide the company with rapid information on capacities, up-side capabilities, inventories in supply lines, component quality as measured by Dell's metrics, and current cost structures. Dell passes on to the supplier direct and immediate customer feedback that is gathered in part through its Premier Pages. The feedback covers such areas as quality in the field, current forecasts and future demand, special technical requirements, and end-use market pricing.

The type of collaborative partnership exemplified by Dell Premier Pages is a starting point, or a portal, for future innovation in the era of the Internet. Any innovative process will have to begin from a point where time and distance have been shrunk and development speed is unimpeded. The quality and directness of the relationship, the speed with which you can channel information, and the dynamic forces that you create will determine the long-term sustainability of your position in an industry with notoriously short life cycles. Like Dell, you will have blurred the traditional boundaries between buyer, seller, and supplier and will have created a radically new creative enterprise.

The process by which Premier Pages become the bridge between the gift and the sale is depicted in the next diagram:

Dilemma 7: Premier Pages: The Bridge between Gift and Sale

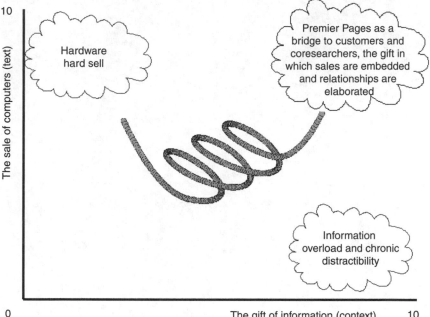

What Dell has done is to leave behind the hard sell of hardware and, by gifting to all members of its network the relevant information, promote computers and the relationships that convey that information. The computers are the text within the context, helping to structure and move information across the bridges of knowledge that join all the members of Dell's ecosystem. In the progressive, mutual revelation of deep needs, these bridges become preferable to all others. The wealth of knowledge that ties together members of this network would be very hard to duplicate or reconstitute. The Net binds its members by hundreds of threads.

Chapter 12

—◆—

Global Brand, Local Touch: Stan Shih, Acer Computers

Peter Prud'homme

THE TAIWANESE COMPUTER company Acer is perhaps the best example of a globalized ethnic Chinese company. Acer's success made company cofounder, chairman, and chief executive officer (CEO) Stan Shih one of Asia's most admired businesspersons in the 1990s. By 1989 *Fortune* had mentioned Shih as "one of the 25 people you ought to know when doing business in Asia," and Shih was selected by *Business Week* as one of the top managers of the year for 1995. Despite recent difficulties as a consequence of the East Asian financial crisis, Acer seems to be well positioned for the twenty-first century, and Acer's strategy often is quoted as a model for other East Asian companies. This makes it interesting to study Shih's globalization strategy: gaining a competitive advantage by reconciling cultural differences. Does this help Acer exploit opportunities, neutralize threats, and adapt to the quickly changing environment of the global information technology (IT) industry?

Acer has been recognized as having a unique globalization strategy since the beginning of the 1990s. Vogel (1991) mentions Acer as an example of a "world-class company." Kao (1993) cites Acer as an example of an ethnic Chinese company that became a "global player" while retaining key elements of traditional Chinese business culture. *World Executive Digest* dubbed Acer's strategy "the fourth way of globalization," differentiating it from the American, European, and Japanese ways. Although recent literature pays attention to a "Chinese model" of management, that model is not well documented in comparison with Western and Japanese management models. Management guru Peter Drucker pointed out that Western organizations could learn from Chinese models: "Chinese companies will be an important object study for Western managers: just [as] the Japanese succeeded in changing the modern corporation into a family, I think that the overseas Chinese will succeed in changing the family into a modern corporation."

Traditional Chinese business consists of small companies with intense familial network connections. The challenge for network organizations in a globalizing world is to cooperate as small units in such a way that knowledge circulates freely and they keep their autonomy but at the same time gather sufficient power to become a "global player." Stan Shih seems to have succeeded in creating this type of flexible network. Acer, originally founded in 1976 as Multitech, is arguably the most globalized Taiwanese company. It has more than 28,000 employees, is an important player in more than 30 countries, and belongs in the top 10 global computer companies. The interview with Shih revealed that his successful strategy has been less about changing the family into a modern corporation and more about reconciling aspects of traditional Chinese business culture and Western corporate culture. Shih, born in 1944, is not a Westernized Asian businessperson. He studied at a Taiwanese university and made his career in Taiwanese companies. People describe his character as modest, tolerant, and generous. He ascribes his success to his willingness to learn not only from positive examples but also from negative teachings and his willingness to trust his employees and appreciate different opinions. About solving conflicts between subordinates, Shih says, "I never make a decision before I understand the overall situation. I involve subordinates in the reconciling of their differences."

In 1993 Stan Shih emphasized (Kao, 1993) that many of the strong points of Acer, such as its stability at senior levels, are related to elements of traditional Chinese business culture, relying more on intuition and the opinions of trusted employees than on figures and establishing work relations with other ethnic Chinese companies. The characteristics of traditional Chinese business culture are well documented (Tai, 1989; Serrie, 1986; Rothstein, 1992; Redding, 1996). An analysis reveals that these characteristics reflect orientations on the seven dimensions of the Trompenaars model. It turns out that those orientations fit very well with the Chinese cultural orientation according to the THT database (and are opposite to American cultural orientations).

UNIVERSALISM   PARTICULARISM

Traditional Chinese business culture is *particularist*. Chinese managers are proud to be extremely flexible and adaptable. Not much value is attached to a formal organization chart. The people who form the organization, interpersonal relations, and informal contact between managers and staff are much more important. Particular circumstances and relationships are stronger than abstract rules.

INDIVIDUALISM   COMMUNITARIANISM

Traditional Chinese business culture is *communitarian*. Companies often started as family companies or at least have characteristics of family companies. People regard themselves primarily as part of a group, not as individuals. This reveals a strong communitarian orientation with important consequences for how business is organized. For instance, meetings in traditional Chinese companies are not places to make decisions but places to check opinions.

SPECIFICITY   DIFFUSION

Traditional Chinese business culture is based on *diffuse* relationships. An essential concept in traditional Chinese business is *guanxi:* networks in and between companies that work on the basis of trust between people with family ties or people from the same region or language group. These networks are used to obtain easy access to capital, establish business contacts, and share and disseminate information. All aspects of the relationships in these networks are interwoven, and the "diffuse" whole is more than the sum of its parts.

NEUTRAL   AFFECTIVE

Traditional Chinese business culture is emotionally *neutral*. There is a strong orientation toward making money by working extremely hard and an emphasis on frugality and discipline. Being able to control one's emotions is considered an important quality of managers and leaders.

ACHIEVED STATUS   **ASCRIBED STATUS**

Traditional Chinese business culture is oriented toward *ascribed status.* Status is attributed to leaders who adopt a paternalistic style. The development of human potential takes place on the basis of a belief in the "educability" of employees and the ascribed status of knowledge. The spoke-and-hub style of many ethnic Chinese companies (spokes around the hub of a powerful founder) allows for a traditional leadership style in which the leader combines the roles of ruler, father, and teacher.

SEQUENTIAL TIME   **SYNCHRONOUS TIME**

Traditional Chinese business culture is characterized by a *synchronous time orientation.* Not much attention is paid to formal planning. Making quick decisions is the key.

INTERNAL CONTROL   **EXTERNAL CONTROL**

The Chinese are willing to make exceptions and make many ad hoc decisions to cultivate long-term relationships with customers. Traditional Chinese business culture is oriented toward *external control.* Chinese businesspeople are inclined to adapt to external forces instead of resisting them. Chinese businesspeople are the entrepreneurs in many Southeast Asian countries. They are famous for entrepreneurial skills that are based on the ability to see business opportunities in their environment and the ability to translate new developments into the satisfaction of customer needs.

These business culture patterns traditionally determine the way small and large Chinese companies work and have been an important factor in their success (Deyo, 1978; Goldberg, 1985).

A Short History of Acer

Phase I

Stan Shih cofounded Multitech, the predecessor of Acer, with five friends, among them his wife. He wanted to let go of the traditional Chinese family-owned style of business, but when he lists the success factors in the early years of Acer's internationalization, it becomes clear that that success was very much based on a Taiwanese style that made use of traditional Chinese characteristics. Acer's success factors in phase (between 1976 and 1986) were the following:

- Extreme flexibility and adaptability to the needs of customers. Shih stresses that flexibility has been an essential Taiwanese survival characteristic for centuries because of Taiwan's "immigrant culture." *Flexibility* and *adaptability* are key terms in Taiwanese management in general. The background of the claim that "members of the Taiwanese workforce have an educational preparation and a cultural background that make it easy for them to adapt to new situations" (*Doing Business with Taiwan R.O.C.*, China External Trade Development Council, 1995) is that there are no standardized rules for management practice in Confucianism. Management is based on highly personal and particular relationships between employers and employees. Taiwan's economy is based mainly on small and medium-size enterprises in which management can work without standardized rules. In phase 1 Shih's Acer was very much a typical Taiwanese company with an emphasis on *particularist* values.
- Shih's philosophy of "creating the Dragon Dream" intended to motivate Acer's staff (at this stage almost exclusively ethnic Chinese). Creating the Dragon Dream refers to Shih's dream of being instrumental in creating what was to become the first multinational Chinese firm; this reflects the Chinese *communitarian* orientation.
- Collective entrepreneurship, which consisted of exchanging opinions, reaching consensus at the management level, and taking risks together. These achievements were possible because of the *diffuse* relationships in the network of Acer's managers.
- Acer's "poor young man's culture," the term used by Shih to emphasize his focus on low cost, frugality, and discipline (reflecting a *neutral* orientation).
- The capability of making fast decisions because of clear mentoring relationships. In the early days Acer's employees referred to their superiors as *shi-fu*, literally "teacher-father," reflecting the *ascribed status* orientation.
- Acer's "first followers" principle. Shih's product strategy for Acer was to be not the first *on the market* but the first *to follow*. Being a quick follower of competition and "cloning" competitors' products instead of focusing on his own product planning was a key factor in Acer's success. Shih explains: "We would rather wait until technology becomes mature and then quickly follow up." Speed was of the essence in the success of this strategy. The speed of change within the IT industry played right into the hands of a

company like Acer, where the staff was used to a *synchronous* time orientation, working in short bursts and quickly changing directions in an *externally controlled* manner.

- Manufacture under original equipment manufacturer (OEM) agreements—that is, equipment made to another firm's specifications and marketed by that firm under its own brand names. OEM business is characterized by low margins and low risk because the marketing risk and stockholding risk are taken on the customer side. In OEM business margins tend to be small, but as long as the quantities are large, it is possible to make a good profit. OEM business fits very well with the Chinese saying "The capital has to be big, the risk small." Shih made use of Acer's externally focused environment when he chose this strategy. During the 1950s and 1960s Taiwan's economic development was very much dependent on American support. Major U.S. multinationals were stimulated to use Taiwanese companies as OEM subcontractors. The establishment of export processing zones after 1966 in Taiwan, where regulation was minimal because production was for export, led to a boom in Japanese investment and in electrical and electronic goods. The presence of many small and medium-sized enterprises stimulated a network economy with an export orientation. The focus on OEM contracts, exports, and external markets in Acer's first stages of development fits very well with the Taiwanese culture's orientation toward *external control*.

The use of aspects of traditional Chinese culture probably was a strength in the first phase of Acer's international development; the threat was that this would become a weakness when further globalization was required. Particularism, communitarianism, and ascribed status orientation, taken to the extreme, often make Chinese organizations too dependent on the charisma of the founder and on personal relationships. Having few rules and procedures and many exceptions can become a problem when the company starts to work with Western employees who expect job descriptions, personnel manuals, and standard criteria for promotions.

The focus on particularist behavior is also responsible for the problem that Chinese companies generally have in finding enough skilled managers for global marketing. Focusing on OEM strategies was not good for the brand image of Taiwanese companies and made it difficult to get rid of the low-quality, low-price image of "Made in Taiwan." Speed can be an important source of competitive advantage for a company like Acer, but it also can be a hindrance to globalization. Taiwanese companies are used to ad hoc decisions and to moving people around a lot. For foreign staff members, changing all the time can be very confusing; they are used to more stability. Taking the external control orientation to the extreme can lead to a lack of direction and long-term focus. The Chinese saying "People are never poor for three generations, and people are never rich for three generations" reflects the experienced difficulty of sustaining long-term success. The perception of Western staff is sometimes that the Taiwanese management has no clear direction and just follows the external environment with a "we sell everything" mentality. It was clear that further globalization required change. The implementation of a new strategy led to a difficult phase 2 in Acer's development.

Phase 2

Phase 2 of Acer's development (1986–1992) was marked by an aggressive globalization strategy and the hiring of outside managers. Shih hired a former IBM manager to be the company's president, and Acer made such major acquisitions as the American company Altos. The former IBM manager's confrontational style was in contrast to Acer's consensus style. This phase ended with the departure of that manager from Acer, a restructuring operation that included the layoff of employees in 1991–1992 and the merging of Altos into Acer America. It was clear that trying to copy the strategy of big Western companies had been a failure. According to Shih, "The logic of success that worked in large companies was not viable for us." The operational costs for high-paid (American) *individuals,* the absence of a sense of crisis, the blurred division between authority and responsibility as well as between reward and penalty, and the inability of employees of acquired companies such as Altos to adapt to Acer's corporate culture were important stumbling blocks.

Looking back, the choice to adopt Western business practices seemed to be correct, but problems arose because there was no connection between the successful strategies in Acer's first phase (building on traditional Chinese business culture) and Acer's strategy in the second phase (trying to emulate the success of big Western companies). Shih recognized that he was confronted with a dilemma, but he was still optimistic about solving the crisis: "When we are forced into a dilemma by our opponent, we either make a wrong move and lose the whole game or make a smart move to solve the crisis." He recognized that to be successful in the long term in a globalizing world, Acer required a different strategy: "Following the footsteps of first-class companies will only make us second-class or third-class enterprises. To conduct effective globalization, we have to develop a management model of our own." The implementation of his own management model marked the start of the third phase of Acer's development. This "fourth way of globalization," as *World Executive Digest* called it, could also be described as a reconciliation strategy. An analysis of Acer's globalization strategy in its third phase of development shows that Shih intuitively reconciled aspects of traditional Chinese business culture with aspects of Western business culture on all seven dimensions.

Phase 3

Phase 3 (1992 to the present) saw the development of Shih's management modes, which turned him into a global player by reconciling global practices with elements of traditional Chinese management. This was done in seven principal ways.

Reconciling Universalism and Particularism: Acer's Global Brand–Local Touch Strategy

Shih saw the need to implement more universalistic elements in Acer's strategy, such as making Acer known as a global brand name, while retaining the company's strong particularist elements. He therefore designed the "global brand–local touch" strategy. There were many difficulties to overcome. Taiwanese companies are traditionally not strong in establishing trademarks, channel structures, structured market research, and sales policies. Marketing and price setting traditionally are based on personalistic networks, and loyalty is based on mutual obligations. Even an already internationally oriented company like Acer did not have strong marketing policies because of its tradition in OEM, in which the responsibility for marketing is on the purchaser's side.

A history as a small to medium-size company and a family business made it even more difficult for a Taiwanese company like Acer to establish brand names in the international market. Building a global brand image required building up that image over a long period, customer service, and dedicated staff available to answer customer's questions. Taiwanese companies traditionally used price competition as their main marketing strategy. However, frequent lowering of prices is not conducive to establishing a prestigious brand.

Taiwan has suffered for some time from a reputation for low-end products and inconsistent quality. "Made in Taiwan" used to have the image of low price and low quality. The reputation for cloning had led to an image of "me too" manufacturers who imitated designs and compromised to keep prices competitive. Shih managed to make Acer the first Taiwanese manufacturer to change the made in Taiwan image for the better. For some time, because of the bad image, Acer was forced to use creative ways to avoid putting "Made in Taiwan" on its products. Then Acer started its global brand, local touch strategy: the development of Acer as a global brand name with a good reputation, in combination with local assembly, local shareholders, local management, local identity, and local autonomy in marketing and distribution. Acer is now Taiwan's most famous branded product. Global brand, local touch is a good example of the reconciliation of particularism and universalism in business strategy. The particularist local touch part of the strategy consists of the following elements:

- Localization of the business structure. Acer's strategy is to have a majority of local shareholders early in the twenty-first century. Shih wants the majority of ownership of the local operations to be in the hands of local investors. He envisions a company owned by local investors and quoted on national stock markets. The final goal is a "worldwide alliance of borderless global companies" within the Acer group: the "21 in 21" concept, or 21 companies for the twenty-first century (for instance, Acer America, Acer Peripherals, Acer Europe, Texas Instruments Acer, Inc.)—publicly listed companies with local shareholders in the majority, each with access to the full Acer group technology but each following its own marketing strategy: "global coverage, locally focused regional offices."
- Local assembly. Acer reversed the trend toward centralized manufacturing centers. Instead, it seeks to have local assembly centers close to the customer. Nationally based, highly autonomous companies combine high-quality ingredients according to local demand.
- Local identity and local management with local autonomy in marketing and distribution (*Far Eastern Economic Review*, Jan. 26, 1995). Shih demands of his local managers that they be pragmatic and accountable, a good example of reconciliation between Taiwanese particularism and Western universalism.

Diagrammatically, Acer's reconciliation can be conceived of as follows:

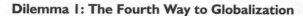

Dilemma 1: The Fourth Way to Globalization

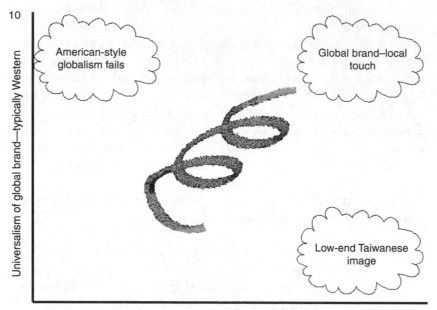

It is crucial to grasp the fact that Acer and Shih have *universalized their own preference for particularism*. They have assumed that most other countries want Acer to be particular and also exceptional in their ways of investing, assembling, marketing, and so on. One country of refugees and immigrants is appealing globally to migrant cultures, which are the creators of so much wealth. With one-third of Silicon Valley's wealth being created by Indian and Chinese immigrants to the United States since 1970 (Saxenian, 1999), Acer's strategy looks like a winning one.

Reconciling Individualism and Communitarianism: Individual Stock Ownership and the Dragon Dream
The Chinese family form of communitarianism has never been without strong individualist features. After all, families are small, and family members benefit individually from the success of family businesses. Shih's initial appeal to "realize the Dragon Dream" was an attempt to move community pride beyond the family and make the Chinese "dragons" a force in the world community. This worked well in the early stages of growth but less well as Acer spread from continent to continent. Making a Taiwanese company world-famous was not the

first thought in the minds of American and European employees. Another way had to be found to give non-Chinese protagonists a stake in Acer's prosperity. A generous stock option plan for all employees gave them ownership of local stock quoted on local stock exchanges. They were part of Acer America or Acer Europe with an individual stake in the local community even as they built the Dragon Dream.

Shih continues his strong support for the local communities in which Acer is based through the Acer Foundation, but in addition, each employee (and his or her family) has a personal financial stake in the success of the regional company. The reconciliation between individualism and communitarianism can be diagrammed as follows:

Dilemma 2: Dragon Dream with Personal Stakes

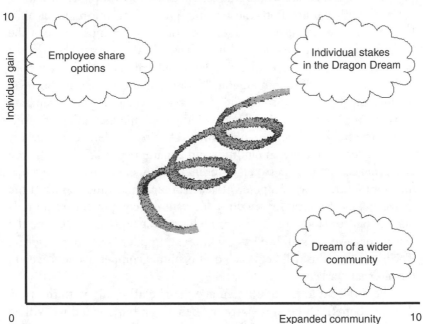

The Taiwanese communitarian orientation that Acer starts with is widened still further, but as Western economies are included, each individual is given an additional personal stake in the Dragon Dream.

Reconciling Specificity and Diffusion: Acer's "Client-Server" Structure
Shih designed a flexible "client-server" model to make Acer's network organization structure work. *Client-server* is the term originally used for

the computer structure in which the connection of several personal computers (PCs) in an office with servers performing different functions leads to the establishment of a complete and flexible network. Client and server are closely but flexibly connected to each other. PCs act as independent clients, and the servers on the network are ready to provide the appropriate resource. Shih used the client-server relationship as a metaphor for Acer's structure: The product-and-technology-oriented business units (servers) provide technology and products for the regional business units (clients). The most basic principle is that each unit accomplishes what it can handle, asks for support from other units on more complicated matters, and is ready to act as a server and support other units at any time.

The client-server structure allows each business to become an independently and separately operating client as well as a support-providing server for other units. Both the product groups and the regional units have autonomy and specific targets, but the relationships between the business units are diffuse, and all units have direct access to the support of the Acer Group. There are no superior-subordinate relationships between units. Each unit is in an equal position and can conduct business without having to go through headquarters. Acer even has a separate department, Acer Open, that deals with the sales and marketing of products from other Taiwanese companies. The loosely knit client-server structure leads to many ambiguities and apparent contradictions. There is internal competition between different units. Acer Open and a regional unit, for instance, may compete with each other in the same market. If the management of a local region does not want the components of a product unit because those products are no longer the best, the latest, and the least expensive, it is allowed to pick other suppliers with better terms. The idea is that this will help each unit maintain competitiveness even in the internal market.

The different units should manage their relationship with the view that "my benefit will be my partners' benefit and in the end we will be able to share the benefit." Shih compares the role of the CEO in this network with that of the operating system of a PC. The center of the network defines a few general features, such as pricing and the brand name, and stimulates the units to establish cooperative relationships and work effectively for their common interest. If a unit is not competitive anymore or refuses to work in partnership, the client-server structure makes sure that Shih will discover this in time to reverse the trend.

Acer's Aspire computer was an example of successful cooperation between different business units, in which communication did not go through headquarters. The ambiguity inherent in the structure does not seem to disturb Shih. If the resolution of a contradiction is difficult, he does not appear to push himself hard to untangle it. Instead, he tries to think up a way that will permit him to live with the contradiction until the timing is right for the settlement. This approach requires time and patience. Shih observes, "Never make a decision before you understand the overall situation. If it is unnecessary, make no decision at all."

This client-server culture has the structure of *collaborative competition* (co-opetition). Specific servers compete to cooperate diffusely with clients. It can be diagrammed as follows:

Dilemma 3: Collaborative Competition

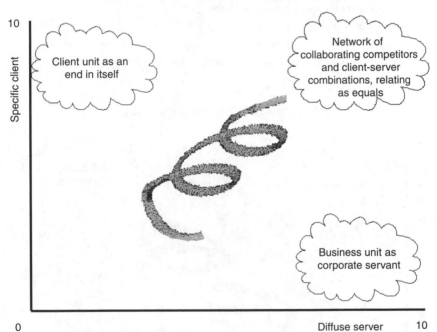

Reconciling Frugality with Kindliness

Not every reconciliation achieved by Stan Shih follows our seven dimensions exactly. It is important to give credit to the leader's original thinking rather than to our model. We see our model as a reflective theme, not as a surefire technique that has only to be followed. Shih and Acer gave great prominence to what they called "a poor young man's culture." This phrase was difficult to translate literally into other languages, and there were several misunderstandings when that was tried. Perhaps the closest equivalent in English would be "young, lean, fit, and traveling light," very much characteristic of the value of a Chinese immigrant who carries his or her most important possessions between the ears and comes without land, baggage, or attachments beyond the family. The immigrant is "poor" in the sense that young people and students are poor in possessions but rich in potential.

After several unsuccessful attempts to convey this idea, Shih settled for "a Commoner's Culture," people without privileges who were eager to earn their own way in the world. At the same time, commoners' frugality and economizing were balanced by kindliness toward all employees. They were there to contribute to prove themselves, but kindliness was facilitative of quality and excellence.

There is a partial correspondence with our fourth dimension, neutral versus affective, but Shih is really saying something more, and the subtlety of his distinctions is captured in the following diagram:

Dilemma 4: A Commoner's Culture

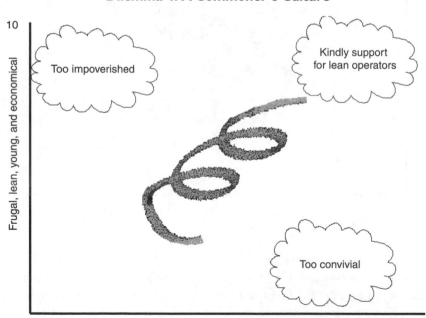

10

Frugal, lean, young, and economical

Too impoverished

Kindly support for lean operators

Too convivial

0

Kindly, generous, and supportive

10

By giving kindly support to those who travel light and economize, Acer has built a fit and lean culture for effective operations.

Reconciling Achievement and Ascription: Managers Are Mentors Who Conceal Nothing from Their Pupils

One of the mysteries of East Asian business success is how nations so much given to ascribed status can create such successful learning organizations. Surely, to ascribe to people a status instead of letting them earn it through achievement is counterproductive. Not necessarily. A vital metaphor for business in this part of the world is the mentor-learner relationship. If your main purpose is to impart knowledge that leaves your pupils wiser and more independent, the ascription of tutor or mentor is both effective and benign. This is a form of ascription that stimulates, and is vindicated by, the achievement of learners. You are mentoring *for* achievement. Shih advocates a leadership style that he describes as "being a tutor who conceals nothing from the pupils." This leadership style has paternalistic elements in the sense that a leader is supposed to know all the details of the work. However, entrepreneurial achievement is encouraged and rewarded by entrusting employees with the running of small business units. The Chinese expression "Better the head of a chicken than the tail of an ox" reflects the view that leadership of a small unit is preferable to subordination in a larger one.

Shih is famous for his tolerance of errors, which he calls "tuition payments," provided that they are not repeated. Error and experience are the best teachers; hence, authority must be delegated downward as far as possible so that subordinates have the opportunity to err, learn, and succeed on their own. The employees' learning and self-advancement will directly help the company. Errors have important information content and memorability, and so they should be studied, not swept under the carpet.

The dilemma is diagrammed in the next figure:

Dilemma 5: The Path to Realization

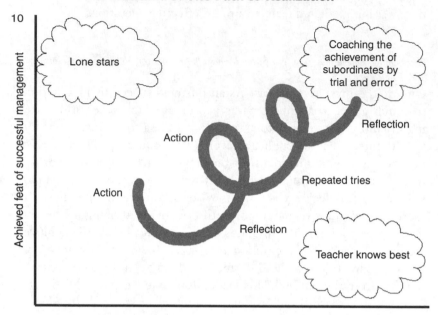

Achieved feat of successful management

0   Mentoring by ascribed tutors who delegate powers and allow errors   10

Every move to the left involves action. Every move to the right has mentors and learners reflect on that action. Instead of oldsters clinging to past achievements, dedicated tutors are eager to pass the torch to the "poor" young men and women coming up behind them.

Reconciling Sequential and Synchronous Time Orientations:
Acer's Fast-Food Business Model
Shih's "fast-food model" is a perfect example of reconciliation between sequential and synchronous time orientation. He also refers to it as the "McDonaldization of the manufacturing process," in which Acer's "boards and drives" substitute for "burgers and fries." The idea of McDonaldization came to Shih's mind when he had a meal in a McDonald's branch on a business trip. He realized that a computer company can learn from the McDonald's system and apply it to the manufacturing and sales of computers. McDonald's has a unified brand name, a simple menu, and systematic, consistent operation. The differences from Chinese restaurants struck Stan Shih; those restaurants are also inexpensive but are not known for consistent quality from one to another. Acer combines standard ingredients (the PC components: hard disks, CPUs,

memory chips, software packages, computer housings, keyboards) with consistent quality and assembles the computers in a flexible way that is adapted to local customers' tastes and needs. The components come via different routes, depending on the extent to which their specifications change because of innovation. The result is a low risk of inventory depreciation and "freshness" of essential components:

- Motherboards, which change rapidly in design and price, are shipped by air from one global factory ("the central kitchen") to other sites, mostly in East Asia.
- Hard disks, CPUs, and memory chips come in from a regional supplier.
- The computer housing, power supply, and floppy-disk drives, which do not change rapidly in their specifications, are shipped by sea to the local assembly factory.

The consequence is that the local branches always have the newest technology available and become a "fast-food store" that assembles fresh PCs. Acer has some 40 assembly centers all over the world. The final assembly of the PCs takes place under a modular assembly system, according to standard procedures, ensuring the quality of the product. Parallel supply processes (synchronous) are combined with a sequential assembly process. The result is that the customer gets "fresh" PCs and Acer has lower inventory costs.

Acer's secret formula for success in the fast-food business model is speed, as it was when the company's focus was on OEM business and on cloning IBM PCs. Speed is also behind the success of Acer as a PC-component manufacturer. When a computer manufacturer makes a change in the CPU of a chip, changes in the motherboard inevitably follow. Waiting until the specifications for a new motherboard are officially released and going step by step through all the various procedures means that it will take about six months from the time that specifications for a new CPU are revealed to complete a design for a new motherboard. But Acer can put out a design in only three months. This is much more efficient and reduces the time it takes to get new products to the market.

Acer component manufacturers grasp the first opportunity to design a product in order to gain a competitive advantage even though the first design may not be perfect. Sometimes they can begin production after only a few small changes. This small investment risk is necessary to be first in the business. Acer is happy with the competition that exists between Taiwanese firms to lower their prices and deliver speedier service. This competition has always forced them to develop new competencies. Acer now promotes its "global logistics management systems," which it had to develop when it was a "just-in-time" OEM supplier for global players. Coordinating business between big suppliers requires the ability to reconcile a sequential with a synchronous time orientation, and Acer made that ability one of its strengths.

Sequential time has to do with sheer speed; cutting three months out of the time needed to design a new motherboard is an example of time cut in half. Synchronous time is about *timing,* getting a product there when the customers want it, neither sooner nor later, to save on inventory and carrying costs. Acer borrowed an emphasis on speed from the West and an emphasis on precise timing from the East, particularly the Japanese, and then reconciled those two visions of time. The dilemma is illustrated in the following diagram:

Dilemma 6: Speed yet Synchronicity

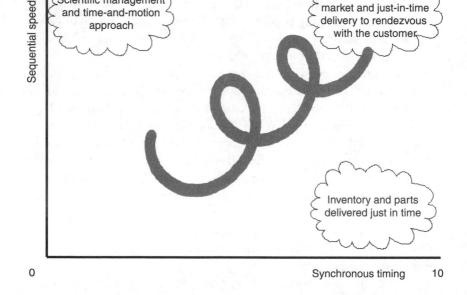

The reconciliation is to speed your and your customer's *time to market* yet get it there *just in time.* Even the customer may fall behind schedule, and so the trick is to "pull" products toward an agreed *rendezvous* in the future, adding or subtracting resources to catch up or slow down. Acer appears to have mastered this art.

Playing Go: Acer's Reconciliation of Internal and External Sources of Control

Shih uses the traditional Chinese board game Go to describe Acer's successful globalization as the "Go game strategy." Go fits an outer-directed orientation: "I will gradually encircle and constrain your moves."

Shih uses Go to explain his strategy. In Go you occupy peripheral positions, especially the corners of the board, before surrounding your opponent. You can control the corners with fewer resources yet still be able to surround your opponent. The game is won when your opponent can no longer move. Similarly, says Shih, an entrepreneur should secure a firm foothold in a niche market before entering a big market.

Acer adopted a globalization strategy in which the firm started in small but growing markets that were not immediately interesting for the big players, markets where Acer could win with fewer resources. Thus, Acer managed to obtain top market positions in countries such as South Africa, Malaysia, the Middle East, several Latin American countries, India, and Russia. These are countries that were not seen as priorities by major American, European, and Japanese PC firms. The strategy worked well, and Acer became a global player by starting from the periphery. When investing in Russia, Acer took the idea of playing from the corners a step further. Most other international computer companies invested in Russia itself, facing difficulties and risks involved in transport, customs, regulations, government intervention, and the opening of local offices. Acer built an assembly operation in Finland, close to the Russian border. Russian distributors would collect the products at the factory. Acer thus avoided many troublesome issues.

Shih developed his strategy as a *response* to the moves of the bigger players, gaining undefended ground and growing with the often rapid rates of economic development in emerging economies. Because computerization is an important part of infrastructure development, these emerging nations would associate Acer with their own economic "miracles" and breakthroughs, and Acer could become a permanent, even traditional, part of their growth and strength. Not only is it easier to penetrate an emerging economy, you are carried along on its dynamism and momentum—a typical outer-directed strategy.

The company has built successful local partnerships in Mexico, South Africa, Brazil, Chile, Thailand, Malaysia, and other countries. Shih is famously unconcerned with losing control to foreign partners—

a feature of outer-directed characters. He believes that wherever his equipment is good enough, Acer's influence usually will be enough. "I would rather lose control of the company and make money than wrest back control and lose money," he explains.

While long experience working for OEMs on a contract basis has made Acer outer-directed, recent experience with original design manufacturers (ODMs) has made Acer more inner-directed. The diagram looks like this:

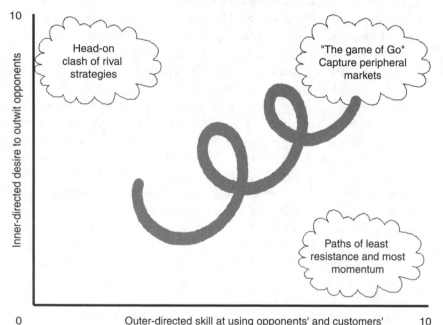

Dilemma 7: Riding the Dynamisms of Growth

It goes without saying that Go, like chess, is a game you aim to win. It is the *means* of winning, the choosing of those "corners" where the influence of a small investment of force can be relatively high because defenses are relatively weak, that illustrates the outer-directed paths to an inner-directed goal.

Despite the seven forms of reconciliation that have made Acer so successful and Shih so adept a leader, scores of interpersonal difficulties and misunderstandings typical of any global company remain. Westerners still complain that the "playing field" is not properly marked out and refereed, that they have no clear criteria for promotion, and that Taiwanese senior managers are relentlessly ambiguous. Shih's reluctance to make decisions, his means of forcing others to take up this responsibility, is still misconstrued as abdication. Feedback on how well a job has been done is insufficiently warm and definitive, say Western employees. That your superior is your mentor, not your boss or judge, is sometimes misunderstood, as is the indirection of many of Shih's policies.

That the Taiwanese type of management can reverse many Western conventions and that these mirror-image priorities work as well as they do tell us that "East is East and West is West" but perhaps the twain can meet, after all.

Chapter 13

—•—

Weathering the Storm: Sergei Kiriyenko, Former Russian Prime Minister

Allard Everts and Charles Hampden-Turner

IN OUR QUEST for leaders for the twenty-first century we ventured beyond the realm of the established economies to the former Soviet world. How has reconciliation been practiced there? We decided to concentrate on Russia, the largest entity of the former Soviet bloc, the motherland of the largest group of the Slavic people and the cradle of both the Russian Orthodox Christian faith and Soviet socialism, a huge country still in economic distress but with a population of 150 million people who take pride in its rich history and its norms and values—its Russian soul.

How can one go about being successful in Russia, where, according to Western observers, the social fabric is ruptured and the economy and the people crave stability? In most of what we hear and see about "successes" in Russia, the reconciliation of value dilemmas seems to play a marginal role. Where can one find successful leaders, managing by reconciling value dilemmas, in this vast and still overwhelmingly Byzantine-style empire—managers who can lead the change Russia is going through? With Russia's isolation finally breaking down thanks to foreign-language education, the Internet, and travel, many people in the new generation must be developing respect for values that differ from the Russian ones—a respect necessary to bridge the gap dividing them from their political and economic counterparts in the West. We decided to interview one of those Russians.

On the advice of our friend Dr. Jurn Buisman[1] and with his extensive introduction, we were fortunate enough to interview Sergei Kiriyenko. He is, of course, best known as the former prime minister of the Russian Federation, appointed at the astonishingly young age of 35. Before that he was the founder of the Social and Economic Bank Garantiya, where he was so critical of the management of NORSI oil that the governor made him president so that Kiriyenko could demonstrate his own advice! He moved from there to government circles in Moscow, where he was briefly first deputy minister, minister of fuel and power, and then prime minister. He was elected to the Duma (Parliament) in 1999 and retains his reputation as a brilliant financial reformer.

Our reason for seeking out Kiriyenko and featuring him is significantly different from our criteria for selecting other leaders in this book: We wanted at least one case in which the dilemmas confronting a leader were overwhelmingly fierce and intractable. However important conventional business success is, we must pause to admire those who fight against force fields and dilemmas of ferocious intensity that would disable lesser persons.

By interviewing Sergei Kiriyenko, we were satisfying our search for a leader caught in a maelstrom of conflicting political pressures. Even if he did not "succeed" in the conventional way (although he did so brilliantly at first) and as a manager, he could give us a graphic account of the dilemmas that menaced him. Tragedy has always been a lesson full of drama, because dilemmas reveal a soul in purgatory and are clear and forceful: "To be, or not to be." In Kiriyenko we sought a Russian soul who could vividly describe the trials inside the maelstrom of Russia. How do you "manage" in a country where that concept barely exists? How do you "reform" in so weak a democratic tradition? In our quest to discover his tribulations we were not disappointed, but we were also surprised to discover a brilliantly innovative leader who thor-

---

[1]Dr J. A. W. Buisman is the director of the Benelux branch of the Foreign Investment Promotion Center (FIPC) of the Ministry of Economy of the Russian Federation. The FIPC was created by the Russian government in 1995 to stimulate foreign investment in Russia and to bridge the cultural distance between Western business initiatives and the Russian federal and regional government institutions at the top decision-making level.

oughly deserved his promotion to his country's premiership, even if that position proved impossible to deal with.

We broke our own rules in another way in this interview, although doing so had a fortunate outcome. We usually try *not* to reveal the models we are using so that the leaders who talk to us are not affected by any suggestions we have planted. In this case Kiriyenko was hesitant to speak to us at all, and so to intrigue him we had aspects of our model translated into Russian and sent to him. When we met in Stockholm, not only had he read some of our work, he had begun to organize his own experiences and memories along our dual axes, to which he took like the proverbial duck to water. Indeed, much of what he said was structured around several of our dimensions. We were surprised and flattered.

Kiriyenko at NORSI

Analysis

Kiriyenko began by taking an unusual position on one of our dual-axis charts and by writing in the parties to the conflict, as shown in the following diagram:

Dilemma 1: Crisis at NORSI

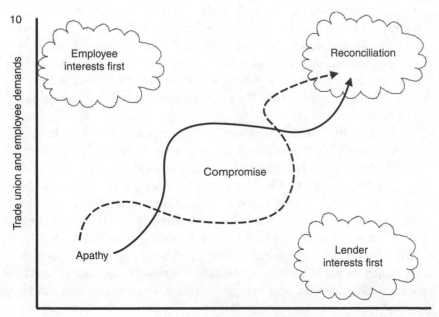

To our surprise, Kiriyenko immediately went for the apathy position (lower left in the chart). This was the mood he had encountered in assuming the leadership of NORSI Oil. In our experience apathy is more notional than real, since the very presence of a dilemma usually means that someone is excited about something. If apathy were total, it would be difficult to see how we would discover a dilemma in the first place: The person would be too bored to tell us anything! But Kiriyenko stuck to his opinion. When he took charge of NORSI Oil, the several interests were uninterested and apathetic, and that was the main problem. He explained: "Because in Russia the skills needed to reconcile [a difference of opinion or a conflict] barely exist and because you can lose badly if you try to gain something at someone else's expense, apathy is extremely common. You just hang on to what you have, trying to change nothing for fear of making things worse. The compromise position [at 5,5 in the diagram] was *not* so common. In order to compromise, you need two defined positions in the first place, and the parties did not have that. They just wanted things to stay as they were and not get any worse. Actually, the culture is not good at compromising either. For that you have to have expectations and then be willing to split the difference. Instead, typically, positions are not taken, and so there is nothing to compromise, nor was there any surplus to be divided."

Of course, the other side of apathy is the trauma of a fierce fight between interests, with one or perhaps both sides losing everything. Apathy is chosen because the alternative—conflict—is so dangerous and so traumatic, especially with gangsterism on the rise. Russia had been moving *backward* economically at the time of the NORSI story. There was less for everyone, unless the sides began fighting, and then there might be nothing at all. We asked for more details, and Kiriyenko complied:

"NORSI Oil Company owns one of the biggest refineries in Russia. When I assumed its presidency, I already knew it was bankrupt. There were the following dilemmas: The monthly costs exceeded the income; the trade union tried to raise the salaries, as did the management; the authorities wanted to raise taxes; the creditors wanted the debts to be paid; and the oil suppliers wanted lower refining costs. It was a vicious circle. For example, the trade union wasn't willing to talk about reducing the expenses for the social security system or reducing the cost of the numerous social enterprises around the refinery (blocks of apartments, holiday retreats, hospitals, etc.). Fifty percent of the costs had no relation at all to the refinery production. The authorities were unwilling to reduce taxes. Debts surpassed the value of the plant by 1.5 trillion rubles, but at the same time the authorities objected to the plant's going bankrupt because, as a result, 10,000 people would lose their jobs. Finally, the managers didn't want to change course; they would just borrow more money, thus creating a classical debt pyramid. This, by the way, increases the power of the director, because he can decide which debts to pay, thus creating an additional possibility for corruption! As for the oil suppliers, they are interested only in their own businesses. The more complex the shipping of the refined products is, the easier it is for the oil suppliers to make a personal deal with the director. Worst of all, nobody wants to normalize the situation. You can try to mark the different positions on the graph, but there is no wish to find a compromise. No one is even going to look for one."

It was not just apathy, but paralysis! The system was slowly subsiding into a wealth-diminishing spiral disequilibrium, but to rock the slowly leaking boat was to risk catastrophe. Everyone clung to a bit of the boat as the subsidence continued, and no one bailed.

Radical Action

"You have to accept where people are now," said Kiriyenko, "and that was at [the lower left of the diagram]. We had to break them out of that state. The only way was to abolish the whole company. Because the system was in apathetic equilibrium, with no one daring to let go, we decided to end the existence of what they were clinging to. I got the agreement of Governor Nemtsov of the Nizhny Novgorod Oblast that everyone be told that the plant was closing. We set up a new management company with a controlling stake in the share capital of the plant and signed an agreement that this company would control everything, such as the flow of commodities and finances, and would have final management responsibility.

"The immediate result was *more* apathy! Whereas before no one had wanted to move, now no one felt *able* to do so. There *was* some regret expressed that they had not tried to reach agreement earlier and that this was the consequence. They had forfeited their chance to influence events; now we acted unilaterally. We formulated new rules. On December 1, 1996, all debts were frozen: salaries, taxes, debts to old lenders, debts to oil suppliers, and so on. We stated that new money generated from refining new oil could not be used to pay and service old debts. Fifty percent of this new revenue would go into the improvement and maintenance of the plant so that it would become more productive, and 50 percent would go to defray debt in a publicly transparent manner, via a Council of Lenders, which published its decisions. In this way, NORSI would stop the steady erosion of its effectiveness and could start to make progress. These rules were strictly applied. I was in trouble if I broke my word. Everyone and everything was hanging on this new dispensation.

"We deliberately paired off the parties and got them to negotiate with each other, seeing that there was not enough for everyone to get all of what was owed to him or her. Negotiating at least moved them from apathy to compromise. For example, the trade unions were forced to negotiate with the tax authorities and lenders. After all, if no one earned anything, no one could pay taxes, and so unless the authorities relented somewhat on the company's back taxes, there would be nothing to collect from the employees. Lenders and suppliers were also invited to negotiate. If the lenders stopped lending, the company would be unable to pay its suppliers; if the suppliers cut NORSI off, the demand for loans would dry up.

"Even with my encouragement for them to negotiate with each other, they often could not do it. So I offered agreements to individual interests: If they agreed, they got some of their claim; if they did not agree, they had to wait. It was just as well, because NORSI did not have the money at that time to meet all claims—even compromised ones—so those who held out actually helped it over its cash-flow crisis. Gradually, however, all the parties began to accept agreements. I presided over the agreements and the resulting flows of funds. In the early stages I favored the unions and employees because I needed allies, needed the company to cohere, and needed production to improve quickly. As things picked up, however, I swung to the side of the suppliers and creditors. Now that NORSI could generate some income, it was its turn to be repaid. At all costs, I had to prevent everyone from reverting to apathy. If I could help the various interests create new agreements and if they discovered that skill in negotiation made a difference to their futures, they would begin to gain some mastery over their fates and see that each interest needed the other to cooperate."

The Upward Movement on the Chart

Whereas all the parties had earlier been clinging to shares of the refinery's meager and diminishing income, now NORSI generated more income to share. Production had increased 300 to 400 percent. With 50 percent of income being plowed back into improvements in plant operations, NORSI was at last adding value. At long last there was something to compromise *about* something more than continued failure of which no one wanted a share. In fact, several parties got a smaller *percentage* share than they had received before, but because the income had grown so much, they actually did much better.

The next diagram tracks NORSI's progress.

Dilemma 2: Progress at NORSI

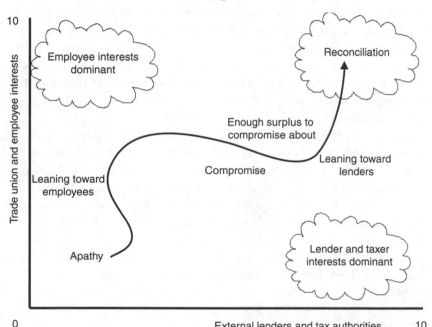

We see that Kiriyenko's first move was toward unions and employees: He had to get them productive. No sooner had they begun to generate a surplus, however, than he leaned the other way. Suppliers and lenders had to be paid, and taxes were needed to shore up the crumbling infrastructure. But above all, there was *now something worth agreeing about*, a greatly enlarged income stream, even if the result was a compromise (at the middle of the chart). This was a huge gain over the earlier apathy. We marvel at Kiriyenko's intuitive skills (and cold-blooded determination). With no tradition of management studies to inform him, he had grasped the idea that he had to wend his way between internal and external interests to provide them with reasons for negotiating with one another. With a surplus to distribute, the system came to life.

Kiriyenko continued: "After six months I got all the interests together around the table and confessed that I had had to play them off against each other and that those who had not agreed had had to wait." His next move was just as bold: "As of now, my individual agreements with them would cease. They would get what they had agreed upon with each other. I think it was a new experience for them to strike a new bargain with their environment and live by that agreement. If those agreements were fair, the income to be shared would grow. They had grown up under centralized coordination, with rules not agreed on among parties but imposed from the top, and so they had had no practice in reaching agreements and had no motivation to do so. When centralized imposition from above began to disappear upon the breakdown of the Soviet system, the various interests froze into apathy. Nothing in their experience had taught them to reach agreements independently.

"Their initial attitude toward change was not that it might improve productivity but that one of the other interests was 'after our share' and had lobbied me to that purpose. They would therefore oppose all change on principle and hang on to the remnants of what they had. What we taught them, I believe, was that they could build up a business via voluntary agreements and jointly take charge of their destinies. Instead of waiting for a ukase, an edict from above that was traditional since tsarist times, they could realize that no more edicts were coming. They were on their own. They had an autonomous company created by their own interests."

External versus Internal Control

Kiriyenko found one of the authors' dimensions particularly apt for the situation NORSI faced: inner-directed versus outer-directed (Dimension 6 in Chapter 2). The Russian people, in general and historically, have had their fates decided by external powers. NORSI Oil was just one typical example of this trend. Even the amount of money to be spent on the company's kindergarten was decreed from hundreds of miles away, not by parents, unions, or managers on the spot.

When we asked Kiriyenko whether the old archetype of the fatalistic Russian was true, he answered as follows: "My hypothesis is that at present in Russia, what motivates people is changing. The main thing for the middle and older generation is to avoid mishaps. That means that to break the immobility you might need, if not a shock, at least a threat—and maybe sometimes a shock. The younger generation and the successful businessmen are now motivated by success, and for them we need a positive stimulus—not a stick but a carrot."

At NORSI, therefore, Kiriyenko had to make things worse before they could get better. He had to abolish the company *and* the ukase on which everyone was dependent. He had to say, in effect, "There is no company or edict coming to save you—only what you yourself create." In November 1996 NORSI was losing 25 billion rubles a month. Six months later, when Kiriyenko left to become first deputy minister for fuel and energy, NORSI was *making* 25 billion rubles a month. He had totally turned around the enterprise by eliminating that on which everyone was trying to depend. This is shown in the following diagram:

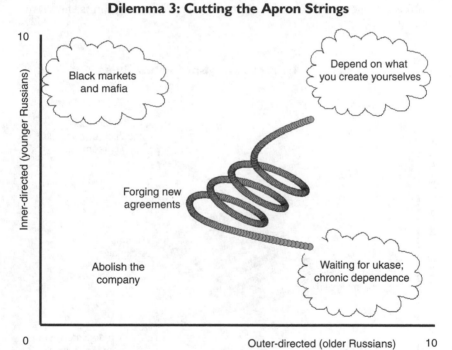

Dilemma 3: Cutting the Apron Strings

The act of abolishing the company forces everyone to negotiate for mere survival new and better agreements through which to halt the losses, or even to profit.

"There is even an application of your rules versus exceptions dilemma," Kiriyenko explained [universal rules versus particular exceptions in Chapter 1]. When he took over NORSI, several of its creditors were getting paid in preference to others. In fact, if you are a large strategic company, owing people money is a power game. You pay your favorites and ignore the rest. You force loans from banks by threatening not to repay earlier loans. Those you like can creep to the head of line and collect money that belongs to others. Why would NORSI avoid chronic indebtedness when that gave it so much power to make or break lenders and suppliers?

When Kiriyenko established new rules and canceled and then re-scheduled all the old debts, there was an outcry. He was cursed, black-mailed, sued, and threatened with physical assault! As some people saw it, the rules had been abrogated, and they resorted to physical coercion. But he promulgated new rules, drew everyone's attention to them, and refused to be intimidated by anyone. One by one they came around, until everyone was playing by the new rules. This situation is shown in the following diagram:

Dilemma 4: From Cronyism to New Rules

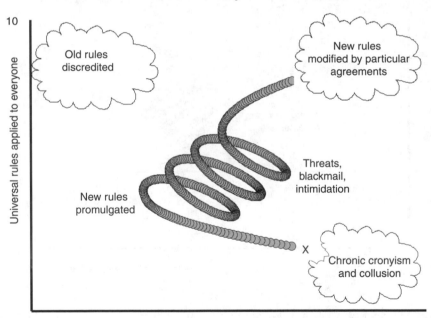

The system was at X when Kiriyenko took over. There was chronic cronyism and collusion between NORSI and "special" creditors. The old rules had been discredited, and so personal favors ruled the roost.

Kiriyenko promulgated new rules, whipping up a storm of threats, blackmail, and intimidation, but by letting the new rules be legislated by the interests themselves, he gradually won acceptance for a home-grown profitable system in which rules covered the particular concerns of all the parties.

After Kiriyenko left NORSI to become first deputy minister in Moscow, oil prices hit bottom. NORSI was struggling again, but he was credited with creating the cushion that allowed the company to survive. As Kiriyenko describes it: "When I was received by Prime Minister Chernomyrdin, he asked how things were going at NORSI Oil. Classic bore that I am, I told him. It took 45 minutes to answer what was, on reflection, only a polite inquiry! But even if his initial impulse was politeness, I succeeded in intriguing him, because he had once worked at the Orenburg refinery. When I had finished, he said, 'I wonder if we could do for the Russian economy as a whole what you did at NORSI Oil.' I thought he was kidding at the time, but when I became Russian premier some time later, I discovered he was serious."

At the national level the debt pyramid and the cronyism were the same, only on a vaster scale, and so was the solution. Could Kiriyenko get the interests bargaining with each other and creating new rules originating within those interests themselves? As it was, Russian prime ministers came and went with Yeltsin's constant changes of tack. When Kiriyenko had to leave, he pleaded to keep the key experts essential to long-term change. Thanks to the combined efforts of Chernomyrdin, Kiriyenko, and, later, Primakov, some continuity of reform survived even as prime ministers were chopped and changed.

Earlier Experiences in the Social and Commercial Bank Garantiya

Kiriyenko's ideas for turning around NORSI did not come out of the blue. After graduating from the Academy of National Economy in Moscow with a degree in banking and finance in 1992, he founded the Social and Commercial Bank Garantiya in 1994. The bank's name suggests that Kiriyenko was seeking a balance between Western commercial imperatives and the social objectives to which the old Soviet system had given lip service but had failed to achieve. His university studies had convinced him that banks had for the most part ill served their depositors and customers and that trust was at a very low ebb and had to be restored if the banking system was to serve the Russian economy. He believed in making money through the fulfillment of social objectives, and so he deliberately set out to create a bank worthy of social trust that made money only insofar as it satisfied its depositors.

Russian banks had for many years served specified industries and had an oligopoly, if not a monopoly, in key industries. They perpetuated a closed shop. You could not get into an industry without financing. Finances, however, were typically in short supply, with banks being prisoners of debtor customers that did not want any new enterprises in their industries and that dominated those banks through their failure and continued indebtedness. Like drowning people in a pool, they clutched each other in a lethal embrace. It was an example of the vicious circle and destructive vortices typical of unresolved dilemmas, as shown here:

Vicious Circle of Ever-Greater Dependence on Underperforming Industries

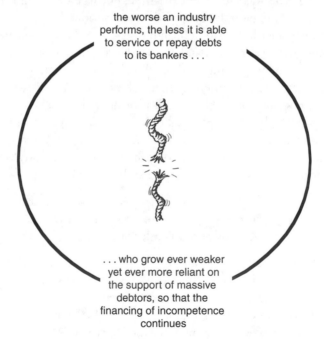

the worse an industry performs, the less it is able to service or repay debts to its bankers . . .

. . . who grow ever weaker yet ever more reliant on the support of massive debtors, so that the financing of incompetence continues

Kiriyenko realized that he had to start from scratch with a customer base that was not already captive to failing institutions. From his youthful experience as the secretary of Young Communist Leagues in the Red Sormovo Plant and in Gorky (now Nizhny Novgorod), Kiriyenko had retained his idealism. It should be possible to serve the people and at the same time generate a surplus to serve even more of them. Banking was the field in which status was mostly *ascribed*, he told us, using the fifth of our seven dimensions. Bankers simply "were" officials in a highly centralized system. That bankers might *achieve* by means of intelligent, well-judged lending and thus grow bigger was very new to Russia at that time and very rare.

A Bank for Those Most in Need

Kiriyenko chose as his new customers some of the most exploited and distressed of his fellow Russians. He targeted older citizens with pensions, savings, and retirement income. Although many of them had worked all their lives, inflation had reduced their pensions to pittances, if indeed the pensions were paid at all. Many industries were defaulting. Many pensioners had fallen victim to pyramid schemes in which those at the apex increasingly exploited those at the levels below until the whole collapsed in scandal. "Elderly people tended to save more, and so they were a source of income for us, but they were also more bemused by economic changes, more likely to be cheated, and more distrustful of banks," said Kiriyenko. "Our social research showed that these customers needed more than a safe place to deposit their savings: They desperately needed someone to advise, protect, partner with, and represent them. They needed a financial institution to trust with what remained of their savings.

"We began to specialize in the support of Russian pensioners, training our staff especially for that purpose. This included the delivery of cash to the pensioners' homes so that they would not have to venture outside if they found that difficult or risk being robbed in dangerous areas. But we still needed a bold initiative to distinguish us from other banks—to guarantee that we were on the pensioners' side and would stay there. We set up a supervisory council to represent depositors and other customers. This was our guarantee that we would not do—indeed, *could* not do—anything against the depositors' interests, because the council had to approve any move we wanted to make.

"At that time interest rates were very much an issue because they could go up or down, and if they did not stay ahead of inflation, depositors could lose. Those were times of financial turbulence. Among the specific duties of the supervisory council was approving or, as it happened, disapproving changes in our interest rates. I was not at this stage aiming for reconciliation. I was still fighting apathy and the accompanying despair. Many of our depositors had been through hell. What I was aiming for was a fair compromise between the interests of those who were relatively powerless and our own interest in building up the bank and increasing the number of our customers.

"The way the supervisory council behaved, routinely siding with our customers against us, was costing us a lot of money. Other banks could adjust their rates to market conditions better than we could, but I was not prepared to disempower depositors or abrogate the decisions of the council even if that had been legal. No one else was even compromising with depositors; everyone was taking advantage of them. That the council was standing up for depositors' rights was winning a lot of attention, and the number of our customers increased rapidly.

"Even so, it was a classic compromise along a straight line. What depositors won, we lost. If we had won, they probably would have lost. But I cannot overemphasize what compromise meant to the parties concerned. We were making money as a bank, and the gains were being shared between the bank and its customers. That was a rare event in the economy of that time, and it still is. That we had some gains to divide up between us, that pensioners did not lose, as routinely happened, that their council got its way and we backed off—all these were rare events, and people took notice." We can diagram the situation as follows:

Dilemma 5: Compromise and Beyond

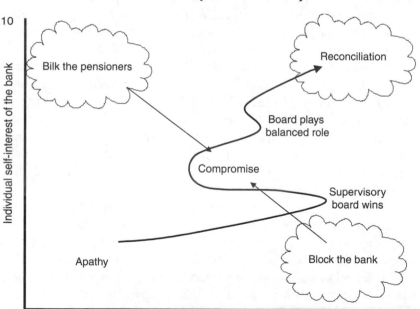

There is a straight-line compromise between bilking the pensioners and blocking the bank, with the bank on one side, pursuing individual self-interest (individualism), and the supervisory council on the other side, upholding the community of pensioners (communitarianism). The S-shaped line first moved from apathy rightward, as the supervisory council was encouraged to win several disputes. Unless this had happened, no one would have believed that the council was anything but a front for the bank's own interests. After the council had won two or three rounds, Kiriyenko approached it and had it examine the numbers. He showed what the council's "victory" had cost the bank on at least one or two occasions and pointed out that those monies had also been lost to the depositors, to whom they rightly belonged. When the council made its judgments, inquired Kiriyenko, could it look more broadly at the prosperity and survival of *all* the parties, the bank included? If the bank went bust, the pensioners would lose their only friend in the financial world. Surely it was in the interest of all that all survive, the council and the bank included.

A Sensible Long-Term View

After that talk the council stopped acting only in the short-term interests of the depositors in all conflicts and stopped merely maximizing the pensioners' immediate returns. It saw the sense of making interest rates responsive to the changing markets and began to achieve a vital balance between different interests. Perhaps it was not exactly reconciliation, but the bank was on its way! It had moved beyond the straight line of win, lose, or compromise. The bank made it clear that it was concerned about the pensioners, and so their council should be concerned for the bank, if only because such concern would help the bank continue to cooperate and extend aid to some of Russia's most exploited people.

In place of the vicious circle described earlier, there was now a virtuous circle:

Virtuous Circle of Benefits to Pensioners and Bank

the better the bank can
serve pensioners, kept up to
the mark by the supervisory
council of depositors, the
more . . .

will be the pensioners
who offer to invest their
savings, trusting in the
fairness of the bank's
representation; thus,
armed with fresh
deposits . . .

The Pension Oil Scheme

An extension of the activities of the Social and Commercial Bank Garantiya was the Pension Oil Scheme. In Kiriyenko's words, "Because we had started with pensioners' personal deposits, it was not long before the bank started providing services to the Nizhny Novgorod branch of the Russian Pension Fund, which appreciated the fact that its own depositors trusted the bank more than they did other financial institutions." It was extending the rapport that the bank had achieved with its own supervisory council.

"The bank was asked to look into a major problem facing the fund. There appeared to be a conflict involving the central pension fund in Moscow, which did not receive enough monies from the pension fund in Tyumen. Tyumen is a major oil-producing region. Thanks to those oil activities, the Tyumen branch of the pension fund is a net contributor to the central fund. Moscow should then distribute the funds to the recipient regions of the federation that generate insufficient funds to pay local pensions. One of those regions is the Nizhny Novgorod Oblast."

"We found that the oil companies were not paying on time, and so we set out to study why payments were in arrears. The problem turned out to be not a shortage of oil but a dearth of buyers for oil. At that time [1994] the oil companies had a sales problem. There was oil but no money to pay for it. The oil companies were ready to pay the pension debts by delivering oil, but neither the central pension fund nor the Tuymen pension fund wanted oil. And of course you can't pay pensions in oil. As a result, the oil companies were fined for making late payments and thus accumulated even larger debts. Then we realized that in Nizhny Novgorod there is the NORSI Oil refinery, which was receiving insufficient amounts of oil for refining because the parties were not confident about being paid and there was no one to make payment guarantees. Then, as a final factor, there was the governor of Nizhny Novgorod, who had two problems: the delay of pension payments and his refinery, which operated under capacity and generated no taxes.

"I at once saw that here were some potential clients for the bank: NORSI, the government of Nizhny Novgorod, the Russian pension fund, and the oil companies of Tyumen. Unfortunately, they were all fighting with each other and were thus perpetuating a crisis in which pensioners were being starved of their entitlements. We did not have a solution for the whole federation, but we did have a local solution: The governor of Nizhny Novgorod would guarantee that when oil from Tyumen arrived at NORSI, the proceeds from refining would go to the Nizhny Novgorod pension fund. This local pension fund, via the central fund in Moscow, could then guarantee the pension fund in Tyumen that it would get its money from the oil companies that were delivering oil to the NORSI refinery.

"Through the governor's guarantee, all parties won. Oil companies were no longer fined for delayed pension contributions and could settle their debts with the Tyumen pension fund. The refinery got oil and began operating again. The Nizhny administration received its taxes, and pensions in the region could be paid on time. The Nizhny pension fund received pension contributions from the refinery, and even the Tyumen pension fund benefited from the scheme, because the salaries of its employees depend on the income generated through the scheme.

"Only for the central pension fund in Moscow was there a certain disadvantage: Now all the funds would go straight to the Nizhny branch. However, Nizhny now received money that otherwise would not have been received at all. The Pension Oil Scheme certainly won many new clients for the bank."

Russia's Major Problem: Change at the Center, not the Periphery

Impressed by Kiriyenko's ability to structure an approach to solving major dilemmas in such a way that all parties seem to benefit in one or another way, we asked him about the future. If one day he were again to be at the helm of Russia or in some other position of high responsibility, would his ability be sufficient to reform that enormous country, to help it move from the old into the new world—to help it keep moving toward wealth? He reminded us: "You remember that in talking about the bank I drew a picture showing the management of the bank at the center, the staff around it, and, outside the circle, the depositors with whom they needed to reconcile? Russia is worse. . . . It's *concentric* circles everywhere [see the accompanying diagram]!

Concentric Circles of Governance

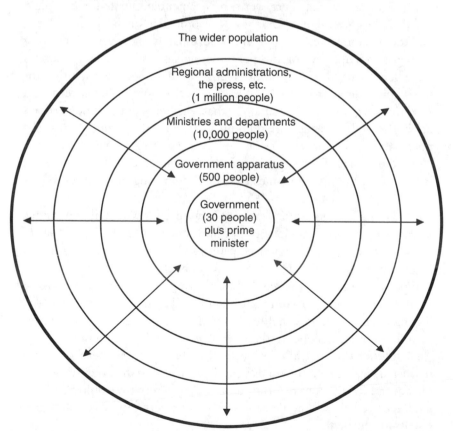

"The smallest circle represents the government with its members: 30 people and the prime minister at its center. Then we have the apparatus of the government, 500 people; then the ministries and departments, 10,000 people; then the regional administrations, 1 million people; and so on. The problem is that the population sits only in the outer circle. Social and economic changes can be organized near the center, the 'inner circles' of the system, but we have so far failed to bring with us those beyond the first few circles of influence."

Kiriyenko went on to say: "When I was prime minister, I managed to solve the problems in the first circle and maybe in the second. We did design the right economic program, as the year [1999] has shown. Inside the circles, nonetheless, there were huge contradictions and conflicts of interest—for example, the balancing of the budget and social expenditures. It was also necessary to get on the same line with the IMF [International Monetary Fund] and foreign lenders, and the two inner circles managed to do so within four months. But then my mistake was to underestimate how many circles there are between the two inner circles and the outer circle representing the population and public support. When we crossed into the third circle, there was no time to mobilize the public support needed for our action. To cross the border of each of the circles takes more and more time, and the contradictions and the methods for creating agreement in each are of a different nature as well. For instance, in the inner circles agreement was reached on the basis of economic interests, but further on it was necessary to coordinate political interests.

"Using your value-dimension model, I would say that in the nearest future the most important dimensions for Russia will be the contradiction between individualism and communitariarism, external and internal control [Russia inside and Russia for the outside world], and the nation's attitude toward time. It is necessary to have a synchronous approach to the issues that face the country, because the problem in Russia is that most of the people are ashamed of the past yet don't see the future. They live in the present moment, and that is the problem: They live in the same apartment they are repairing. These are the greatest contradictions. They can be solved through political means but not quickly."

Thus went the stellar rise of Sergei Kiriyenko to the premiership of the Russian Federation. Sadly, some systems are too much for even the most talented leaders. What used to be called "the contradictions of capitalism" and might now be called "the contradictions of post-communism" were finally too strong for one of the country's most able administrators. In the end only *some* dilemmas are within our own cognition; many lie *between* us and other people in our culture. The force fields within cultures can be fearsomely strong and divisive. The would-be reconciler is among the foremost casualties.

Kiriyenko seems to be only too aware of this, aware of his own vulnerability and limitations. His personal vulnerability is not something that seems to bother him, but the fate of his ideas on economic and political reform does. Therefore, we were not surprised to learn that just one week before the latest elections to the Duma, his political party, the Union of the Right Forces, lined up with the supporters of Putin. This alignment was a final proof of Kiriyenko's reconciliatory capabilities, adapting his impressive abilities to create a concept for a new economy in Russia with the popular support he was unable to mobilize on his own.[2]

[2]On May 18, 2000, it was announced that Sergei Kiriyenko had been appointed plenipotentiary of the president of the Russian Federation of the Volga District. As one of the seven new "supergovernors," he will be in charge of 15 republics and regions between Moscow and the Urals.

Chapter 14

—◆—

Toward a New Spirit: Edgar Bronfman, Seagram

Fons Trompenaars, Todd Jick, and Charles Hampden-Turner

*I*T IS NO coincidence that we hear so much today about the missions of companies, their values, cultures, and purposes. We are advised to study *Living Companies* (Arie de Geus, 1998) and companies *Built to Last* (Collins and Porras, 1997). This is much more than rhetoric and public relations, for the fact is that leaders can no longer tell subordinates what they should do. Problems and challenges are too complex and too numerous. There is insufficient time to refer most issues to the top of the organization, and no mind is capacious and knowledgeable enough to be able to make hundreds of judgment calls a day.

What has to happen is that leaders must manage the *culture* of the corporation: its values, mission, purposes, strategies, and aims. Then autonomous agents within the context of that culture will make decisions that respond to those cultural aims. Rather like a director shooting a film, the leader does not tell the actors how to act but describes the setting and the meaning of the situation and lets the characters loose to interpret their roles. The leader also recognizes quality in performance and moves on to the next take when quality has been achieved. The leader may not know how to handle a camera, but he or she knows good camera work. The leader may be incapable of rigging lights but knows when a set is properly lighted. Values are used to set parameters (or soft goals) so that initiatives can be taken within them.

Shared meaning, values, and culture are all the more important when sites and operations are geographically dispersed. When the industry is in flux, when environments are turbulent, and when times are tough, it is even more important to know who you are, what you value, and where you intend to go. Edgar Bronfman, chief executive officer (CEO) of Seagram, faced such a situation. In addition, he was convinced that the firm's culture and values would have to change if the company was to engage its changing environment successfully. What follows is an account of Bronfman's program for change.

What Bronfman Faced

Culture and Values: What Are They?

Values are embedded in culture. The culture of an organization is the pattern of *what actually happens* on a routine basis—what has been seen to work well and is therefore admired and rewarded, what achieves internal integration and external adaptation, and what is passed on to newcomers as "the way we do (or don't) do things around here." This definition is taken from Edgar H. Schein (*Organizational Culture and Leadership,* 1997), and it has several implications. Culture is *not* just what a CEO dreams up, extols, or tells people to do. The values espoused by an organization may or may not be realized in practice. What managers say they do, what they actually do, and what customers experience are not necessarily the same. Not all talk is walked. Not all aspiration is realized.

Seagram's Challenge: The Necessity for Change

Joseph E. Seagram and Sons, Inc., is a major player in the global beverage industry and has diversified into entertainment. The history of Seagram was a classic example of a company whose founding values and implicit practices seemed outmoded and counterproductive in the face of significant marketplace challenges. The Seagram Company was founded in 1924 with a single distillery in Canada and became a major player in the beverage industry for more than 70 years. Seagram developed a loyal consumer following with premier products and premier brands such as Chivas Regal, Glenlivet, and Mum Champagne. Primarily operating in North America and Europe, the company successfully positioned itself in these growth markets for decades.

By the late 1980s, however, the entire $16 billion industry was facing a "new sobriety." Young, up-and-coming executives and entrepreneurs drank water, especially at lunch. The new "high" was work and achievement. Spirits, being highly intoxicating, failed to keep pace with wine, and a health-conscious public turned to wine and fruit juices. Seagram acquired Tropicana in 1988 to keep up with this trend as liquor sales fell. Higher taxes, campaigns against drunk driving, and social criticism of the marketing of spirits proved major challenges to the industry. Bronfman began to repeat his message throughout the company: "Better business results cannot be achieved by business as usual." His vision for Seagram was that it should be "the best-managed beverage company." When he assumed the roles of president and CEO in February 1995, he told 200 senior managers, "I have a vision and a belief that we will be best managed. We will be focused on growth, be fast and flexible, and be customer and consumer oriented. We will honor and reward teamwork; we will lead, not control. We will be willing to learn. We will develop, train, and motivate our people. We will be honest with ourselves and each other. We will manage on the basis of the values we articulate and share."

To realize that vision, Seagram would have to transform itself radically, change the way it thought and acted, reposition itself strategically, diversify, and "reengineer" its processes. Values were to be the medium and the currency of those changes. Over the next five years values were to play a major role in transforming the culture. What had been a proud and successful culture of individualism, entrepreneurship, authority, functional pride, and personal relationships was "in transition" to a new culture built around such new values as teamwork, innovation, and a focus on the consumer. Indeed, the value of innovation would become very dramatic as major strategic changes—multibillion-dollar acquisitions in the entertainment industry—emerged as strong evidence that change was sought.

Seagram's success in the future would derive from this very different portfolio of businesses and a far more global enterprise. Its young and visionary CEO had visibly taken significant risks and laid major new bets for the company. To succeed would require aggressive development of the company's brands and products, as well as people to exploit the new businesses and improve the old ones. But as the plans for reinventing Seagram were being fashioned, it became more and more clear that the company had to change every aspect of the way it had been managed. Indeed, it was then that Bronfman set the goal of being the best-managed company and a growth goal of 15 percent per year—both highly aggressive targets. Toward those twin ends, he was very clear about the need to reconcile top and bottom, hard and soft, and the long term and the short term. But before it could integrate and reconcile these orientations, the company needed to be reengineered.

Reengineering the Company While Developing Its Values

Bronfman was quick to grasp that reengineering was not a magic formula. You cannot change industrial processes without the guidance and understanding that values bring. As he described it, "It was essential from the outset that we would integrate the hard and soft sides of the change process. Reengineering per se is useless. Just looking at values and behavior is not much better. The combination with the right timing is what makes a winning team."

Dilemma 1. Hard Reengineering versus Soft Values

Seagram engaged the Boston Consulting Group in the mid-1990s to assist it in a major reengineering effort. The initial goal was to manage Seagram's business processes and operations more effectively and to reduce costs, yet there came to be increasing recognition that significant barriers to progress existed. The new processes required numerous changes in how people behaved and interacted with each other—indeed, a new culture. Seagram would have to unlearn its old culture, which was characterized by silos, risk aversion, a rigid hierarchy, and limited communication. The company would have to learn how to be more innovative, cooperative, communicative, and customer focused.

Bronfman articulated the conviction that for values to change in a permanent way, *behavior must change first.* People value what they have experienced as accomplishments. They value the results of the accomplishments, the rewards for the results, the admiration received as a consequence, and the processes involved, but the key remains behavior, because the way aspiration is transformed into reality is through behavior. Seagram would finally consummate its values when it began to perform, and Bronfman's target was growth of 15 percent per year, a very sizable improvement on what he had inherited: virtually flat and even declining performance.

The dilemma that Bronfman faced and that his statements acknowledge is that reengineering without values to guide it turns employees into "retrofitted mechanisms" (see the following diagram). But merely espousing values may not work either if the underlying hardware is not being used effectively. "Love-in on the *Titanic*" (see the diagram) should remind us that if the ship's present course and speed are going to sink it, all the culture in the world and all the beautiful people on board will not keep that from happening. Your relationships must give you access to the wheelhouse or they are doomed.

Dilemma 1: Culture as Patterns of Valued Behavior

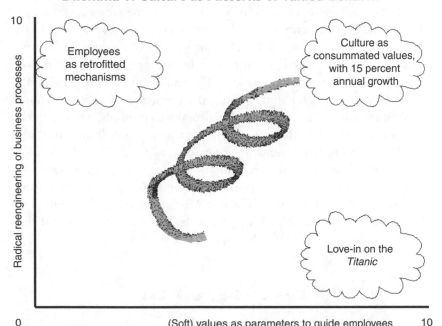

10

Radical reengineering of business processes

Employees as retrofitted mechanisms

Culture as consummated values, with 15 percent annual growth

Love-in on the *Titanic*

0   (Soft) values as parameters to guide employees   10

The helix moves clockwise because you start with soft values and then realize them through the reengineering of hard processes, which in turn makes the soft values operational. Culture arises from values consummated through action. In this case Bronfman made 15 percent growth his target.

Dilemma 2. Top Down versus Bottom Up

If you want core corporate values enshrined in actual behavior, you cannot impose that by fiat. Bronfman had the right—even the duty—to propose the values that Seagram should serve, but then those values had to be negotiated and discussed with the people whose conduct he was trying to influence. He engaged in an intensive top-down *and* bottom-up process to reach agreement on the right wording and the right implementation. Bronfman explains: "I found it crucial to start conceptualizing the basic values myself. I knew where I wanted the company to be heading, but I couldn't do it alone. So we developed a very time-consuming but effective process that included all the employees at Seagram."

Thus, the output of the management conference was refined and redrafted by the top 15 executives. That in turn was reviewed and critiqued by over 300 employees in 8-to-10-person focus groups. Those employees represented a vertical cross section of the entire company—all businesses, all functions, and all levels. They were asked not only to give feedback on the values draft but also to identify behavioral examples of the values in action and make suggestions about how to introduce and communicate those values. The employee version of the draft was much simpler and shorter than the original and also was more understandable to all levels and all cultural backgrounds. Those inputs then were fed back to the top executives, who again redrafted the values. With this draft, the company appeared ready to finalize the six values: a consumer and customer focus, respect, integrity, teamwork, innovation, and quality (see Exhibit 1). Along with the values there was a summary of "values in action," a checklist of behavioral examples for living the values (see Exhibit 2). There also was a strong view that the values had to be measurable in order to be practiced.

Exhibit 1: Seagram Values

VALUES
As Seagram Employees We Commit To the Following Values:

CONSUMER AND CUSTOMER FOCUS
Everything we do is dedicated to the satisfaction of present and future consumers and customers.

RESPECT
We treat everyone with dignity, and value different backgrounds, cultures, and viewpoints.

INTEGRITY
We are honest, consistent and professional in every aspect of our behavior.
We communicate openly and directly.

TEAMWORK
We work and communicate across functions, levels, geographies, and business units to build our global Seagram family.
We are each accountable for our behavior and performance.

INNOVATION
We challenge ourselves by embracing innovation and creativity, not only in our brands, but also in all aspects of our work.
We learn from both our successes and our failures.

QUALITY
We deliver the quality and craftsmanship that our consumers and customers demand—in all we do—with our products, our services and our people.

BY LIVING THESE VALUES,
we will achieve our growth objectives, and we will make Seagram the company preferred by consumers, customers, employees, shareholders and communities.

Exhibit 2: Seagram Values in Action

Consumer and
Customer Focus

➡ We demonstrate through our actions that consumers and customers have top priority in our daily work.
➡ We treat each person we deal with as a customer.
➡ We work continually to understand our consumers' and customers' requirements and anticipate future needs.

Respect

➡ We seek ideas and contributions from people, regardless of their level.
➡ We have a climate where issues are openly discussed and resolved.
➡ We have a balance between our professional and private commitments.

Integrity

➡ We deliver what we promise.
➡ We disclose facts even when the news is bad.
➡ We make decisions based on what's best for the company, rather than personal gain.

Teamwork

➡ We share across borders, across affiliates and across functions to learn from one another.
➡ We work together to achieve consistent, shared goals.
➡ We consider the impact our activities have on other areas of Seagram.

Innovation

➡ We create an atmosphere where continuous improvement and creative thinking are encouraged.
➡ We look for new ways to remove layers of bureaucracy to enable speed and action.
➡ We have patience with new ventures and recognize there will be failures.

Quality

➡ We produce results that consistently meet or exceed the standards of performance our consumers and customers expect.
➡ We consistently improve our processes to better serve our customers.
➡ We get the job done accurately and on time.

One might ask why employees would take so much trouble to discuss, negotiate, and finally agree on the core values inscribed in the two exhibits. Are the values not largely rhetorical? With the generalizations so wide and abstract, is what we have not a solemn agreement on the desirability of motherhood and apple pie? Many corporate missions might indeed be so abstract as to mean almost nothing and to constitute mere frosting on the cake, but we would be unwise to put Bronfman's in this category, because something else is happening here—something that helps explain the alacrity of the negotiators and the 15 percent growth target that later was achieved. The values *are* indeed soft and *do* leave latitude for interpretation, but *therein lies the autonomy of managers and Bronfman's delegation of responsibility to them.* With broad parameters you have considerable discretion from the bottom up in satisfying customers and realizing the values through several alternative means. What these values call for is not obedience to set procedures but self-generated solutions. To focus on customers and their satisfaction leaves all managers with considerable latitude in how that satisfaction is best delivered. The leader is not directing that specific actions be taken but is indicating a process of discovery in which customers are the vital source of information. The values support a process of inquiry into what the environment wants and how those wants are changing. Bronfman is *modeling* the same bottom-up elicitation of knowledge that he wants his managers to employ with customers. The reconciliation of top down with bottom up is diagrammed in the next figure:

Dilemma 2: Confluence of Top Down with Bottom Up

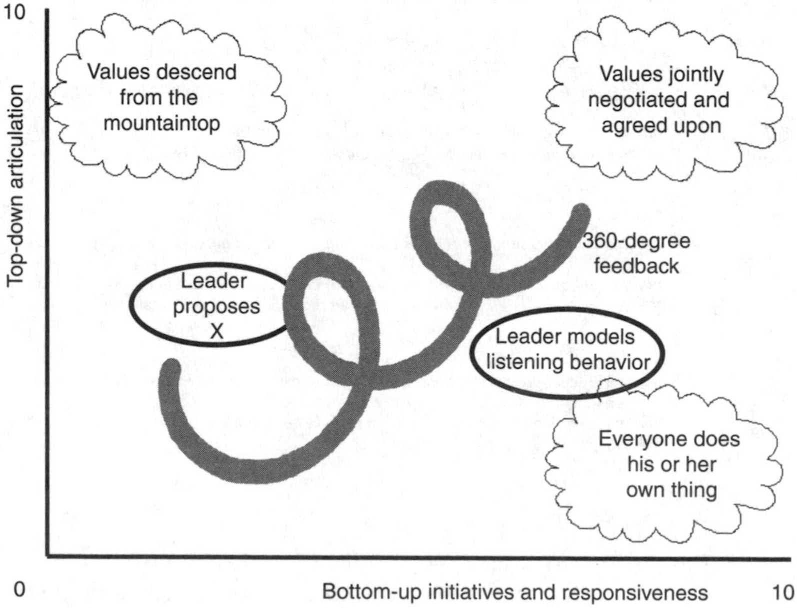

Note that Bronfman has led the process of defining values. The helix starts near the top left of the chart, but this is no imposition: He proposes a set of values, and his managers come back to him with their own revisions and suggestions. Bronfman listens to them just as they should be listening to customers and incorporates many of their requests. Exhibits 1 and 2 are jointly negotiated and agreed upon, with the result that managers will try to live up to what are *their own* values.

Focus groups met at several levels to gauge the reaction of managers and employees to the statement of values. At "cascade meetings" local chiefs met with their direct reports, and comments, suggestions, revisions, and redraftings were collected. One theme emerging from the focus groups was whether "management is really serious about living the new values themselves." In short, workers were waiting to see whether their supervisors were going to behave differently or whether getting the workers' reactions was a verbal exercise to make people feel good. To make the values statements operational and credible, a 360-degree feedback system based on the values was designed and administered to everyone (see Exhibit 3).

Exhibit 3: Directors' Reports

Value Total		
	Total	4.14
	Supervisor	4.57
	Peers	3.96
	Directors' reports	4.21
	Self	4.71

6. This executive is approachable and friendly.		
	Total	4.67
	Supervisor	5
	Peers	4.75
	Directors' reports	4.5
	Self	5

1. This executive seeks ideas from people regardless of their level in the organization.		
	Total	4.44
	Supervisor	4
	Peers	4.5
	Directors' reports	4.5
	Self	4

3. This executive is careful to consider another person's idea before accepting or rejecting it.		
	Total	4.11
	Supervisor	4
	Peers	4.5
	Directors' reports	4.5
	Self	4

4. This executive explains issues and answers questions when communicating.		
	Total	4.11
	Supervisor	4
	Peers	3.75
	Directors' reports	4.5
	Self	5

5. This executive treats people fairly when they make a mistake.		
	Total	4.11
	Supervisor	5
	Peers	3.75
	Directors' reports	4.25
	Self	5

2. This executive supports people in their efforts to balance their professional time with their private lives.		
	Total	3.78
	Supervisor	5
	Peers	3.75
	Directors' reports	3.5
	Self	5

7. This executive provides periodic feedback to tell others where they stand in terms of performance.		
	Total	3.78
	Supervisor	5
	Peers	3.5
	Directors' reports	3.75
	Self	4

Three-hundred-sixty-degree feedback consists of asking peers, supervisors and workers to give feedback on the individual's demeanor—in this case, the individual's capacity to "live the values." The advantage of this tool is that it highlights upward, downward, and lateral styles of communication and identifies both those with a tendency "to bow to the wishes of authority and tread on the people beneath them" and those who organize the grass roots against those in authority. Bronfman used a virtuous circle to encompass the entire culture of change:

Bronfman's Virtuous Circle

The concepts at the opposite sides of this learning circle were in tension with each other: values versus business processes and behaviors versus results. Each acted as feedback for the other. Values led to improved business processes, which in turn confirmed the new values. Behaviors led to better results and increased growth, which engrained those behaviors which had proved effective and eliminated those behaviors which had not.

Dilemma 3. Values Training as a Form of Consultancy and Learning

The new focus on values also was incorporated into training programs; toward this purpose, the Center for Executive Development in Cambridge, Massachusetts, designed two values training programs, each of four days' duration. The first program, "Leading with Values," targeted the top 200 managers; the second, "The Seagram Challenge," reached approximately 1000 middle managers. Each program focused on the meaning and application of the six values in everyday Seagram life and in best-practice standards from other companies. Participants discussed small case studies of Seagram situations in which the values were effectively put to the test. In addition, participants received 360-degree feedback about their own behaviors related to each value, were provided with a private coach to discuss their findings, and were encouraged to develop personal action plans. Finally, each value was assessed on a companywide basis in terms of the perceived amount of "talk" about it and the perceived amount of "walk." Participants were asked to summarize their recommendations for improvements for the company and to close the gap between the walk and the talk as well as the gap between "today's walk" and the desired amount of "walk." The recommendations were presented to and discussed with one or two senior executives, often Edgar Bronfman himself, during the last half day of each training program.

Traditionally, training programs simply impart a lesson that senior managers want their workers to learn. But in this case seminars were designed so that trainees could consult with senior management and assess and monitor the ongoing progress of the values project. That kind of training does not happen "on the side" but is part of a process by which leaders learn along with participants. In effect, training is one more opportunity for supervisors and workers to exchange top-down and bottom-up information to negotiate their differences.

Bronfman commented: "These discussions are very useful. The only way to translate values into behavior is to challenge ourselves as leaders continuously and to allow ourselves to be challenged by those who want to follow us. As leaders we need to keep on pointing at what is valued behavior and what is not. People should not learn this from being fired, when the message comes too late for them, but from the many small ways in which we celebrate what is consistent with our values and discourage what is not."

The dilemma of how to train workers while also educating the educators, or "talkers," is set out in the next diagram. Educators present and reinforce the values, but trainees explain how and why some of those values are difficult to translate into action, and they make representations and recommendations on how to "walk the talk" more effectively. Each side has half the answer. Educators know which values they are trying to instill. Participants in the seminar know the practical difficulties and the pitfalls in the way of making some of the values viable. What happens, for example, when customers want something different from what they should get? How are staff in the field to mediate conflicting loyalties? Training continues the process of making values work in practice. It is a conduit through which customers communicate with the top of the corporation via managers in the field.

Dilemma 3: Training as Consulting to the Corporation

10

Filling the trainees with knowledge about values

Talking down to pupils

Balancing talk with walk; reviewing values in action

Walking as usual

0

Responding to trainee suggestions, criticisms, and experiences of operating day to day

10

Dilemma 4. Those Who "Succeed" but Violate Values: Reconciling "What" with "How"

Many participants in values seminars take it as a sign of Bronfman's seriousness that those who violate values, however "successful" they may be according to traditional criteria, are sanctioned for their violations. Suppose your commercial results are good but you acted in the wrong way—breaking promises, hiding facts, and conning the customer? Bronfman had a chart, borrowed from Jack Welch at General Electric, that dealt with this issue (see Exhibit 4).

Exhibit 4: The 2 × 2 of Personnel Actions

	Inappropriate values	Appropriate values
Make the numbers	Type I Former heroes	Type II New heroes
Miss the numbers	Type IV Newly unemployed executives	Type III Potential heroes

People could *make the numbers* or *miss the numbers.* In the old dispensation that was all there was to it. Those who *kept* missing would soon *go* missing. Making the numbers was everything. Top management was not too fussy about how this was done or whether values were violated. Under the new values-driven system, the "former heroes," or Type I, were to be disciplined on account of their inappropriate behavior while those who fulfilled the values but had yet to make the numbers were "potential heroes," or Type III. Those who *both* missed the numbers *and* violated values now had two reasons for unemployment, as in Type IV, while the "new heroes" (Type II) both made the numbers and personified the values in the ways they behaved.

We have reproduced Exhibit 4 in the exact style Seagram uses, but in fact, it can be represented as a dilemma without altering its sense. We use the following diagram to illustrate—if more illustration is needed—that outstanding leaders think in terms of dilemmas:

Dilemma 4: Reconciling "What" with "How"

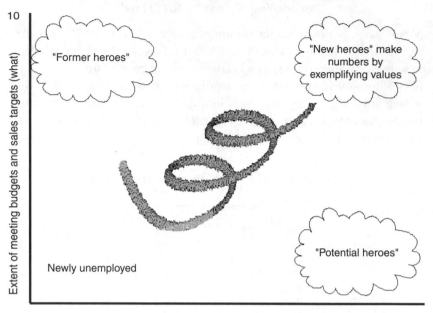

The helix is counterclockwise and moves first to the right, because Seagram wants managers to start by modeling its values. Then, through modeling the values, the managers go on to make their numbers. The "former heroes" may have short-term results to their credit, but they have achieved them through violations of good conduct that before long will weaken the organization and harm the development of its people and customers. Together, these visible symbols of the rewards for exemplary values behavior and the costs of values violations were crucial in reinforcing and sustaining the values. There were always disagreements about who truly deserved an over-and-above award or who deserved to be fired, but the signal was sent that there would be consequences to living or not living the values.

Several issues are still in the process of being discussed. Should those "living" the values be rewarded for this alone—even the potential heroes? Is it not true that living by values is its own reward and should not require additional compensation? Should the entire workforce below management be participants in the values discussions?

Results

Communication of Values in Action

Finally, the corporate and business unit communications managers developed plans to highlight the values in executive speeches, corporate magazines, off-site conferences, annual reports, and letters from the CEO. For example, the quarterly corporate magazine, *Premiere,* included stories of successful values in action—highlighting one or two values in each edition. Even as times and individuals changed, terms such as *Team Seagram, consumer focus,* and *innovation* appeared regularly through the end of the decade of the 1990s.

What Happened? Outcomes and Results

There was no formal evaluation of the impact of the values change, but there are several data points—qualitative and quantitative—that together add up to a qualified success overall. What follows are comments made by Seagram executives in interviews:

> **Reengineering did not just spot gaps in our knowledge and processes; it also discovered a host of hidden talents, roles, and capabilities. We are already reaping the benefits of reengineering in terms of improved business practices and working culture as well as cost savings as part of a continuous drive toward excellence. (Donald Gaynor, reengineering leader)**

> **Cultural change was crucial to improving our performance as we seek to be flexible, innovative, and fast to market. For this to happen, people need a common denominator and clear reference points for behavior—hence, our values-in-action program. (Steven J. Kalagher, president and CEO, Seagram Spirits and Wine Group)**

> **Regarding teamwork, there has been more cross-departmental cooperation. Employees from the sales and manufacturing areas have come together in workshops and learned about one another's job challenges and responsibilities, which has led to a greater respect among and across departments. (A Seagram manufacturing manager)**

> **Our surveys of customers have shown that Seagram's external customers are more satisfied, validating our commitment to the value of a customer and consumer focus. (A Seagram marketing manager)**

> **Some of the traditional militaristic methods that were a common complaint among employees have been replaced by flextime options and casual workday attire. This is a big part of what the respect value is all about. (A Seagram employee)**

In addition to citing these comments, one can point to some quantitative measures of success. Customer satisfaction surveys, training workshop evaluations, and the innovative acquisition of new businesses all indicate market improvements in Seagram's performance. The values have served as a critical impetus for all these initiatives. Indeed, the overall growth rate of the company—attributable to many factors besides the values, of course—increased in the late 1990s. Finally, all the values workshops and discussions have sparked enthusiasm in a group of employees who have the potential to become future leaders and key contributors to the company's success.

Expectations have been raised—and by no means always met. Despite some of the positive changes that occurred in Seagram since the values program was implemented, there remained some underlying skepticism among employees. Despite the fact that this four-year initiative—continuing to date—has been the longest in Seagram history, employees still question whether their managers are truly living the values. Conflicts between day-to-day behaviors and decisions based on some of the values continued to exist and understandably sent disheartening messages within the organization.

For example, to some of the old guard at Seagram, respect means keeping your mouth shut and your head down and treating those who rank above you with awe. Some of the newer, younger, and more innovative thinkers interpret respect differently and feel that they are disrespected by their elders. Another value that is subject to some criticism is teamwork. For some, the existing bonus system still essentially says, "Rank has its privileges," and as a result, "Team Seagram," which is meant to cut across vertical and horizontal boundaries, appears unachieved—as yet.

In sum, the experience to date with values and reengineering has created a lot of good results, but some obvious gaps remain. The reinvention of Seagram's business strategy and business processes is palpable. Seagram has become both a beverage company and an entertainment company. It has transformed numerous fundamental business processes through reengineering. But in the creation of a new "genetic code," labeled as values, there is still work to be done. Indeed, this is hard work that takes many years to bear fruit, and Seagram has made undeniable progress to date. However, as was stated at the outset of this chapter, it is easier to focus on the restructuring, the buying and selling of businesses, and the cost-cutting efficiencies than it is to change the daily work habits and attitudes of thousands of employees. Nonetheless, the long-lasting results of change will occur only when the values are indeed the instinctive habits of the new company and, as such, become institutionalized.

Discussion and Implications of the Seagram Case Study

Seagram's example provides an in-depth look at how to implement values by using management as a critical component in a restructuring and reinvention effort. The details of the process were examined because it is by the details that the success or failure of an effort is determined. What are the general lessons from all this? There are two ways to put this example in perspective: one for the pragmatic practitioners and the other for the reflective practitioners.

What differentiates successful from unsuccessful values-based management? What is common to companies that succeed, and what is common to those which fail? The way a company implements its values program is a critical determinant of whether the program succeeds or fails. Implemented properly, a values program can become the essence of a company. Implemented improperly, it can become the subject of mockery and make the shortcomings of the company more glaring.

Successful values-based management efforts tend to share some characteristics. First, value systems cannot be imported; they have to be homegrown. In doing so, first and foremost, a company must make sure that its values are aligned with its strategy and are seen as a vehicle to help a company build competitive advantage. Second, values typically are balanced between "soft" and "hard" issues. This balance ensures that values are linked to real business and customer issues. Third, proposed values are discussed in detail, and their relevance to the company is debated. If employees contribute to the process, they are far more likely to support and live the values. Richard Pascale, in *Managing on the Edge*, supports these observations as well:

> **Experience teaches us that an effective statement of vision, values, and guiding principles cannot be hammered out by the public relations staff or the human resources [personnel] department. Nor do they blossom from crash efforts of an executive task force. Values are truly a "no pain, no gain" proposition. If top management doesn't agonize over them and regard**

them as a psychological contract between themselves and employees and society, such statements are little more than empty words. But if hewn from discussion and introspection, values come to be internalized as honored precepts of behavior. They serve like the North Star—valuable guiding lights that orient an organization and focus its energies.

Once they agree to a set of values and aspirations, people must be equipped, trained, coached, and reinforced to live the values. In the case of Seagram there was a clear evolution of training efforts to help reinforce the values. In the beginning there were the Leading with Values and Seagram Challenge programs, which were designed to create awareness and build commitment. Then the Living the Values program was instituted to provide a forum for employees to talk about values, and later the Seagram Discovery program emerged to address specific "how-tos."

In putting all these elements together, one can see that the implementation of values-based management ultimately requires a broad repertoire of change levers, all of which are aligned and all of which are crucial. Exhibit 5 summarizes the key elements discussed here and serves as a road map for practitioners of change. The exact sequence and the specific details vary from company to company. However, it is by the effective use of these levers and by disciplined execution that the success of values-based management is realized.

Exhibit 5: Values Management Levers

Dilemma 5. Values Can Evaporate Like Spirits: How to Keep On Connecting

More recently, the question has arisen of how to keep up the momentum. When everyone has agreed on the values in action and after most have been through seminars and raised issues of implementation and practicality, where does the company go from there? One direction was to create additional learning initiatives. A program called Living the Values provided a forum for ongoing discussions. Those who had taken the seminar three years earlier faced new challenges on the ground. Because the challenges had not yet been exposed to the values test, the executives who had taken the seminar could benefit from a refresher course, while the values could be assessed for their relevance to new markets and new developments.

A program called Seagram Discovery targeted new recruits to the company: those who had not attended the original seminars. The values were supposed to be the keys to better performance, but simply believing in them was not by itself going to raise performance. Values had to be imaginatively deployed and mobilized. New ways of "respecting the customers" had to be discovered and tried. The values "came to life" when they made a major difference in the performance of a job. Values also could be interpreted from a variety of viewpoints and perspectives. Ronny Vansteenkiste, head of organizational learning and change and the designer of Seagram Discovery, said, "This program forced people to put on a different lens and see things from other angles. We needed to expose people to such a program in order for us to become innovative. They needed to see the bigger picture."

The process of integrating values with behavior and walking the talk is not a once-only breakthrough. You do not "get it" and then keep the new knowledge safely in the bosom of the corporation. The task of reconciling values with actual conduct never ends, and it keeps coming apart unless it is carefully maintained. Bronfman recently likened values to spirits, which all too easily evaporate into a heady sensation in your nasal passages. Once again demonstrating use of dilemmas, Bronfman condemned both "vaporous spirits" *and* "acting without principle"—that is, acting without knowing or asking yourself why you are behaving that way. The following diagram illustrates the dilemma:

Dilemma 5: Multiple Interpretations of Core Values

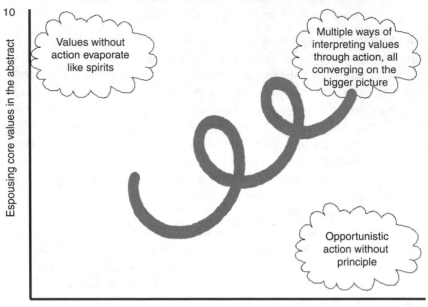

What helps integrate the many ways of serving customers is the underlying principle of respect. The search for new ways to ground values in new realities never ends. Values need to be renewed in all their manifestations.

Commentary

Measuring the Driving Values

There is an old adage that states that what gets measured in a company literally "counts," but values are typically too soft and vague to measure and thus are "of no account." Values are given lip service, but when all the data come in, either you have made the numbers or you have not; your unit either is profitable or is not. Unless attainment of values is measured with equal rigor, it can become so much "noise."

Values-Based Management as a Trend among Successful Companies

The companies that have engaged in values-based management the longest, such as Johnson and Johnson (J&J), have shown that it is indeed a combination of balancing the effort to reinforce with an effort to reinvigorate. Every few years J&J engages in a companywide exercise to challenge and improve its credo of corporate values. Ironically, the words seem to end up largely the same, but the dialogue that occurs serves to refresh and reinvigorate and thus enable people to recommit to the values. Thus, there emerges a delicate but effective balance between *preserving* what people believe to be critical standards of behavior and decisions and continually *challenging* people to find ways to improve them.

Ironically, then, values-based management can both help create change in organizations, as was stated at the beginning of this chapter, and itself be subject to change and challenge. For most companies the challenge of instituting and living values is formidable, but the ultimate challenge for the most successful companies is finding how to keep the values alive through refreshing, reinterpreting, renaming, and reiterating. These "re" words are therefore just as applicable to values-based management as they are to the companies that are facing change pressures and opportunities. Thus, Motorola's "Individual Dignity Entitlement" has no fixed definition but evolves over time through structured dialogues between the supervisor and the person supervised. It is a process of values renewal.

There are many such indicators if you are determined to identify and use them. For instance, *communicating up, down, and sideways* was measured by the 360-degree feedback instrument already touched upon, but this concept had to be eased into use gradually because its verdicts can hurt the managers who are assessed. The discovery that your subordinates dislike you—that, say, women or minority group members find you arbitrary and unpleasant—can be quite a shock. Accordingly, in the first year of operations a manager's score was a private affair between that manager and his or her coach, but in the second year scores became known to the manager's superior and became an official part of the assessment. This meant that in effect everyone had a year's grace to put right negative feedback on values in action.

Visible Actions and Symbols

Another way of supporting *values in action* is to bestow public praise on those whose measurable performance best exemplifies core values. Which field office has been rated the best by customers on the basis of what criteria? Not only should measures of customer satisfaction be publicized, those with the highest ratings should receive honor and acclaim.

Recruitment and Promotions

The process of recruiting for Seagram must advertise for people willing to serve the described values, and during the interview process potential recruits can be asked about initiatives they envision that would fulfill those values. Can they think of ways to make their values work in practice?

Assessment and promotion should employ instruments based on the values. In the case of Seagram several managers were put on "probation" not for underperformance but for not exemplifying the values. This had a profound effect on the culture; values were important after all.

In our view, all micromeasures should themselves be in a dilemma format. Hence, when assessing a manager, you ask, "How bold was your aspiration for the previous year?" "How well did you meet those aspirations?" "What did you achieve?" and "How did you achieve it?"

Education and training have been discussed already. Suffice it to say that the presentations to top management at the end of the seminar should be an occasion to reward the best. Furthermore, there is no reason why initiatives should stop at the door of the classroom. Good presentations can be repeated to key groups of decision makers, and smart teams can be kept together to champion their solutions.

Finally, *leadership behaviors need modeling*. Apart from what you say, fellow managers notice what you do. Indeed, there is much to say for changing your behavior *first* and then, when you have colleagues intrigued with your new conduct, explaining your reasons. If you want staff to listen to customers, it is more effective to listen to staff yourself than to preach a sermon on listening. If you want punctuality at the office in the morning, look to your own arrival times. Actual behavior is much easier to measure than is the utterance of noble sentiments.

Performance Management Systems and Business Plans

Among the easier values to measure is quality. How many broken cases? How many returns? How many late deliveries? What about in-process inventory, carrying costs, and inventory turns? How many customers complained? Do they now believe that their complaints were respected and the problem was remedied? Which were the outstanding teams in the last quarter? Who do those teams believe were their most valuable players in enhancing team performance? Who sponsored the most successful teams, empowered them, and delegated authority to them? Who was chiefly responsible for recognizing the innovative capacity *of others?*

The more ways you can find to measure values, the more reliable will be the pattern that emerges. How and why does a certain person repeatedly sponsor a team, give it a goal, and get wonderfully innovative solutions out of it? We know the values involved—respect, integrity, teamwork, innovation, and quality—but they do not say what crucial judgments the sponsor has made to keep getting superior results. The behaviors that serve these values need constant rediscovery. How do you set goals that "stretch" your group without exhausting or disappointing its members? Values are the avenues of inquiry at the end of which lie realizations of that inquiry.

Rewards can take many forms, but it is perhaps inadvisable to dangle carrots or wield sticks, because they may detract from the logic of discovery involved in bringing values to life. Most values carry their own rewards; your customers will reciprocate your respect for them, and teams can make their star members feel ecstatic about themselves. Rewards are very important for another reason also: Any group or person solving a problem deserves the attention of the corporation so that the solution can be taught. Rewards are not so much the motivators of problem solving or of learning in themselves as they are *signals about who has succeeded and who should now get additional resources to follow up that success.* Those who have brought core values to life need to be highlighted so that others can learn to emulate them and duplicate that feat.

Conclusions

We have seen that values-based management is essentially a participative process in which managers negotiate wide degrees of freedom and latitude in exchange for being assessed according to behavioral indices of how those values have been exemplified in practice. Managers are judged both by results and by the process used to achieve those results. They must "make the numbers" by using methods that clearly derive from the core values involved.

Throughout the entire change process there must be a reconciliation of reengineering with values parameters (Dilemma 1), of top-down articulation with bottom-up initiatives (Dilemma 2), of filling trainees with values with responding to their criticisms and day-to-day experiences implementing those values (Dilemma 3), of *what* has been achieved commercially with *how* it has been done socially (Dilemma 4), and of the abstract core values being espoused with an ever-increasing variety of initiatives that bring those values to life in different ways (Dilemma 5). Bronfman's record speaks for itself.

An Ironic Postscript

Most of our chapters have "happy endings," with all indicators pointing upward. In June 2000 Vivendi, the French entertainment group, made a successful bid for Seagram, and once again all is uncertainty. But values-based management is well designed to help business units survive such experiences—to know amid the turmoil who they are and what they stand for.

Chapter 15

——◆——

Change within Continuity: Karel Vuursteen, Heineken

Dirk Devos and Charles Hampden-Turner

KAREL VUURSTEEN, PRESIDENT of Heineken, took control of a company that had been successful for a number of years, but the prospects of continuing that level of success were uncertain without a renewal of the values of the company. He could not afford to let go of a profitable past, but neither could he continue without making significant changes. He faced the problem of redefining his company in quickly changing circumstances—the ever-recurring dilemma of change with continuity and the challenge of renewal.

Karel Vuursteen: A Professional CEO

One of the authors met Karel Vuursteen in Amsterdam at his office overlooking the canal and facing the old brewery, now a museum and the site of Heineken's new business academy. Although he sits amid the elaborate carvings of the Heineken dynasty, Vuursteen is the first chief executive officer (CEO) to run the company without family members on the supervisory board or executive board. Yet he must somehow reconcile the interests of that family with the professionalism required and expected of a CEO who has been chosen for merit, expertise, and achievements. He has been spectacularly successful, as we shall see.

Heineken's Global Leadership Platform recently flagged some serious problems. There was growing pressure on prices and margins in the firm's retail food outlets. The company's capacity to influence consumers was limited, especially in hotels, restaurants, and other outlets. Much of the growth was in less attractive markets, and the fragmentation of markets had raised marketing costs.

Heineken undertook an extensive exercise in postulating scenarios. Two axes of uncertainty were the relative strength of retailers and the globalism versus regionalism of markets, as shown in the following diagram:

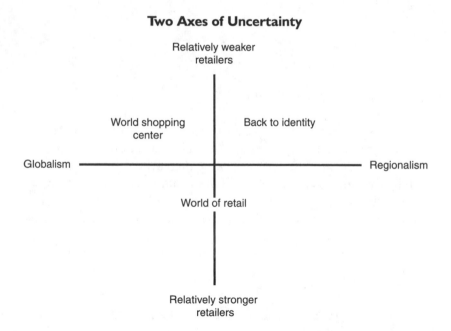

Two Axes of Uncertainty

The following table describes the scenarios in more detail.

SCENARIO	ENVIRONMENT	BEER MARKETS
World shopping center	Continued globalization Free trade Solid economic growth	Powerful global brands Strong local brands Few global brewers
Back to identity	Strong regionalism Strong tariff barriers Slow economic growth	Stable global brands Strong local brands Network of brewers
World of retail	Mediocre economic growth Powerful retail chains Cheap, fast brewing technologies	Strong private-label brands Stable local brands Low-cost producers

In facing these alternative futures, whose salience probably was a question of degree, the Global Leadership Platform saw several strategic dilemmas:

- What would be the consumers' strength of preference between high quality and low cost?
- Would free trade be stronger than protectionism, or vice versa?
- Would regulation facilitate or restrict the beer business?
- Would consumer behavior be group and community oriented or more individualistic?

We will leave these issues for the moment to pick up on the leadership dilemmas described by Vuursteen, but we will return to them in the context of his concern to see how the reconciliation of certain key dilemmas can contribute to the reconciliation of others. Vuursteen and the author discussed three major dilemmas the leader saw himself confronting and needing to reconcile:

1. Rapid growth versus the shareholding interests of the Heineken family
2. A premium branded global product versus a cheaper local-regional product
3. Stability and tradition versus innovative products and markets

Finally, we shall turn to issues flagged by the Global Leadership Platform and the exercise in postulating scenarios and ask what else might need to be done to meet the concerns expressed in these issues.

Dilemma I. Rapid Growth versus the Shareholding Interests of the Heineken Family

The company is still controlled by the Heineken family, and Vuursteen's duty remains to the family (as well as to public shareholders). He is an agent of the owners, obliged to serve their interests, but the owners are of two kinds: private and public. The family-held shares constitute a majority. The members of the family see Heineken as a legacy to their children, grandchildren, and great-grandchildren—indeed, as a legacy to the nation and the global beer industry. Short-term positive results are welcome, but they occur in the broader context of Heineken's contribution to economies and lifestyles and its overall reputation and market position.

"Clearly," Vuursteen states, "I'm not hired by the Heineken family[1] to dilute its share in the company, and so there is a very exciting tension that I have to manage: not dilute the interest of the Heineken family yet grow fast enough to satisfy my public shareholders while remaining world class. I have to be both a caring father and a champion of high earnings." Some people, including certain colleagues in the company, find his policy too cautious. They believe he should sell more shares to the public, increase investment funds, and go for growth at all costs. They think he is insufficiently daring. But his aim is for controlled growth, sustainable returns, and being true to Heineken's origins as a family company that aims to improve the human condition. He is not about to attenuate the family's control of what it built over three generations.

Vuursteen continues: "There is a way of satisfying both sets of obligations, and that is to increase our value per share. That way, both public and private shareholders are better off."

Vuursteen's success in carrying out this policy should not be underestimated. Since he joined Heineken, net profits have tripled from 300 million Dutch florins to almost 1 billion. The company's nominal growth since 1980 has been 14 percent per year, or 11 percent when corrected for inflation; that amounts to doubling in size every seven years. Above all, earnings and value per share have risen since Vuursteen took charge. The dilemma looks like this:

---

[1]The role of the family and business is discussed further in Chapter 19, in which different family business sociotypes are considered.

Dilemma 1: Growth versus Family Interests

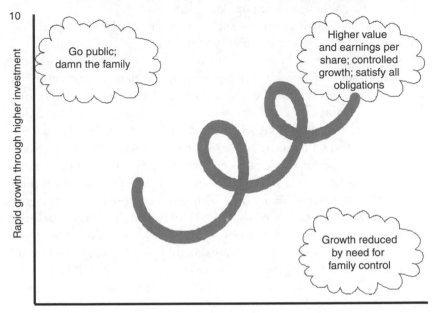

By making each share more valuable and boosting earnings per share, Heineken rewards public shareholders, yet the Heineken family remains in control of its legacy and tradition. Those who originated the company and shared its fate for three generations have rights and obligations superior to those of a pension fund that bought the shares last week and might well sell them next week. Vuursteen has to mediate between these very different stakes.

Dilemma 2. A Premium Branded Global Product versus a Cheaper Local-Regional Product

We have elaborated this dilemma slightly by melding Vuursteen's chief concern, brand versus brewer, with the Global Leadership Platform's concern about premium quality versus low cost and with the issue arising from the scenario-postulating exercise involving globalism versus regionalism. The successful brander tends to earn a global premium, while the successful brewer has a more regional, word-of-mouth appeal based on production processes that initially delight only neighbor-hoods nearby, although their popularity may spread.

Vuursteen explained to the author that the marketing of beer is quite complex. Heineken is the only premium lager beer brand with a truly global presence. At the same time, it must be aware every day of the importance of local roots for beer marketing. Every country, every region, has its own beer tradition, and that specific tradition largely determines how the company can integrate a beer portfolio into the existing traditions of the local market while adding the Heineken brand on top of it as the international premium brand. "We surf on the power of the local beer roots when we enter a new mar-ket," says Vuursteen. Heineken believes it has good reason to do it this way. "Look at Coca-Cola in Brazil," urges Vuursteen. "It never got the soft-drink position Coca-Cola has obtained in other markets, because it neglected regional tastes. We should be aware that local responsiveness is connected with local eating and drinking habits that are deeply rooted." Yet sheer volume and economies of scale are cru-cial in the beer business, which operates according to a very simple logic:

$$\text{Profit} = \text{operating profit per hectoliter (22 gallons)}$$
$$\times \text{ volume of hectoliters}$$

Heineken believes that it has the best brewing technology in the world, but the throughput from using that technology is vital also; it has to push volume through high-quality processes. In 1886 the company developed the famous Heineken A-yeast, which gives its lager a dis-tinctive taste and is the core of its brewing process to this day. Heineken was the first export beer in the United States to offer lager in small bot-tles, making that move in 1933. With Prohibition just ending and the number of refrigerators in the home increasing, the firm won a sizable share of the U.S. market.

The Branded Brewer

Heineken's typical strategy for expansion reconciles the company's pre-mium brand with local brewing traditions. Heineken acquires regional breweries, and it is good at transferring its brewing know-how to them while maintaining the taste that won local acceptance. Using its outlets, customers, and goodwill, Heineken continues their brewing traditions while superimposing its own premium brand. This strategy enables Heineken to encompass both low-cost products and premium products and to convert some consumers to the latter while the company supplies a wide spectrum of demand. Both premium and lower-priced brews push up total volume. In countries where Heineken cannot command high volumes, it aims for a niche position among premium beers and strives for leadership.

Compared to with its competitors, Heineken uniquely combines branding strategies with brewing strategies. Interbrew and South African Breweries are typically strong in brewing, investing chiefly in production and distribution. Anheuser-Busch is among the top branding companies, with its powerful Budweiser brand. Heineken invests heavily in both branding and brewing; its brewing technology gives it economies of scale, and its brands, global and regional, constitute a family, with each member having both a local identity and enough autonomy to grow beyond local roots to a broader presence.

Traditionally, Heineken followed the American pattern of earning premiums with "export lager." In that multiethnic society imported European beers had a special cachet as the authentic flavor of the old countries. Now, however, Heineken is challenging this entrenched belief on the grounds that local product and local sourcing give it regional advantages without the sacrifice of premium qualities. The company exports know-how, not necessarily or always beer. Over time Heineken has switched from *central control* to *decentralized coordination,* which reconciles branding with brewing and globalism with regionalism. When Vuursteen took over the company, he had a discussion with his predecessor, who advised him, "If I were to choose between brewing and branding, I would have to choose branding."

That was in the early 1990s. Vuursteen is now glad that he did not make a definite choice of either one. When you go through a scenario-building process, you realize that you might have to rely more heavily on one than on the other, but you cannot predict which will be more effective. You then see that you require both, with the relative emphasis dependent on circumstances. In a "world shopping center," for example, you need branding above brewing, but in "back to identity" you need all the brewing expertise you can muster. It is irresponsible not to develop both themes.

Can we diagram Vuursteen's dilemma, together with the dilemma seen by the Global Leadership Platform? We believe we can. The conflicting values read as follows:

Dilemma 2: The Branded Brewer

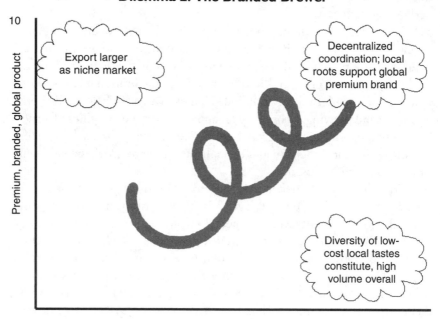

The actual process is a bit too complex to be captured by this diagram. Roots in the local community give Heineken immediate knowledge of local beer-drinking habits and distribution networks. Those facilities are then reorganized to deliver not simply staple brews but also premium branded products. The mix of local and global brews maximizes volume throughput, while advanced brewing technologies make quality relatively cheap. More of this complexity can be captured by devising a virtuous circle:

The Virtuous Circle

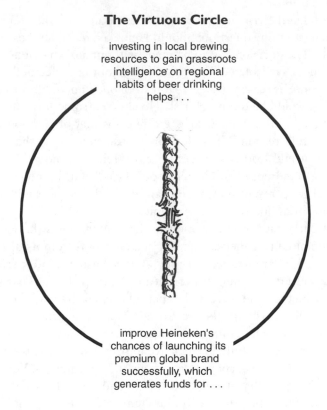

investing in local brewing
resources to gain grassroots
intelligence on regional
habits of beer drinking
helps . . .

improve Heineken's
chances of launching its
premium global brand
successfully, which
generates funds for . . .

Dilemma 3. Stability and Tradition versus Innovative Products and Markets

The Heineken tradition is incredibly valuable but also potentially frail. For over a hundred years it has appealed to people's taste buds, but those sensing devices do not explain why people enjoy Heineken and what commands their loyalty. Because this patronage is in part mysterious, Heineken interferes with it or introduces sudden changes only at its own peril. When you are unsure of what you have, you can lose it easily. When changes must be made, it is unclear what is fundamental to Heineken's reputation and what is peripheral. Historically, the company's reputation has been maintained at great cost.

Vuursteen provides an example: In 1993 Heineken had a problem with glass particles in its bottles. It needed to decide whether to recall all the bottles from all its distribution channels in 21 countries. Heineken had no data on how much this operation would cost. Nor could it judge the risk, because experts came up with different views. Vuursteen faced one question: Should Heineken recall all these bottles, yes or no? The decision had to be made without any knowledge of the consequences. He isolated himself and one hour later decided on a full recall action. His reasoning was that if even one human life was endangered, that would be too much risk. He also saw some possible benefit in quickly admitting a mistake, even if it was that of the bottler, and accepting full responsibility for the consequences. Perhaps ready admission would lead customers to trust Heineken more in the long run. Those hundreds of millions of bottles carried its brand, and so the brand had to act responsibly. Heineken survived that crisis with greater respect for itself and from other people.

In its early days of exportation to the United States the Heineken family promised its American agents that all profits from its operations there would be reinvested in the export business: 50 percent in Heineken advertising and 50 percent in Heineken USA. That pledge, together with the bond it created, is part of Heineken's heritage and tradition. It will not lightly be destroyed. That is an example of how Heineken's approach to innovation is cautious. It changes one thing at a time and watches carefully for negative impacts. Of course, we are talking less about facts than about perceptions and appearances. Vuursteen's view of change is that it must maintain continuity: There are lots of changes out there, but Heineken must remain true to what people like about it even as markets and environments shift.

Vuursteen continues: "In a funny way we are still searching for what has always been important in our appeal to consumers. We know we are successful, but we don't know just why. The real fight is for consistency to maintain whatever our attraction is. We may have to change to remain consistent. This applies especially to processes. Can we do things better, cheaper, and quicker with the same results as before? Can we draw on more talents to preserve our quality? We recently launched a design competition on the Internet for the improvement of beer-can designs. We received top-quality work."

One way of innovating that is not dangerous is to clear a space for a totally new approach, one that is separate from Heineken's existing success and will not endanger it. Look at the Volkswagen Beetle: In the early 1970s the Golf (Rabbit) was created. It was the first expression of a new archetype. It was needed because the Beetle was outdated. So when somebody comes to Vuursteen and says, "I want to create something totally new in the beer market," he is inclined to say, "Go ahead and do it; let's create the free space you need and create this new world, but don't touch the heritage and the present success of our leading products and brands."

This dilemma is expressed in the following diagram:

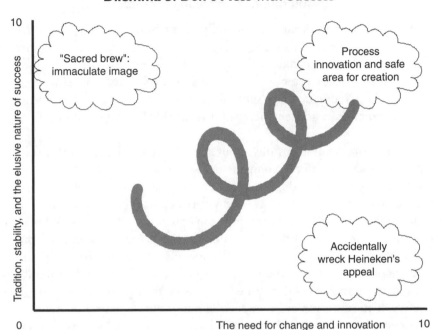

Dilemma 3: Don't Mess with Success

Heineken is highly successful, but the reasons for its success are elusive. That customers like the brand is clear; *why* they like it is less clear. Vuursteen might decide to change nothing for fear of damaging the "sacred brew," or he could embark on wholesale innovation and accidentally wreck Heineken's appeal. Instead, he has very cleverly embarked on two forms of innovation that are relatively safe: *Process innovation* searches for better and newer means of creating the same result, and *reserving a safe area for creation* allows new beverages to be invented from scratch without involving Heineken's premium product in the experiments, much as the Golf grew up beside the Beetle.

This completes our discussion of Karel Vuursteen's three principal dilemmas, but in addition, we can observe an obvious affinity between our second dimension, individualism versus communitarianism, and a very similar concern expressed by the Global Leadership Platform on how consumer behavior might evolve.

Dilemma 4. Individualism versus Communitarianism in Markets

Traditionally, beer brands are heavily advertised on television to the *mass market* (a market of aggregated individuals who do not know each other but who share a liking for Heineken's products). Heineken's export lager grew up in the U.S. age of mass marketing and is one of its outstanding success stories. Surveys show individualism growing in affluent parts of the world. Do we need anything more?

The story Vuursteen told about the glass particles in bottles suggests another side to the company. Most economists will tell you that self-interest and individualism are sovereign and superordinate in commercial affairs, but that is not how Vuursteen behaved in the crises he faced and not how Johnson and Johnson behaved when a deranged person put cyanide in bottles of Tylenol. In both cases, all units of the product were withdrawn and the company took responsibility for the errors of others. When the chips were down, Heineken was a family company concerned with families of customers. Its *first* duty was to the safety of those customers; only second did its duty to enrich shareholders come into play. Crises teach us what our real values are; as Johnson and Johnson remarked, all the money due to shareholders comes from satisfied customers.

In both of these cases the community judged the companies by the social concern they exhibited. For both, sales climbed rapidly after the crises were resolved. Vuursteen had to ask himself what the Heineken family would want and what he himself stood for. In both cases the answer was the coherence of community and individual concerns. Individuals benefit as a consequence of first caring for customers. In crises you learn what economists do not teach.

The dilemma can be drawn as follows:

Dilemma 4: Community Concern versus Self-Interest

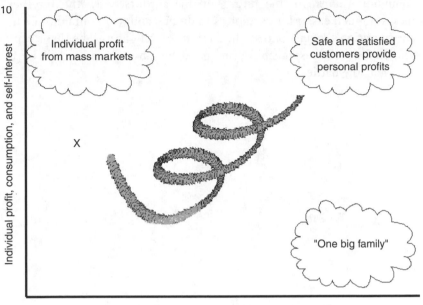

The conventional economic view is at X, where there are short-term profits to be made from mass-market appeals, but when a crisis struck, Vuursteen was challenged to understand that his prior obligation was to the community. "Prior" is not necessarily the same as "most important," though: Prior means "before." Before you make profit, you take good care of customers so that the flow of custom is restored; then you integrate communitarianism with individualism once more. Vuursteen was correct in his belief that this crisis might in the longer run turn to Heineken's benefit. What customers infer from such incidents is the supplier's commitment to *them*. They are impressed, as well they might be, by sacrifices made to protect them. We tend to judge others by their intentions, not by the absence of mistakes. We have learned this from our third dimension: specificity-diffusion. Mistakes are specific, but if they occur in the diffuse context of continuing care and good intentions, we often forgive them.

What are the prospects for the balance between individualism and communitarianism in the future? In the authors' view the Internet makes it much easier for customers to discuss and form opinions about a corporation's social conduct. In the future it might well be that a reputation for social responsibility and good neighborly conduct will be at least half the battle.

Chapter 16

———◆———

The Challenge of Renewal: Hugo Levecke, ABN AMRO

Dirk Devos and Charles Hampden-Turner

ONE OF THE authors (DD) has known Hugo Levecke, the chairman of the managing board of ABN AMRO Lease Holding (AALH), for 17 years. Over that period Levecke's reputation has become formidable: Whenever he was given a leadership task, dynamic growth, improved service, and superior financial performance resulted. The two met at the Okura Hotel in Amsterdam, where they discussed strategic innovation and its inherent dilemmas. Levecke took the lead, warm and enthusiastic as always. The largest part of ABN AMRO Lease Holding's business is in car leasing: 72 percent of the company's profits come from it, and 78 percent of the firm's assets are in it. Lease Plan (AALH's core brand) is among the founders of the car-leasing industry in Europe. The "open calculation concept," in which the costs of leasing are broken down, compared with those of outright purchase, and shared with the customer, has been widely imitated and has contributed significantly to the success of the industry. In many markets Lease Plan was the first to offer global systems to manage the entire fleet of a company's cars. Together with GE Capital, AALH is one of the few international players with a global presence.

ABN AMRO started as a team of 25 entrepreneurial front-runners some 20 years ago; now 5000 strong, the company faces some major challenges in a changing industry, for the car-leasing industry is in the throes of transformation. One can see from a list of its 1000 top clients that more than 60 percent are international companies. There is a tendency toward transnational harmonization of car-leasing policies, and there is pressure for cost management. Margins and fleet-management fees are under pressure, and customers expect tight control of exploding car-leasing and maintenance costs.

On top of all this car manufacturers are becoming players as well and have started their own car-leasing businesses. In mature markets the fleet-management product tends to become a commodity, and operational risks, especially the decrease in the residual value of the leased vehicles, are increasing. The introduction of the euro and of e-commerce will make markets much more transparent than they ever have been; price comparisons will become easier, and operational risks will increase.

As early as 1996 Levecke warned the company's directors about these changes. In his speech at the directors' meeting in Rovaniemi he discussed a number of options with his colleagues. His purpose was to raise issues and pose questions, not to propose solutions. Among the options, should the group

- Switch to commodity pricing and positioning? While doing so would match market conditions, it would waste all previous efforts toward becoming a highly profitable market leader.
- Fully exploit the remaining differentiation options and new-product extension strategies? Would clients really notice the difference and be prepared to pay for it? It could be too little, too late.
- Aim for market expansion strategies, bringing in higher-margin business from new markets to offset the lower-margin business from older markets? This strategy risks being slow and expensive, and eventually one must run out of new markets.
- Create product development strategies, opening entirely new markets and channels as a toehold in new industries and to generate new profits?
- Focus on internal cost productivity? By working in a different way, one may be able to liberate capital resources that will fund

innovative breakthrough projects, allowing new margins to develop. However, this completely depends on the willingness and ability of the existing team to change its daily way of working.

Although these arguments and reflections were heard and acknowledged by the directors, nothing really changed. ABN AMRO Lease Holding was cocooned by its strongest competitive force: the autonomy and entrepreneurialism of its business units. The company had grown up in this way, so why change a winning formula? The freedom of each local company to respond to local conditions had proved highly effective in the past.

Two years after the Rovaniemi meeting, Levecke was asked to chair the managing board. He was convinced that the company should reinvent itself, and he realized that the major challenges were (1) to persuade the same leaders whose local autonomy had been the recipe for past successful reinventions of the company and (2) to develop new patterns of mutual assistance and information sharing. The company needed a single global strategy, although with local adaptions where necessary; all units had to cooperate in its realization. The strategic goal was to be among the top three automobile-leasing companies worldwide *and* in each local market where the company did business. The new overall strategy would encompass an integration of new-product development with internal and external cost-cutting strategies. An example of a new product is Fleet Management Consultancy for transnational accounts. An example of a local adaptation is consumer leasing as it has been introduced in France: CARPLAN is a joint venture with Carrefour, the biggest megastore in France. The distribution of the product is the key factor in success. Manufacturers are very surprised by this development.

As we sat together in the Okura Hotel in Amsterdam, Levecke asked me, "What will happen when brains meet emotions?" He had been strategizing for nine months with unit heads, and he believed that the rational case for what he had proposed had been made and accepted in principle. But what about the emotions? Could the unit heads bring their hearts to this far more interdependent way of doing business? Had the managers not *earned* their autonomy through skill, hard work, and results? All this was a dilemma for Levecke. He had been part of this group. Many directors were his personal friends; he had personally recruited nearly half of them and urged them toward autonomous decision making. Indeed, he was part author and exemplar of the paradigm of radically decentralized operations. Now he was asking them to change their patterns of work. They would be reporting to him, at least on questions of shared strategy. His relationships with them would change, and some of the trust and mutual respect they had developed over the years could be put into jeopardy. Might relationships turn sour?

Together, Levecke and the author inventoried the key changes necessary—the shift from left to right in the following table:

FROM	TOWARD
Managing an operation	Leading a transition
Working on issues that we know rather well	Discovering new issues that we don't know as well
Exploiting a successful formula	Reinventing a successful formula
Local entrepreneurship	Transnational leadership

Levecke said, "I realize that this is demanding a huge transformation of the business. It is about changing our deeply held beliefs, our daily habits, the way we are used to working. There are no easy or secret tricks. Business transformation will require personal transformation in the way we all lead, and each of us is going to hurt inside emotionally—and that includes me. No one will be privileged. We are going to have to go through an intensive leadership development program with our minds open and vulnerable. This is not a linear progression or a rollout of tested techniques but a process of trial and error and of mutual support and understanding for the lessons learned from it. From time to time all of us will be asking each other, 'Why are we doing this?' "

Listening to Levecke, I appreciated his honesty and concern for his friends in their directorship roles. But had he underestimated new ways of tapping into their entrepreneurial energy, new sources of pleasure in risk taking? Might not this new paradigm be an additional source of satisfaction for all concerned? We talked about the four core transitions and considered them in turn. Looked at more closely, the four transitions were really dilemmas, because *leading the transition* could not possibly replace *managing an* (*existing*) *operation* (which would have to follow rapidly upon any transition). The same applied to the other three transitions. The group must, for example, *reinvent a success formula,* but it would then have to *exploit the* (*new*) *success formula;* nor could the group stop *exploiting the* (*old*) *formula* while *reinventing* it.

Dilemma I. Managing an Operation versus Leading a Transition

How can our operational qualities help us better lead the transition? And how can the transition improve our operational qualities? Leading a transition while managing operations is like playing simultaneous chess games. The leaders of ABN AMRO Lease Holding needed to drive current business along with key projects while connecting at a transnational level and advancing the transition process. How was this to be done? An important clue is contained in Chapter 1, where Fons Trompenaars and Charles Hampden-Turner discuss centralization-decentralization and argue that both can be achieved simultaneously, *provided that they operate at different levels.*

The levels that concern us here are those of action and information. Activity of an entrepreneurial kind must remain radically decentralized, as has always been the case since the company's founding. In this respect, the company does not have to change. Managing an operation proceeds as before, with local judgment, skill, and autonomy as strong as ever—perhaps stronger! In contrast, the new centralization, which leads a transition, takes place at the level of information. ABM AMRO Lease Holding *acts locally, but thinks globally.* No one's right to act innovatively is infringed upon, but the information from all such initiatives is shared by all. A "scoreboard" is created that records everyone's autonomous activities and the results those activities have achieved. We now know and share what was tried, what succeeded, what failed, and especially *what was learned* from the initiative.

The answer, then, is not to work *harder* but to work *smarter.* Before you make a deathless decision and put your reputation on the line, you have the benefit of studying similar or identical initiatives that tried to achieve the same goals. In this way you do not have to repeat mistakes and may be able to steer around pitfalls.

In addition to a companywide scoreboard that records initiatives and results, it is important to have periodic meetings. It should be the right of any director to call in any other director for, say, five "consulting days" per year. You form teams consisting of directors or the specialists reporting to them who have had the experiences most similar to the initiatives being attempted by a business unit. Hence, the French director who pioneered CARPLAN with Carrefour in France is a member of the strategy teams trying to do something similar in Germany, the United Kingdom, and the Netherlands. Teams must always have a strategic purpose and seek to move information from one successful project to help create another. These meetings are not committees of people representing other people who have to report back but persons empowered to act so that a team takes direct responsibility for the strategies it recommends. The dilemma and reconciliation can be illustrated as follows:

Dilemma 1: Using Information to Learn

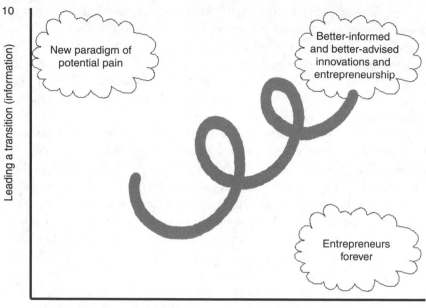

There is no reason for the sense of entrepreneurship to be any less simply because each director now has an intelligent audience to admire and critique each initiative. There will always be local variations in what needs to be done, but the shared global strategy means that any initiative by a local business unit could become a potential breakthrough for all of them. Now the initiatives of all the units have ramifications beyond their own countries.

Dilemma 2. Working on Issues That We Know Rather Well versus Discovering New Issues That We Don't Know as Well

How can we know that we do not know? How can what we know already help us explore? We must follow Gary Hamel's advice in *Manifesto for Revolutionaries* and "challenge the orthodoxies." There are a number of ways to open yourself up to what is new and to what you need to know and to determine which of your assumptions deserve to be challenged. We have already discussed the scoreboard, which compares strategies with the results achieved. What we now need to do is *interrogate* that strategy and those results. Ask those attending team meetings to set the agenda. They may see different priorities or read the information available in different ways. One advantage of asking questions is that you develop hypotheses, which your data then confirm or reject. Data should not be confused with information or knowledge. Information is a *response to a question.* Knowledge is a response so important that it can have wide applicability to many processes, markets, and customers and is therefore stored and shared across the business. For instance, a vital issue in any networked company is *who knows what.* There may be a vast array of experience, information, and success based on these initiatives across the company, but unless you know where such knowledge is located, you will not be able to bring the right people to the crucial issues.

Finally, you have to ask what the current results posted on the strategy scoreboard *dis*prove. What might no longer be true, judged by the most recent achievements? You cannot keep planning without "*unplanning,*" without saying, "Well, that turned out to be wrong!" A final advantage of a knowledge-creating company is that errors and failures are useful information from which other business units can learn from and which do not have to be repeated.

The dilemma looks like this:

Dilemma 2: Interrogating Strategic Results

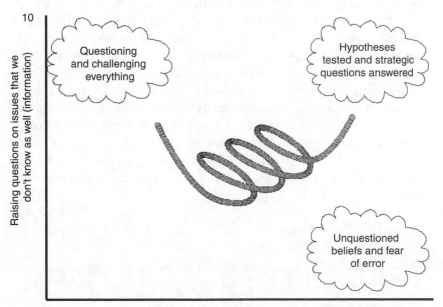

In this model all business units share and compare their results, which are systematically interrogated to see whether they fall short of the strategy or whether the strategy fails to illuminate and model the results. We can improve our performance, revise our strategy, or do both.

Dilemma 3. Exploiting a Successful Formula versus Reinventing a Successful Formula

To some extent this dilemma is resolved by the two earlier reconciliations. Giving each business unit entrepreneurial freedom to maximize returns on the open calculation concept was the original formula for success. Now we must reinvent the formula by investigating what these businesses have discovered that could be generalized across the whole group and again lead to a fundamental breakthrough in the car-leasing industry.

Levecke recognizes in his strategy for the future that car leasing has a life cycle of birth, growth, and maturation. It is possible for mature businesses in developed countries to anticipate the growth pains and advantages of the countries following behind them. Many of these emerging countries may seek to leapfrog the earlier stages of development and go straight to leasing in its more sophisticated forms. Nothing decrees that we should all make all the errors of all our predecessors. It makes sense to cut straight to the leading edge. Perhaps the quickest way to learn is to regard all successful entrepreneurial initiatives as potential strategies for other business units to follow, what Henry Mintzberg has called *emergent* strategy. These successful initiatives could be more than local successes; in rare circumstances they could be strategic models that can be generalized to other units and used in the design of a megastrategy. In short, entrepreneurial success can have something to teach us and can have principles that inform us. Within local success formulas could be a new reinvented formula for global success. The dilemma looks like this:

Dilemma 3: Tradition and Exploration

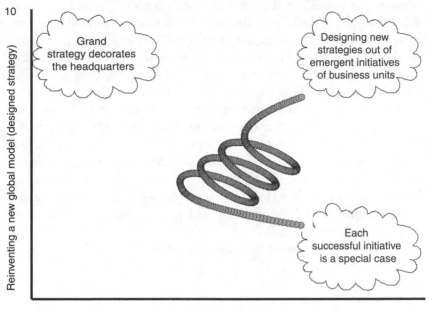

At the top left we have the "grand strategy" as a decorative flourish by company headquarters. Given Levecke's values, there is little danger of that. At the bottom right there *is* the danger that every regional success will be regarded as a unique testimony to entrepreneurial genius, never to be repeated. In fact, all successful initiatives *have something to tell us about the success of other units.* They may be based on principles of success that can be generalized. Ideally, Levecke should design his global strategy *out of* the successful initiatives of business units.

Dilemma 4. Local Entrepreneurship versus Transnational Leadership

How, then, can the power of local entrepreneurship help us develop transnational leadership? And how can the development of transnational leadership reinforce local entrepreneurship? We have already seen that local successes can have lessons for a global strategy—that with many business units, the good and the mediocre can learn from the best and replicate at least some of their moves—but the process also works the other way around. Transnational leadership can become a repository for models of success and, armed with these solutions, can think through problems and dilemmas. Headquarters is a kind of *central nervous system* that integrates into one brain the news coming from all localities and is able to communicate this knowledge to each business unit. Headquarters celebrates and enshrines what some business units have done and stretches and motivates others.

In addition, there are huge cost savings to be made from having one headquarters buy 200,000 cars a year from manufacturers and share information technology facilities and strategic training. The more these costs are pushed down and shared, the more competitive every business unit can become. Through a bulk-purchasing agreement, every unit can be more competitive in its local markets. Through success in local markets, headquarters becomes better and better informed about what works and what does not.

The following diagram illustrates this point:

Dilemma 4: Leading Transnationally

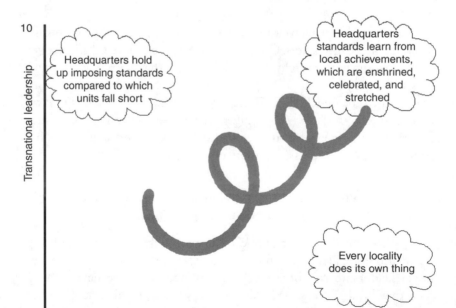

At the top left headquarters upholds such imposing standards that business units fall short. At the bottom right each unit "does its own thing" and remains incomparable. The ideal is for headquarters to have standards inspired by extant achievements, to celebrate those achievements, to encourage emulation, and so to excite the ambition of all other units to excel in turn. Hugo Levecke seems to have intuited all these processes. Headquarters and the business units have shared responsibility for all of the following:

- *Stretching ambitious goals.* This is achieved by using the scoreboard to show what level of improvements is possible and by urging businesses to aim high. It is motivational to have your achievements recorded and advertised.
- Accepting the *discipline* of comparing all actions with results and all ideas with real outcomes.
- Developing the *trust* of people you learn from, teach, evaluate, and applaud, advising them and sharing consequences with them.
- Coming to *support* other business units with similar problems and challenges—business that can benefit from your successes, learn from your errors, and be encouraged by your understanding.

In a few years Hugo Levecke has redirected his company from being a financial services provider toward the global number-one position in the fleet management industry, with a portfolio of 1.2 million cars.

Chapter 17

———◆———

Keeping Close to the Customer: David Komansky, Merrill Lynch

Fons Trompenaars and Charles Hampden-Turner

*T*HIS CHAPTER FEATURES a leader who is prominent in global financial services, Dave Komansky, chief executive officer (CEO) of Merrill Lynch, one of the premier U.S. investment bankers. Three or four American-based investment banks now dominate global markets, with the weight of American shareholders behind them.

The Historical Context

The Bull at Bay

Merrill Lynch's symbol, the bull, which stands outside the company's Wall Street offices, is famous throughout the world. Its two horns remind us of the dilemmas that face business leaders, of the bear that shadows the bull, and of Merrill Lynch's latest dilemma: its confrontation with discount brokers using the Internet, especially the challenge posed by Charles Schwab.

The Wall Street Journal recently analyzed one of the greatest dilemmas the management of Merrill Lynch has faced in its existence of over 70 years. Company founder Charles Merrill believed that opportunities in the financial markets should be accessible to everyone. His life's mission was "bringing Wall Street to Main Street." "Indeed, Charles Merrill revolutionized financial services in the twentieth century with the simple yet powerful promise that the client's interest would always come first," explains Herbert M. Allison, Jr., president and chief operating officer of the firm. "Today we are pleased to show how we'll carry that vision into the twenty-first century as the preeminent financial adviser for client achievement in what is fast becoming a 24-hour-a-day financial world. This is a natural extension of the client-focused strategy that has attracted over $1.5 trillion in client assets worldwide over the past several decades."

Yet there were unresolved issues in early 1999 that sparked much discussion and debate within the organization on how to prevent a loss of market share to competitors. What was urgent was to renew Merrill's mission of keeping closer to customers than did its rivals. The Internet could be an additional means to that closeness; hence, in the spring of 1999 colorful brochures entitled "Key Things You Can Do with Merrill Online!" were mailed out to clients. This led to the following comment in *The Wall Street Journal*:

> **Customers can transfer funds between Merrill Lynch accounts. They can view their statements. They can track gains and losses in their portfolio, and read Merrill research reports. They can even shop via direct links, from books from Barnes & Noble and vines from Virtual Vineyards. Buy and sell stock? Uh, no. To do that, they still need to call their Merrill Lynch stockbroker and pay fees that often are several times the cut-rate commissions paid by investors using Internet accounts from a growing number of upstart firms.**

The consequences soon became clear. The frequency of calls to Merrill Lynch brokers declined sharply. Clients who wanted just 1 or 2 trades had figured out that they could make 5 to 10 trades for the same price with discount brokers. Most did not close their Merrill Lynch accounts but used them for long-term holdings that they rarely traded.

Merrill Lynch's lack of on-line trading facilities had started a serious erosion in its market share during 1998. The issue had come to a head by May 1999. It was clear that Charles Schwab, a relatively new and dynamic discount broker, was training its customers to be their own brokers and traders, using the Internet. This was clearly a problem for Merrill Lynch, which with 15,000 brokers all earning at least six-figure salaries in U.S. dollars—and some seven figures—was the world's largest brokerage house, charging its customers millions in fees in return for the advice of top professionals.

Charles Schwab's appeal goes beyond discounted fees. Indeed, compared with rival discount brokers, it is *not* among the cheapest. Schwab's appeal is that it transfers its own professional expertise to customers. It is that rarity among professionals, a firm that educates customers in its own secrets so that they can in time, if they wish to, become fully independent. This could be a losing strategy if it did not draw an ever-increasing number of "pupils" eager to be taught, who replace those who have "graduated." Schwab is in the "customer mentoring" business, as opposed to the financial services business. For many elderly Americans and people between jobs, managing their own share portfolios is their "last and most meaningful employment," providing funds they can leave to their families to ensure their continuing influence. Schwab was helping customers help themselves in the time-honored American tradition.

David Komansky saw that this challenge would have to be met, yet he could not risk alienating his army of professional brokers. Increasingly, however, financial services were being unbundled: You could buy top information and research and then pay as little as $5 per trade on the Internet. This was far less than the brokers' inclusive fee. Furthermore, brokers' judgments are not infallible. In the hurly-burly of stock fluctuations it is not unknown for the Dow Jones average to outperform professionally managed portfolios. Luck is quite a leveler.

Merrill Lynch's response to its dilemma was to refocus its efforts on reconciling new technology with customer service. Its strategy was announced by John Steffens at the Forrester Conference in May 1999: "By combining technology with skilled advisers, clients are given the convenience of interacting when, how, and where they want." Komansky clarified the policy: "Anyone, anywhere, at any time can log on to the Internet to get free quotes, market data, and stock picks from a variety of chat rooms. Yet at Merrill Lynch we are confidently making unparalleled billion-dollar investments in our financial consultants, research analysts, technology, and products. We're doing this because we know that success in the on-line world—as it was in the off-line world—will be defined by *meaningful content* for the individual. Only now, in a world with almost unlimited access and bandwidth, this content can be delivered in more effective ways—and its value grows exponentially. That is why we are confident in our investments and bullish on the future of financial advice."

The Importance of Personalized Service

What the new technologies made possible, besides the opportunity to lower costs, was the personalization of service. John "Launny" Steffens, Merrill Lynch's "Mr. On-Line," created for the company a Trusted Global Advisory (TGA) system that would synthesize more than 50 data sources and make possible a process of matching the requirements of customers with the latest market opportunities. Merrill Lynch's financial consultants would have this information at their fingertips and could create optimal client advice within minutes.

Komansky spoke of "leveraging technology to deliver value" and of "elevating advice to a new level through a collaborative platform modeled on choice and empowerment." While the TGA system is for consultants, not clients, Merrill Lynch Online is a Web site for clients to discuss investment issues. The company has found that informed clients are better customers who ask better questions and get better answers. On-line dialogues grow deeper and more intelligent. This helps empower clients. Komansky seeks to improve and multiply these dialogues and conversations by moving some of TGA's resources to Merrill Lynch Online. An additional tool is the Global Investor Network, which allows clients to join discussions through video and audio channels. These links are just beginning, but the goal is to make every tool that facilitates the investment process available on-line. Despite this, the value of skilled financial consultants is meant to increase, and they are to hold on to a valuable share of the market by catering to a wide range of individual needs through their willingness to spend more or less time on investment decisions.

"On-line," Steffens points out, "there is no single type of advisory relationship that will serve all clients well. Clients can inform their financial consultant as to what kind of advisory relationship they seek. At one extreme we have clients with little time or interest in managing their own financial affairs. They wish to be kept informed but want a professional to decide. It is a question of time, that perishable asset. Investing is better left to those with the means to inform themselves in minutes while the client is freed up for his or her own favorite activity." At the other end of the spectrum are clients who actively manage their investments and come up with their own investment ideas. For them the financial consultant serves as a sounding board, an educator, a personalizer of information, and a source of new ideas.

A computer cannot by itself provide the level of service, the dialogue, and the personal focus of a human adviser. Only advisers can attain the wisdom, judgment, and habit of personal service that views each client as a whole person with dreams and ambitions.

Clients are not confined to one adviser: They can speak with specialists and consult experts in specific fields. Quality advice is not "consumed" in the usual way. Rather, it enlightens clients and provides access within Merrill Lynch to the most qualified persons available to improve the clients' investment opportunities.

From Phase I to Phase II

Komansky sees two distinct phases in the Internet revolution. Phase I is reconciled by asking, How will on-line services revolutionize existing service models? To that end Merrill Lynch Direct was launched in late 1999. The service offers after-hours and in-hours direct trading. Investors can buy or sell stocks at $29.95 a trade. But Phase II is already upon us; it is reconciled by asking, How will on-line services be revolutionized by ever-higher client expectations? It is a mistake to think of technology as the sole driver; clients want more.

Steffens explains: "If you don't maintain a laser focus on helping your clients thrive and find freedom in a complex financial world, no one is going to stay at your party very long. We are looking outside our walls to bring better execution and extended hours of trading to our clients. We're doing all this—and we're doing e-commerce— because the big picture matters to clients, and sweating the details counts. The relationships we're building through these efforts are sticky, rich, and profitable. A lot of people doing business on-line are more than happy with what they've found, but there's another segment that's mad as hell, and they are not going to take it much longer. It's in Phase II of the Internet revolution that clients will ask, 'What have you done for me lately?' They will demand a richer level of content and a higher level of service than are currently offered by many on-line services."

An important characteristic of the Internet is its density of information. Complex products, such as books on Amazon.com, sell well on the Internet because reviews, comments, and discussions revolve around them. Giving clients access to this wealth of materials about investment, along with a means of navigating through that knowledge, could be Merrill Lynch's priceless advantage. Once again Komansky is articulate on the topic: "I believe the trump card to these bundles of information will be *access* to trusted advice. Choice and openness are vital but not enough, because the choices are so limitless that you are overwhelmed. What is hard is to find personal meaning among all the data and to guide the client through this morass so that direction and commitment are possible."

While it is still too early to discover whether these strategic syntheses of technology and personal service have worked, early indications are positive. Wall Street seemed impressed by Komansky's newly built strategy. As of late 1999, Merrill Lynch had pulled even with the market capitalization of Charles Schwab after having briefly lost its place to its archrival. Merrill Lynch's new policy of "click and mortar" has won many admirers on Wall Street, and Forrester Research placed the company's Web site second among a dozen or so on-line competitors in "effectiveness for investors." In the words of the report, "Up to now Schwab has been setting the pace in on-line brokerage. Merrill, though, is a bolt from the blue."

Despite some hostile comments, Komansky has launched Merrill Lynch's campaign for its services by highlighting the "human achievement" of the investment advisory process. As one ad put it, "Computers are plastic and metal and sand. People are brilliance and discernment and vision." That is intended not to put computers down but to emphasize how well they are utilized and by whom. Merrill Lynch believes that it is creating a comprehensive framework that will revolutionize the concept of personal financial services in America. Clients will be able to customize the global power of the company for their own purposes and preferences. Merrill Lynch is proud of the versatility of services available under one roof, backed by its history and reputation and by its globalism, intelligence, and financial strength.

We are now in a position to diagram the dilemmas that Merrill Lynch has recognized and reconciled. We are also in a position to suggest a dilemma that the company may not yet have recognized or reconciled. Finally, we consider an ingenious idea and, turning around our usual procedure, ask, What dilemmas does this reconcile?

The dilemmas are as follows:

1. Low-cost specific data and transactions versus rich, meaningful, diffuse personal relationships
2. The individuality of the client versus the concentrated power of Merrill Lynch's global community
3. The profit-maximizing model versus the client-mentoring model
4. The influence of London versus the influence of the regions
5. Capitalism versus the ideals of democracy
6. The private sector versus the publicly funded education sector

Dilemma 1. Low-cost Specific Data and Transactions versus Rich, Meaningful, Diffuse Personal Relationships

The challenge to Merrill Lynch has come in part from the unbundling of services into specific pieces. You can buy information, research, trading facilities, and advice from separate sources yet find the combined fees perhaps less than those paid to Merrill Lynch's six- and seven-figure professionals. The Internet is overflowing with data, but that is not the same as having knowledge or information. We are *informed* by facts relevant to our questions and concerns. We *know* when we get answers to our propositions and hypotheses. The vaster the Internet becomes, the more customers will need a guide to what is relevant to their concerns.

Instead of relationships being eclipsed by the Internet, they will become more and more important in interpreting data flows as what is available keeps growing ever larger than what is relevant to each client. Hence, in Phase II we will discover that intelligent dialogue about the bewildering complexity of financial markets forms and changes the Internet rather than that the Internet changes the financial markets. We need *high tech,* but we also need *high touch.* The more those numbers rain down on you, the more you need to talk to someone about them.

The dilemma can be diagrammed as follows:

Dilemma I: Guidance through the Maze

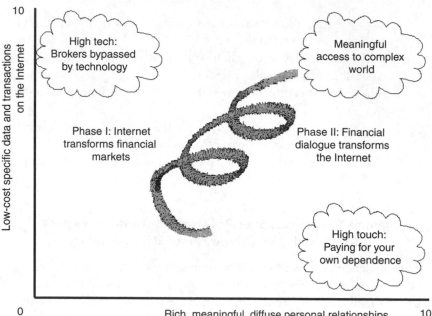

In 1998–1999 Phase I was in full swing, with the prices of specific trades and reports falling and Schwab and others making inroads, but in 2000 and 2001 Phase II has been setting in, with a complexity so vast that meaningful access through professional relationships is becoming vital.

The dimension of specificity-diffusion is the third of the seven dimensions introduced in Chapters 1 and 2. In this case it is heavily qualified by other considerations.

Dilemma 2. The Individuality of the Client versus the Concentrated Power of Merrill Lynch's Global Community

One good reason the Internet will not sweep all before it simply by communicating data is that every customer is different. Some want high risks, others low; some want growth stocks, others dividends. Some have specialized interests in technology, media, energy, or engineering;

others feel more secure with diversification. Some have ethical concerns about tobacco or armaments; others rely on the invisible hand of the market to provide the greatest good for the greatest number. Some investors would say, "I do not keep a dog and bark myself." That is, they employ professionals to do what they personally do not want to do or are not qualified to do. Some investors want to participate in or influence the professional's decision; others want professional advice on choosing for themselves. Just as there are degrees of participation, there are degrees of transparency versus privacy. Some customers would *like* other people to know just how wealthy and successful they are; others use professionals to keep their affairs private. They believe it is boastful or dangerous to flaunt their wealth and may even ask that their mail to be sent to a post office box or be bundled up for personal collection.

Whichever way you look at it, customers vary in a myriad of ways and may treat a broker like a Buddha or a butler. It is because customers are so diverse individually that it takes a global community to bring satisfaction to each person, and it requires deep relationships of mutual respect to find in that community the people and resources the client most requires. Within any networked community of professionals there are literally thousands of meanings for individual investors rather than one message for everyone who can download it cheaply.

Merrill Lynch's strategy has been to devise two parallel systems: TGA to inform professional brokers and Merrill Lynch Online for investors. This division ensures that investors get better and better informed but that the professional community retains an important edge in sophistication and expertise and is not second-guessed on the basis of the same information. The likely success of the strategy depends in part on how well individual customers are profiled. Do they want someone to talk things over with? Do they aspire to professionalism? Do they want someone they can trust to get on with things without bothering them? What is their trade-off between security and gain? Customers of a particular type need appropriate service. They have the right to set their own goals and objectives and have them pursued. The dilemma is diagrammed in the next figure:

Dilemma 2: The Search for Personal Meaning

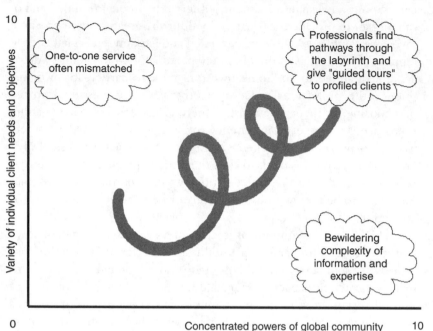

Given the vast expansion in world trading, Internet information, initially so intriguing, will rapidly become overwhelming, with a host of contradictory opinions making it harder, not easier, to decide. Far from substituting for professionalism, this complexity and chaos will increase the demand for "guided tours" through the labyrinth by professionals aware of client idiosyncrasies (upper right in the figure). One-to-one service (upper left) is not enough because the client and the financial consultant can be mismatched. Nor does the overflow of information (lower right), however easy to access, guarantee understanding and relevance; rather, professionals earn their salaries by "managing chaos" on behalf of individual interests.

Dilemma 3. The Profit-Maximizing Model versus the Client-Mentoring Model

We come now to a dilemma that Komansky has perhaps missed but that could be crucial to the competition between Merrill Lynch and

Charles Schwab. We say "perhaps" because Komansky certainly knows more than he says within our hearing.

It seems possible that Charles Schwab is not just a discount broker but an *educator* of those who wish to develop professional expertise. The job of advising on investments has two different tests of effectiveness. There is the profit-maximizing model, in which you look at how effectively stocks perform and ask whether the input of costly professional advice pays for itself in better returns, and there is the client-mentoring model, which involves the transfer of professional expertise from experts to clients with the purpose of turning those clients into experts in their own right. The latter process can be cheaper because it involves clients acting by themselves rather than paying others to act, but that is not its main attraction. What attracts clients is that *their autonomy and expertise are being developed to put them in charge of their own wealth.* The fees are less commissions than they are tuition fees. The outcome sought is not "to have my money work for me" but "to have me work with my money."

This helps explain why many other "discount brokers" have made little headway against Charles Schwab, which is by no means the cheapest. If clients believe they are paying "tuition fees," they will pay more now to benefit more later, and their satisfaction will come from steadily increasing their autonomy in managing their own wealth and steadily increasing their responsibility for the size of their wealth. (This is very much "the American way," and Schwab's appeal is perhaps cultural.) Clearly, this does not appeal to *every* client. Many have more enjoyable things to do with their lives than trade stocks. For others, however, that is a job from which they cannot be retired or fired, and doing it well is very important.

Merrill Lynch should not surrender this market to Schwab, and no one should underestimate the significance of this development. Traditionally, professionals have kept their secrets from their clients, profiting in part from the esoteric nature of professional jargon to make clients dependent on them. Schwab might well be the first to make a determined attempt to professionalize clients themselves. George Bernard Shaw once said, "All professions are a conspiracy against the laity." All but one, perhaps. The revolution in customer service may involve sustained mentoring and education. Although such customers will eventually cut their ties, could each be replaced by two or three who are eager to learn? We have tried to convey this in the next diagram:

Dilemma 3: Professionalizing the Client

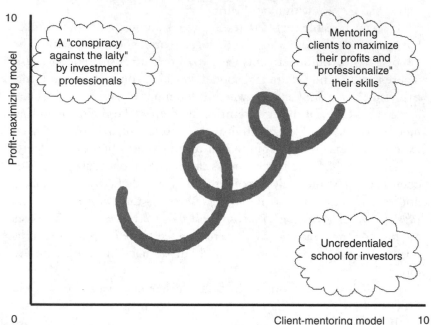

Provided that you make it clear that you are emancipating your client in the longer term from continued reliance on Merrill Lynch, you can legitimately charge educational fees. The criterion of success is still profit maximization, but *the agent of investment decisions is the client,* your pupil (upper right in the figure). The "conspiracy against the laity" (upper left) sees professionals scheming to stay ahead by withholding from clients all that they know. The uncredentialed school (lower right) is committed to tuition but makes no effort to compare its efforts with performances by seasoned professionals. "Pupils" should not be encouraged to "graduate" and go solo until they have proved their capacity to perform against the best. The internal "league standings" would be part of the education and part of the thrill.

If capitalism is really to work at its full potential, we need ever more sophisticated investors in ever more specialized areas. We believe that Merrill Lynch has yet to counter Charles Schwab's major appeal. In the discount issue Merrill Lynch has started a false hare.

The Global Investment Challenge: A Simulation

Sometimes there are ideas so good that we instinctively applaud them. Only later, often through the disciplines expounded in this book, do we realize *why* they are so good and how many dilemmas they resolve. The test of a really good idea is its simultaneously and multiply resolving dilemmas facing a whole industry. Let us consider idea that was recently implemented at Merrill Lynch in the United Kingdom and then use dilemma theory to assess it.

The company recently launched an investment simulation, or game for schools, called the Global Investment Challenge (GIC). Any secondary school in the United Kingdom is free to enter and play. Each team of players, supervised by a teacher, is given a hypothetical £1 million ($1.6 million) to invest. All the teams compete with one another in regard to the gains achieved by their portfolios of investments. The winners get an all-expenses-paid trip to Merrill Lynch's New York headquarters. In this game, no one can lose (money) but the winners get treated to the Big Apple. Yet much of the thrill is in the process, not the prize. Each team and its teacher receive a packet containing stock and bond information, instructions on how to play, and forms on which to enter a portfolio of selections. The game is publicized, and local teams are reported on and supported by local newspapers. Investments are global in range and in scope, and so students must be aware of world trends and events that could affect prices, and they must become aware of the sheer diversity of possible investments.

Teams buy or sell shares on five occasions during the course of the game, and in making those choices they have access via free phone service to Merrill Lynch's leading analysts in the fields in which those analysts specialize. These analysts advise the team approaching them much as they would a genuine client. Probably, the analysts want "their team" to win the trip to New York. Throughout the contest it is possible to discover where you stand in relationship to rival teams, with last-minute changes in prices tipping the balance. Excitement runs high.

In 1997, 75 students from 16 schools participated, and valuable publicity was gained when Steven Byers, secretary of the Department of Industry, awarded the first prize, in Newcastle, to a team from a local school. By 1999 three games were being run for 1700 students from 133 schools.

What might this game accomplish for Merrill Lynch? It could help to reconcile at least three dilemmas:

a. The influence of London versus the influence of the regions
b. Capitalism versus the ideals of democracy
c. The private sector versus the publicly funded education sector

The Influence of London versus the Influence of Regions

The United Kingdom is notoriously overcentralized, with London, a magnet for world money, overshadowing the regions and the provinces. This is especially true for towns like Newcastle, once the site of great shipbuilders but long since in industrial decline. Such regions not only need help with their educational efforts, they also need an understanding of world competitive pressures. They need to understand how and why investments are flowing from their own capital city to enterprises the world over. If regional school pupils can learn to think like investors, they may also learn what attracts investment to their region and what does not. At the height of Britain's industrial revolution such provincial "capitals" as Liverpool, Newcastle, Glasgow, and Sunderland were models of civic pride and prosperity. Can they rebuild their fortunes? Although the GIC is a modest contribution to a huge historical imbalance within the British economy, where financial services ride high and manufacturing struggles, every little bit helps, and proper general understanding of investment flows could be the key to future policy.

Merrill Lynch sees its game as an attempt to repay the communities, where much of the company's talent is nurtured and subsequently drawn upon. The demand for workers with knowledge is exponential. Komansky calls this "good citizenship." Among the advantages accruing to the company is a greater brand awareness in the regions, which have been slower to take up investment opportunities than have London and the "home counties" (the areas adjoining London). Merrill Lynch recently set up a number of regional offices.

The dilemma is illustrated in the following diagram:

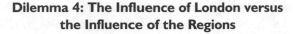

Dilemma 4: The Influence of London versus the Influence of the Regions

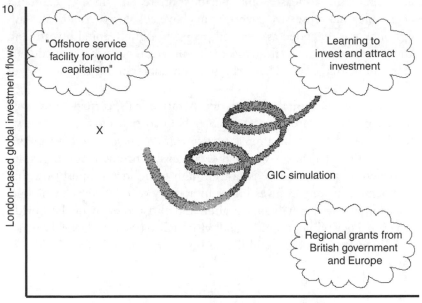

London's somewhat ambivalent reputation is as an "offshore service facility for world capitalism." In a world where geographic contiguity no longer matters, Taiwan might get much more investment from London than does the northeast region of the United Kingdom, including Newcastle. What such regions *do* get are government grants and European funds for regeneration—monies for which their relative poverty qualifies them. Yet these measures are only stopgap solutions to the problem—the lack of attractive investment opportunities—and this is where Merrill Lynch is helping. The GIC simulation is an enjoyable way to learn about the real world of capital flows and about how to get your share to your region.

Capitalism versus the Ideals of Democracy

The next two resolutions are ones that we as writers consider important even if Merrill Lynch has not specifically cited them. A lot of leadership ability is tacit, not explicit. Leaders can be better than they know.

All democratic nations today are also capitalist, but not all forms of capitalism are democratic. For example, in Chile, Argentina, Greece, and Spain, in at least some periods of recent history, capitalist economies and repressive governments have cohabited. American slavery once was defended as a sacred property right. Capital investment, which reallocates funds from losers to winners, is not necessarily democratic in its outcomes: There is a marked tendency for the rich to get richer.

To reconcile capitalism with democratic ideals, certain steps must be taken. First, shares must be *widely* held so that most citizens own them. Second, the citizen must *participate in the investment process.* Pension fund capitalism, in which the citizens' retirement resources are managed by professionals, is not enough to build a property-owning democracy. As long as investing is an activity of relatively few people, the capitalist system will appear alien and elitist to many of the world's citizens. They will not understand why their parts of the world are not as affluent as others and will blame investors. The dilemma looks like this:

Dilemma 5: Capitalism versus the Ideals of Democracy

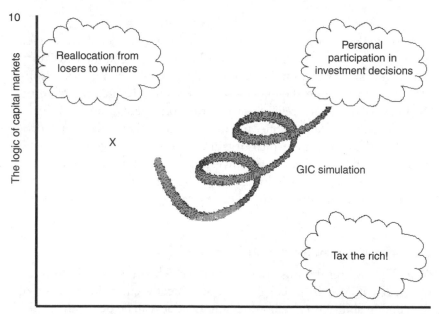

The reallocation of resources from the less successful to the more successful has antidemocratic possibilities unless investment in those successes is widely distributed through the population. This is more the case in the United States than in the United Kingdom and more the case in the United Kingdom than in most of Continental Europe, but most citizens need more than a financial stake in investment flows—they need an understanding of those flows and the ability to exercise personal judgments about where to invest. It is here that the GIC simulation makes an important contribution. As of now the idea is perhaps more important than its impact, which is relatively small. But "investor education" might be essential to making world markets not unjustly skewed against poorer regions. The fact is that you must understand this system in order to share in its advantages.

The Private Sector versus the Publicly Funded Education Sector

In most developed nations general education is paid for by public funds taken out of taxes. This has given teachers and their unions an ambivalent attitude toward capitalism. They judge, with some justice, that idealistic, nonmonetary reasons for a teaching career are routinely exploited by low salaries. The dynamics of supply and demand are such that markets punish teachers for having dedication to people rather than to financial objectives. "Idealism plus peanuts" is a teacher's typical reward. Not surprisingly, education professionals and associations show a preference for left-wing political parties and hesitate to educate their charges about the potential of capitalism. That one of the purposes of schools is to prepare students to take their places in a capitalist economy is regarded with some distaste.

The dilemma is laid out in the next diagram:

Dilemma 6: Synergy of Mutual Respect

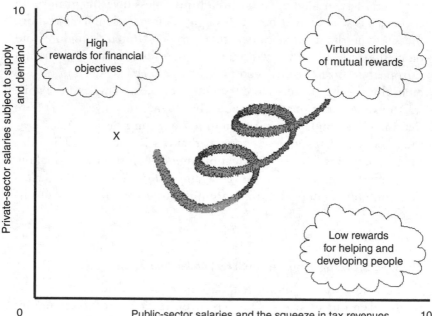

We do not wish to pretend that a simulation game for children is "the answer" to the historical antipathy of the teaching profession to the multitudes in the private sector who are much better rewarded for comparable skills. Resolving this societal dilemma will require much more effort and money, but the GIC simulation is at least an indicator of what creative solutions can accomplish. Every teacher won over to exploring what investment flows can teach is a gain to that economy and that region. It is not Merrill Lynch's mission or responsibility to change the world, but those with the ambition to do so could benefit from studying these examples of artful reconciliation.

Chapter 18

—◆—

Managing the Internationalization Process: Kees Storm, AEGON

Fons Trompenaars

KEES STORM, NOW chief executive officer (CEO) of AEGON, the Dutch insurance giant, devised his own system of management in 1990, when he was responsible for AEGON's Dutch market. He called it "Management by Betting." The system consisted of estimating what was genuinely possible for the company to achieve and then having Storm make a friendly bet that the managers could not do it. If Storm lost, the company won anyhow. It was a win-win situation. Forecasts tended to be very conservative, with managers anxious not to fail and thus aiming low. Storm wanted to throw down a challenge: "I'm betting that you fail; show me differently!" He wanted to take the trauma out of failure and give pleasure to those confounding him. The stakes were usually symbolic—a bottle of good wine—but this strategy has lasted for 10 years.

AEGON has certainly put on a winning performance. Its share price rose 173 percent in 1998 and is up more than 400 percent since 1997 and more than 3000 percent in the last 10 years. The price stands at 40 times earnings and 6 times book value. AEGON is one of the highest-rated insurers in the world, second only to AIG in overall market value. AEGON is number two in the United States. The company's total assets have passed $200 billion.

AEGON avoids both hostile takeovers in the glare of publicity and auctions. Auctions tend to be expensive for shareholders when you have to beat all the other bidders and offer a price that no one else will top. Storm prefers private negotiations, out of the limelight.

The Process of Internationalizing

AEGON is internationalizing rapidly. The members of its boards hold American, British, Dutch, German, and Belgian passports. The company has come a long way since the 1980s, when an American colleague remarked of its culture, "If you ain't Dutch, you ain't much."

Internationalization has been accomplished by means of radical decentralization. Storm explains:

"We have a very decentralized company, and our units have almost complete freedom to decide what is good for their own business. We manage our company together with our main-country managers. We meet four times a year to discuss the framework of our plans. Local freedom is high because we have jointly internalized some shared rules of the game, such as 'Make a plan and stick to it.' Financially speaking, our acquisitions are quite simple—simpler than those in other industries. We have a minimum ROI [return on investment] of 11 percent after tax in mind, and so in our quite stable piece of the service industry we can calculate these numbers with some certainty. The real challenge lies in the social and business integration of the acquired company. Our portfolio is nicely spread between insurances that thrive on longevity and those which don't. We have funeral insurances, so-called home services, and pensions. They nicely balance each other. The intermediate salesperson has regained a position in our service industry by expanding the scope of what he or she offers. It is almost like becoming a full financial consultant."

Fitting into Local Markets and Regional Opportunities

AEGON operates in five key countries: the United States, the Netherlands, the United Kingdom, Hungary, and Spain. The country units operate in such an independent way that each of them could decide to go beyond its own borders. AEGON USA, for example, started a joint venture with the largest Mexican bank, Banamex. AEGON the Netherlands started to sell certain specialized types of financial services in the German and Belgian markets. AEGON started to sell insurance services in Taiwan and the Philippines and is represented in China and India.

Storm sees decentralization as essential because of the diversity of local laws and customs: "Our local approaches are a result of the dependence of our services on local laws and cultural habits. We have taken this very far. Despite the fact that we are very Dutch in our roots, we have no Dutch men or women in our foreign activities. Each local business unit has a unique knowledge about the markets and knows its opportunities. The *management of this knowledge* is therefore crucial for the success of our decentralized business. In our internationalization process we have no intention of putting as many flags on the globe as possible. We would rather focus on some 10 large markets where we can grow significantly. I think it is important for the members of the management team to be physically available in the countries in which we do business. This is particularly important in the start-up phase of a new acquisition. We will internationalize in a restricted and focused way. We are now listed on six stock exchanges: Amsterdam, New York, London, Frankfurt, Zurich, and Tokyo. That is very important for the capital-funding needs of the company. At the present moment more than 75 percent of our people work outside the Netherlands. To be able to attract the best people for the top jobs, we have introduced English as the working language at AEGON."

Integrating and Managing Knowledge from All Regions

AEGON doesn't focus on regions only: Each business unit is concentrated in one specific segment of the market, one specific country, and one specific distribution network. At AEGON there are many examples in which the local experience in a new service area was quickly used in another part of the organization. This is made possible by an excellent information technology (IT) and communication system and a strong shared corporate culture that encourages the exchange of ideas. Selectively moving a small number of people across business units reinforces this culture.

What follows in this chapter are essentially Storm's reflections on AEGON's role in internationalization.

AEGON developed so-called inner circles—networks of specialized managers (IT managers and financial specialists) by which knowledge is exchanged across business units. Moreover, it established a way for all of its 30,000 people to get a chance every three years to communicate with all the executive board members. Every three years the board pays a visit to all the company's offices, meets the people there, and presents and discusses future plans. It is amazing how many people ask questions in a variety of areas on these occasions, and the board hears what issues are alive in AEGON's family. In a program it calls "Optiek," AEGON is trying to minimize hierarchical layers just by meeting people around the globe in a personal way.

AEGON headquarters develops principles of global strategy by studying local successes and discussing to what extent they can be generalized to other regions around the world. The value and relevance of these global strategies are widely debated. AEGON is probably one of the very few organizations—maybe the only company of its size—that organizes all-ranks meetings in every country to give every employee a chance to meet the members of the executive board in person at least once every three years. It also gives everyone an opportunity to hear the group's strategy from the horse's mouth. Global strategy would not work unless employees had a stake in global success and cared how units in other regions fared. Accordingly, employees are encouraged to join a global stock option program, and more than 90 percent have chosen to do so. Stock options also give the whole company a stake in being consistent and in implementing methods that have proved to work in one or more regions.

AEGON has a very loyal group of people with close relationships and respect for cultural differences. It tries both to radiate consistency by making its strategies, goals, and results as comparable as possible, and to have its people challenged by the achievements of its best groups. AEGON wants quick feedback about what is working and what is not and what feels good or bad. If people make plans, they should stick to them; otherwise they cannot learn about any shortcomings or even determine whether the plans were too modest. As usual, Storm bets that the people cannot beat their targets, and they rise to the challenge. AEGON also has "bonding events" such as marathons and golf tournaments—whatever works.

Stick to Your Knitting

So complex is this process of studying what works, what does not, and why from region to region and across numerous insurance products that AEGON could not possibly make sense of it all unless it *stuck to its knitting*—that is, operated in the insurance industry business alone. Of course, there are connections to industries such as banking, but these links are tactical and ad hoc.

Storm explains: "We date banks but do not intend to marry them. We are trying to prove that this is best for the organization. Many banks have merged their activities with insurance companies. Up until now not doing this has paid off [for AEGON]. I think merging banks and insurance companies is the mistake of the century. It would be like driving two cars at the same time. It is the convergers who end up against a tree. Therefore, we stick to our knitting—which, by definition, does not make us contrarian but consistent. We also believe that giant mergers or takeovers resulting in companies that employ hundreds of thousands of people will prove to be unmanageable and will fall apart sooner or later. We will gladly pick up some of the parts if that happens in our industry."

The Importance of Stakeholder Value

Storm has strong views on the folly of being narrowly fixated on shareholder value, although paradoxically, AEGON is often regarded as an exemplar in this regard.

AEGON often is seen as an Anglo-Saxon company because of its focus on shareholder value. Storm has "never heard such a stupid dichotomy as shareholder versus stakeholder value." Value creation starts with the customer. AEGON's primary task is to fulfill the needs of the client and expand the circle of satisfied clients. This can be achieved only if you have motivated employees with the resources to do their work properly. And to have the proper resources, you need to have access to the capital markets. For AEGON that is crucial. This access can be created only by rewarding the capital resources properly. Value creation is a process that involves many stakeholders, and leadership consists of trying to find a balance between all the stakes. Whenever one stake prevails, the whole circle becomes vicious. Instead, Storm intends to create a learning spiral "resembling a Catherine wheel in which all the rockets combine to rotate the display." He sees this balance of stakeholders "firing together" as a form of democracy.

Storm is one of the very few leaders we have run across who is explicit about the reconciliation of values. "This famous discussion between stakeholder value versus shareholder value," he said, "should be finished, in my opinion. Value creation starts and ends with the client in our conviction, and to satisfy your clients and keep them satisfied, you need motivated employees. Where you have motivated employees, you will make great returns for your shareholders. If you then tie the stakes of the shareholders, employees, and customers together through our famous share options, you will create a *value circle* that increases its revolving speed continuously." All this results in an ever-faster Catherine wheel.

The notion of the Catherine wheel can be diagrammed as follows:

Storm's Value Circle

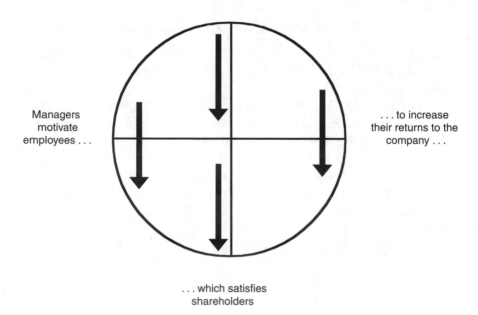

... to better satisfy
customers by means
of stock options, which
encourages the employees

Managers
motivate
employees ...

... to increase
their returns to the
company ...

... which satisfies
shareholders

Dutch Codetermination

AEGON was strongly influenced in its employee participation efforts by Dutch codetermination laws and by the institution of workers' councils. As Storm explains, AEGON did not have to institute them in countries where they were not mandatory, but its Central Works Council gave AEGON such good advice that it exported the spirit to the whole global system. Industrial democracy is so much a part of how the firm exchanges ideas and shares experiences that AEGON does not always need to give it legal expression. Among its most enjoyable activities are friendly competition between business units to see which has better ways of working. AEGON learns a lot that way. The company uses IT to "keep score," but nothing beats personal contact and meeting people in other units. AEGON's slogan is "Respect people, make money, and have fun."

While being interviewed by *The Scotsman* on March 21, 1999, Storm had to leave in a hurry on other urgent business. He left behind a giant doodle of intersecting circles of roughly rectangular placement, all overlapping at a central point. The newspaper wrote of "the urge to interpret the doodle as a subconscious expression of his strategic thinking." Each circle was presumably another business unit, largely free but joined to the center.

Dilemma Analysis

Two dilemmas stand out from various interviews and accounts of AEGON given by Kees Storm. We call these *learning from decentralized unit performance* and *the synergy of stakeholder value*. Storm probably intuits the resolution of many more dilemmas, but his statements give us clues to at least these two conscious reconciliations.

Dilemma I. Learning from Decentralized Unit Performance

All units are radically decentralized in order to fit the legal and cultural requirements of particular markets. They are encouraged to make plans, to beat the bets Storm makes that those plans are unattainable, and to record their best possible performances, which are then studied, discussed, and emulated by the company inner circles, which ask, What is comparable across such performances and what is unique to one? Differences are respected, but the search for consistency never ends. Can best practices be followed and duplicated—if not precisely then at least approximately? And what do these many successes have to teach us?

We diagram this dilemma in the following figure:

Dilemma 1: Learning from Decentralized Performance

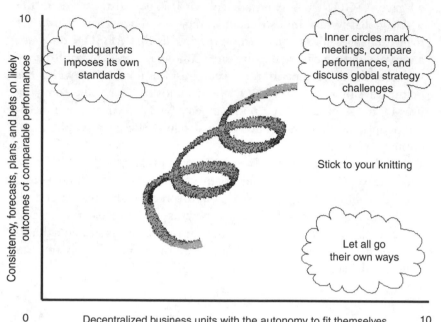

On the vertical axis is the combination of the drive for consistency, comparability, and betting on targets. On the horizontal axis is the combination of the high level of decentralization, autonomy, and fitting to local conditions. Each of these emphases would fail if it were exclusive of the other. You cannot make *everything* consistent when regional conditions are so varied. The company rightly shuns a headquarters that imposes its will, but you cannot let every unit diverge and lose itself in noncomparability.

Thanks to the Inner Circles, the all-ranks meetings, and the forecasts (matched to results) on which Storm lays his bets and gets others to do so, AEGON discovers many ways of succeeding and consistently seeks to have units inspire and learn from each other's examples. However, this learning process is complex, and so AEGON must "stick to its knitting" or lose track. You cannot add to the existing degree of diversity by mixing the contrasting cultures of insurance and banking.

Dilemma 2. The Synergy of Stakeholder Value

Storm sees nothing but foolishness in extolling shareholder value above the rights and duties of stakeholders. This is because the outcomes for all the stakeholders are interdependent, and you cannot emphasize any single stake selectively without damaging the whole system and precipitating a regressive spiral. Once again we must not confuse "importance" with "priority." You can argue that shareholder value is most important to you—that is a question of ethics, and we prefer to leave ethics to those in touch with divine inspiration. But if we ask which has priority—which value must logically come first—there is no doubt that motivating employees to satisfy customers *precedes* increasing returns and paying profits to shareholders. The reason for this order of precedence is that customers supply the monies that shareholders later receive. If employees are for any reason *not* motivated and customers are *not* satisfied, there is no money for shareholders to receive. The dilemma is illustrated in the following diagram:

Dilemma 2: The Synergy of Stakeholder Value

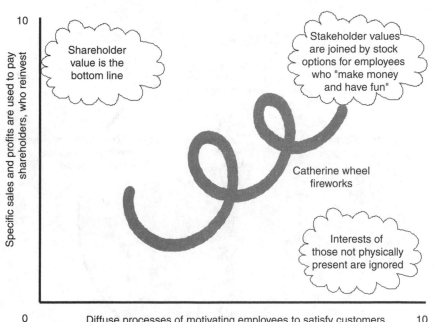

Note that the *clockwise* spiral is in this case obligatory: The money customers pay you for satisfying their needs is given to shareholders, who reinvest it, allowing the processes of motivation and satisfaction to continue. We have also reintroduced our own Dimension 4, specificity versus diffusion. Shareholder value tends to be specific and countable;

motivation and satisfaction are more diffuse. Diffuse processes can be overlooked too easily.

In the diagram, specific sales statistics and profits for shareholding are on the vertical axis and diffuse processes of motivating employees to satisfy customers are on the horizontal axis. The bottom line (upper left in the diagram) can be taken too far, but it is also possible to ignore the interests of those not physically present [i.e., the shareholders (lower right)]. By operating his "fireworks display," illustrated earlier, Storm first motivates employees to satisfy customers and thus raises sales and profits for shareholders, who reinvest in AEGON as a result. Stakeholder values are synergized at the top right by stock options that give each interested employee a stake in the shareholders' profits so that employees "make money and have fun."

It was Storm who warned against the "vicious circle" of celebrating shareholder value too exclusively. We next diagram one way that could happen:

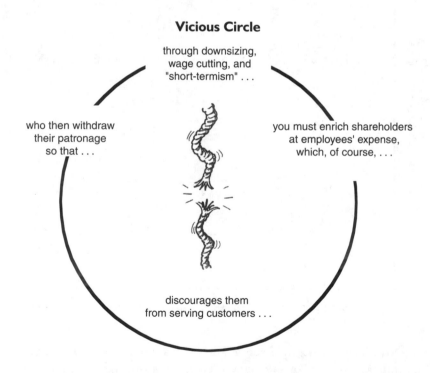

Vicious Circle

through downsizing, wage cutting, and "short-termism" . . .

you must enrich shareholders at employees' expense, which, of course, . . .

discourages them from serving customers . . .

who then withdraw their patronage so that . . .

The ship sinks by the stern (where the employees are), but everyone else later drowns as a consequence, even shareholders, who in the end are worse off for being favored above the rest.

Chapter 19

——◆——

Innovating the Corporate Dynasty: Rahmi M. Koç, the Koç Group

Jo Spyckerelle and Charles Hampden-Turner

*I*T'S NOT OFTEN that you find a profile of a Turkish business leader. Almost as rare is the large-scale family-owned conglomerate known as the Koç Group (KG). If we want evidence that the ways of capitalism vary in different parts of the world, we need look no further than KG. It is extraordinarily successful within the Turkish cultural context and is jokingly referred to as "the third sector," after the public and private sectors. Koç businesses employ 45,000 people, and their turnover is equal to 5.5 percent of Turkey's gross national product (GNP). The group is also a significant contributor to charities and to education. We examined the Koç Group because we were particularly interested in the effects of globalization on a country that is at the crossroads of Europe and Asia. We also wanted an insight into how a business leader behaves in a very pronounced family culture.

Rahmi M. Koç succeeded his father as chairman of the board in 1984 at the age of 53. The head of the family and the founder, Vehbi Koç, remained active as honorary chairman until he died in 1996 at age

94. The difference between family ownership and public ownership could not be more clearly drawn. The founder had towered over Turkey's business sector for three-quarters of a century. The Koç Group is a business dynasty only two years younger than the Turkish Republic itself.

Now Turkey is eager to become a member of the European Union and has taken the first steps by joining the customs union. How will Rahmi M. Koç and his group fare in the global economic system they are in the process of joining? Will the group prosper in the new environment? In this larger world conglomerates are out of fashion and large family-owned companies are looked at with some skepticism by the financial markets. When we spoke to Koç in the elegant old Harem Building, with its magnificent view of Istanbul, he spoke of the following dilemmas:

1. Whether to continue with family succession or become a public company
2. Whether a "national champion" with strong regional loyalties can withstand the competitive pressures of global rivals
3. How to find the correct balance between the private sector and the public sector
4. How to reconcile the pressure on Turkey to be democratic and to practice free trade with playing its cards effectively to catch up with the rest of Europe
5. How to take into account both the Turkey that is a marginal state and the Turkey that is a tinder box of conflicting loyalties
6. How to reconcile local success with the search for new directions for the nation

Dilemma 1. Family Succession versus Public Ownership

Koç explains: "I have been head of this company since 1984. I had no choice. It was my destiny. The company grew up after the 1920s in a relatively closed economy. We won the 'first mover' advantage in several fields and were preeminent in the Turkish economy in energy, construction and mining, banking and financial services, retailing, consumer durables, automotive supplies, motor vehicles, and tourism.

"I have now succeeded my father but ironically face another succession crisis, that of the third generation of the family. Only 18 percent of U.S. and 25 percent of European family firms make it into the third generation, and it will be interesting to see if we succeed. My three sisters run different parts of the business, but what remains to be seen is whether the next generation and the one after that want to rise to the challenge. On the other hand, it is a pity to observe that the loyalties of nonfamily executives are not as strong as they once were.

"One obvious alternative to trying to groom successive generations of family members to serve the company is to switch to public ownership. But this has turned out not to be as simple as we had hoped. The Koç name has a formidable reputation in Turkey for its leadership, integrity, corporate culture, nationwide production, distribution, after-sales service, and foundations. We are quoted on the exchange in Turkey, but when we tried an initial public offering (IPO) in the United States in 1998, we withdrew because we did not agree with the value they put on our company.

"Much of your local reputation does not always travel well to global centers of finance. In 1998 the markets were in shock from the East Asian meltdown and the Russian default, and our IPO was so long in preparation and so badly timed that international investors declined to invest in emerging markets such as Turkey. We were valued at $2.2 billion, as against the $5.6 billion we are generally valued at today on the local stock exchange. It was a moment of truth: the way the markets treat an offering they do not really understand from a region thought to be in turmoil and hence risky.

"Many of the virtues of a family company do not register with shareholders: our long-term commitment to our country, our concern with the environment, the value of our reputation for integrity, the years of loyalty among customers, consumers, and the family. It was a shock to see these intangibles disregarded and undervalued. The team responsible for this debacle was released from their company. We felt they had let us down in the eyes of the world."

We should note here that another possible reason for the low valuation was the markets' known dislike of conglomerates, but probably more important was Turkey's high rate of inflation. All in all, the transition from family ownership to partly public ownership for a company this size is not easy. Western shareholders do not understand the reasons for the strength of family ownership in Turkey or the suitability of this form to local conditions. KG believes that its hard-earned reputation for integrity is in no way inferior to the so-called transparency of public companies, which all too often is contrived by creative accountancy.

We can illustrate Koç's dilemma with the following diagram:

Dilemma 1: Family Succession versus Public Ownership

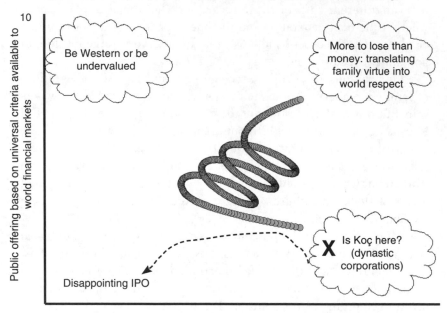

Public companies are judged by universalist criteria and allegedly are transparent. They supply the same "facts" to everyone. Family companies are judged by particularist criteria; allegedly revered and trusted in their own cultures, they are more opaque and have very special relationships to key persons, whom they may treat differently.

What Koç has to do is make the strengths of his family dynasty appeal to public shareholders despite the differences between Turkey and Wall Street. Educated in business administration at John Hopkins University, Koç is no stranger to American ways and is determined to demonstrate the virtues of his company to the world markets. One handicap is that Turkey still lacks financial rating agencies, and so it is not always clear how the wider world will regard KG or what its criteria of judgment will be. The story that has to be told is how one preeminent Turkish family constitutes both the backbone of and the gateway to the Turkish economy and deserves respect for that reason alone, although there are many others.

Those who have more to lose than money (i.e., their reputation, a good name with neighbors) can be expected to act honorably, and KG has a track record of 75 years of fair dealing. A word should also be said about the dismissal of the IPO team. When a family's reputation is at stake, together with that of the Turkish nation, those who embarrass it in public bring censure on themselves.

Dilemma 2. Can a National Champion with Strong Regional Loyalties Withstand the Competitive Pressures of Global Rivals?

KG is very much a homegrown champion. Can it, despite its impressive but local size and large resources, stand up to the competitive pressures faced by truly global players? The sheer amount of giving to charities, including the Vehbi Koç Foundation with assets of over $650 million, the Rahmi Koç Foundation, and the Suna and Inan Kiraç Research Fellowship, is impressive. Can a company so immersed in giving also satisfy shareholders and customers, or will it fall victim to global rivals with lesser obligations to national infrastructures? The truth is that Turkish markets have not been truly open in the last 20 years or so; the danger is that KG might be outclassed by global competitors that have been under more pressure to be efficient.

Koç believes that KG can meet the competition head on and "either do something no one else does or do it better than others." He believes that his joint partnerships with global giants such as Ford and Fiat are truly equal and mutual in their benefits and that those partnerships can help guarantee that KG will share global strategies with the big boys. For Fiat, KG manufactures the Palio, Marea, and Brava family of cars at Tofas. For Ford, the Ford Otosan venture with KG is unique. Otosan will be the sole manufacturer of Ford's brand-new light commercial vehicle, which is aimed especially at regional markets, and exports will start in 2001. In total, KG has joint ventures with 21 global partners. The Koç brands Beko/Arçelik (durable goods) and Ram Store/Migros (supermarket and retail chain) are extremely successful in Western Europe and the former Soviet countries, respectively.

KG's strength lies in traditional ties of loyalty. Some of its long-trusted dealers are also in their third generation of ties between respective families. Can this last? Will the rising generations feel the same way? Will they prefer a relationship with KG, which does so much for Turkish society, or will they prefer to ally with a global player vying for KG's markets?"

Koç was not sure of the answer, but we pointed out that Japanese consumers pay 20 to 30 percent above world prices, in part because national companies are public benefactors and major contributors to learning and development. So long as KG commanded local loyalties, it would be hard to enter the Turkish market without a respected local partner. The family could not renege on its charitable giving at this point; the only viable strategy was to utilize the loyalties won by its generosity and make it hard for others to enter local markets without the guidance and blessing of KG. The partnerships with global players would help win respect and make KG privy to global strategies. The dilemma looked like this:

Dilemma 2: Global Competition versus Local Loyalties

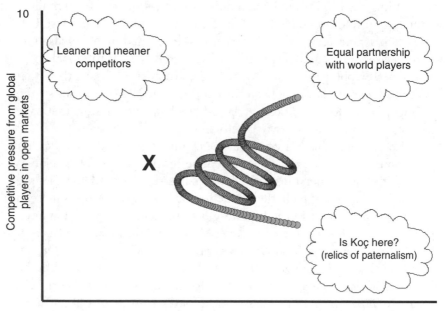

The danger is that the leaner and meaner competitors (top left in the diagram) will tempt Turkish society to abandon its loyalties. The converse danger is that KG could become a relic of paternalism (bottom right), still giving generously but less and less able to afford such kindly concerns.

Koç's answer seems to be to partner with global players and in the process become their full equals and learn all about their thinking and strategy, their manufacturing techniques, and their market intelligence—above all to join them in exporting so that KG grows into a genuinely global player itself rather than just a national powerhouse.

Dilemma 3. The Private Sector versus the Public Sector: Finding the Right Balance

Like many countries left behind by the wave of industrial revolutions that transformed Western countries in the nineteenth century, Turkey was mobilized and had its fortunes revived by its government. Kemal Atatürk was the originator of the new Turkish republic that arose from the collapse of the Ottoman Empire, and the English expression "young Turks" is a lasting tribute to the reforming zeal of Turkey's new republicans. In a pattern that has repeated itself among nations that found themselves behind industrially and then started to catch up fast, those efforts were orchestrated by the government. The original ideal was a good one, Koç explained. Governments could *start* things going and then spin them off to the private sector before they ossified and became bureaucratic. Alas, the ideal was not always adhered to. If the government had sold its telecommunications business several years ago, it would have been worth much more than it is worth today. Quite soon the springboard becomes deadwood.

In Turkey the state is the largest employer and accounts for a large proportion of the economy. Government is not merely the employer of last resort; it needs to keep its own electoral supporters on its side. For many years, because of extensive budget deficits, lending to the government has been a guaranteed source of profit for banks. In a recent scandal several failing banks that were due to be taken over by the government gave generous loans to selected cronies, safe in the knowledge that the state would assume their debts. One thing that prevents the timely spin-off of government initiatives to private enterprise is the sheer number of politically motivated deals. Given this regrettable situation, Koç seeks to redress the balance within his own publicly oriented initiatives. The money given to charity—to universities, hospitals, schools, and museums—is, whenever it is practical, managed by his own system. He does not believe in dropping money into public institutions where it falls through the cracks.

If he does not actually manage a school he endows, he makes sure it is close to one of his plants so that trusted managers can keep an eye on it. The Turkish nation has not yet given its private sector the scope or the people to be effective, but at least KG is doing its best to establish a balance. It has shown most dramatically by its own example that public projects are best performed by private initiatives and that the public interest is safe in the hands of at least one corporation. It is not just a matter of charity and meaning well but a matter of good management and the effective use of funds. There is no good reason why social caring should not be businesslike and the Koç foundations have demonstrated this truth. The dilemmas involved can be illustrated as follows:

Dilemma 3: Public versus Private

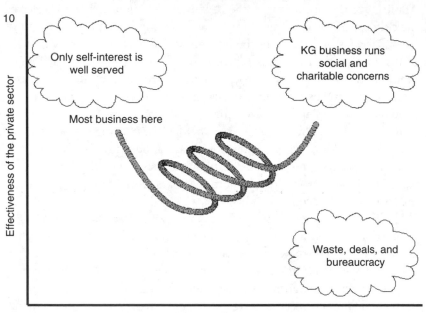

Most businesses are near the upper left in the diagram: effective but narrowly self-interested in their aims. It has been the achievement of KG and its foundations to combine business with social caring and to show the nation that big government may not be necessary after all.

Dilemma 4. Pressure to Be Democratic and Practice Free Trade versus Playing the Cards Effectively to Catch Up

We put it to Koç the notion that no nation ever achieved economic leadership through free trade. The United States, for example, hid behind the Monroe Doctrine of disengagement from Europe for much of the nineteenth century and then became an arms supplier in two world wars. Its Cold War defense expenditures were massive and subsidized its airlines, its microelectronics companies, and high tech generally.

Free trade is the slogan of nations once they have reached supremacy and want no markets closed to them.

Singapore, South Korea, Malaysia, China, and the Pacific Rim nations have all grown rapidly by radically modifying the free-trade doctrine. What should Turkey and KG do about this dilemma?

Koç replies: "God has given every country some cards to play, but Turkey's situation is particularly difficult. We have cheaper labor but are accused of 'dumping' when we use it strategically. Global companies tend to dictate terms, especially the price of raw materials. They can and do dump on us to gain market share.

"At the moment global companies, with some exceptions, are transferring their profits and wealth to their home countries. When this is reversed, the pressure on KG will become intense.

"I agree that certain nations have come from behind successfully, but most of them are a long way from being democratic. South Korea has been in a condition of martial law with an aggressive northern neighbor for 35 years or more. There are no strikes, and there is a clear division of sectors. Singapore is not genuinely democratic and has been ruled by a benevolent dictator for most of the years since its independence. Because East Asia was a frontier in the Cold War and has weak democratic traditions, considerable variations from orthodox free trade were tolerated. China, as of now, manages to have a communist government alongside markets partly open to the West.

"None of these concessions are offered to Turkey. We are expected to be a European-style democracy and a full signatory to human rights legislation as a condition of entry to the EU [European Union]. This includes following the rules of the World Trade Organization and letting global players enter our markets. South Korea has created by government policy vast economies of scale and powerful concentrations of high tech, but if Turkey or KG were to attempt it, this would almost certainly be ruled illegitimate. The irony is that Europe is not really liberal in trade and erects barriers to the outside world; nor is it genuinely a single economy or a single market. Turkey does have cards to play, among them a highly skilled workforce and excellent manufacturing quality, but whether we will be allowed to play these cards remains to be seen. At the moment we are expected to live up to free trade and democratic ideals that our competitors have not consistently attained themselves. In order to join, we have to be 'better' than those we are joining! It is a tough assignment. Someone gets drunk and makes a lot of noise in the middle of the night, waking up his neighbors. When asked to be quiet, he replies, 'We live in a democratic country.' When he gets arrested, he complains that his human rights are being ignored! We are trying, but it is hard."

The truth is that to take off, infant industries need a period of protection as they develop their muscles for world competition. Current trade rules render this almost impossible to achieve, except informally through "nontariff barriers" erected by customer loyalty. Turkish industries could be subject to head-on assaults before they are ready to meet them.

The dilemma illustrated in the next diagram shows the bind in which Turkey as a culture and economy, along with KG, finds itself:

Dilemma 4: Free Trade versus Catching Up

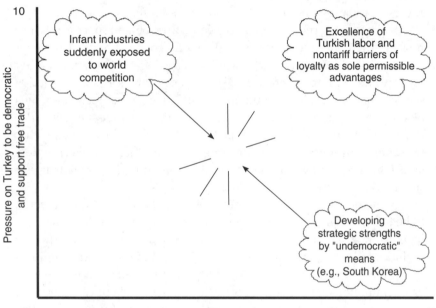

On the vertical axis we see that the price of admission to the EU is to behave in a way that European democracies have idealized but not fully attained. On the horizontal axis we see that nations such as South Korea have been allowed to "cheat" on the probably unrealistic rules of free trade because of their continuing states of emergency and front-line position against a communist state. Turkey is barred from using such strategies.

The two incompatible pressures collide in the center of the diagram; in truth, KG and the Turkish economy may not have enough cards to

play. We should not think of dilemma theory as always allowing reconciliation. Often the external forces are too great, and whole nations are
tossed from one horn of dilemmas to the other. What KG *does* have are
very skilled workers and fiercely loyal customers who realize that the
fortunes of KG and those of the Turkish nation are closely bound
together. Whether this will be enough remains to be seen.

Dilemma 5. Turkey as a Marginal State versus Turkey as a Center of Potentially Conflicting Loyalties

Turkey is on the very edge of Europe, yet it was a loyal ally of the West
throughout the long years of the Cold War. Turkey is where Islam
meets the West. It was the scene of the Crusades and the site of Con-
stantinople, which was sacked by East and West repeatedly.

Two views are possible. The first is that Turkey and KG are "marginal Europeans," on the frontiers of European economic wealth and
"civilization." It is in Turkey's interest to join the club of relatively
wealthy nations despite the fact that it may always be regarded with
some suspicion as not "really" European. The opposing view is that
Turkey is a potential tinderbox, vulnerable to the fate that recently be-
fell Lebanon, which, after years of peace, turned into a nest of religious
and ethnic hatred and burned itself down in internecine strife. It is such
fears that cause Turkish business to be labeled "high risk." Although
Turkish culture presents the moderate face of Islam, it is feared that
this may not last, that religious divides may fracture at the point where
they must; thus, Turkey lies not just on a geological fault line (there
were terrible earthquakes in 1999) but on a cultural fault line as well, so
that Jihad may clash with McWorld, a seemingly faithless fast-food
emporium.

Koç is particularly insightful and visionary on this issue. He sees
Turkey as a "peaceful Lebanon," the dream that once was but then died.
He points out that many "crossroads" nations have prospered: Switzerland historically; Austria when it bordered on the Iron Curtain; Hong
Kong, which gave access to China; Finland, which was linked to both
the West and the Soviet bloc. At their best crossroads states allow different cultures to mingle peacefully and engage in trade. Turkey stands
at the frontiers of the Middle East, Islam, Russia, and Europe. As a sec-
ular state, it could reap the benefits of its multicultural, multireligious
nature, providing a safe bridge over potential fault lines.

Turkey is multilingual. It has adopted the EU's legal framework,
particularly the defense of intellectual property. It is also developing a

hugely popular tourist industry, evidence that people feel safe while visiting this exotic clime. Such schemes as duty-free goods and efficient car rentals are highly successful and help the country earn foreign currency.

The dilemma and its reconciliation may be expressed as follows:

Dilemma 5: Marginal State versus Tinderbox of Conflicting Loyalties

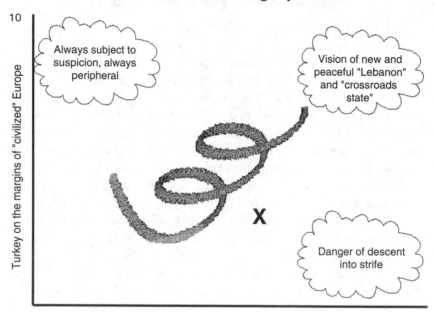

Turkey as a tinderbox of conflicting loyalties

Although this is very much Koç's vision, he is not too optimistic that the Turkish government will help bring it about: "Governments have been nationalistic rather than cosmopolitan. Liquor and tobacco are still monopolies; salt and beer were demonopolized to a large extent some years ago. As of now I doubt that we have the strategy to be like Hong Kong.

"There was a fashion in the 1970s to push up the birthrate, to become 'Big Turkey,' with a population rivaling those of India and Pakistan. Then, after a change in government policy, measures were taken to bring the birthrate down to 1.2 percent.

"On the export front, incentives have been on again, off again, and we have been accused increasingly of 'unfair competition' with Europe and have been subject to antidumping regulations."

Dilemma 6. Local Success Has Reached Its Limits versus Finding New Directions

Koç's last dilemma is less about Turkey than about KG, although the fortunes of the two are closely intertwined. Given KG's large market shares in the national economy—in several cases reaching 50 to 60 percent and rarely less than 35 percent—there is not much more "success" to be had locally without so dominating various industries that KG will be undone by its own market power and be accused of oligopoly. Although it is difficult and perhaps undesirable for KG to increase its local size, there is still much to be done in export markets through the development of local brands that can withstand competition. (That Koç knew what he was talking about was strongly suggested at the end of our interview, when he took a telephone call from the prime minister.)

What is urgently needed, as he sees it, is to close the gap between education and the workplace. On-the-job training should begin at the university so that what is learned there can be tested, developed, and renewed in the world of work. KG recently divested its relatively low-knowledge textile business and is concentrating on helping the Turkish nation manage sophisticated knowledge so that it informs new products and services. To that end, the New Business Development department of KG (a part of the Strategic Planning Group, which acts as an internal investment bank for the group) is strategizing for the long term and looking into alternative futures. One possibility is a trans-Caspian pipeline project that could carry natural gas from Turkmenistan under the Caspian Sea. Another is to bid for the state telecom monopoly, Türk Telekom. Another ambitious project is a standardized and integrated customer database of literally hundreds of thousands of the business customers of KG. When it is complete, this should be an invaluable source of intelligence about who does what in Turkey.

Whatever it decides to do, KG hopes to mobilize a sizable part of Turkish business to follow its lead in the twenty-first century. Schools, hospitals, museums, research centers, and businesses will organize the knowledge that will constitute the core competences of the new millennium. The dilemma and its resolution looks are illustrated in the following diagram:

Dilemma 6: Domestic Success versus New Directions

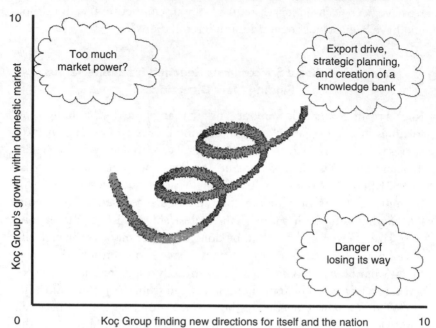

As a major player in Turkish economic development and a potential mediator in what has recently been dubbed *the clash of civilizations,* Koç looks down on the Bosphorous with a keen vision of what the twenty-first century may bring.

Chapter 20

━━━◆━━━

Leading through Transformation: Sir Mark Moody-Stuart, Royal Dutch Shell

Jo Spyckerelle and Charles Hampden-Turner

M ARK MOODY-STUART (now Sir Mark) became a member of the Committee of Managing Directors (CMD) of the Royal Dutch Shell Group of companies in 1991. By 1998 he was chairman of the CMD. He was fated "to lead through interesting times," although just how interesting (and turbulent) came as a surprise to everyone, himself included.

During those years Shell was totally transformed. It closed its major regional headquarters in Rotterdam, Houston, Hamburg, and Paris and Shell-Mex House in London. It reorganized itself internally. Senior Shell managers think in terms of dilemmas, and so the word is not strange to them. One of the authors (CH-T) wrote "The Dilemmas of Planning" for the CMD in 1984, and the idea of confronting dilemmas and reconciling them as a challenge of leadership appears to have stuck. Speeches made by senior officers are full of dilemmas.

Moody-Stuart confronted the following issues:

1. Internal versus external orientations and the trauma of Brent Spar

2. Truth and communicability: the judicial murder of Ken Saro-Wiwa in Nigeria
3. Excessive decentralization versus the need for global action
4. Trust me, tell me, show me
5. Shareholders versus stakeholders
6. The multicultural, multivalued meritocracy

We will look at these events one at a time.

Dilemma 1. Internal versus External Orientations and the Trauma of Brent Spar

Before we spoke to Mark Moody-Stuart, we had received extensive briefings on background issues from some of his senior officers. Some of what they told us is paraphrased in the passages that follow.

The oil industry (Shell included) has long tended to look inward. Shell's ear was not to the ground. It had integrity and a Calvinist conscience, but it was *insider* integrity, *insider* rationality, and *insider* judgment that was more expert than anyone else's and more likely to be correct. It would always come as a shock to Shell when the oil industry was criticized. Shell managers saw such issues as matters of technical expertise, and about that they knew better than did any critics. After all, they had the facts and the outsiders did not. These facts were typically technical, not social, issues and had the rational-empirical substance that engineers love. Of course, it was recognized that the decisions would have a social impact, but that only made it more important that they be technically sound. That sociopolitical events in the external world had logics of their own was not always clear to Shell in those days.

In part, this came about because upstream was more profitable than downstream: Exploration and production were much more profitable than retailing. Shell divisions made money in inverse relation to their proximity to consumers, and this fact reinforced an inward-looking technological bent. In addition, there was a cultural tendency for the engineers to be Dutch and the accountants Scottish, so that the profitability of upstream activities was widely known and admired. The British tended to be more commercial, treading on the back of the old empire. It was this inner-directed technological mind-set that got Shell into trouble over the Brent Spar, a massive, obsolete oil storage and loading buoy in the North Sea that Shell planned to dispose of by sinking it in a deep part of the Atlantic.

Shell had done its homework, costing out all the options for disposal and calculating them from multiple points of view, including the environmental impact. As far as Shell could measure the impact, disposal in a relatively deep undersea trench was best for all stakeholders compared to the alternatives. The safety of the operation was a major concern. Of course, getting rid of a huge metal structure is not trouble-free: There are always some costs. The British government had endorsed the calculations, and its Department of Industry was on Shell's side. Shell had consulted widely. What could go wrong? Plenty, as it turned out. Moody-Stuart takes up the story:

"We allowed ourselves to be placed in a false position, and this made it imperative *not* to sink the buoy. Greenpeace had accused us publicly of leaving 4000 tons of oil sludge and sediment in the core of the spar. Because Greenpeace had dramatically occupied the spar, the world assumed that that organization had looked and measured the amount of sediment. We knew that this report was wrong, but if we had sunk the buoy, we could never have disproved the accusation, and we would have been blamed ever after for polluting the water as the oil seeped out. On top of this accusation came another from a German expert that toxic pollutants were to be dumped at the same time. That expert claimed in an affidavit to have sealed the drums himself! We knew the charge was crazy, but once the spar was sunk, we would be accused of drowning the evidence. We could refute these charges only if the spar was open to inspection.

"Thus our famous 'U-turn,' which gave the appearance of our being irresolute and unsure of our position, was forced on us by false accusations and the need to establish our credibility. We had to withdraw from a solution we believed—and still believe—to be technically correct. Were we right? Within our own logical framework we were, but there are other frameworks out there in the world external to oil. And these were slower to grasp. Admittedly, they were emotional arguments, but they also had a logic of their own.

"What really had a big effect on me was a statement by the Swedish minister for the environment. She said, 'Actually, I believe Shell's arguments. I accept them completely. But how can I talk to our schoolchildren about the importance of recycling materials when one of the world's largest companies simply topples its own huge wastes into the sea?' And I saw at once what she meant—that her logic was impeccable also, albeit different from ours. I learned that one can be absolutely right technically but that real decisions must take account of personalities, agendas, emotions, beliefs, symbols, and appearances.

"When people ask me, 'Don't you think you were right all along?' I cannot entirely agree with them. Decisions must take into consideration how the people with whom you are consulting think. And because people think about and value things differently, there is always a dilemma—a need to reconcile diverse logics."

Sinking the Brent Spar in the vicinity in which it had originally stood could convince the watching world that if Shell was a huge litter-bug, dumping that for which it had no more use, at minimum inconvenience to itself. In this context wild stories about the poisonous contents of the spar gained a credibility they did not deserve. It must have seemed as if Shell were hurrying to dispose of the evidence of its "crimes," except that there were no crimes and the process had already taken years, with the actual sinking being only a culmination.

However, it is crisis that sells newspapers and attracts audiences to television, and so when the disposal was only hours away, the furor intensified. When Greenpeace finally apologized for its wildly inaccurate report about the oil platform it had occupied, it was too late. The audience had shifted its attention.

There are two dilemmas here: inner-directed technological expertise versus the outer world of sociopolitical appearances and truth versus communicability. We will deal with the first of these two now and postpone the second until after our discussion of the Nigerian crisis.

Shell's inner-directed technological expertise is far stronger than its grasp of sociopolitical appearances. This dilemma is a slight variation on the inner-directed versus outer-directed dimension discussed in Chapter 2. The situation is set out in the next diagram:

Dilemma 1: Internal versus External Orientations

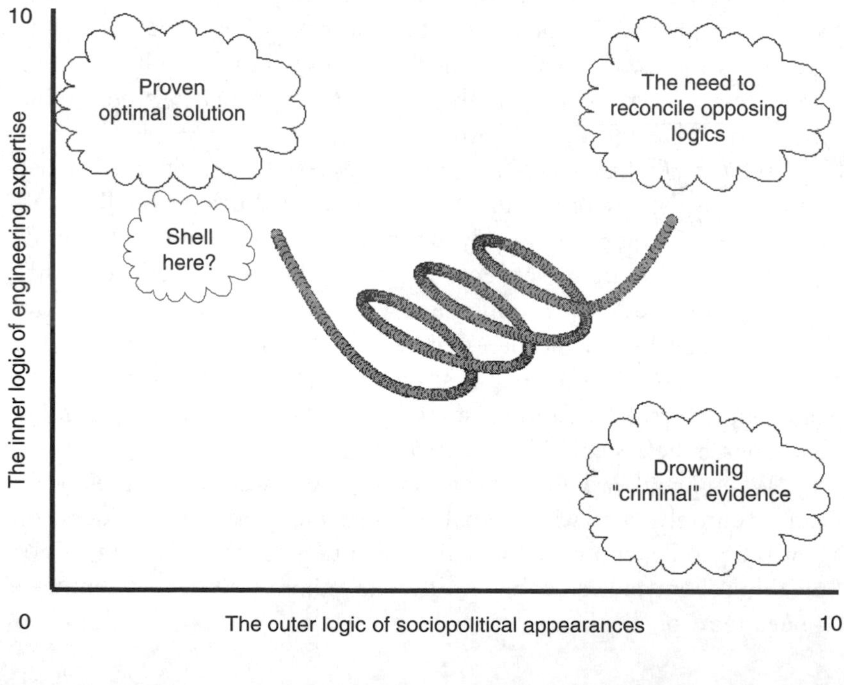

The inner logic of engineering expertise (y-axis, 0 to 10)

The outer logic of sociopolitical appearances (x-axis, 0 to 10)

Proven optimal solution

The need to reconcile opposing logics

Shell here?

Drowning "criminal" evidence

We have tentatively located Shell toward the upper left of the diagram, indicating that the company was strong in inner-directed technical expertise but much weaker at understanding the external world of sociopolitical appearances. Organizations such as Greenpeace require scandals to "raise consciousness" about environmental issues and recruit members. Boarding the Brent Spar amid crashing waves made them look like "cockleshell heroes," braving the elements to discover the (unfortunately false) truth.

Shell is relatively unsophisticated in this world of heroic postures and media "spin." While enraged protestors vent their righteous wrath, Shell spokespersons read the deliberations of a committee from prepared scripts. Even if the second is more truthful than the first, the first *seems more authentic and spontaneous.* It is the utterance of the underdog "thinking only of the environment" against the might of a profit-making giant corporation.

What Moody-Stuart is calling for are decisions that take into consideration *all* logics (upper right in the diagram): the internal logic of inexpensive, safe disposal *and* the concern of the Swedish minister of the environment, trying to teach schoolchildren not to throw debris into the environment we all share. All major corporations take public positions, if not on purpose then by default. Shell must learn the logics of such positioning.

In that connection, we now come to the second scandal that plagued Shell: the execution of an environmental campaigner by the Nigerian military junta.

Dilemma 2. Truth and Communicability: The Judicial Murder of Ken Saro-Wiwa in Nigeria

The execution of Ken Saro-Wiwa had to do with two conflicting issues: the truth of what actually happened and the communicability of that truth. When you speak the truth, will you be believed by the Nigerian government, by your own employees, by the indigenous people, and by the world community? Dilemmas are not just a mental exercise for resourceful leaders; they can be murderous crosscurrents in world politics that drag under anyone caught between them. Saro-Wiwa was the chief victim, but Shell's reputation suffered too, if only to a lesser degree.

Ken Saro-Wiwa was an environmental activist and the representative of a minority Nigerian tribe not favored or represented by the Nigerian military junta. The junta had seized power from an unelected civilian regime. Installed by the previous military government, it was in the process of being expelled from the Commonwealth. The environment in which Saro-Wiwa's tribe lived was allegedly polluted with crude oil; prompted by Ken Saro-Wiwa and the environmental campaigners who supported his cause, world newspapers and television programs were full of pictures of stagnant pools and twisted broken pipes, although the real damage was questioned by *The Times* and *The Independent.* The latter publication pointed out that Shell controls only about 10 percent of the delta, which puts the reported "devastation" in perspective. Here was a brave, lonely African protester imprisoned and charged with treason for protesting an intolerable state of affairs. Was this ghastly tangle of leaking pipes Shell's work? If so, was Shell also complicit in the death of this "troublemaker," who drew attention to the company's environmental record? Was this not an unholy alliance between a junta that cared only about its royalties and a company seeking profits that decided that Saro-Wiwa was in the way? In a world that judges by appearances Shell was in the dock of world opinion.

We asked Moody-Stuart for his view of this dilemma. He was typically forthright. Commenting on our background interviews, which had revealed that the locals sabotage the pipelines themselves, he demurred at the word *sabotage:* "I don't think that is the right word. These people are totally excluded from the benefits of their society and get virtually none of the massive oil revenues we pay their government. It is their frustration at not getting any share of this wealth while living in the middle of the disturbance it causes that drives their behavior.

"If there is a mess, we pay them to clean it up, and the more the mess, the more we pay. They break up the pipes for many reasons, sometimes only to get back at an arbitrary and illegitimate government that is not of their people. Perhaps if that government loses enough revenue, it will make concessions. Getting your money directly via a foreign company which keeps its promises is infinitely preferable to hoping that money paid to your overlords will eventually reach you. A stinking environmental mess is preferable to not earning and not eating at all, and these are desperate circumstances."

We asked Moody-Stuart whether he had noticed these appalling conditions when he was in Nigeria in the late 1970s and early 1980s. His voice grew lower and softer: "Oh, yes.... There were community disruptions when I was in Nigeria. At that time Shell's effective tax rate was 98.5 percent. Of every million units of local currency we generated, we kept barely two thousand. I remember the community coming to me in a rage, saying, 'It's not fair. Unless we too receive something, we'll just shut down this operation.' I used to pull out my charts on which the division of income was presented, but they said to me, 'You are like the millionaire's son. We know *you* don't have the money, but if we hold you for ransom, maybe the millionaire will notice us.'

"So I used to say, 'I promise you I will pass on your message. I absolutely guarantee to repeat what you tell me to the government. But if the government clamps down and if the population is provoked, we could all lose.' "

Our background interviews revealed some of the reasons why the Nigerian government might continue to ignore its own people even when an oil company passes on the message. Oil companies are, after all, among the residues of the colonial era. They are not political organizations, and no one elected them. They are tolerated for one reason only: their technical prowess at locating and extracting oil. The difference between the best and worst companies is several hundred million in revenue, and so you choose the best and try to forget that they are part British.

Why white technicians should be thought influential with black politicians in regard to Nigeria's sovereign interests is hard to explain. That white foreigners are campaigning for Saro-Wiwa is a reason *for* executing him and emphasizes the effectiveness of his "treason": "He has set the world against us!" The political impotence of a white technical expert in a former colonial country should be highlighted. If the expert asks for a political objective, someone will make sure that he or she does not get it. To "fight for the life of Ken Saro-Wiwa" is to seal his doom! No astute black politician will be seen making concessions to former colonial masters.

What Shell did was try to influence the junta "behind the scenes," a tactic that did not succeed in halting the execution but was the only avenue of influence that would not be gleefully snubbed. Moody-Stuart continues: "Brent Spar and Nigeria both acted as magnifying glasses that clarified where we were not succeeding. We were not connected to the several publics with which we interface on issues that were highly symbolic.

"On many such subjects the public mind is schizophrenic. On the one hand, it wants instant, clean energy; on the other hand, it also seeks the freedom and independence of traveling when and where it wants. We wish to be wealthy but bewail the gap between rich and poor. We want to grow economically, but not at the expense of the environment. Between these opposing views, Shell finds itself situated. Until the parties agree with each other, we are liable to be the football between contending sides."

The underlying dilemma is between truth and communicability. Not everything that is true is easily communicable. The sheer extent of the gap between the Nigerian government and its own people, who in their desperation break up pipelines, is true but not easily communicable, because no constituencies want to hear that message—no groups gain from publicizing it. There are no heroes opposing villains; instead, there are victims turned villains as the legacy of past oppression lingers.

We can diagram this dilemma as follows:

Dilemma 2: Truth and Communicability

The uncomfortable truth is that the military rulers in Nigeria will kill for the vast riches of "black gold" supplied by oil companies, and the profits will be sent straight to Switzerland or Luxembourg to fatten their overseas accounts. The truth is bitter and ironic. What the press wants are people to love and to hate: heroic Saro-Wiwa versus the "complicit" company, not the "exploited turned exploiter." The fact is that Gandhi, Nelson Mandela, and Martin Luther King, Jr., are exceptions; most exploited people bite back when they get the chance! Mobutu repeats King Leopold's plundering of the Congo.

From our background interviews we got an idea of what Shell is planning to do about situations such as that just recounted. These ongoing dilemmas must be publicly discussed with the press, politicians, and the public before the crises that are symptomatic of the dilemmas strike. You know something is likely to go terribly wrong if you are the only visible white agent of an increasingly oppressive government. However, you also know that jobs and income will be lost to other nations' oil companies if you simply pull out. These dilemmas must be engaged before they explode in Shell's face. Shell is prepared to sponsor an examination of the problems. So long as the public is fragmented into mutually hostile camps, though, Shell is likely to be cut.

Moody-Stuart has changed the whole mood of the company in this regard. He explains: "If our society is fractured, this is no good for us. I say to our people, 'If someone comes to you with a problem, never say, "That's not my problem; I'm a businessperson." If it's a problem of our society or of the world community, it's our problem too, and sooner or later we'll be caught in the middle if we are not prepared to deal with it.' The question is, What can I contribute? All those comfortable boundaries are gone. It is not a 'Nigerian problem,' a 'technical problem,' or a 'matter for the government.' It's *our* problem, because we are abroad in the world.

"You can no longer say, 'We pay our taxes to the Nigerian government. We run an open, honest, audited business.' It isn't that we are responsible personally; it is that we are part of the process, and if the money is siphoned off for illegitimate uses, that social system eventually will fracture, and we will be in the middle of it. Pulling out is no answer either. These countries have a single chance in their entire histories to use their oil revenues for economic development. If they blow it, that is forever. We have to give them that chance.

"You cannot give up talking to any regime you are enriching; we have to keep trying. We have an obvious personal interest in fair and stable elected governments, but we cannot hector them. We instead point out our shared interest in a peaceful, prospering nation with shared wealth."

Dilemma 3. Excessive Decentralization versus the Need for Global Action

So how did it happen that Shell shed so many of its national headquarters?

Shell is justly famous for its scenarios, which consist of three or four "alternative futures," each one coherent, persuasive, and reasonably probable. In the early and middle 1990s the scenario writers were telling the leaders of the Shell Group that there were three contending visions of capitalism: that of North America and the North America Free Trade Agreement (NAFTA), that of East Asia, using a more cooperative model of catch-up capitalism; and that of the European zone, soon to be unified by a single currency.

No one tells Shell managers which scenario to believe. The whole point of scenarios is to be ready to engage *whatever* future emerges. What *does* happen is that group decision makers check from day to day on which vision of capitalism's future is becoming more true and more influential. It was soon obvious that American-style global capitalism was the type most in the ascendancy by virtue of the long boom and the sustained success of the U.S. economy, whose ceaseless innovation appeared to have ended the cycle of boom and bust. In contrast, East Asia suffered a financial crisis, and the euro lost ground to the dollar.

In this emerging new world, was Shell's traditional model of decentralized multinationalism the right one? There were excellent reasons for Shell's traditional decentralization. The automobile had come into its own between World Wars I and II, when nations were divided by steep tariff barriers. Oil has long been regarded as a strategic commodity, and it was advantageous for nations to have their "own" oil supplies. That Shell took on the coloration of different localities was long regarded as a competitive advantage. If the Hague was under German occupation, London was not. During the Vietnam War Shell was to many people the most acceptable oil company—for instance, Shell Oil of Houston was separated from Royal Dutch Shell.

But times change. Sir Mark takes up the story:

"The old Shell business model served us well and was well suited to the world as it was 30 or more years ago, with strong, autonomous national business units, with money accumulating to those units which managed their regions, and so on. That was right for a world in which communications were still slow, boundaries were firm, tariff and nontariff barriers were still high, and governments were influential in economic affairs. It was demonstrably successful, because we started way behind Exxon and caught up. The problem we faced in the 1990s was that boundaries and barriers were falling. Communications were instantaneous, markets were globalizing, and you had to respond far faster than before.

"One key point was that we neither decided to nor intend to 'sacrifice local marketing' in the process of centralizing and globalizing. I sincerely hope we have not done so. The strategy is not to diminish our local reach and intelligence but to centralize information about those local initiatives. A great many things are best done locally, but we must think globally about them and respond globally, where necessary, to events anywhere in the world. The old system was too slow to react. Something happened. There were many different opinions, and by the time we had an agreed-upon policy, the situation had changed yet again.

"What we have done is to vest executive authority for a business and nonexecutive authority for all the other businesses in the country in one person so that he or she, say, is both in charge of our exploration, production, and gas business in the United Kingdom and also, as country chairman, represents all Shell businesses in the United Kingdom in dealings with the government. When we were closing the Norwegian refinery, it was the country chairman, who happened to be the executive responsible for our EP business, who handled all the government public relationships. He knew all the local players. You cannot parachute a foreigner from the center into Norway to do that kind of job.

"When we closed national headquarters, we did not thereby withdraw from our involvement in those countries. Instead, we moved *closer* to actual customers and to local operations and made sure that they informed our global strategic activities about what was happening on the ground. The offices are now closer to customers and retailers and are not located in big towers.

In fact, Shell embarked on a process of making each of its research units justify itself in terms of the customers' demands instead of assuming that any piece of interesting research would pay off eventually. All research staff members were exposed to courses in "marketing for nonmarketers," which showed how to estimate the value of your own activities in market terms. Each project became a profit center searching for customers and had to look to its own bottom line. The fact that you are decentralized in your localities does *not*, unfortunately, mean that you look outward to customers and markets.

Mark Moody-Stuart believes that the move to greater centralization and globalism was the right decision, but he believes it could have been communicated better: "The old habits of patiently negotiated consensus and voluntary compliance with suggestions proved too slow, especially when it was these very practices that were to end. There was the usual resistance—the usual talking in circles. We finally decided we had to change and could not wait for everyone."

The dilemma of centralizing the previously decentralized structure is illustrated in the following diagram:

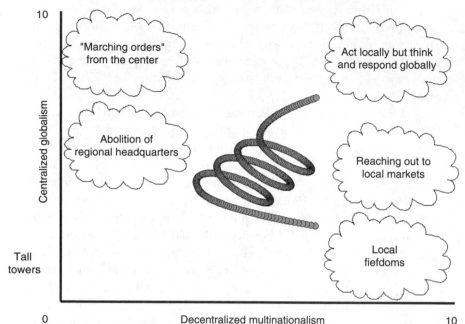

The diagram shows how Moody-Stuart aims to increase centralization *without* reducing the group's range, scope, or local flexibility. His aim is nothing less than to increase Shell's outreach to customers while better coordinating the knowledge that flows from such operations. This will enable the group to act swiftly and in concert.

Dilemma 4. Trust Me, Tell Me, Show Me

It is an axiom at Shell that the world is changing from "Trust me. I know what I'm talking about and my business is too complicated to explain anyway," through "Tell me—explain to the world what Shell is doing," to "Show me that you are doing what you say you are doing so I can check up on you." The original formulation was by Sir John Jennings, a senior officer in the group, but Moody-Stuart saw it being used by a union speaker at a United Nations conference called by Kofi Annan to launch his "Global Compact" where industries, unions, and nongovernmental organizations (NGOs) came together to support the compact. He was fascinated to see the distinction come back to him through a union spokesman, who said we had moved from a "Trust me" to a "Show me" world and that unions and NGOs now wanted to be shown. It gave Moody-Stuart pleasure because it was a sign that Shell had engaged the public world of opinion formation, to which it has so long felt itself a stranger.

Moody-Stuart sees "trust me, show me" as a dilemma but one that is readily reconcilable by making Shell's operations as transparent as possible. It is how he plans to run his restructured organization. Managers are held publicly responsible for cost containment and better capital utilization, with clearly defined targets, and are encouraged to show each other, the corporation, and the public what they have done.

Shell is now a "three-legged stool" with objectives having to do with return to shareholders, environmental audits, and social impacts, but all three are in the "show me" world. It is not enough to do something; you must also arrange for its verification and demonstration. Moody-Stuart explains that there are *two* levels of "trust me": "trust me without looking at the evidence" and "trust me because you have seen the evidence repeatedly and do not want to bother rechecking." He explains: "But [it] is a different form of trust; it is a trust based on complete openness—absolute transparency of reporting—so that people trust you because they can see what is happening. Very interestingly, you come back to trust via the show-me tactics."

This dilemma is illustrated in the following diagram:

Dilemma 4: Trust Me versus Show Me

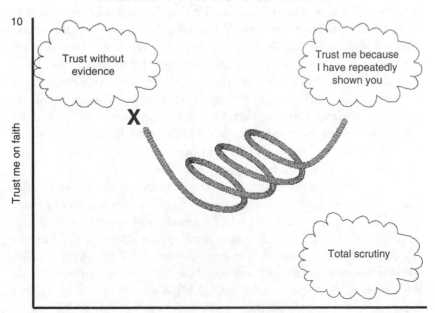

What this means is that Shell's knowledge and reports must be in demonstrable form, open on request to outside scrutiny.

Dilemma 5. Shareholders versus Stakeholders

Among the rude shocks that rattled Shell's foundations was the dramatic incident that occurred in 1998 when the financial markets wrote Shell down from $180 billion to $140 billion. Moody-Stuart had been chairman of the CMD for just a year. It was a shock for him and for everyone. Shell was being challenged by the shareholder community.

In fact, the financial markets had their reasons. Several competitors were making a 15 percent to 17 percent return on assets, while Shell had been languishing in the single digits. A sizable part of the oil industry was making less than its cost of capital, and shareholder protest was a matter of time. Even so, $40 billion was a huge reduction in the group's estimated value, and characteristically, Moody-Stuart fought back.

Exxon was the model of capital efficiency, whereas the model of flexible public recognition of the need to change patterns of oil consumption was British Petroleum (BP). Moody-Stuart decided that Shell was going to be as capital-efficient as Exxon. Our background interviews also suggested movement on alternative sources of energy, which is BP's rhetorical position. He explains that Shell unashamedly looked at Exxon's example of capital efficiency. For years Exxon had been making the same net income as Shell, but with $25 billion less capital. That is not true anymore; Shell has closed the gap. Moody-Stuart agrees with Lee Rehman of Exxon that in this way Exxon has given all the players a lead and shown the industry what is possible.

Nonetheless, Moody-Stuart insists that pleasing shareholders is only part of his task. His three-legged stool includes social ramifications and environmental impacts. He does not want Shell to be like Exxon in all respects, as there are other areas where he believes Shell to have the lead. He judges that BP has been a great communicator—a great packager of the message.

Moody-Stuart immediately set to work to increase Shell's capital efficiency. The closing of national headquarters offices was not unconnected to this issue, because each office had a grandeur of its own, with all the trappings of national pride, not to mention prime urban sites. Value was not created by these monuments; it was destroyed. BP had abandoned its London headquarters much earlier. Moody-Stuart explains that the commitments Shell made to the outside world were very simple: "(1) We are going to sort out our portfolio and remove unprofitable and less profitable activities. (2) We are going to increase our capital efficiency by cutting capital expenditures and completely changing the capital allocation process so that the higher expected returns outcompete the lower ones rather than having all proposals try to reach a threshold. We no longer optimize locally but compete globally. (3) We have targets to cut costs and continue cutting while improving operations."

Here is where the trust me–show me dilemma joins with the shareholder-stakeholder dilemma. Moody-Stuart is adamant that transparency is internal to Shell so that outsiders can peer inside: "What has changed is personal accountability. Every bit of the cost structure, from the top down, is broken up into pieces and is allocated to specific individuals. We are not so much concerned with blame and punishment as with everyone knowing who is responsible for which cost reductions and realizing that this is being accomplished on all sides. We want to be sure that the person with the responsibility also has the power—the levers of change—in his or her hands. It rapidly becomes clear if responsibility and power are mismatched, and then changes can be made.

"When everyone starts to use these powers effectively, the whole process accelerates; savings made in one place have ramifications in another, and it becomes easier to save money. The move to 'Show me' comes full circle back to 'trust me'—trust that everyone is working hard to use the assets more effectively. These methods are not confined to the capital-allocation and cost-cutting processes. Indeed, we aim to show the same kind of thoroughness and attention to detail with the other two 'legs of the stool': environment and social impact. Here too responsibilities are individualized. An NGO would not bother to speak to us a few years ago because it did not trust us. Such persons are now *shown* by the persons responsible what is being accomplished, what the targets are, and when they will be met. If Shell cannot make these targets, we explain why and how much longer it will take, but it is rare that we do not keep our promises."

Moody-Stuart continues: "NGOs are increasingly working *with* preferred oil companies in order to prove to industries and governments that social and environmental targets can be met at reasonable costs. We want to be chosen by these NGOs, and we want to join with them in proving what is possible. If they have a big enough stake in joining with us to get things done, maybe we can count on their support in future crises. Part of increasing our social intelligence is to work with those who have personal agendas so that we understand the cross currents of opinion in the world."

Every year from now on Shell will make three reports: on finances, on the environment, and on the social impact of its operations. None is to be sacrificed to the others. The funds saved by means of better capital utilization can be spent in all three areas. As Moody-Stuart wrote in his message from the chairman in *Shell Report 2000,*

> **My colleagues and I are totally committed to a business strategy that generates profits while contributing to the well-being of the planet and its people. We see no alternative.**

The image he uses is that of the surfer who does not know which of the big waves moving toward him or her will hit; Shell is ready for all three scenarios and the crises associated with each one. The trick is to keep your balance in heavy seas. The dilemma can be visualized as follows:

Dilemma 5: Shareholders versus Stakeholders

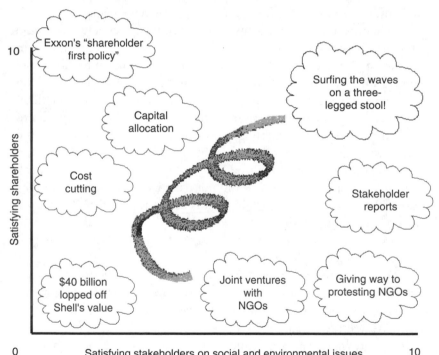

"Surfing the waves on a three-legged stool" is, of course, a mixed metaphor that is doubtful in terms of literary quality. But we must accustom ourselves to such hybrid concepts if we are to appreciate fully the need to reconcile values generally believed to conflict with each other. The mixed metaphor is the gateway to the realization that shareholders and stakeholders can both be satisfied. Literary elegance will have to take a back seat to creative resolution.

Dilemma 6. The Multicultural, Multivalued Meritocracy

Moody-Stuart is passionate about meritocracy but also concerned about the framework against which "merit" is judged. Traditionally, Shell has attracted some of the finest minds in core disciplines, and they do not stop learning when they come to work—in fact, they have barely begun. The big payoff of scenario planning was never the accuracy of the predictions made but the fact that every manager who used scenarios had three or four guesses about future outcomes rather than just one. You learn through conjectures and their refutations. With three or more guesses, refutations come thick and fast and learning is accelerated. Moody-Stuart, however, knows better than to believe that "merit" is universally understood around the globe and that we all agree easily on what an employee "deserves":

"When I talk about getting genuine national and cultural diversity into Shell, people remind me that this is a company run on merit. What I am 'really' talking about, they claim, is quotas—getting so many people from this or that place, based on ethnicity. If you go out to fill a quota, you will get some people who would not have made it otherwise, and that harms the merit principle."

Actually, Sir Mark is not talking about quotas at all but about a much more subtle issue: *Who says what merit means?* People succeed in different ways, in part because their personalities are different but largely because different cultures value different attributes. Shell has to see that merit itself is culturally defined. Thus, when an Anglo-Dutch corporation claims to promote people on the basis of "merit," these yardsticks are defined and invented by the founding nations of Royal Dutch Shell. These people are asking a world of diverse peoples to succeed *as they define it.* That is not something to be ashamed of—every company sets standards—but it is something to be aware of. To what extent has Shell accidentally narrowed the definitions of competence? Is an element of being global diversity not just of people but also of standards so that multiple forms of intelligence can find the respect that is due to them?

Moody-Stuart says: "We do not get Nigerians on the CMD, or most other nations for that matter. Genuine diversity is not a race with multinational entrants and Dutch, British, and American judges. It is crucial to discover what different cultures most value and to ask whether these values could benefit all of us. That is a genuine meritocracy, with multiple definitions of 'merit' so that employees can excel in their own ways.

"And Shell is making progress—generally, better progress than its rivals. There are 96,000 employees, speaking 51 different languages, from 135 countries. Seventy-one percent of the employees, well above the average for big corporations, say 'Where I work, we can question our conventional way of working.' Sixty-eight percent endorse the view that 'Leaders in my unit trust the judgment of people like me.'"

Sir Mark continues: "Shell must move toward having a dialogue of national and cultural groups. I had an American journalist ask if he could write up an interview in a personalized way, as it was easier for both him and his readers if things were personified. I agreed (there is not much choice with journalists!) as long as both he and his readers understood that it was a gross oversimplification. You cannot run Shell, or even work in it, without depending on thousands of other people. If X wants to be an individualist, fine, but other people must provide the other values. The CMD filled in the Myers-Briggs indicator the other day, and I'm proud to say we were all over and at different ends of the four continua. That's how it should be: unity from diversity."

Moody-Stuart's sixth dilemma is illustrated in the following diagram:

Dilemma 6: Multicultural Merit

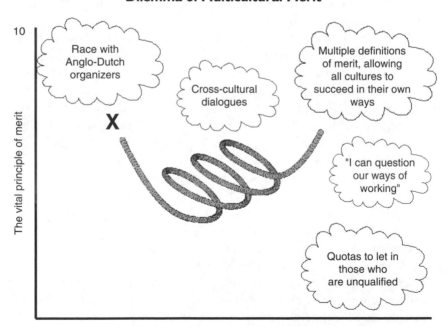

At the top left we have the present situation, which is fairly open and quite competitive, but the standards come mostly from two or three cultures and the judging is Anglo-Dutch and Anglo-American. At the bottom right we have the quotas that Moody-Stuart has rightly rejected. At the top right is the reconciliation, a multivalued world of multiple competences and forms of intelligence in a perpetual dialogue.

Let the last word be the peroration of Mark Moody-Stuart's report:

Compiling and verifying this report makes us measure our progress in a rigorous way. Our aim is to give you the necessary information to form a view. This year we have combined the group health, safety, and environment report with the Shell [financial] report to provide you with a consolidated overview of our activities. Read on. Judge for yourself and then tell us how we stand.

Keeping the Family in Business or Keeping the Business in the Family: Stuart Beckwith, Tim Morris, and Gordon Billage

Peter Woolliams and Charles Hampden-Turner

*T*ODAY'S MAJOR CORPORATIONS have a world presence so strong that we are tempted to believe that multinationals rule our lives and our economies. Each has a host of smaller service industries that feed off it. Even education, training, consultancy, and research are organized by large players. We might be led into thinking that the only place for world-class leadership is among these giants. But we would be wrong. Most of the world's corporations and most employment are within family-owned companies. It is the entrepreneurial sector that creates most new jobs and is the major engine of innovation. Even when a small company is acquired, it remains a creative nucleus for the economy as a whole. Indeed, the French essayist Montaigne once said that there is scarcely any less trouble running a family than governing an entire state![1] This chapter will address four major topics:

---

[1] *Essais,* 1580, 1, 39.

1. The small or family-run business as a genre
2. Stuart Beckwith, an entrepreneur who is a consultant to other entrepreneurs
3. Tim Morris, an entrepreneurial support service provider to small businesses
4. Gordon Billage, who had to lead the founding division of his company into new areas of business

The Small or Family-Run Business as a Genre

Small businesses are in many cases the acorns from which the giant oaks grow. In new environments with new logics, such as the Internet, recent start-ups dominate the medium. This is because the giants have difficulty *unlearning* the assumptions that made them great originally, while entrepreneurs think and act creatively.

The governments of the G8 nations and other countries are busy incubating or otherwise facilitating small businesses with various enabling measures, including tax concessions, industrial parks, and rule waivers. Considerable resources and effort therefore are being focused on supporting and helping small to medium-size enterprises worldwide.

There is some difficulty defining what is meant by a small, or family, business. In the United States the term *family-run business* (FRB) can be synonymous with the term *small to medium-sized enterprise* (SME). In Europe the latter term usually refers to organizations that employ fewer than 200 people and that have an annual turnover of less than £15 million. We can also identify some larger successful corporations with only a few major shareholders, all of whom are members or descendants of the original family. Finally, we can identify small to medium-sized businesses in which a small team of principals is in continuous intimate interaction even though the principals are not actually related (as in a true family). Whichever definition we choose, the statistics remain impressive and remind us that we ignore small business at our peril.

In 1996 *The Economist* reported that SMEs account for 40 percent of the U.S. gross domestic product (GDP) and 66 percent of Germany's while employing 60 percent of the workforce in the United States and 75 percent in Germany. A slightly earlier study found that SMEs account for 70 percent of Portuguese companies, 75 percent of British companies, 80 percent of Spanish companies, and 85 to 90 percent of Swiss companies.

Even when a family-owned company goes public, the influence of the family can persist by virtue of significant shareholding and managerial standing within the company. Donelly (1995) found that 20 percent of the Fortune 500 manufacturing companies retained a significant family influence.

Family-influenced businesses have several characteristics that public companies are criticized for having lost. They usually are managed for the long term because the family itself seeks to perpetuate its line and its wealth. There is a tendency for employees to be regarded as family and for top management to seek to leave a legacy to the generations that follow. The family might also seek to make a lasting social contribution to its town, state, or nation.

Under the broad definition of an FRB used by Goldberg (1995), some 95 percent of all businesses could be so described, although many of these are small and employ fewer than six people. The following chart shows the percentage of all businesses that have been categorized as FRBs (Thornton, 1999). SMEs are in addition to these percentages.

Percentage of Family-Run Businesses

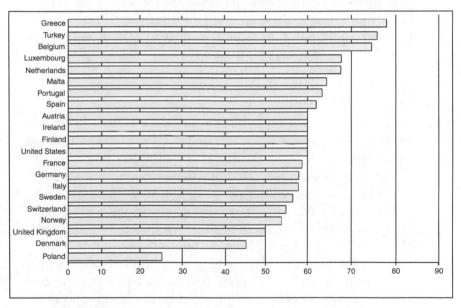

This pattern is replicated around the globe, with China, Japan, South America, Australasia, and Africa relying even more on the family. China's "town and village enterprises" typically are originated by prominent families, with the assistance of local community members. These enterprises, not the state-owned behemoths, are the ones responsible for nearly all of China's record growth rates. Taiwan was the country least affected by the recent Asian banking crisis, in part because of the pre-dominance of its small family firms, which are largely self-financing.

Family-run companies have also been shown to outperform public companies on the stock market. Leach (1994) cites a number of longi-tudinal studies by Stoy Hayward carried out between the 1970s and 1990s, showing that during that period $1 invested on the Dow or Financial Times Stock Exchange (FTSE) in 1970 would have grown to $8.72, whereas $1 invested in a family business would have risen to $11.11. Westhead and associates (1995) suggest that the main reason for this superior financial performance is a tendency to be more focused than nonfamily counterparts in seeking to maintain and enhance the lifestyles of the owners.

Buried within the myriad of small businesses around the globe, then, is an enormous number of successful leaders. Some are known as successful and effective leaders only by their immediate family mem-bers and friends. Many employees and local economies owe their whole lifestyle, prosperity, employment, personal finances, and career to these leaders. Rarely do the leaders appear on the world stage, in the press, or in the other media. Some do receive publicity, but often only in the local newspaper, perhaps as a result of a charity or philanthropic event.

Characteristics of FRBs/SMEs

Before we consider leadership in small businesses, we must first ask how such businesses differ from larger corporations. We find them different from other businesses in that their directors, managers, and other em-ployees often share a family relationship, the ethics and behavioral pat-tern of which are to a greater or lesser extent carried over to the workplace. In many, the family subsystem dominates the business man-agement system. This effect is seen by some researchers, such as de Vries (1997), as a built-in Achilles' heel that can render the interaction between the family and the business incompatible and cause friction and conflict.

On the other hand, it is often said that family businesses are more humane places to work than is the stereotypical bureaucratic organiza-tion. Generally, there is more concern for the welfare and satisfaction of employees and the community, and family businesses usually pay wages higher than the industry norm. Yet family businesses often are risk averse. Donckles and Frohlich (1991) concluded that FRBs tend to be more successful when they are positioned in niche markets. Leach (1994) attributes this kind of success to this genius of the founder, whereas Degolati and Davis (1983) disagree, reasoning that the small size of most FRBs keeps them from competing on the basis of economies of scale, and so they instead search for a niche in which they can rely on customer loyalty.

In this chapter we will consider three leaders as representatives of this important community of FRBs/SMEs. We have chosen them to illustrate how many of the underlying concepts, propositions, and frameworks on which this book is based apply to that world as well. In drawing these comparisons, we note the following facts:

1. FRBs and SMEs are like the early stages of large organizations. We can seek to derive generalizations that will be applicable to any type of organization as it develops.
2. In many large corporations what actually goes on at the top is like a small family business. The senior executives are in continuous close and personal contact with each other. Often their contact with other staff members and other parts of the organization is limited, and they behave like family "insiders" despite being involved in feuds with wider interests.

Stuart Beckwith, an Entrepreneur Who Is a Consultant to Other Entrepreneurs

Stuart Beckwith is the founding entrepreneur and managing director of the BCIF group of companies. His organization provides a "one-stop" center for business training, consulting, and recruitment that is targeted mainly at small or family-run businesses. Over the last 15 years BCIF has grown from nothing while helping more than 9000 new businesses become established. Beckwith has both developed his own organization and helped thousands of sole traders or partnerships develop into viable, self-sustaining businesses. The corporate ethos of BCIF, deriving from his style and personality, has been to synergize the contribution his organization can make by cooperating with the many other (often government-initiated) agencies that provide help to small businesses. BCIF works in close partnership with those government departments and with staff agencies, accountants, tax and planning advisers, and banks and venture capitalists. In an earlier career Beckwith was a senior lecturer at a major British business school, specializing in small-business entrepreneurship. In the early 1980s he left the security of his tenured post to face the challenges of the commercial world. This chapter will provide some extracts from an interview with him by one of the authors.

> **PW: How would you cope if you were starting out today rather than 15 years ago? Wouldn't it be much more difficult in today's much more competitive world?**

SB: In fact, I think it is easier today. There are so many sources of help, many of which are free (i.e., publicly funded). Also, technology means you can quickly position yourself on the Internet, across the world, with e-mail and accommodation addresses, and give the impression that you are already established and successful, almost from (and with) nothing.

PW: What have been the main dilemmas you have faced or have observed with your customers?

SB: Without doubt it is the interaction between the demands of the family and those of the business. I have observed families breaking up through the demands of the business and businesses failing through the demands of the family. In our business I employ some of my sons, and my wife is also a senior executive. I have always been conscious of the need to find ways to integrate these apparently competing demands.

Family-Business Sociotypes

If we examine these opposing values, we find the following dilemma occurring frequently:

Four Sociotypes of Family Businesses

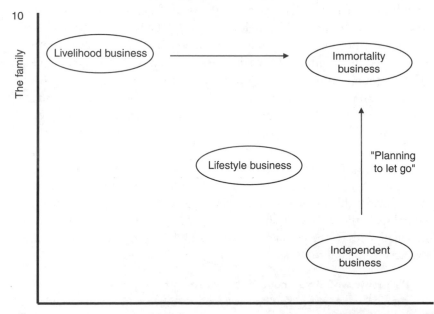

The diagram provides us with a typology that explains the appearance of small-business sociotypes (after Swaffin-Smith, Woolliams, and Tomeko, 2000). Let us consider these four types in turn.

The Livelihood Business

In a *livelihood business*, the family is dominant. For some family members, the activity may not even be recognized as business. Because the demands of the family are paramount, the prime concern is to accumulate personal assets rather than retained profits in the business. In many cultures it is often the women who take the key role, with a man taking the role of the "front man." Many pass the business on to another member of the family when it has fulfilled the needs of the family in terms of funding the upbringing of children. Even more frequently, the business withers or dies and doesn't pass to the next generation. Often, in developing countries, an FRB is subsidized by family members who work overseas on condition that it employ other family members who otherwise would not have employment, might not have a specific role, and might not be the best people for the job. Terms of payment for nonfamily employees are usually not comparable to those for family members who work for the business. Children can be under pressure to join the family business, to "carry on your father's mission." Other FRBs discourage their children from working in the business or employ low performers to insulate their children from the demands of the external job market. Children often work in the business as they grow up simply by virtue of being a member of the family. Sometimes they work for their keep and are not paid enough to make them independent of the family.

Investment funds are often borrowed from friends and family, who see them as a stake in the family's future. The funding is seen as a personal loan to an individual, with little or no expectation of an economic return. In many cases the lenders realize they are making a gift, but it is easier to regard it as a loan, making it a vote of confidence. The financial and control systems are simple, with an emphasis on cash, not profit. Cash generation is required to cover living costs and investment in personal assets. In many cases the balance sheet does not differentiate between personal and business wealth. The next generation often finds it difficult to enter and develop the business because there has not been enough investment to develop it.

FRBs often have no real management systems. Intuitive decisions are often based on dealing with people who are known intimately. Families decide for themselves which of their members will become involved in a business decision. A manager in a larger corporation might play tennis with fellow employees during lunch hour but is able to separate personal relationships from necessary business decisions. If these sports partners had to be dismissed or relocated, the clean disjunction of work from play would help the manager make the necessary decisions on purely business grounds.

In a livelihood business the equivalent situation is the owner-manager's playing tennis or soccer with employees to whom he or she probably is related, perhaps by marriage. Here the relationship is not separate from the business. It is more difficult to return to the office and make decisions injurious to a member of the family. Investments might have been made on the expectation that family members would be provided with employment. Any damage to one relationship could have ramifications for others. A family firm has all its eggs in one basket. A conflict originating in the bedroom or the boardroom will affect both, but it is the family that will be put first, even if the business suffers.

The Independent Business

The *independent business* has its own identity and makes demands on its members and on the family to support that business even at the cost of some family relationships. There is a clear distinction between the family and the business. The business is often well financed from a variety of sources, but with an emphasis on medium- and long-term returns. There are well-developed financial procedures, with review by representatives from all major stakeholders. The accountancy function generally is performed by professional outside practice.

There is usually a business strategy that is clearly positioned for growth. There is a greater tendency toward strategic thinking, having budgets associated with it and motivating a shared attitude toward achieving sales targets. Family members are entitled to *opportunities* for success and promotion but not to *automatic* preferment. The system is meritocratic, and ownership, management, and control stakes frequently are traded for diversity and growth.

The demands of the business often place stress on relationships within the family. Family members who are less well educated or less effective in business (e.g., they fail to meet sales targets) may be replaced by external employees who are skilled or experienced personnel. These decisions can easily give rise to rifts, to close family members not speaking for years, and even to the breakup of marriages. Once again the eggs are all in one basket, but here the survival of the business is put first, and the family can be sacrificed.

The Lifestyle Business

We see the *lifestyle business* operating as a compromise between the competing demands of the family and the organization serving as a market. As with any compromise, there is always some loss on both sides: Family life has to give something, yet business performance never reaches its full potential. It could be that what is essentially a hobby or a form of self-expression is generating income. These small businesses can be primarily backdrops for how the principals present themselves publicly and may only secondarily serve family or business values. Some are extensions of the "life spaces" of the protagonists.

Those involved might argue that their main concern is to fulfill themselves and earn enough to subsidize a degree of self-actualization. The contribution they can make to the building up of wealth both in the family and in the business may be limited. The business often is financed through personal assets or through not having to pay domestic or other personal bills. Cash (survival) to maintain the lifestyle and sustain the enterprise is the main issue. The lifestyle business can move toward independence over time if funds exceed lifestyle requirements. It usually dies with the person whose lifestyle it enhances.

Products or services vary considerably, originating as they do from individuals' interests or hobbies, and therefore are wide ranging. The initial focus of the business might be on the short term, fulfilling personal goals through producing the best. Many take high risks because of their dream visions of themselves, and the business could have an uncertain future through aspirations exceeding achievement. Grand plans are part of the lifestyle. We return at this point to more comments from Beckwith.

> **PW: Do you observe that the businesses you interact with tend to follow one of the preceding three sociotypes?**
>
> **SB: Very much so, and I have always been conscious of the need to avoid conflict between family and business demands in my own companies.**
>
> **PW: To probe the nature of these relationships, we sometimes ask, Would you expect your employees to help you paint your house or give you support for a domestic event outside of work?**
>
> **SB: I think I can safely say that there wouldn't be any dilemma on the part of my staff. In fact, we had a move recently, and many**

people offered to help. There was no recording of who helped and who didn't. Some nonfamily members helped, and some family members did much less. It just wasn't an issue. No one, I am sure, felt uncomfortable about the situation—except perhaps me! I didn't want some people to see inside my house and see how much expensive furniture I might have! On another occasion different members of our team would help.

PW: So how does your style of leadership bring about this integration between the business and family values.

SB: It is not a simple thing. It is about continuously striving to bring this integration about. It is more than just policy or a decision framework. I make sure my sons, for example, have clear roles at work—yet we have a drink afterward on several evenings. We can discuss business when we are together socially, and we can discuss family matters during work time. In fact, I would say that the family bonding has helped develop the business and that the business has helped strengthen the family.

PW: Do you foresee the time when you will need to step down or retire?

SB: Yes, and I am conscious of the problem created because many founders won't let the next generation get on with things. The original owner wants to stay on and interfere. I see this all the time. They try to use their status and family position (probably now akin to a grandfather or "godfather") to get their own way. This often conflicts with younger middle managers, who have new ideas, recognize changes in the marketplace, and are keen to exploit new technology.

PW: So how have you resolved this tension between your role derived from your status and the technical competence of the high-performing managers you are developing?

SB: I recognize the importance of "planning to let go." I can use my "status" to ensure that we do have succession plans in place and that the business will not depend on my personal presence in the future. I also recognize the need for change and that BCIF in the future will be much different from what it is now.

The Immortality Business: A Plan for Letting Go

We can identify a fourth stereotype: the *immortality business.* Here the demands of the family and business and the tension between the aging founder and the younger achievers are reconciled. The founder achieves immortality of a kind by living through his or her successors. Unlike most family businesses, these companies won't suffer the "Italian syndrome," in which family businesses tend not to survive to the third generation. In fact, most small businesses don't even survive the loss of the founder.

We have observed that family members often own a part of the business in a custodial role. They are willing to forgo short-term profit to ensure that the business continues, and their family history is intimately tied up with the history of the business. They share power and build up assets, both in the business and in the family. There is a possible opening in the business for all members of the family who want one and importantly, they recognize that fairness is not the same as equality. They might even consider unrelated staff members as "sons or daughters of the house."

Family members play a variety of roles. They can be owners (shareholders) and members of the family but not work in the business. They can be family members working in the business, but with no ownership stake. They can be just family members but related to owners or people working in the business. They can have a strong psychological attachment to the business. What they have to pass on are "genes" of knowledge and experience. Even so, letting go is very difficult; even the most loyal progeny mix your ideas with their own.

Some family members may try to originate policies, using professional managers who are qualified in particular functions to carry them out. Such policies include both agreed-upon relationships between family members and professional rights and obligations. "Inside" decisions can be routinely checked against "outside" advice.

In the end our only lasting powers come from our influence and from the organizations that empower our ideas. A family business aspiring to immortality must ask, What is our legacy? and must give subordinates the autonomy to renew that legacy in a new century. Pressure for change will come from changing market conditions, from family members who want to do more (or less), from those seeking to withdraw or add capital, and from major nonfamily contributors who feel they are being shortchanged for their efforts. The "right" balance is an ever-shifting one.

The number of family businesses found in each category varies from culture to culture, usually with the relative importance the culture places on the individual and the family. But there is little doubt that all values find fulfillment at the top right of the diagram representing the four sociotypes and that the struggle to reconcile is a crucial aspect of value creation.

Tim Morris, an Entrepreneurial Support Service Provider to Small Businesses

In an earlier career Tim Morris worked in banking for one of the larger banks providing corporate lending to client companies. In those days the bank was interested only in covering its own risk with the borrower's home and savings. Morris led a change toward lending on the basis of professional risk assessment and understanding and helping to develop a better business plan.

Later he left banking and became the managing director of the Greystone Group. Greystone was originally in the business of purchasing and managing service stations (gasoline filling stations). Morris excelled at this venture and gained a reputation with the major oil companies as a highly successful entrepreneur and a shrewd station operator. He was able to develop and lead an extensive team that would seek out service stations that were underperforming. He would complete a comprehensive review, including customer and traffic surveys in the vicinity and a study of local planning developments, before purchasing a station. He would add a retail store to the business of basic gasoline sales. Revenue would grow quickly while the relative costs of operations fell.

It wasn't long before the Greystone Group owned a string of service stations. Reflecting on the classic question "What business are you in?" led Greystone to realize that it was in the property-development business rather than in gasoline retailing. The value of each service station purchased had increased beyond the rate of property-price inflation or gasoline revenues. The codirectors wanted to diversify Greystone into purchasing hotels and residential property, but they reached a point at which their quest for growth outstripped the scope of their specialized expertise. At the same time, the property market looked increasingly uncertain. For this reason, Morris made his exit and established a new venture he control by himself. He is now the founding entrepreneur and managing director of MMP Business Management, Ltd., which he established some six years ago. MMP is a business management company that provides the back office for a range of diverse organizations that want to grow a distinctive competence full time.

For example, a local restaurant might be started by a restaurateur or a chef. Such persons know about serving people, about good food, and about providing an ambience that will give diners a satisfying experience. What they don't know about (or simply are not interested in) is how to connect an electric cash register to a local area network of personal computers so that the next morning they can see the business results from the night before. Here, Morris's company helps: It provides all the know-how and services that are necessary. Let's talk with Morris about how he does this.

PW: Why is MMP so successful after such a short time?

TM: There are many reasons, but it is clear that people want to get on with what they know best and leave the rest to someone they can trust. Banks don't help anymore—they just want to rip off their clients. Traditional accountants are useless and think their only job is to produce a set of accounts at the end of a year that satisfy the tax authorities. So we have a wide range of clients and help them execute their businesses. It may be companies selling replacement windows, electrical contractors, small manufacturing or engineering companies, and so on. They may be sole traders or larger SMEs employing up to 100 people. We are their "office." We also act as intermediaries between banks, the tax authorities, and problem customers, negotiating prices and terms with suppliers, all on behalf of our clients.

PW: What was important when you started?

TM: We recognized that technology was playing and is going to play an increasingly important role in all businesses. Although I (and my core team) were IT [information technology] literate, we knew we needed to get up to speed with the very latest—and keep up to date. We needed this enhanced technical competence fast. We also needed some instant credibility. The new, young, and hungry entrepreneurs we wanted as our clients don't all play golf. Yes, we wanted to develop relationships, but we needed some instant status.

PW: Did you see the need to get both instant technical competence and status to be a contradiction—even if it was just because of what you could afford at the time?

TM: Yes, at first. We thought of expensive offices, a prestigious address, and high-quality printed literature and promotional material. We also thought about attending local universities and colleges that could give us the enhanced technical competence— although it would take a little time.

PW: So how did you reconcile this dilemma between novelty and credibility?

TW: I decided to set about studying for and passing the Microsoft exams. The course material is available electronically, and what we needed was a high level of capability in Microsoft Office products, networking, Internet, e-mail, databases, and so on. I also knew that if we were successful in passing the exams, we might get Microsoft's approval.

After a three-month, very intensive study period, both I and my wife passed a range of Microsoft exams. As a consequence, our company became instantly "Microsoft approved." We were able to use the status of Microsoft by branding all our literature as "an approved Microsoft solution provider." This immediately brought us clients who thought we must be good (and differentiated from other, "cowboy" companies). Because we were technically up to date, we could indeed provide them with the technical help they wanted and solve their technical problems. This was more than just basic PC [personal computer] awareness. We were competent with hardware (bar codes, scanning, and networking) and software (accountancy and office systems). This instant "status" gave us initial inquiries, but the clients stayed with us because of our technical competence. In fact, even Microsoft passes on business leads to us in our specialty area. Many follow the typology you describe: Our clients may be lifestyle, livelihood, or independent businesses.

PW: What sort of contracts do you have with them?

TM: We don't use a written contract. They pay us a fee each month for our services. We may renegotiate the fee if the volume or scale of what we do for them changes. If they are not happy with our service, we just tell them to stop paying for it.

PW: So you take away the hassle of the administration. Is that it?

TM: No, it is much more. It's all about control. We are continually surprised at how many small businesses don't know how much cash they have in the bank, what payments [to creditors] are due in the near future, and what debtors they have. They seem to be trying to catch a flight with last month's departure screen display board! I couldn't sleep at night if I didn't know exactly where my business was! On the other hand, we find owner-managers who are obsessive about being in control. Just because they started the business and it has been running successfully, they think it will go on forever if they continue to apply their "magic formula."

PW: Are you a control freak?

TM: No, it is a matter of avoiding the extreme. For those who are all fatalistic and think that everything depends on luck or the economy, we try to encourage them to get their business under control. We produce a daily (or sometimes weekly) snapshot of income and expenditure and exactly where they are. This gives them a greater degree of control. We do the same thing for our own business, of course. At any time, at the click of a mouse, I know exactly our cash bank balance, our creditors, and our debtors. Conversely, for those who think they are in control, with simplistic administrative systems, we try to show them that they are not—because in the medium term they may be vulnerable to the external environment.

PW: So does this mean you are concerned with overall concepts and a holistic view?

TM: Yes and no. We also need to be concerned with details. I remember that in our gas stations, fuel was delivered by volume. One hot day I realized that we were getting less in our delivery from the oil company supply because of the thermal expansion (and therefore lower density) on hot days. We assessed this and negotiated volume and cost corrections due to temperature variations on deliveries to us. What we thought was simply a matter of principle and of scientific interest turned out to be significant in real revenue terms over a year. It's being concerned with this level of detail that makes being in business for an entrepreneur so exciting. Knowing that we have made things sharper, more profitable, and more efficient is where we get our kicks.

In the end, it's not just about money—we can eat only three meals a day. You can be an entrepreneur only by doing it, by making mistakes and learning from them. The buzz comes from doing something your own way, with no one else around to tell you how. In our MMP business today we are continually using small detailed costings and margins to make the overall company more efficient. In turn, by making the overall company more efficient, we can focus on the smaller things that make a difference.

PW: So is your business (and your clients) concerned with the short term or the longer term?

TM: In fact, and if the truth be known, we often get new clients because they are in trouble. They may be overtrading or facing a cash-flow crisis. There is a temptation to focus on the short term: How are we going to pay the workforce next week? How can we pay the next tax bill due? Implementing only short-term emergency measures would mean that we could never climb out of the hole. Similarly, if we only take a medium-term or longer-term view, a creditor may petition to suspend the business from trading.

We have to use the short-term emergency actions to set up guidelines for longer-term sustainability. Just because we produce cash position statements each morning for our clients when we take them on doesn't mean we stop doing that when the crisis is over. We still do it every day. The short-term action becomes the long-term operational characteristic, and so the clients don't get caught unaware the next time.

In the same way, we identify where they want to be in two or three years. We then use the long-term goals to encompass any short-term emergencies. The long term must *include* the short term.

It pays to be honest, believe me. We make a point of keeping our promises and never letting people down. If it is good news or bad news, I like to be straight. I like to have a relationship with my clients that is more than just a business relationship. This means I can tell the truth even though it hurts. Take it from me, in the long run, it pays!

PW: How do you benefit from all of this?

TM: Apart from monthly fees that start to come in from month 1, we often try to negotiate an equity stake in the client's business. It also means that we accumulate wealth in the longer term rather than fees being just an alternative to salary earnings.

PW: What next?

TM: Although some of our clients (or their businesses) may not be here in the future, we certainly shall. We think the world of work and business is changing faster than many pundits think. While technology is one of our unique selling points, we accept Dale Carnegie's view that only 15 percent of financial success comes from technical business knowledge and that 85 percent is skill in human engineering. It is our ability to lead people that really helps our clients, and as we help our clients, MMP goes from strength to strength.

Analysis of MMP's Dilemma Resolution

Tim Morris and his company have a keen eye for one of the central dilemmas of entrepreneurship: Most entrepreneurs are interested *in only the most original aspects of the enterprise.* They have an idea; they want to make that idea a reality; and the other aspects of organizational existence—keeping accounts, filing taxes, meeting payrolls—are felt as almost an affliction, a necessity dragging the entrepreneur away from the work that he or she finds most exciting. There is a desperate need to find someone willing to do such "boring" and "routine" functions. Those surrounding the entrepreneur and identifying with him or her may be equally bored with maintenance activities, so that such activities frequently are done badly by a marginal person who is not liked or admired in the organization. This helps explain why MMP tells clients not to pay the monthly invoice if they are dissatisfied. In truth, very few clients can afford to do without help, and so this generous attitude is very rarely exploited. The dilemma, as the following diagram shows, is between what the entrepreneur *likes doing* and *dislikes doing.*

Dilemma 2: Likes and Dislikes

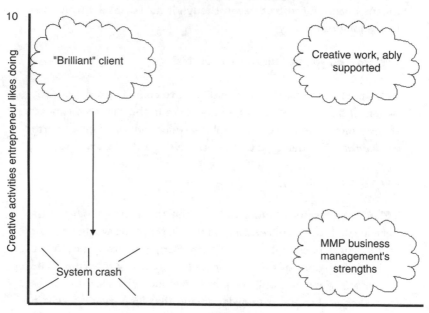

In the preceding illustration we see that MMP provides a strength and reliability that complement creative work, allowing it to continue without the system crash (bottom left) to which "brilliant" clients (top left) are prone.

We should be careful about our labels. What is "boring" for a high-tech entrepreneur is interesting and challenging for MMP Business Management. Microsoft Office is an exciting field of new applications for those wrapped up in it, and Morris and his wife are entrepreneurs too. They get their thrills in their own ways. Nonetheless, clients benefit from getting on with the leading-edge aspects of their own work while gaining high-quality support for necessary functions.

Morris is also extremely insightful regarding two contrasting types of entrepreneurs: those who *over*control and those who *under*control. For each kind of client, he has a different treatment. The undercontrolling client we have already encountered: The attitude is "Leave it to lesser beings." There is important and creative work, and there is support work, of less importance, done by lesser persons. Such entrepreneurs leave the control to others and disparage control per se. This is shown in the following diagram:

Dilemma 3: Undercontrol and Overcontrol

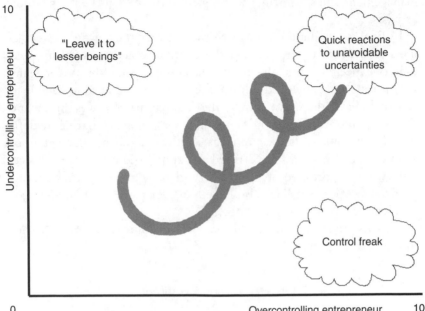

There is a second, contrasting tendency. Many an entrepreneur has "made it" because a set of original ideas was mobilized within a single mind. These ideas could be ordered and sorted, with perfect control over their disposition; all of this resulted in breakthrough success. It is very easy for such entrepreneurs to associate success with their total control of key elements. As the company expands, those "key elements" come to include other people, and we have the makings of the control freak (bottom right). Morris moderates this "control freakery" by constantly informing the entrepreneur of variables beyond his order control—variables that *cannot* be changed or countermanded but *can* be responded to and taken advantage of. He moderates the "leave-it-to-lesser-beings" entrepreneur by compensating for this snobbery through innovative office products. He is also privy to very important inside information, and if he chooses to invest in his clients, there is probably no other investor with his quality and accuracy of information. There are advantages in being both underestimated and concerned with detail!

Famous examples of the two types of entrepreneur are Edward Land of Polaroid, who tended to disparage and neglect all functions except his own inventive leadership, and Henry Ford, who ended his reign as an avid supporter of Adolf Hitler, keeping his factories full of management spies, informers, and gangsters hired to beat up union activists.

A final reconciliation for Morris was between the newness and riskiness of his own enterprise and the continuity and security his customers expected. After all, he was accepting responsibility for some very private and privileged information. They would need to be able to rely on him. Of these two contrasting characteristics, it was the second that posed more difficulty. His company was young and daring by definition; how could it also become trustworthy and reliant? His ingenious solution was to get himself certified and approved by Microsoft Office, borrowing the prestige of an industry giant and even getting clients referred *by* Microsoft. This also gave him ever more efficient and economical ways of running an office.

Morris's reconciliation of this novelty-reliability dilemma is set out in the next diagram.

Novelty versus Credibility

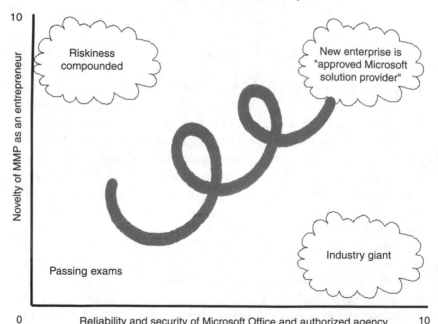

Morris had essentially gained access to an unending stream of innovative office management tools. Unless Microsoft fell behind, he would be able to surf on its success. What the client thought of as "support"

was for Tim Morris continual innovation in its own right. The obvious danger is at the upper left in the diagram, where riskiness is compounded by having one fledgling company rely on another. By passing exams and getting his company guaranteed by Microsoft, Morris gets the best of both worlds (upper right). Note that this is superior to a direct relationship with an industry giant (lower right), because so large a company probably would not bother with small, risky enterprises of the type MMP tries to help.

Gordon Billage, Who Had to Lead the Founding Division of His Company into New Areas of Business

Gordon Billage is chief executive officer (CEO) of Clifford-Thames (Holdings), Ltd., a successful, dynamic, and growing SME that employs some 300 people. Under his leadership, Clifford-Thames has grown from a printing company to a printing and communications company and is now repositioning itself as a "support services enterprise." Billage is leading a major push away from traditional print and toward technology data management and the delivery of information across a variety of media. The current overall objective of the group is to realize a shareholder value of £25 million by March 2003. We now present parts of an interview with Billage.

PW: How would you classify Clifford-Thames?

GB: We are not a family business, but most of our senior management has been in place for many years after our buyout, and we operate as a personal and closely knit team. We have climbed out of being a traditional very small business and are now a substantive SME, with sales of approximately £20 million a year. The last few years have been difficult trading, but I am anxious to lead our team into the next phase. My problem, as ever, is that I know what we want to do but cannot always see how to do it. Corporate culture and change have taken up my time over the years.

PW: Let's go back a few years. You were founded as a "high-quality printer," but by 1993 you already had a range of diverse operations. What has been your corporate culture?

GB: While printing was always rather authoritarian—you get an order and carry it out as instructed—our communications company warranted a more open and participative style of manage-

ment. Reconciling these factors with the group has been—shall we say—interesting. We introduced a total quality approach back in 1991, mainly because certification was required by some of our major customers. It didn't come from the heart.

PW: How did you lead the workforce?

GB: Beginning in 1994, we introduced an annual employee survey to involve the workforce and provide an input to our decision making and planning. In early surveys people saw it as a chance to air their grievances. However, over time the feedback became more constructive and has been a major factor in getting everyone committed to a shared vision. By 1996 we were described by one of our major clients as the furthest advanced in quality operating systems in Europe. We took this to mean furthest in "continuous improvement" rather than simply obtaining ISO 9000 certification.

PW: Does your certification bring customers because of the status of ISO 9000?

GB: Meeting ISO standards helps us acquire and satisfy other customers who do not actually insist on them. It shows that we have processes and procedures to meet customer requirements that we follow. Because we maintain this thrust and constantly review what we do, this means that we can position ourselves as a star "quality company."

PW: Did you just follow standard TQM [total quality management] procedures to introduce this philosophy?

GB: The original steering committee was a mix of strong personalities. Some wanted change, and some wanted to keep things the way they always were. Attendance at meetings was variable. Many things we tried showed up opposing value systems. "Management by walking about" was welcome but also was criticized. ("What's he doing? It's not a royal tour!")

PW: Did this lead to the in-house publication *Prospect*?

GB: We already had *Prospect* but saw that we could use it to improve communication between management and the workforce. We carried several articles over a period about the competing demands of change versus stability, following procedures, and including everyone.

PW: What about the technology of printing?

GB: We are all aware of the changes in this industry. On the one hand, we have the advances in digital typesetting and printing, resulting in lower costs and faster turnaround. At the other extreme, high-quality, high-volume printing presses are enormously expensive. It's only when they run 24 hours a day, 7 days a week, that return on investment becomes achievable. New technology means greater efficiency and leaves us with less margin to compete at price levels created by the more efficient presses. It also means more flexibility and a quicker setup for short runs.

PW: So which did you choose?

GB: Both! We are continually upgrading and replacing our major presses as well as using digital low-cost systems for lower-volume jobs. We have to have both because our customers want solutions, and we have to have the range of options to satisfy their needs.

PW: It appears that you have had to reconcile change with stability, high-cost, high-volume technology with low-volume, low-cost technology, and the status of ISO certification with achieving results by continuous improvement. Is this still the position?

GB: At this stage the real dilemma originates from our role as the parent company in the degree to which we direct and dictate to our operating subsidiaries or adopt a more passive coordinating role.

PW: Centers have the potential to add or destroy significant shareholder value. The key question is, therefore, How does one go about designing and creating a center that can fully exploit common opportunities without damaging the individual integrity of units?

GB: There is little general advice or guidance about the role and structure of a corporate center. Even traditional research in university business schools tends to focus on functional activities and does not appear to have a general framework. Given this, many centers opt for a simple rationale: that small is best. This tends to produce an atmosphere of cost reduction rather than value creation.

Many organizations have struggled to transform headquarters. In my experience, it is not simply a matter of deciding what is best, because what is appropriate changes continually and shows up at the unit level.

PW: How do you see your leadership role at the center of Clifford-Thames?

GB: My role is to continually reconcile the universal needs for growth, to follow the corporate plan, and to achieve universally agreed-upon organizational goals with the particular needs, talents, and circumstances of the operating companies.

I believe that the center's influence should be positive so that strategic value opportunities can be exploited. For this, we need to stay sharply focused. Compromise alone is insufficient and tends to drift toward the traditional role of administrator.

PW: What are the general principles by which you lead?

GB: The agenda must follow corporate strategy. Recently we undertook an exhaustive strategy review for the period 1999–2003. We must be lean, responsive, flexible, and benchmarked. We translate "pressure" into business unit goals. Overall, we are creating a partnership of expertise within our organization. We see our customers as having a series of continuing relationships with us over time—not just a quick sale but a valuable source of information for improvement.

I see my CEO role not as simply designing the center but as leading that continuous improvement, which we learned from our earlier days with TQM under John Cumberland's stewardship. Together with our chairman, Ed Hough, we must now seize opportunities and learn from and instruct our operating companies while maintaining a "feel" for the uniqueness of each business. If we can continuously reconcile these objectives, we can create additional value that easily outweighs the 2 or 3 percent cost of the center.

Although we have achieved growth in the last few years, trading has been difficult, and bottom-line profit has not kept up with our growth. Unlike some of our competitors, we have survived, and we are increasingly confident about the future as we continue with our business transformation. It is the pride and passion shared by members of my senior team that will deliver results and that make our success theirs.

Small Business and Entrepreneurship

We selected the leaders in this chapter because they were successful entrepreneurs in small but growing businesses and because they could comment about others as well as themselves. If there had been space, we could have included many others in small-business enterprises, the following:

- Hashem Al Refaei from the United Arab Emirates, who integrated his technical knowledge of IT with the status conferred by his family relationship with his sheikh ruler.
- Stan Landi from Pisa and his coffee bar, which is frequented by the older generation (pensioners) during the day and yuppies by night.
- Su Yo Kuk (Taipei) and his interest in fish; in his shop, he sold not only fish for cooking and eating but also aquarium fish for pets.

Most previous rigorous research studies of entrepreneurs and of leadership by entrepreneurs attempted to identify their psychological characteristics. However, these approaches ignored the interdependencies between the leader and his or her staff and the ways in which the crucial dilemmas are reconciled. We cannot study these leaders in isolation, investigating only their personal characteristics. It is not a case of *what makes an entrepreneur,* but of *what an entrepreneur makes.* The real leadership component of entrepreneurship is understandable only in context. We must be concerned with the interaction between the followers and the more general processes through which purpose and commitment are generated and sustained within the evolving organization.

It is frequently found that entrepreneurs have not had a formal academic education; often (especially in their mature years) they wonder whether they might have been even more successful if they had been to college or received some other relevant business education.

However, education traditionally recognizes only a Cartesian approach, that assumes that all problems need only more time and money to be solved and that managers (rather than leaders) can solve problems only by using a deductive logic of problem solving that consists of eliminating all factors that cannot be strictly controlled or accurately measured. What remains is a solvable problem in an isolated system with no relevance to the real world. Real problems that real entrepreneurs face are composed of the contrasting values in these chapters. Managers can't cope with these issues by using an either-or logic of exclusive options. If at any one time (like a binary computer that is "off" or "on" they can give allegiance only to one extreme or the other, the result is a loss of realism and integrity. Choosing between exclusive objects does not meet the requirements of living systems.

The opposites that leaders wrestle with, such as growth and decay, put tension into their world, sharpen their sensitivities, and increase their self-awareness. The problem cannot be "solved" in the sense of being eliminated but can be wisely transcended. Small and family businesses need stability and change, tradition and innovation, public and private interest, planning and laissez-faire, order and freedom, and growth and decay. Successful leaders get surges of energy from the fusing of these opposites.

Thus, entrepreneurs must exhibit adequacy (*adaequatio*) in order to resolve dilemmas; that is, the understanding of the knower must be adequate to the thing being known (*adaequatio rei et intellectus*; Plotinus). Some people are incapable of appreciating a piece of music not because they are deaf but because of a lack of *adaequatio*. The sense of hearing receives as its input nothing more than a succession of tones; by contrast, the music is grasped by active intellectual power. Some people possess such powers that they can grasp an entire symphony simply by reading the score; to others it is just a noise. The former is *adequate* to the music; the latter *inadequate*.

For all of us, there exist in organizations only those patterns and dynamics for which we have sufficient *adaequatio*. Entrepreneurial leaders possess *adaequatio* for reconciling dilemmas. For example, they don't try to win an argument. Real leadership isn't about winning arguments. Human actions and opinions aren't changed by arguments—win or lose. As Sir Ross Smith said,

> *A man convinced against his will*
> *keeps the same opinion still.*

What finally creates wealth are the *relationships* between people and what they value. A product or service is a distillation of reconciled values offered to customers through relationships.

Chapter 22

—◆—

Transcultural Competence through 21 Reconciliations

Fons Trompenaars and Peter Woolliams

Introduction

The aim of the research on which this book is based was to discover how outstanding leaders manage knowledge effectively. Our core finding is that great leaders reconcile seemingly opposing values—that's what they do, that's what makes them effective, and that's what makes them great. Senior leaders appear to know how to integrate objectives to deliver results. Successful leaders rarely give orders; rather, they create a culture of reconciled values. It is this underlying, encompassing process that is essential for real success: It delivers benefits and bottom-line business results. From extensive evidence gained both through direct data gathering and through close partnering with the client companies, we have identified a new, overarching process that we term *transcultural competence.*

In this chapter we seek to generalize into a robust operational and practical framework what is behind the behaviors exhibited by high-performing leaders. This exercise is intended to make cultural and other value-system differences tangible so that their consequences can be made explicit. In that way we can all have access to a common basic model; we can all attempt to reconcile dilemmas with a chance of reaping the benefits.

This Trompenaars Hampden-Turner (THT) framework encompasses the three *R*'s: *r*ecognition, *r*espect, and *r*econciliation.

Recognition

The first step for leaders is to help all players *recognize* that there are cultural differences—to recognize their importance and how they have an impact.

Culture, like an onion, consists of layers that can be peeled off. We can distinguish three layers. The *outer* layer is what people primarily associate with culture: the visual reality of behavior, clothes, food, language, the organizational chart, the handbook for human relations policies, and so on. This is the level of explicit culture. The *middle* layer refers to the norms and values that an organization holds: what is considered right and wrong (norms) or good and bad (values). The deepest, or *inner* layer is the level of unquestioned implicit culture. This layer is the result of human beings organizing to reconcile frequently occurring dilemmas. It consists of basic assumptions as well as many series of routines and methods developed to deal with the regular problems one faces. These methods of problem solving have become so basic that, like breathing, we no longer think about how we do them. For an outsider the basic assumptions are very difficult to recognize. Understanding the core of the "culture onion" is the key to working successfully with other cultures and to successful alliances and cross-border collaborations.

Thus, while we instantly recognize explicit cultural differences, we may not recognize implicit cultural differences. This explains why cultural *due diligence* is usually absent from the management agenda of pre- and postmerger acquisitions. Our research, especially evidence from practical experience, has led us to develop diagnostic instruments and validate models to reveal and measure these basic assumptions. They are grounded in the seven-dimensional model of cultural differences we have developed over the last 10 years and are at the core of this new transcultural competence framework.

Respect

Different cultural orientations and views about "where I am coming from" are not right or wrong—they are just different. It is all too easy to be judgmental and to distrust those who give different meaning to their world from the one you give to yours. Thus, the next step is to *respect* these differences and to accept others' right to interpret the world in the way they have under the historical conditions that have made that right for them.

Because of the different views of the world and the different meanings given to apparently the same constructs, we find that these differences manifest themselves as dilemmas. We have two seemingly opposing views: those of contrasting cultures and those of the knower and the known—the researchers' model and the informants' model.

Reconciliation

There is a growing conviction that wealth is created in organizations by reconciling values—by supplying customers ever more potent synergies of satisfaction. Our model helps identify and define behaviors that make value-generating leadership effective. This new approach will inform leaders and managers about how to guide the people side of any organization. It has a logic that unifies differences. It is a series of judgments that makes possible effective interaction with those who have contrasting value systems. It reveals a propensity to share an understanding of others' positions in the expectation of reciprocity and requires a new way of thinking that is circular as opposed to linear and sequential. Only recently has cybernetic thinking become acceptable to Western mind-sets.

Major Dilemmas in Need of Reconciliation

Reflecting on the principal chapters of this book, we find that there are 21 stereotypical dilemmas that our sample of leaders have reconciled. In genuine leadership, it is necessary to challenge the status quo, a process that induces dilemmas. The seven-dimensional model is a means to elicit, describe, and frame the major dilemmas organizations have to resolve when faced with the need to integrate people and systems.

The 21 dilemmas can be categorized as derivatives of each of the seven dimensions (although what derives from what is an issue in itself).

For convenience and clarity, we have grouped the leaders' dilemmas under seven heads:

1. **The universal or the particular.** Do people in the organization (or in collaborating organizations) tend to follow standard-

ized rules, or do they prefer a flexible approach to unique situations?

2. **Individualism or communitarianism.** Does the organization (or do collaborating organizations) foster individual performance and creativity, or is the focus on the larger group's achieving cohesion and consensus?

3. **Neutral or affective.** Is the display of emotion controlled, or are emotions displayed overtly?

4. **Specific or diffuse.** What is the nature of the involvement (personal relationships) in business? Do specific propositions get defined first, out of which a more diffuse relationship may develop later, or do you have to get to know your business partner before you can get down to specifics?

5. **Achievement or ascription.** Are status and power based on your performances, or are they determined more by, for example, which school you went to; by your age, gender, and family background; by your potential; or by the worthiness of your aspirations?

6. **Internal or external control.** Are you stimulated by your inner drive and sense of control, or do you adapt to external events that are beyond your control?

7. **Sequential or synchronous in regard to the past, present, and future.** Do you organize time in a sequential manner, doing one task at a time, or in parallel, keeping many tasks in progress at the same time?

When you are faced with cultural differences, one initial but effective approach is to compare the profiles[1] of the two parties to identify whence the major differences originate. In practice, the major origin of cultural differences between your organization and the new partner often lies predominantly in one or two cultural dimensions. By reconciling the dilemmas deriving from the differences along those dimensions, organizations can begin to reconcile their cultural orientations. *Recognition* of these differences *alone* is insufficient.

In performing our critical review of how our 21 leaders operate, we found more than 100 such dilemmas that were reconciled, but we have selected 21 of the most persistent and now summarize them according to our seven-dimensional model.

---

[1] A profile is a culture map, in which each party scores along each of the seven dimensions.

Dilemmas Deriving from Universalism versus Particularism

Universalist cultures tend to feel that general rules and codes are a strong source of moral reference. Universalists tend to follow the rules even when friends are involved and to look for "the one best way" to deal equally and fairly with all cases. They assume that the standards they hold dear are the "right" ones, and they attempt to change the attitudes of others to match.

Particularist societies are those in which particular circumstances are more important than rules. Bonds of particular relationships (e.g., family or friends) are stronger than any abstract rule, and response will differ with the circumstances and the people involved.

There are many examples of the universal-particular dilemma affecting our leaders. The dominant one is the global-local dichotomy. The question faced is, Shall we have one *standardized* approach, or shall we try the local, *particular* approach? There are differing views on whether we are becoming more nearly globally universal and alike or are becoming more influenced by particular (and unfamiliar) national cultures.

The Global-Local Dilemma

The global-local dilemma can be set out in the following diagram:

The Global-Local Dilemma

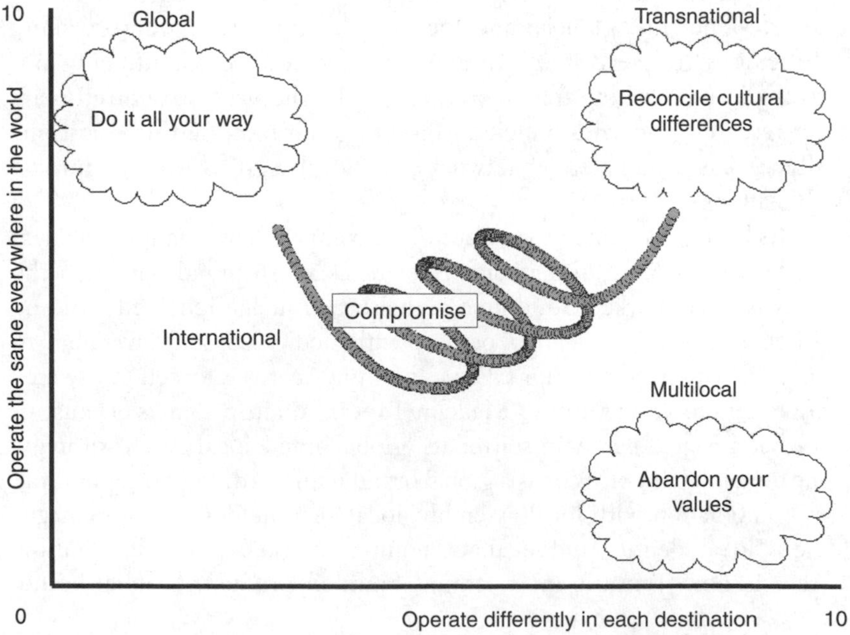

A corporation reconciling the horizontal and vertical must make a conceptual leap. The answer lies in *transnational specialization,* allowing each nation to specialize in what it does best and be a source of authority and leadership within the global corporation for that particular vein of excellence. The reach is truly global, but the sources of major influence are national. International alliances need to look for a similar logic: It is the result of linking particular learning efforts into a universal framework, and vice versa. It is the connection between practical lessons in a context of intelligent theories. In this dialectic we integrate best practice, whatever its origin, and learn from the diversity of models, adopting, adapting, and combining the best. However, such a solution is not easily achieved and needs the involvement of senior leaders.

The first example we shall examine concerns the dilemma that Stan Shih of Acer Computers reconciled. He seems to have reconciled universally his preference to be particular. In this way, he was able to build a strong brand image out of Taiwan, which frequently is seen as a manufacturer of low-quality goods.

Reconciling Universalism and Particularism: Acer's Global Brand, Local Touch Strategy

Stan Shih saw the need to implement more universalistic elements into Acer's strategy, such as making Acer known as a global brand name, while retaining the company's strong particularist elements. He therefore designed the "global brand, local touch" strategy. There were many difficulties to overcome. Taiwanese companies are traditionally not strong in establishing trademarks, channel structures, structured market research, and sales policies. Marketing and price setting traditionally are based on personal networks, and loyalty grows from reciprocal obligations.

Its history as a small to medium-size company and a family business made it even more difficult for Acer to establish brand names in the international market. Building a global brand image required building up that image over a long period, with dedicated staff available to answer customers' questions. For some time Acer was forced to use creative ways to avoid putting "Made in Taiwan" on its products because of the bad image. Then Acer started its "global brand, local touch" strategy: the development of Acer as a global brand name with a good reputation, in combination with local assembly, local shareholders, local management, local identity, and local autonomy in marketing and distribution. Acer is now Taiwan's most famous branded product. "Global brand, local touch" is a good example of the reconciliation of particularism and universalism in business strategy.

The particularist, "local touch" part of the strategy includes the following elements:

- Localization of the business structure
- Local assembly
- Local identity and local management, with local autonomy in marketing, distribution, and shareholding

It is crucial to understand that Acer and Shih have *universalized their own preference for particularism.* They have assumed that most other countries want Acer to be particular and exceptional also, following their ways of investing, assembling, marketing, and so on. One country of refugees and immigrants is appealing globally to migrant cultures, which are the creators of so much wealth. With one-third of all Silicon Valley's wealth being created by Indian and Chinese immigrants to the United States since 1970, Acer's strategy looks like a winner.

A second major dilemma we have found in this area of rules versus exceptions is the reconciliation wrought by Jim Morgan at Applied Materials. In a world where speed is crucial, you cannot wait to get everything right the first time. Morgan has designed organizational processes that accelerate learning by pouncing on mistakes and correcting them fast.

Jim Morgan's Fast Learning Process through Errors

According to Jim Morgan, chief executive officer of Applied Materials, the successful corporation of the twenty-first century "will foster a culture resilient in the face of setbacks, which also rewards success." This process involves reclassifying what was acceptable last month as unacceptable this month and doing better. Errors never go away, because the bar keeps rising and because you keep trying new things to see what works better. This is why Applied Materials has always been very close to first-class customers such as Intel, AMD, ST, and Philips. It needs their tough verdicts to improve rapidly.

Morgan has always encouraged his people to take risks, and he forgives failure because mistakes are inevitable in the new emerging world. It takes courage to live with your mistakes in order to transcend them and move on, learning as you go. Applied Materials, as the largest manufacturer of semiconductor-producing equipment (the machines that make the circuits), cannot have any mistakes in its machinery. Every little mistake has enormous consequences, and so each must be found and eliminated.

This learning process—the error-correcting system—comes with the following dilemma: If errors are made by the score and few learn from them quickly enough, we are left with a situation in which we wallow in repeated errors. Errors are fine but need to become an input to possible improvement. On the other hand, Morgan knew very well that an organization full of "perfect persons" would not learn rapidly enough in a changing world. At Applied Materials Morgan created a culture in which error-correcting systems for continuous improvement and ever-rising standards were developed. Every error needs to be an opportunity to improve rather than the cause of shame or disgrace. People must be empowered to monitor and improve themselves, reflecting on their work and rethinking it. Beyond this tension lies the capacity to improve continuously and even to redefine improvement.

The second example deals with the efforts by Rahmi Koç to utilize global learning to gain local market share. His stance was directly opposite from that of Coca-Cola and McDonald's, which try increasingly to transform local learning into global products. His company, one of the largest Turkish conglomerates, developed joint partnerships with global giants such as Ford and Fiat that helped guarantee that Koç shares global strategies with the big boys.

What values has Koç reconciled? And is that possible in a company that is known to be part of a closed economy standing for an uncompromising approach: "Be as close and loyal to your clients and suppliers as you can be." (It is interesting to note that it was the foreign operations of Koç that gave a stimulus to recovery in Turkey.)

There is much to learn from Koç. He showed how a national champion with strong regional loyalties can withstand competitive pressures from global rivals. One might have thought he would nominate a decentralized approach as the main lever for success, but look where he ended. It is not global at the cost of local or vice versa. It is not even global and local. The main success criteria are how to improve local activities *through* global Learning and how to apply locally what has been developed globally. It is a type of thinking that we observe repeatedly among our 21 leaders and call "through-through thinking." It is quite different in sequence from the approach of companies that started globally.

The Transnational Koç Created by Rahmi

The Koç Group is very much a homegrown champion. How could it stand up to competitive pressures from truly global players?

From the sheer amount of donations to charity, can a company so immersed in giving *also* satisfy shareholders and customers? Rahmi Koç has avoided becoming a victim to global rivals with lesser obligations to national infrastructures. The danger was that global competitors could outclass Koç.

Koç, as a twenty-first-century leader, was able to meet this competition head on and "either do something no one else does or do it better than others." Koç's strength lies in traditional ties of loyalty. Some long-trusted dealers are also in their third generation of ties between respective families. Rahmi showed that this could last. He identified that Japanese consumers pay 20 to 30 percent above world prices, in part because national companies are public benefactors and major contributors to learning and development. As long as Koç commanded local loyalties, it would be hard to enter the Turkish market without a respected local partner. The family could not renege on its charitable giving at this point; the only viable strategy was to utilize the loyalties won by this generosity and make it hard to enter local markets without the guidance and blessing of Koç. Thus, the partnerships with global players would help win respect and make the group privy to global strategies. The dilemma of global competition versus local loyalties was a tension between the fact that leaner and meaner competitors might tempt Turkish society to abandon its loyalties and the fact that the Koç Group could become a relic of paternalism, still giving generously but less and less able to afford those kindly donations. The leadership of Rahmi is centered in partnering with global players and in the process become their full equals and learn all about their thinking and strategy, their manufacturing techniques and market intelligence. The Koç Group joins them in exporting so that it grows into a genuinely global player itself rather than just a national powerhouse.

Dilemmas Deriving from Individualism versus Communitarianism

The conflict between what each of us wants as an individual and the interests of the groups we belong to is the second of five dimensions measuring how people relate to other people. Do we relate to others by discovering what each one of us individually wants and then trying to negotiate the differences, or do we place ahead of this a shared concept of the public and collective good? It is easy to recognize major differences on this dimension among global players.

We all go through these cycles, starting from different points and conceiving of different means or ends. The individualist culture sees the individual as the end and uses improvements in collective arrangements as the means to achieve that end. The communitarian culture sees the group as the end and uses improvements in individual capacities as a means to achieve that end. Yet if the relationship is truly circular, the decision to label one element as an end and another as a means is arbitrary. By definition, circles never end: Every end is also the means to another goal.

The effective international leader empathizes with the conviction that individualism finds its fulfillment in service to the group and that group goals are of demonstrable value to individuals only if those individuals are consulted and participate in the process of developing them. The reconciliation is not easy, but it is possible.

Reconciling Individualism and Communitarianism

Throughout our study of companies, we have found three major cases in which individual creativity was integrated into teamwork: we define this as *co-opetition*.

First, we find the superb leadership of Christian Majgaard at LEGO. He has created communities of creative individuals by installing processes in which creative ideas are there not to be killed by the bureaucracy but to be celebrated by a diverse set of team members.

The Individual versus the Community of LEGO

At LEGO there is no problem finding enough individuals to generate enough ideas. The challenge lies with the "business system" or community, which has to translate those ideas into the reality of viable products and services. It was not unusual for the community or system to impede the realization of good ideas, especially when those ideas came from senior people, while juniors were expected to be concerned solely with implementation. Majgaard has made a vital intervention in this force field. Ideas originate with individuals, but it is not a good idea simply to pass them down for subordinates to implement. The subordinates are inhibited in their criticism, and consultants will need to be hired to legitimize skepticism. Instead, the originator must work *with* critics, implementers, and builders of working prototypes to help to debug an idea whenever that is necessary.

Majgaard has seen that it is unwise to give higher status to the idea than to its implementers; otherwise, defective ideas will persist, disappointing their backers. Realization is at least as important as idealization, and the two must be reconciled. You must also beware of testing ideas to the point where they are destroyed.

We can interpret this *individual versus community* dilemma by observing with Majgaard's insight that the membership of teams must be diverse, consisting of people whose values and endowments vary, yet these teams must achieve a unity of purpose and shared solutions. Once again we have two polarized extremes: one at which prima donnas are created and one at which solid, viable, safe, unadventurous agreements are the result. According to Majgaard, this creates the potential for coming up with a solution that has benefited from diverse viewpoints and novel inputs, clearing the hurdles of skepticism.

The problem with highly diverse competing individuals is that they may behave like so many prima donnas, singing their own praises. The problem with unity and team spirit, above all, is that diverse and novel inputs get squeezed out. Majgaard's reconciliation is to make the superordinate goal so exciting and the process of creating new shared realities so passionate and enjoyable that diverse members overcome their differences and realize a *unity of diversities* that makes the solution far more valuable.

The second great master in this type of reconciliation is Richard Branson. We found it very difficult to categorize him under one cultural dimension. He seems to integrate all dilemmas through his personality. The one that shines through, however, is his tremendous ability to reconcile the personalities of "David" and "Goliath." He seems to have a great talent for creating public sympathy in favor of the *wronged individual* confronting the *collectivized assailant.* Branson surely heads a large organization, but in the eyes of public opinion he is a man alone facing servants of power, a personality against an institution.

Richard Branson's Integration of "David" and "Goliath": The Victorious Underdog

An important repository for reconciled values is the human personality. To an extent almost unprecedented in world business, the Virgin brand *is* the personality of Richard Branson. Branson often seems to win sympathy by fighting against well-chosen opponents, thus escaping the reputation of a bruiser or a vexatious litigant. He is able to set the scene of his confrontations so as to portray himself clearly as the underdog, likely to attract public sympathy. If he wins, he wins, but even if he loses, he wins sympathy. Although Branson seems to have reconciled many dilemmas, one of the most striking is that he comes out as a Goliath who has the approval ratings of a David!

He has taken on Coca-Cola, PepsiCo, the giant clearing banks, the pensions industry, the U.S. gambling industry, British Airways' 95 percent of British-originated airline traffic, the motor-car cartel (which uses Britain's right-hand drive to overprice domestic vehicles), and the closed system of movie distribution. There is public sympathy for the wronged individual confronting a collectivized assailant. In individual-istic cultures such as those of the United Kingdom and North America, the individual is going to win every time. It is part of folklore that groups conspire against individuals.

Branson starts from his underdog position and uses the sympathy generated to win his fights against compromised corporations. He rec-onciled the dilemma of the victorious antagonist with the risk of fail-ing, of the mighty being who is the proverbial underdog, and of being part of the system while trying to beat the system. Branson, however, very often became the victorious underdog by attaining a deeply satis-fying victory for the underdog against corporate power. Virgin is per-sonalized as the individual who comes to the rescue of the consuming public by confounding the strength of "the oppressor."

Third, we find the very interesting reconciliation by Gérard Mes-trallet, president of Suez Lyonnaise des Eaux (SLDE). While world-wide privatization seems like a new capitalistic dream, paradoxically it was the French who were best positioned to take advantage of it, be-cause for many French managers the proper conduct of private enter-prise has never lacked a sense of public duty and social obligation to the wider community. Mestrallet, an icon of French sophistication, saw in business the opportunity to "continuously take care of the needs of your fellow man." What dilemma did he face in this humble striving? If you are *of* the community, you can be trusted to take care of it only at the risk of being chronically inefficient and underfunded. Conversely, if you are an unelected out-of-town operator, going for profit had pre-viously meant being insufficiently trusted.

Mestrallet: Socially Responsible Privatization

It follows that privatization, as practiced by SLDE, is less likely to lead to local communities being taken advantage of and more likely to be seen as an opportunity to care creatively. Supplies of fresh water and the proper treatment of wastes have historically been responsible for doubling life expectancy in communities. A company dedicated to these tasks is not easy to find in laissez-faire economies, where self-interest is sovereign over public services. However, although smallness and localness assist in the taking of social responsibility, too often the system is chronically inefficient and lacks economies of scale.

SLDE is challenged to be locally responsible *and* a large, efficient investor. Mestrallet is seeking to demonstrate that privatization not only is technically and economically superior but also matches the concern for the local communities shown by contractors on a short leash forever lobbying for renewal of their concessions. SLDE is targeting big cities, where its professionalism can be appreciated. It has current projects in Atlanta, Indianapolis, Gary, Milwaukee, and San Antonio, among others—with favorable comments.

Mestrallet continuously faces the dilemma of *socially responsible privatization versus regulation in the public interest*. On the one hand, we find the risk that deregulation, privatization, and large-scale economies and investments will lead to "rogue out-of-town" operation. On the other hand, we find that too much emphasis on community responsibility runs the risk of developing many small municipalities, close to users and responsible but chronically inefficient and underfunded.

Mestrallet's strategy is brilliant: He is trying to have SLDE commit itself to the communities and municipalities it serves. If the tide turns against privatization, there is still a chance that SLDE could be regarded as an exception, one of the few global operators that serves its customers with honesty and dedication, creating oases in a spiritual desert. This occurs because the private deregulated resources are used responsibly.

Dilemmas Deriving from Neutral versus Affective Thinking

In relationships between people, reason and emotion both play a role. Which one dominates depends on whether we are *affective* (show our emotions), in which case we probably get an emotional response in return, or are emotionally *neutral* in our approach and display. Typically, reason and emotion are, of course, combined. In expressing ourselves, we try to find confirmation of our thoughts and feelings in the response of our audience. When our approach is highly emotional, we are seeking a *direct*, emotional response: "I have the same feelings as you on this subject." When our approach is highly neutral, we are seeking an *indirect* response: "Because I agree with your reasoning or proposition, I give you my support." On both occasions approval is being sought, but different paths are being used to achieve that end. The indirect path gives us emotional support only contingent on the success of an effort of intellect. The direct path allows our feelings about a factual proposition to show through, "joining" feelings with thoughts in a different way.

The expression of opinions in an open and often passionate way by individuals with strong personalities often gels into fairly fixed opposition and sometimes into an adversarial communication style. It is frequently necessary to restate the importance of basic communications skills such as listening.

Reconciling Affective and Neutral Cultures

Overly affective (expressive) cultures and overly neutral cultures have problems relating to each other. The neutral person is easily accused of being ice cold with no heart; the affective person is seen as out of control and inconsistent. When such cultures meet, the first essential for the international leader is to recognize the differences and refrain from making judgments based on the presence or absence of emotions.

This aspect of culture frequently is manifested in the amount of emotionality people can stand across cultures. Kodak introduced an ad selling on the basis of "memories," which Americans love, but the British interpreted it as overly sentimental. It was Michael Porter who said that Germans don't know what marketing is about. In his American conception, marketing is about showing the qualities of your products without any inhibitions. Germans might see this as bragging. It is not accepted unless you sell secondhand cars. The way in which you express positive things in Germany needs to be subtle. This subtlety perhaps escaped Porter.

We always find it difficult to reconcile reason with emotions, neutral left- with affective right-brain capacities. Looking at the essence of the innovative process, we see that many reconciliations are necessary, including the neutral check of one's passion. Hear what Tom Peters said in a 1999 meeting in Atlanta: "It is cool to be emotional nowadays." In investigating, searching, and solving problems, our excitement often points the way to what is later found to be factual and rational. Solutions have an elegance, an aesthetic that warms the heart.

We have found that our great leaders all either had passion as the context in which their reason made sense or had reason as their context in which their passion became meaningful. The first exemplar of this dichotomy is Philippe Bourguignon at Club Med. His insistence that the aesthetic experience of a vacation make sense in a world of calculation rescued the company from a dark period in its history.

Bourguignon's Rational Ingredients of a Personal Dream

Club Med's prodigious growth had overstrained its traditional management structure. It had become intoxicated by its self-celebrations, week after week, and was not keeping track of costs or logistics. The company's downward spiral had begun, and chronic underinvestment made it worse. The company was not competent in the more neutral, "hard" side of the business (travel, finance, logistics, etc.). Resorts were not profit centers, and several had lost money without anyone's realizing it. Opening was often too early in the season or not early enough. Hospitality had been increased without any awareness of diminishing returns. The food and wine expenditure had escalated too far. When what one is looking for is *esprit, ambience,* and all the affective and diffuse aspects of life—leave it to Club Med. But this was also its undersponsored strength. Bourguignon was aware that he had to reconcile these neutral and affective necessities of Club Med. He helped the business refine the art of placing immaterial experiences above the bits and pieces of the material world while ensuring that the bits and pieces paid off.

The wholeness of experience, with its *esprit* and stylishness, is vital, but taken too far (as it was in the early 1990s), the personalized and unique vacation was driven to the point of destruction. Club Med had become a vendor of incomparable experiences, but it couldn't survive in a cost-conscious world. The opposite, more neutral approach, in which elements are standardized into a reliable, high-volume, and therefore affordable holiday, would risk abandoning Club Med's founding values, however.

Because of ever-advancing living standards, the separate elements of luxury and good living are available to more and more people. What is often missing, because it is more elusive, is the integration of these elements into a diffuse and affective sense of satisfaction, a *savoir vivre.* Club Med no longer manages villages as such but instead delivers a shared spirit, a seamless scenario of satisfactions, an *ambience* or atmosphere augmented by food and wine, as do Planet Hollywood and Hard Rock Cafés. As Pascal put it, "The heart has its own reasons, with which reason is not familiar at all."

It was immediately obvious, when we interviewed Hugo Levecke from ABN AMRO Lease Holding, that part of his success story was based on reconciling viewpoints across this neutral-affective dimension. On the one hand, under Levecke the leaseholding division of the great bureaucracy of ABN AMRO had grown into an entrepreneurial and very successful unit, independent of the more rational headquarters culture. On the other hand, what would happen when brains met emotions? Levecke had been strategizing for nine months with unit heads, and he believed that the rational case for what he proposed had been made and accepted in principle. But what of the emotion? Could they bring their hearts to this far more interdependent way of doing business? Was it not skill, hard work, and results that had earned them their autonomy?

All this was a dilemma for Levecke. He had been part of the group. He himself had created the warm and trusting relationships. How could he turn the company around if the relationships he had developed over the years turned sour?

Hugo Levecke: How to Change an Emotional Entrepreneurial Setting into a Neutral, Rationalized one

Hugo Levecke, the president of ABN AMRO Lease Holding, needed to turn around the new division. In the past most of the division's growth had been created by innovative entrepreneurs. With the maturing and internationalization of the business, there developed a need for more interdependence between the units. But could Levecke bring the hearts of his people to join him in this most calculated approach? He knew that there are no easy or secret tricks. Business transformation requires a personal transformation in the way we all lead; this would hurt all concerned emotionally—and that included him. He was aware that he could not turn to a linear progression, a rollout of tested techniques; rather, he faced a process of trial and error in which mutual support and understanding for the lessons learned would be required from everyone.

The major dilemma Levecke had to reconcile was the need for a rational and neutral approach in business with not losing the hearts of those people, including himself, who had grown the company through their entrepreneurial and pioneering spirit. Levecke found the source of reconciliation in monitoring the leading process of innovation and entrepreneurialism intellectually. People had to work not harder but smarter. He focused on improving the quality of internal communication and establishing a rapid exchange of knowledge at all levels of the organization. For this purpose he developed a companywide scoreboard that records initiatives and results. Moreover, he introduced periodic meetings at which teams consisting of directors or the specialists reporting to them exchanged the most common experiences resulting from the initiatives being attempted by a business unit.

Teams were organized around strategic purposes and sought to mine information from one successful project to help create another. In this way, people were empowered to act so that the team could take direct responsibility for the strategies it recommended. Thus, the dilemma of taking risks while your heart was in your mouth was qualified and controlled by cool calculation that compared one bold initiative with another and drew sober conclusions. Levecke's achievement was to create a process in which the sense of entrepreneurship survived simply because each director now had an intelligent audience to admire and critique each initiative.

The third and last major challenge in the area of the affective-neutral dilemma is what Anders Knutsen did at Bang and Olufsen, reconciling neutral technical excellence with the emotional appeal of products. Beautiful audiovisual information had to be conveyed on instruments worthy of their content in the same way that the instruments of an orchestra carry the spirit of the composer and express his or her feeling. To counterbalance the strong influence of scientifically oriented research and development, teams were sent to the United States and elsewhere to try to capture the ineffable qualities of new sounds and sights so that they could be faithfully rendered.

Anders Knutsen: the Integration of Two Strong Traditions

Bang and Olufsen had two strong traditions. Knutsen knows very well that there is an aesthetic and emotional commitment to the beauty of sights and sounds recorded and played by both employees and clients. On the other hand, there is a strongly developed tradition of engineering and technological commitment to brilliant scientific solutions. This dilemma is rich and contains many subdilemmas, the main one being the affective and neutral approaches. The client's model actually touches on three of our dimensions: the two dimensions making up the diffuse and affective experiences of particular art forms and the specific neutrality of scientific and universal solutions. They are often at odds with one another, tilting the balance of power now this way and now that.

Knutsen knew very well that neither a technical dominance nor a pure focus on a diffuse and emotional feeling for music, visual arts, and pure aesthetics would get the company out of trouble. It is in "Idealand" that various values meet, clash, and achieve a final harmony. Each group champions its own values until they find inclusion in a larger system and in a more creative synthesis, watched over by a principle of parsimony that seeks to cut costs to the bone. The synthesis of values must be spare, rich, and elegant yet pricewise. "Idealand" was supported by Anders Knutsen because he saw it as a vehicle for harmonizing values into viable ideas and offering them to customers.

Dilemmas Deriving from Specificity versus Diffusion

The next of our seven dimensions concerns the degree of involvement in relationships. Closely related to whether we show emotions in dealing with other people is the degree to which we engage others in *specific* areas of life and single levels of personality or *diffusely* in multiple areas of life and at several levels of personality at the same time. In specificity-oriented cultures a leader segregates out the task relationship with a subordinate and isolates it from other dealings. But in some countries every life space and every level of personality tend to leak into the others. This dilemma is also significant in small family businesses (Chapter 21), in which dilemmas arise when there is tension between family bonds and business demands.

At the global level the dilemma shows itself clearly in the alliances that can be observed between many of the major airlines. In our work with British Airways and American Airlines, the model helped the parties recognize and respect the different ways in which they define the relationship with their passengers. It is typically American to emphasize "core competencies" and "shareholder value." In contrast, British Airways and Cathay Pacific emphasize service, with hot breakfasts, champagne, and the like. Thus, in this "One World" alliance, the options are as follows:

1. Go for "serving the cattle with Coke and pretzels."
2. Not only serve hot breakfasts but add massage and shoe polishing and "go bankrupt on the flight."
3. Compromise and "serve the hot pretzel" so that it becomes certain that one will lose *all* clients.

Reconciliation is the art of trying to define those specific areas to provide a more personal service and deepen the relationship. Jan Carlzon of SAS called this the "moment of truth." The future of the alliance will depend on one particular reconciliation: the competency of the employees of the airlines at consistently choosing those specific moments to deepen the relationship in the service being provided. A compromise will lead to a business disaster (and we have often seen them in alliances of any kind).

Three Major Dilemmas of the Specificity-Diffusion Orientation Resolved by Excellent Leaders

At first glance, the dilemma of specificity versus diffusion is very difficult to reconcile. However, we have seen in our research that this form of reconciliation is one of the most rewarding. For instance, Dell's success in the computer industry has been highly dependent on this kind of integration.

Let us look first at the main dilemma Michael Dell approached and how it partly explains his major success in the industry. Because Dell was a latecomer to the computer industry, he had to do something entirely different, something that would differentiate him from competitors. Among many other things, he decided to bypass distributors entirely. He would sell directly to customers, establishing a unique advantage over other computer suppliers. Speaking directly with customers instead of using intermediaries caused information on changing customer needs to reach the company more quickly and with greater clarity and urgency. It was possible to learn firsthand the strategic aims of major corporate customers. The model of direct selling received a welcome and powerful boost from the Internet, which was first used to sell a Dell computer in June 1996. Thus, you can get down to each customer's problems in *specific* detail yet at the same time serve a *diffuse* array or spectrum of needs and people. Above all, specific computers swim in a sea of diffusely communicated information.

Dell's Dilemma: A Broad Spectrum of Customers versus Deep, Personalized Customer Relationships

Michael Dell had to come to grips with the dilemma of selling either to a broad array or to a special group with which deep relationships were developed. In fact, his newly developed Direct Selling Model had the advantage of being very broad and at the same time deep, personal, and customized.

Dell broke with the conventional wisdom that you aim either for many customers, making your profits off volume, or for just a few clients with complex problems and specialized needs who require very complex high-end service (for which you can charge heavily). The first strategy is cheap but superficial. The second is intimate and personal but typically niche oriented. The risks are obvious. If you go for the first strategy, distribution channels may clog very quickly and there is no differentiation between you and your competitors. This strategy runs the risk of swamping the intermediaries. On the other hand, focusing on creating a very narrow but deep strategy risks creating severely limited opportunities in small niche markets.

The reconciliation that Michael Dell created was as powerful as it was simple. By using direct sales via face-to-face interaction, telephone, and the Internet, he reconciled breadth with depth and complexity. The genius of direct selling on the Internet is that you reach an ever-increasing spectrum of customers *and* can use the Net to give personalized, detailed, information-rich services to those customers on Premium Pages for each one.

The Internet is uniquely suited to information-rich products, which can be embedded in an ongoing community of discussants and can be woven around with dialogues on details and special opportunities. You can serve the whole spectrum of Net users while still going deeply into specific problems.

David Komansky of Merrill Lynch faces a major dilemma in this arena. The struggle to integrate the specific culture of Internet-based business activity with the diffuse and deep relationships that financial consultants have developed with their clients is still ongoing, but we are confident that it will lead to success. How will he do it?

Going for the Clicks That Stick

The challenge to Merrill Lynch has come in part from the unbundling of services into specific pieces. You can buy information, research, trading facilities, and advice from separate sources at combined fees possibly lower than the single fee paid to the firm's six- and seven-figure professionals. The Internet is overflowing with *data*, but this is not the same thing as knowledge or information. We are informed by facts relevant to our questions and concerns. We "know" only upon receiving answers to our propositions and hypotheses. The larger the Internet becomes, the more customers will need a guide to what is relevant to individual concerns.

The dilemma can be analyzed as follows: On one axis we find low-cost specific data and transactions on the Internet. The risk here is that you create a high-tech solution in which your staff of brokers is bypassed by technology. On the other axis we find the rich, meaningful, diffuse personal relationships that brokers have developed with their clients. It maintains a high-touch environment in which customers overpay for their dependence.

Komansky is working in a setting where complexity is so vast that professional relationships become vital to discovering meaning and negotiating the maze. Instead of relationships being eclipsed by the Internet, then, they get more and more important in interpreting the possible meanings of data flows as what is available grows ever larger than what is relevant to each client. Hence, in this phase of the Internet we will discover that intelligent dialogue about the bewildering complexity of financial markets is a formative influence on financial markets.

We need *high tech,* but we also need *high touch.* The more those numbers rain down on you, the more you need to talk to someone about them. Merrill Lynch can use the Internet to give better personal service (via high tech) to its high-touch customers while simultaneously using it to identify those high-tech customers to whom it makes good business sense to offer high touch.

A third dilemma in the area of degree of involvement has been reconciled very clearly by Kees Storm of AEGON, the large Dutch insurance company. It is a very important one; we believe that the old dilemma of shareholder value versus stakeholder value will be wonderfully reconciled in the twenty-first century. The new forms of capitalism will be reconciled with an old form, Marxism. It will be an interesting century in which Storm will play a pioneering role.

Kees Storm: The Synergy of Stakeholder Values

Kees Storm has frequently communicated his belief that there it is foolish to extol shareholder value above the rights of and duties to stakeholders. This is the case because the results of all the stakeholders are interdependent, and you cannot increase emphasis on only one without damaging the whole system and precipitating a regressive spiral. Storm did not confuse importance with priority (i.e., which value must logically come first); there is no doubt in his mind that motivating employees to satisfy customers precedes increasing returns and paying profits to shareholders. The reason for this precedence is that customers supply the money that shareholders later receive. If employees are for any reason *not* motivated and customers are *not* satisfied, there is no money for shareholders to receive. Shareholder value tends to be specific and countable; motivating and satisfying are more diffuse. Diffuse processes can too easily be neglected or even overlooked. On one horn of the dilemma we find specific sales and profits used to pay shareholders who reinvest. The risk here is that you will end up in "the bottom line" for stakeholders who never share. On the other horn we find diffuse processes of motivating employees to satisfy customers. The risk here is that the interests of those not physically present (shareholders) are ignored. Storm has integrated these two tensions at a higher level by joining stakeholder values with stock options for employees, who "make money and have fun." By operating his fireworks display, Storm first motivates employees to satisfy customers, raising sales and profits for shareholders, who reinvest in AEGON as a result.

Dilemmas Deriving from Achieved versus Ascribed Status

All societies give certain members higher status than others, signaling that unusual attention should be focused on those persons and their activities. Some societies accord status to people on the basis of their achievements; others ascribe it to them by virtue of personal character-istics such as age, class, gender, education, mission, and position. The first kind of status is called *achieved* status, the second is called *ascribed* status. Achieved status refers to *doing*; ascribed status refers to *being*.

Achievement-oriented cultures market products and services on the basis of performance. Performance, skill, and knowledge justify authority. These cultures will make those products into a standard only when they have proved superior in the market through competition.

Ascription-oriented cultures often ascribe status to products and services. Particularly in Asia, status is attributed to products that "nat-urally" evoke admiration from others, for example, highly educational technologies and projects deemed to be of national importance because they build infrastructure. The status is generally independent of actual accomplishment.

This contrast generates dilemmas when partners have different traditions about how people move up the ladder in the organization. In achievement-oriented cultures your position is best secured by continuous performance and by what you know. In the worst case, you are only as good as your last performance. In ascribed cultures senior-ity and long-term loyalty are much more important, as well as whom you know and the noble aspects of your endeavors. This dilemma has been a fundamental issue for Stuart Beckwith, who is the found-ing entrepreneur and managing director of the BCIF group of com-panies. His organization provides a "one-stop" center for business training, consulting, and recruitment targeted mainly at small or fam-ily-run businesses. One of the main dilemmas he has reconciled, both within his own organization and for the organizations he helps, is that of the family-driven "livelihood business" versus the "independent business."

Creating a Legacy through Immortality Businesses: Stuart Beckwith

Over the last 15 years BCIF has developed from nothing by helping more than 9000 new businesses become established. Beckwith has been concerned with the development both of his own organization and of all those he has helped grow from sole traders or partnerships to viable, self-sustaining businesses.

The main dilemma he faced as a leader of BCIF and a consultant to his clients concerned the ascribed status that is so dominant in a family business. Here it is important to be well connected and to have the right mentors from the family coaching you. In a *livelihood business* the family is dominant. For some family members, the activity may not even be recognized as business. There is a clear line between the family and its business. Members are judged purely on their performance and achievements. Beckwith said during an interview, "Without doubt, it is the interaction between the demands of the family and the business. I have observed families breaking up through the demands of the business and businesses failing through the demands of the family. In our business, I employ some of my sons and my wife is also a senior executive. I have always been conscious of the need to find ways to integrate these apparently competing demands." Reconciliation was found in the *immortality business*—making sure your business is a lasting legacy to your children and grandchildren.

By being conscious of the problem that many founders won't allow the next generation to get on with the business, Beckwith recognizes the importance of "planning to let go." He uses his "status" to ensure that his customers have succession plans in place and that the business will not depend on the founder's personal presence. He also recognizes the need for change: In the future BCIF will be very different from what it is now. In an immortality business the demands of the family and business and the tension between the aging founder and younger achievers are reconciled. The founder achieves "immortality" of a kind by living through the successors and leaving them to interpret what he or she has taught them.

A family whose business aspires to immortality must ask, "How can we renew ourselves?" and must give subordinates the autonomy to redefine the legacy in a new century. Pressure for change will come from changing market conditions, from family members who want to do more or less, from those seeking to withdraw or add capital, and from major nonfamily contributors who feel that they are being shortchanged for their efforts. The "right" balance is ever shifting.

Since our original interviews with Beckwith, he has broken up the evolving monolithic BCIF group into a number of components, each of which focuses on a number of core business competencies. By giving his children the opportunity to drive new ventures, he has further reconciled his need for survival with his family needs.

Another excellent example of reconciliation between achieved and ascribed status is the profit-oriented versus nonprofit status of BUPA realized by Val Gooding. Should you have a yield of 25 percent profit to shareholders and have to compete with Internet stocks on the AEX, or should you make enough return to take care of the old and frail? To care about the people you serve is a precursor to success. You must ascribe status to them initially.

Val Gooding's Provident Association

There is much discussion about whether "care" should or even can be delivered effectively by those seeking to make therefrom profits that match the rising returns that are increasingly common in the City of London. Or should you instead opt for the stakeholder and look at larger and longer-term goals than the next quarterly gain? For this reason BUPA has no shareholders but is a *provident association*, hovering between for-profit and nonprofit status.

Gooding regards provident status as a strong advantage, provided that she herself can furnish the stimulus for growth and risk that would otherwise come from shareholder pull. Remarkably, she has reconciled the sense of urgency and constant striving for improvement that shareholders often have with the well-known fact that the customer is unambiguously the top priority. Because it takes high staff morale to keep customers happy, employees become the means of satisfying customers. You care for your employees up front, and they will pass that care on to customers.

The dilemma can be analyzed as follows: Most quoted companies, having impatient shareholders, cannot invest for the long term, in which current investments in upgrading equipment and call centers justify themselves 20 years from now. Shareholders want too much too quickly. On the other hand, a nonprofit, customer-oriented approach leads to an organization that is risk averse and too noble of intention to try very hard to succeed.

Gooding has taken BUPA from roughly the vicinity of the latter position to being a company eager to grow as fast as its success allows (with no need to pause for private enrichment) dedicated to worldwide customers, and willing to invest in their long-term welfare—and she has done that so successfully that BUPA now has difficulty finding a way to invest all its surpluses in long-term solutions and global expansion!

Even Richard Branson's rebel stance is a form of ascribed status: He sets out to afflict the comfortable and turns this political gesture into success with consumers.

Gordon Billage: Leading His Founding Division into New Areas of Business

Gordon Billage, as chief executive officer of Clifford-Thames, reconciled many other dilemmas, but in the same way, he used his ascribed status as the managing director to lead the business units from his headquarters role. This enabled him to achieve improved business performance across the company. Not only was his title later changed to CEO, he was given even more ascribed status (courtesy of his local university) by being awarded an honorary degree because of his achievements!

Despite far greater emphasis on ascription or achievement in certain cultures, the two usually develop together. Those who start by ascribing usually see potential in others and treat them in ways that help bring that potential to fruition. Those who start by achieving usually have importance and priority ascribed to the next project. Hence, all societies ascribe and all achieve, after a fashion. It is once again a question of where a cycle starts. The international leader surfs the crest of this dilemma.

Dilemmas Deriving from Internal versus External Control

The next culturally determined dimension concerns the meaning the actor assigns to the (natural) environment. In cultures in which an organic view of nature dominates and in which the shared assumption is that humans are subjugated to nature, individuals appear to orient their actions toward others. People become "other-directed" in order to survive; their focus is on the environment rather than on themselves. This attitude is known as *external control*.[2] Conversely, it has been determined that people who have a mechanistic view of nature and believe that human beings can dominate nature usually take themselves as the point of departure for determining the right action. The "inner-directedness" of much of the West is also reflected through the current fashion for strategic thinking, as if one were Alexander the Great conquering the known world.

Reconciling Internal Control with External Control

The major issue at stake here is to connect the internally controlled culture, leading to the talent of *technology push,* with the externally controlled world of *market pull* in order to achieve a culture of inventive-

---

[2] J. B. Rotter, *Generalised Expectations for Internal versus External Control of Reinforcement.* Psychological Monograph 609, 1966, pp. 1–28.

ness. Take a consumer electronics company such as Philips: Nobody will deny its great knowledge and inventiveness in its specific technologies and the quality of its marketing. The problem the company faced was that its two major functional areas didn't seem to communicate. The success of an organization is dependent on the integration of the two areas. The push of technology needs to help you decide what markets you want to be pulled by, and the pull of the market needs to help you know what technologies to push.

Leaders Reconcile the Pushes into a Pull

Again, we have found three leaders who have made this dilemma the core of their success. First there is Tim Morris. He is now the founding entrepreneur and managing director of MMP Business Management, which he established some six years ago. His company provides the back office to a diverse range of organizations that want to get on with their key business. One of the main dilemmas he helps his clients reconcile is the need for control of key business processes and the need to let things go in order to be able to focus on key business.

Under- and Overcontrol and the Ability to Let Things Go while Remaining in Charge

Morris believes that companies and their owners need to strike a creative balance between their need to control key business processes and the ability to let go. He said, "It continually surprises me how many small businesses don't know how much cash they have in the bank, what payments [creditors] are due in the near future, and what debtors they have. They seem to be trying to catch a flight with last month's departure screen. I couldn't sleep at night if I didn't know exactly where my business is! On the other hand, we find owner-managers who are obsessive about being in control. Just because they started the business and it has been running successfully, they think it will go on forever if they continue to apply their 'magic formula.'

"It is a matter of avoiding the extremes. For those who are fatalistic and think everything depends on luck or the economy, we try to encourage them to get their business under control. We produce a daily (or sometimes weekly) snapshot of income and expenditure and exactly where they are. This gives them a greater degree of control. We do the same thing for our own business, of course. At any time, at the click of a mouse, I know exactly our cash bank balance, our creditors, and our debtors. Conversely, for those who think they are in control, with simplistic administrative systems, we try to show them that they are not—because in the medium term they may be vulnerable to the external environment."

Morris is also extremely insightful about two contrasting types of entrepreneurs: those who overcontrol and those who undercontrol. For each kind of client he has a different treatment. The undercontrolling leader's attitude is to "leave it to lesser beings." There is important and creative work, and there is support work, of less importance, done by lesser persons. Such entrepreneurs leave the control to others and disparage control per se. But there is a second, contrasting tendency. Many an entrepreneur has "made it" because a set of original ideas has been mobilized within a single mind. These ideas could be ordered and sorted, with perfect control over their disposition, resulting in breakthrough success. It is very easy for such entrepreneurs to associate success with their own total control of key elements. As the company expands, those "key elements" come to include other people, and we have the makings of a "control freak."

Morris moderates "control freakery" by constantly informing the entrepreneur of variables beyond his or her control, which cannot be changed or countermanded but *can* be responded to and taken advantage of. He moderates the "leave it to lesser beings" entrepreneur by compensating for this snobbery through innovative computer-based Microsoft Office products.

Sir Mark Moody-Stuart, president of Royal Dutch Shell Group of Companies, sought to reconcile a major dilemma in this area of inner and outer direction. It can be argued that the reconciliation of this dilemma will account for much of the success of Shell in the twenty-first century.

Beyond the Trauma of Brent Spar

The oil industry, including Shell, has long tended to look inward and often has not monitored the external environment sufficiently. Shell had integrity and a Calvinist conscience, but it was its integrity and rationality and its judgment that were more expert than anyone else's. Even the seasoned leader Mark Moody-Stuart found it a shock when the oil industry was criticized—witness the planned sinking of the Brent Spar. The Brent Spar was a massive, obsolete oil storage and loading buoy in the North Sea which Shell planned to dispose of by sinking it in a deep part of the Atlantic.

Shell saw such issues as technical and in this regard knew better than its critics. After all, Shell had the facts and the critics did not. The facts were technical, not social, issues and had the rational-empirical substance that engineers love. Of course, Shell recognized that its decisions would have social implications, but that only made it more important that they be technically sound. It was not always clear to Shell why external sociopolitical events had so many followers.

This situation originated in part because exploration and production are more profitable than retailing. Shell made money in inverse relation to its proximity to consumers, and this reinforced its inward-looking technological bent. Added to this was a cultural tendency for the engineers to be Dutch and the accountants Scottish. In contrast, the British tended to be more commercial, trading on the back of the old empire. It was this inner-directed technological mind-set that was the root of the trouble over the Brent Spar.

Although Shell had attempted a cost analysis of all the options for disposal, there were emotional arguments that had logic of their own.

Moody-Stuart revealed his leadership qualities clearly when he admitted that decisions must take into consideration how other people think. And because people think and therefore value differently, there is always a dilemma deriving from the need to reconcile diverse logics.

On the one hand, there was the support for the inner-directed technological expertise versus the outer-world of sociopolitical issues, that is, the dilemma of truth versus communicability. Organizations such as Greenpeace exploit scandals to "raise consciousness" about environmental issues and recruit members. Boarding the spar amid crashing waves made them look like "cockleshell heroes" braving the elements to discover the unfortunately false truth. On the other extreme there is the utterance of the underdog "thinking only of the environment" against the might of a profit-making giant corporation.

Moody-Stuart called for decisions which take into consideration *all logics:* the internal logic of inexpensive, safe disposal and the concern of the Swedish minister of the environment, trying to teach school children not to throw debris into the environment we all share. All major corporations take public positions, if not on purpose then by default. Moody-Stuart's leadership created a context in which Shell could continuously learn the logic of such positioning.

A final example concerns a very intriguing reconciliation by Sergei Kiriyenko of more inner-directed younger Russians with traditional outer-directed older Russians.

Kiriyenko: Cutting the Apron Strings

Historically, the Russian people in general have had their fates decided by external powers. NORSI Oil was no exception. Kiriyenko knew that the old archetype of the fatalistic Russian was true and that, at present people in Russia both yearn for and dread change. The main thing for the middle and older generations is to avoid mishaps. To break a log-jam, then, you might need, if not a shock, at least a threat.

The younger generation and the successful businesspeople are now motivated by success. For them, he created a positive stimulus—not a stick but a carrot. At NORSI, therefore, Kiriyenko had to make things worse before they could get better. He had to abolish the company and the ukase (decree from above) on which everyone was dependent. He had to say, in effect, "There is no company or edict coming to save you—only what you yourself create." He faced a situation in which inner-directed younger Russians would create black markets and Mafia-type environments if they were not constrained. On the other hand, he was also working with outer-directed, predominantly older Russians. Here the risk was to be left with people who were waiting for some new direction to save them.

He totally turned around the enterprise by eliminating that on which everyone was trying to depend. Reconciliation was achieved through the act of abolishing the company. This forced everyone to negotiate new and better agreements through which to avoid loss, make a profit, and even survive.

Dilemmas Deriving from the Meaning of Time: Sequential versus Synchronous in Regard to Past, Present, and Future

If only because leaders need to coordinate their business activities, they require shared expectations about time. Just as different cultures have different assumptions about how people relate to one another, they approach time differently. This orientation is about the relative impor-tance cultures give to the past, present, and future. How we think of time has its consequences. Especially important is whether our view of time is *sequential*, as a series of passing events, or *synchronous*, with past, present, and future all *interrelated* so that ideas about the future and memories of the past both shape present action.

Across cultures, we see two ways in which people think of time. For the more sequential people, time is an objective measure of passing increments. The more quickly you act and the shorter the time taken, the more effective you will be competitively. To them, we are in a race with time. Synchronous cultures, on the other hand, like to do things "just in time" so that present ideas converge in the future. The better your timing is, the more effective you will be competitively. To these cultures, time is like a dance.

Toward Reconciliation

The international leader is often caught in a dilemma between the future demands of the larger organization, needing vision and missions and managing change, and the past experiences of local populations. The short-termism that plagues Western and, particularly, American companies often is driven by the needs of the stock markets for annual or quarterly results and profits. The risk of a strong future orientation is failure to learn from past mistakes.

Synchronous people can deliver in time, but they like to do it for *you,* not for your clock, and just-in-time manufacturing has proved that the best way to speed up a sequence is to synchronize it just in time.

Our Leaders' Dilemmas of Time

In our research we have found that the reconciliation of the various aspects of time is crucial. We see that keeping the traditional products that made your name in the first place can jeopardize the creation of new products. We have found that organizing time sequentially makes you efficient but not very effective. Much time is lost. Long-term and short-term thinking need to be united on a higher level.

One dilemma of past and future needs of product development was exceptionally well approached by Karel Vuursteen of Heineken. He needed to integrate the traditions of the Heineken family with the future needs of the company, and he integrated the traditions of the Heineken product with the need for innovation—for example, in the area of specialty beers.

Heineken's Vuursteen: Tradition and Stability versus Innovative Products and Markets

The Heineken tradition is big, but the seeds of decay are in it. For over a hundred years Heineken's beer has appealed to people's taste. Historically, the company's reputation has been maintained at great cost. Recently, however, many specialty beers have entered the market, jeopardizing the big established names in the trade.

In 1993 Heineken faced a problem with glass particles in some of its bottles. The rich tradition of the company asked for a recall of hundreds of millions of bottles carrying its brand. Heineken also faced some difficulties in the introduction of new manufacturing sites in the United States and of Buckler's low-alcohol beer. Great misses like these have cost a lot of money, and so Vuursteen's approach to innovation was cautious. He had to maintain the consistency of Heineken's attraction, and he had to change to remain consistent. One method of innovating in a way that's not dangerous is to clear a space for a totally new approach that is separate from existing success and will not endanger it.

Heineken is highly successful, but the reasons for this success are elusive. *That* customers like the brand is clear; *why* they like it is less clear. Vuursteen's dilemma is the tension between Heineken's tradition of stability and the elusive nature of its success. The risk is that it creates a "sacred brew of immaculate image." He might have decided to change nothing for fear of damaging the sacred brew. At the other extreme we find that Heineken's need to change and innovate could risk accidentally wrecking the company's appeal.

Instead, Vuursteen very cleverly embarked on two forms of innovation that are relatively safe. *Process innovation* searches for new and better means of creating the same result and reserving a safe area for creation. *Product innovation* allows new drinks to be invented from scratch without involving Heineken's premium product in the experiments.

Another dilemma that our leaders seem to reconcile with great talent deals with the intervals between supervisions in the sequence elapsing before synchronization. Through a very interesting approach of sponsoring empowered teams, Martin Gillo of AMD wrought a reconciliation of extremes between the need for the sponsor to be responsible and the need for the team to have time, and hence freedom, to be creative.

Martin Gillo's Approach to Sponsoring the Empowered Team

Advanced Micro Devices (AMD), the large U.S. chipmaker, made a courageous move when it decided in 1995 to pursue chief executive officer Jerry Sanders's vision and build a mega-fab (factory) to produce state-of-the-art microprocessors equivalent to those of Intel in the Dresden region of the former East Germany. From the very beginning Gillo, vice president of human resources Europe, then in Geneva, realized that trying to import and to impose AMD's American culture on Dresden would be a mistake.

In no way can one culture produce an exact copy of another even if it wants to—and it rarely does. Restraint was not easy; many standardized approaches, such as the work of semiautonomous teams, were so successful in the United States that there was a tendency among managers to believe that those approaches also needed to be introduced in Dresden. So successful were team operations in Texas and California that they were defined as a nonnegotiable aspect of operations at the new Dresden Fab.

There is no doubt that teams are vital, because problems in this industry are too complex for any individual to deal with. They even grow beyond the mandate of management. You need teams to learn, through a discourse process, how the problem has to be tackled. The risk of autonomy for the team, however, is that it might deviate from, misinterpret, or defy its sponsor's charge. In this event the authority will be seriously weakened. Alternatively, if the team is not fully trusted by the sponsor, the time between supervisions becomes too short. Letting the team alone for only days makes the autonomy low, along with the risk and the likelihood that the team will come up with something significant.

Gillo has done everything possible to preserve and develop "natural groups"—that is, groups that have learned and experimented together and in whose relationships much crucial information is stored. Gradually, these natural groups are growing in their reputation for discovery. This reconciliation of longer sequences and timely synchronous actions has made big differences in increasing the yield of the Fab.

Generalizability: The Authors' Dilemma

We now seek to make general statements about leadership and the reconciliation of dilemmas that go beyond our particular observations, our interviews, and our analysis of 21 leaders. We have to consider the extent to which our sample is representative of the wider context and the spectrum of managers and leaders across the globe—and independent of any destination or home culture. Throughout, we have sought to avoid any ethnocentric approach in which our new model works only in a single culture.

As authors, we were faced with our own dilemma. Qualitative inductive research based on semistructured interviews (like the ones with our 21 leaders) produces rich outputs that have high *validity*. However, the *reliability* may be low if we cannot transfer these findings from a small sample to a wider population.

By contrast, findings from questionnaire-based instruments can be made highly *reliable* through careful selection and structuring of the sample. However, such reliability on its own does not mean that the findings are *valid*. The dilemma is captured in the following diagram:

The Authors' Dilemma: Validity or Reliability?

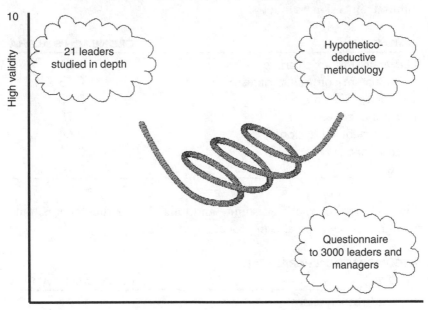

As readers will have learned from the rest of the book, we should not opt for one or the other of two contrasting approaches, rejecting the opportunity to reconcile those extremes. Doing both (interviews and questionnaires) independently is simply a compromise. We sought to practice what we preach by reconciling our own dilemma. We used the findings from initial contacts with our 21 leaders as input to the structure of our questionnaire. Conversely, we used early feedback from our questionnaires to know what questions to ask our 21 leaders.

Thus, the approach in this book was not to derive our model inductively from our 21 leaders. The prima facie case for the *dilemma reconciliation theory* had already been established and published by Charles Hampden-Turner. We sought instead to develop an understanding of what leaders do by using a hypothetico-deductive approach that reconciles the researchers' dilemma. We approached our 21 leaders with a mental model of dilemma theory already in place and sought to collect evidence to extend reconciliation theory by means of a synergy of these leaders with our reconciliation database.

For the questionnaire, we applied statistical tests of reliability (Cronbach alpha analysis) and were able to improve our reliability across each cultural dimension, as follows:

DIMENSION	CRONBACH'S ALPHA
Universalism-particularism	0.71
Individualism-communitarianism	0.73
Specificity-diffusion	0.63
Neutral-affective	0.75
Achievement-ascription	0.64
Internal-external	0.71
Time	0.74

Similarly, the internal consistency and reliability of the dilemma culture-map scales were also improved:

RECONCILIATION PARADIGMS ($n = 2980$)	CRONBACH'S ALPHA
Rejecting other values	0.71
Abandoning your own values	0.65
Reconciling opposing values	0.79
Compromising	0.68

Questionnaire Results from the 21 Leaders

We also invited our 21 leaders to complete a shortened version of our diagnostic instrument. Although this is only a small sample (maximum 21!), we observe (by using the exact tests method for small samples) that our leaders show a higher propensity for reconciliation than does our total database of general managers.

Within the limits imposed by the small sample size from the 21 leaders, the results from those who completed the shortened version of our questionnaire were totally consistent with the conclusions drawn by the authors in each of the detailed analyses given in the body of this book. Our leaders consistently opted for reconciled options when challenged with these dilemmas. In some cases they stood up for their own values across some dimensions, but without fail they opted for a reconciled solution to a problem domain akin to their own business or political life. The following table compares the responses of the 21 leaders with the mean of the sample of respondents with respect to the dilemmas with which they were presented.

Propensity to Reconcile (Percent Selecting a Reconciliation Option)

DIMENSION	OUR 21 LEADERS	MEAN FROM 2980 MANAGERS
Universalism-particularism	75	45
Individualism-communitarianism	75	33
Specificity-diffusion	66	55
Neutral-affective	66	25
Achievement-ascription	80	60
Internal-external	90	30
Time	75	50

Questionnaire Results from Our Database

By extending our framework to our 60,000 managers in the cross-cultural database and the 3000 leaders in the reconciliation, we were able to summarize the more significant findings.

Using the correlation between 360-degree feedback and responses to the dilemma posed, we find that leaders who work internationally or have more international experience have a greater propensity to reconcile, as shown in the following table.

Propensity to Reconcile (percent)

Mean of all managers	35	$p = 0.05$
Leaders working internationally	73	$p = 0.05$

Leaders and managers tend to claim that their own propensity to reconcile is greater than the average in their organizations:

Propensity to Reconcile (percent)

Average of all other managers in their own organizations	38	$p = 0.05$
Leaders working internationally	52	$p = 0.05$

Leaders with a higher propensity to reconcile rate themselves higher in their own self-sufficiency and perceived effectiveness:

Perceived Effectiveness (1 = low, 5 = high)	
Self	3.7
360-degree feedback	2.9

Less experienced leaders, as well as those with a low propensity to reconcile, are more consistent in rejecting reconciliation and tend to retain (and work from) their own value orientation. Thus, their simultaneous score on the seven-dimensional cross-cultural scale is more reliable than is their score on reconciliation.

In contrast, those with a higher propensity to reconcile tend to be more concerned with reconciliation than to worry about their own cross-cultural orientation. Thus, they can start either from their own orientation, to accommodate their own view, or from the opposing value and then return to their own in order to reconcile matters. Thus, their scale in reconciliation is more reliable than is the simultaneous assessment of their cross-cultural orientation.

By way of illustration, a Malaysian may act like a Malaysian as a junior manager, but as he or she becomes more effective globally (develops transcultural global competence), starts to travel, becomes concerned about quarterly reports, and starts to leave behind birth-country value systems, he or she becomes more global.

There is a positive correlation between a leader's propensity to reconcile and the independent 360-degree assessment of his or her interpersonal effectiveness. One's propensity to reconcile also correlates with bottom-line business performance (where those data are available).

Spearman's Coefficient of Rank Correlation		
Correlation with 360-degree feedback	0.71	$p = 0.05$
Correlation with business performance	0.69	$p = 0.05$

Many of the earlier data were not very discriminating. Peer assessment tended to be bland, and there was little variety in the data; for example, 70 percent rated the sample as a 3, and only one or two individuals were rated 4 or 5, 2, or 1. Data collected more recently have greater internal variety. For this reason, it is expected that stronger correlations that are statistically more significant will be obtained. Three smaller samples, from two American clients and one Dutch organization, all show a high correlation.

Some Other Findings

There is a small negative correlation between independent assessment of technical competence and the propensity to reconcile. Junior leaders with a high achievement orientation and an internal locus of control tend to select the compromise option rather than reconcile. Women tend to score higher on compromise than do men and to have a significantly more synchronous orientation to time.

The role or significance of reconciling by starting from one's own orientation or by starting from the other orientation is unclear. As might be expected, leaders (or cultures) with an internal locus of control (e.g., Americans) tend always to reconcile by starting from their own orientation across any other dimension. Those with an external locus of control (e.g., Japanese) tend to start from the opposite orientation and then integrate their own.

Those respondents who are in marketing or sales appear to have a higher propensity to reconcile and tend to start from the opposite (customer?) perspective first.

In conclusion, we claim that we have integrated validity and reliability. However, the final comment must go to Charles Hampden-Turner in the Afterword.

Short Biographies of the Contributors

Peter Woolliams, PhD, is Clifford-Thames professor of international business at the Anglia Business School in the United Kingdom. He has worked extensively as an academic and a practitioner management consultant in his specialist field of international business modeling and analysis. He has an extensive research and publication record and is faculty member of Management Center Europe (Brussels) and Transnational Management Associates, New York. He has collaborated with Fons Trompenaars for some 10 years and has been responsible for the development of the Trompenaars database.

Maarten Nijhoff Asser is a senior manager at Trompenaars Hampden-Turner and heads the U.S. office in Boston, MA. He has a degree in international law and intellectual property from the University of Amsterdam and an MBA in strategy, information, and technology from Theseus International Management Institute in Sophia Antipolis, France. He has facilitated business culture change processes for major multinationals and taught at business schools of international repute, including Harvard Business School.

Allard Everts is a senior manager at Trompenaars Hampden-Turner. He has a master's degree in mining engineering from the Technical University in Delft, the Netherlands. After working in the dredging industry, he moved to the Dutch national steel company. In 1988 he joined a company that specialized in SME and entrepreneurship development. He started working for KPMG in 1993, focusing on the restructuring of former state-owned companies. In 1998 he joined Trompenaars Hampden-Turner to strengthen the consulting capabilities in the field of corporate strategy.

Naomi Stubbé-de Groot has a master's degree in organizational psychology from the State University of Leiden (the Netherlands) and an MBA from Bradford University, UK. She has worked for six years as a senior manager at KPMG and her areas of expertise include intercultural management, change management, organizational culture analysis and development, counseling, and management style development. During 1998–2000 she was managing director of Trompenaars Hampden-Turner.

Peter Prud'homme van Reine has an MSc degree in physics engineering from the University of Delft, the Netherlands, and an MA in cultural and organizational anthropology from the University of Utrecht, the Netherlands. From 1979 to 1993 he worked as a project manager and technology manager for Philips Electronics. His second career was as a business anthropologist, when he joined the faculty of culture, organization, and management of the Free University of Amsterdam. He joined Trompenaars Hampden-Turner as a senior consultant in 1996.

Todd D. Jick is a managing partner of the Center for Executive Development. He was a professor at the Harvard Business School for 10 years and a visiting professor of organizational behavior–human resource management at INSEAD. He has also taught at the Columbia University Graduate School of Business and York University in Toronto. He earned his master's and PhD degrees in organizational behavior from Cornell University and he has a BA in social anthropology from Wesleyan University. He has been actively involved with executive education and consulting in areas such as leadership, executive coaching, organizational change and transformation, values-based management, service management, customer-supplier partnerships, and human resources management. He has been published widely and his latest book, *The Boundaryless Organization* (with Ashkenas, Ulrich, and Kerr), won the Accord Group Executive Leadership "best business book of the year" award.

Dirk Devos is founder of the WOODSHED (*www.woodshed.nl*), a home to strategic innovators and a consulting practice and virtual learning network focused on strategic value creation. Key practice areas include the design of unique value concepts and the creation of living-hero stories. Dirk Devos helps transnational leadership teams clarify the nature of choices to be made: either-or, and-and, and through-through choices. He integrates expert and process consulting and facilitates leadership conferences.

Dr. Park Jae Ho is Professor of Psychology at Yeungnam University in Korea. He has worked as a consultant and trainer in the field of intercultural management, intercultural leadership development, change management, and globalization with major Korean and U.S. companies. He started to work with Trompenaars Hampden-Turner in 1995. In 1990 he was a visiting professor at Harvard, and he was recently invited as a visiting professor to USIU in California.

Jo Spyckerelle is director of Trompenaars Hampden-Turner. After receiving a bachelor's degree in business administration from the Catholic University in Louvain, Belgium, he started working for Arthur Andersen and Co. as an accountant. He joined KPMG in 1982. He became a chartered accountant (Reviseur d'Entreprises) in 1986 and worked for many of KPMG's national consultancy practices. He became a consulting partner at KPMG's International Headquarters in Amstelveen, the Netherlands, in 1995, and joined Trompenaars Hampden-Turner in early 2000.

References

Introduction

Warren Bennis, *On Becoming a Leader.* Perseus Press, 1983.

John W. Hoat, London Business School, quoted in *Financial Times,* October 1, 1998.

R. White, P. Hodgson, and S. Crainer, *The Future of Leadership.* London: Pitman Publishing, 1996.

Chapters 1 and 2

Although dilemma theory is very much our own and has its origins in the 1970s, several other writers, faced with an increasingly turbulent social and business environment, have since come up with analogous concepts. Especially close to our own view yet independently arrived at is Rushworth Kidder's idea that good clashes with good. See *How Good People Make Tough Choices,* New York: William Morrow, 1995. Charles Handy has been pointing out that conventional reasoning does not work. See *The Age of Paradox,* Boston: Harvard Business School Press, 1994, and *The Age of Unreason,* London: Business Books, 1989. Several others have looked to the "new physics" for paradoxical ideas in business leadership; see especially Margaret H. Wheatley, *Leadership and the New Science;* San Francisco: Berrett-Kohler, and Danah Zohar, *Rewiring the Corporation;* San Francisco: Berrett-Kohler, 1998. A very similar theory, again independently constructed, is explained in Barry Johnson, *Polarity Management: Identifying and Managing Unsolvable Problems,* Amherst, Mass.: HRD Press, 1992. The reason for this convergence of independent views is simply that we all face the same problem of seeming contradictions.

Chapter 3

The best and most entertaining source is Branson's own *Losing My Virginity: The Autobiography,* London: Virgin Books, 1998. This is the origin of the two stories retold in this chapter. Attempts to capture the enigma of Branson's leadership include the following:

Mick Brown, *Richard Branson: The Authorised Biography.* London: Headline, 1998.

Des Dearlove, *The Richard Branson Way.* Oxford: Capstone, 1998.

Tim Hanson, *Virgin King.* London: HarperCollins, 1994.

Alan Mitchell, *Leadership by Richard Branson.* London: Amrop International, 1995.

For a ludicrous hatchet job of interest chiefly to those concerned with the treatment of entrepreneurs by Britain's tabloid press, see Tom Bower, *Branson,* London: Fourth Estate, 2000.

Chapter 5

Christine Ockrent and Jean-Pierre Sereni, *Les Grands Patrons.* Paris: Plon, 1998.

Figaro Economie (Oct. 10, 1999), Le Club Med dévoile ses projets de l'an 2000.

The Wall Street Journal (Oct. 10, 1999), Club Med's New Ad Campaign Will Push Family Fun.

Le Soir (Sept. 22, 1999), Philippe Bourguignon a dynamité le Club Med.

The Independent (Sept. 15, 1999), The Accidental Tourist.

Sud Quest (July 13, 1999), Interview avec Philippe Bourguignon: Nouvelle image au Club Med.

The Wall Street Journal (June 30, 1999), Despite 25% Jump in Net, Club Med Won't Relax.

Les Echos (June 3, 1999), En achetant Jet Tours, le Club Med entame son redéploiement.

Financial Times (June 3, 1999), Club Med Buys Jet Tours Amid Talk of Takeover Bid.

Le Monde (June 3, 1999), Le Club Méditerranée passe l'offensive en rachetant Jet Tours.

The New York Times (June 30, 1999), Club Med Gets Serious, Club Med Is Getting a Big Serious.

Chicago Tribune (April 25, 1999), Club Med Looks to Reclaim Paradise: Bikinis to Baby Food to Full Family Focus.

Forbes (March 22, 1999), Paradise Regained?

La Croix (March 3, 1999), Philippe Bourguignon, le nouvel esprit Club Med.

The Wall Street Journal (Jan. 20, 1999), Europe Puts Club Med Back in Black.

Stratégies (Dec. 18, 1998), Interview avec Philippe Bourguignon: Etre-re est un projet d'entreprise.

The Observer (Dec. 20, 1998), Sun, Sea and Wishful Thinking.

Le Monde (Sept. 24, 1998), Les habits neuf du Club Med.

Business Life (July/August 1998), Of Mice and Med.

Le Monde (Feb. 21, 1998), Interview avec Philippe Bourguignon: Le Club Méditerranée mise son avenir sur la qualité de sa marque.

Financial Times (Jan. 28, 1998), Redefining Sun, Sand and Sangria.

The Times (Oct. 15, 1997), Club Med Seeks Brighter Image.

L'Express (July 24, 1997), Interview avec Philippe Bourguignon: Réinventer Le Club Med!

Financial Times (Feb. 24, 1997), Club Med Turns Its Back on Idealism of the Past.

Chapter 7

Per Thygesen Poulsen, *Break-Point: Anders Knutsen and Bang & Olufsen.* 1996.

Chapter 8

Christine Ockrent and Jean-Pierre Sereni, *Les Grands Patrons.* Paris: Plon, 1998.

Chapter 10

James C. Morgan and J. Jeffrey Morgan, *Cracking the Japanese Market.* New York: Free Press, 1991.

Chapter 11

Books:

Jim Moore, *The Death of Competition: Leadership and Strategy in the Age of Business Ecosystems.* New York: HarperBusiness, 1997.

Michael Porter, *Competitive Strategy: Techniques for Analyzing Industries and Competitors.* New York: Free Press, 1998.

B. Joseph Pine, et al., *Mass Customization: The New Frontier in Business Competition.* Cambridge, Mass.: Harvard Business School Press, 1999.

Michael Dell, *Direct From Dell: Strategies That Revolutionized an Industry.* New York: HarperBusiness, 1999.

Web site: www.dell.com

Speeches by Michael Dell:

NetSpeed: The supercharged effect of the Internet. Address at the Executives' Club of Chicago, October 23, 1998.

Maximum speed: Lessons learned from managing hypergrowth. Address to the Comerica Economic Forum, Dallas, Texas, September 10, 1998.

Collaborating in a connected economy: The power of virtual integration. Address at the World Congress of Information Technology, Vienna, Virginia, June 24, 1998.

The PC industry: A robust outlook. Keynote address at the Society of American Business Editors and Writers Technology Conference, Austin, Texas, October 9, 1998.

The Dynamics of the connected economy. Address to Forbes CEO Conference, Atlanta, June 25, 1999.

The Dell advantage. Address to Information Technology Group, San Francisco, March 3, 1999.

Building the infrastructure for twenty-first-century commerce. Keynote address at the 1999 Networld+Interop, Las Vegas, May 12, 1999.

E-business: Strategies in Net time. Address at the National Press Club, Washington, DC, June 8, 2000.

Leadership in the Internet economy. Keynote address at the Canadian Club of Toronto, April 7, 2000.

Building a competitive advantage in an Internet economy. Address to the Detroit Economic Club, November 1, 1999.

Chapter 12

Frederic Deyo, Cultural Patterning of Organizational Development: A Comparative Case Study of Thai and Chinese Industrial Enterprise. *Human Organization* 37(1): 68–73, 1978.

Michael Goldberg, *The Chinese Connection.* Vancouver: University of British Columbia Press, 1985.

John Kao, The World Wide Web of Chinese business. *Harvard Business Review* (March-April), 24–36, 1993.

S. G. Redding, *The Spirit of Chinese Capitalism.* Berlin: de Gruyter, 1996.

Frances Rothstein and Michael Blim, *Anthropology and the New Global Factory.* New York: Bergin and Garvey, 1992.

Hendrick Serrie, "Chinese Business and Management Behavior and the Hsu Attributes: A Preliminary Enquiry," in H. Serrie (ed.), *Anthropology and International Business,* pp. 59–71, Williamsburg: Department of Anthropology, College of William and Mary, 1986.

Hung Chao Tai, "The Oriental Alternative: A Hypothesis on East Asian Culture and Economy, in *The Republic of China on Taiwan Today.* Taipei: Kwang Ha Publishing Company, 1989.

Ezra Vogel, *The Four Little Dragons.* Cambridge, Mass.: Harvard University Press, 1991.

Chapter 13

In preparation for the interview with Sergei Kiriyenko, we approached Jeffrey Deutsch (deutsch@rabidtiger.com), an expert on Russia for many years. Jeffrey was so kind as to send us a summary of Kiriyenko's career. More detailed information on Kiriyenko's earlier and recent activities came through Dr. Jurn Buisman, director of the Amsterdam office of the Russia & CIS Foreign Investment Promotion Centre of the Ministry of Economic Development and Trade of the Russian Federation (fipc@rusnet.nl). His assistants, Dr. Alexandra Boldyreva and Eugenia Lountchenkova, did additional research, and the latter also acted as interpreter during the interview. Finally, background information was taken from various Internet sources, newspapers, and magazines.

Chapter 14

James C. Collins and Jerry I. Porras, *Built to Last.* New York: HarperBusiness, 1997.

Edgar H. Schein, *Organizational Culture and Leadership.* San Francisco: Jossey-Bass Business & Management Series, 1997.

Arie De Geus, *The Living Company,* Cambridge, Mass: Harvard Business School Press, 1997.

Chapter 17

Newspapers:

The Scotsman, (Oct. 8, 1997), Investment Game Attracts a Thundering Herd.

The Scotsman (Sept. 4, 1997), Merrill Lynch Global Investment Challenge.

The Scotsman (August 5, 1998), *Playing to win.*

Speeches by David Komansky:

A bull market in human hopes and dreams. Goldman Sachs Financial Services Investor Conference, New York, November 5, 1997.

America's role in the global financial marketplace. American Council of Life Insurance, Naples, Florida, January 15, 1999.

Bulls, bears, and buffaloes: Merrill Lynch's four decades in Japan. Japan Society Annual Dinner, New York, May 26, 1999.

Leveraging global investments. Merrill Lynch Investor Day Conference, New York, May 2, 2000.

Repositioning in a rapidly changing industry. Merrill Lynch Banking & Financial Services Conference, New York, September 13, 1999.

Testimony on the financial marketplace of the future. Senate Committee on Banking, Housing, and Urban Affairs, New York, February 29, 2000.

The global/local paradox: Comments on the future of the global financial intermediation. Club de Bourse, Paris, January 20, 1997.

The global markets: Good for some or good for all? Economic Club of Detroit, May 24, 1999.

Other Sources:

Winthrop H. Smith, Jr., Expansion of business into global markets. Address at Richard Ivey School of Business University of Western Ontario, November 4, 1998.

John L. Steffens, A new investment paradigm for the digital age. Address at Financial Summit: Investing in the Future of Technology, New York, October 20, 1998.

John L. Steffens, Managing wealth in the new global economy. Address at Merrill Lynch Wealth Management Conference, St. Helena, CA, June 29, 1997.

John L. Steffens, The Internet revolution: Phase II. Address at Jupiter Communications Online Financial Services Forum, San Francisco, September 27, 1999.

John L. Steffens, The role of online advice. Address at the Forrester Conference, Princeton, New Jersey, May 24, 1999.

Chapter 18

Newspapers:

Business Week (July 13, 1998), Financial Supermarkets? Bah.

Financial Times (Nov. 6, 1997), The Laughing Insurer.

Financial Times (Jan. 1, 1999), AEGON Plays on Its Local Strength.

Forum (June 17, 1999), interview with Kees Storm, De Kraanvogel.

International Money Marketing (Dec. 13, 1996), AEGON Grows Service with a Smile.

Management Team (May 5, 1998), Ik Denk Dat het Juist is Dat ik Ga.

The Economist (Feb. 20, 1999), Storm across America: AEGON Buying Transamerica.

The Scotsman (March 26, 1998), The Dynamic Duo, AEGON Buying Scottish Equitable.

Storm Kees Sources:

Hoe cultuur scheppen? CHC.ZW. July 10, 1998.

Hoe international is een internationaal bedrijf? Speech at the Free University, Amsterdam, February 25, 1999.

Investor presentation. Presentation in London, March 5, 1999.

Knowledge management: Tomorrow's key competitive asset? Introductory remarks, World Economic Forum, Davos, Switzerland, February 1, 1999.

Speech at the Borgen meeting, Slochteren, the Netherlands, February 25, 1999.

The clear picture. Speech in Frankfurt, Germany, June 29, 1999.

With Loek Wijchers, *Management Bestek*. Holland Business Publications, 1997.

Zorg, Toekomst en Directeur, *NCD jubileum uitgave*, 1998.

Chapter 20

Financial Times (Aug. 11, 2000), Inside Track: Giant That Sees No Evil: Management Energy.

Financial Times (Aug. 22, 2000), Ban on Dumping Oil Rigs at Sea.

Andrew Rowell, Andrea Goodall, Greenpeace International, Shell-Shocked: The environmental and social costs of living with Shell in Nigeria, July 1994.

Shell Report 2000. Internal document.

Chapter 21

R. Donickles and E. Frohlich, Family Businesses: Really Different European Experiences. *Family Business Review* 2, 1991.

S. Goldberg, Significant Points Leading to Effective Successors in Family Businesses. *Family Business Annual Research Paper* 1(1): 74, 1995.

Manfred Kets de Vries, "Family Business" in *Human Dilemmas in the Family Firm.* London: International Business Press, 1997.

P. Leach, *Family Businesses,* 2d ed. London: Kogan Page, 1994.

Peter Woolliams, and Tomenko Swaffin-Smith, *Towards a Unified Model for Small to Medium Enterprise Business Paradigms.* Anglia: Earlybrave Publications, 2000.

P. Westhead, M. Crowling, and G. Story, The Management and Performances of Family Businesses in the UK. Paper for the Stoy Centre for Family Businesses, Warwick Business School, 1997.

Donckels, Small Business Networks, *Journal of Small Business Management* (April): 13–25, 1997.

Davis, Realizing the Potential of the Family Business, *Organizational Dynamics* 47–56, 1983.

Leach, *Family Business,* 2d ed. London: Kogan Page, 1996.

Degolat, cited in Manfred Kets de Vries, *Human Dilemmas in the Family Firm.* London: Thompson Business Press, 1996.

Donelly, The Family Business, *Harvard Business Review* (March-April) 93–105, 1964.

Goldberg, Significant Points Leading to Effective Success in Family Businesses. *Family Business Annual Research Paper,* Institute of Directors, vol. 1, section 1, p. 74, 1995.

Thornton, Reasons for Failure in Small Businesses. London Business School (Stoy Hayward), 1997, pp. 3–15.

Index

About the Authors

Fons Trompenaars, Ph.D., and **Charles Hampden-Turner, DBA,** are coauthors of *Riding the Waves of Culture: Understanding Cultural Diversity in Global Business* and *Building Cross-Cultural Competence: How to Create Wealth from Conflicting Values.* Trompenaars is managing director of Trompenaars Hampden-Turner (THT) Intercultural Management Consulting, an international management and training consultancy and KPMG Network affiliate that lists Motorola, Mars, Shell, Bombardier, and Heineken among its clients. Hampden-Turner is a management consultant with THT and author based at the University of Cambridge's Judge Institute of Management Studies. He has taught at Harvard University, Brandeis, and the University of Toronto, and is a past recipient of Guggenheim, Rockefeller, and Ford Foundation fellowships. Find out more about THT at www.7d-culture.nl.